Introducing ZBrush®

ERIC KELLER

WILEY PUBLISHING, INC.

Acquisitions Editor: Mariann Barsolo
Development Editor: Stephanie Barton
Technical Editor: Gael McGill, PhD
Production Editor: Rachel Gunn
Copy Editor: Judy Flynn
Production Manager: Tim Tate
Vice President and Executive Group Publisher: Richard Swadley
Vice President and Executive Publisher: Joseph B. Wikert
Vice President and Publisher: Neil Edde
Media Associate Project Manager: Laura Atkinson
Media Assistant Producer: Josh Frank
Media Quality Assurance: Kit Malone
Book Designer: Caryl Gorska
Compositors: Chris Gillespie, Kate Kaminski, Happenstance Type-O-Rama
Proofreader: Ian Golder
Indexer: Ted Laux
Cover Designer: Ryan Sneed
Cover Images: Eric Keller

Library of Congress Cataloging-in-Publication Data

Keller, Eric.

Introducing ZBrush / Eric Keller.

    p. cm.

ISBN 978-0-470-26279-5 (paper/dvd)

1. Computer graphics. 2. ZBrush. I. Title.

T385.K397827 2008

006.6—dc22

                    2008008346

Dear Reader

Thank you for choosing *Introducing ZBrush*. This book is part of a family of premium quality Sybex books, all written by outstanding authors who combine practical experience with a gift for teaching.

Sybex was founded in 1976. More than thirty years later, we're still committed to producing consistently exceptional books. With each of our titles we're working hard to set a new standard for the industry. From the authors we work with, to the paper we print on, our goal is to bring you the best books available.

I hope you see all that reflected in these pages. I'd be very interested to hear your comments and get your feedback on how we're doing. Feel free to let me know what you think about this or any other Sybex book by sending me an email at nedde@wiley.com, or if you think you've found a technical error in this book, please visit http://sybex.custhelp.com. Customer feedback is critical to our efforts at Sybex.

Best regards,

Neil Edde
Vice President and Publisher
Sybex, an Imprint of Wiley

For my dog Blue

—Eric Keller

Acknowledgments

I'd like to thank the editors at Sybex and Wiley for helping make this book a possibility. In particular, thanks to Mariann Barsolo for her support. Thanks to Stephanie Barton for her excellent editorial work. I'd also like to thank Gael McGill, my tech editor, for agreeing to much more than he anticipated. And thanks to all the folks on the book team who brought it all together: Rachel Gunn and Judy Flynn. ■ Special thanks goes to the folks at Pixologic for creating such a wonderful program. Thanks to Ryan Kingslien for his help and Scott Spencer for his inspiring teaching and artwork. Thanks to everyone at ZBrushCentral.com for their enthusiasm and all the fantastic creations they upload every day.

About the Author

Eric Keller is a freelance animator working in Hollywood, California, at some of the finer design and effects studios. He got his start in the field of digital visual effects developing animations for scientific visualization at the prestigious Howard Hughes Medical Institute, where he had the opportunity to work with some of the world's leading researchers. He has been a professional 3D artist for 10 years and has been using ZBrush since 2004. Along with molecular visualization, bacterial invasion, and cellular function, Eric has pitched in on numerous animations for film, commercials, and television. Eric used ZBrush to create the surrealistic intracellular environment sequence seen at the end of the feature film *Invasion*. He has also been a guest lecturer on animation and scientific visualization at Harvard Medical School. He has written articles and tutorials for numerous industry magazines and authored *Maya Visual Effects: The Innovator's Guide* (Sybex, 2007).

If you have questions, you can email Eric at kellerrific@yahoo.com or check out his website, www.bloopatone.com.

CONTENTS AT A GLANCE

Contents

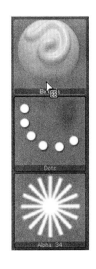

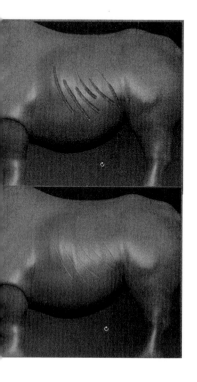

Introduction

ZBrush is an easy program to use once you know how. Learning how to use it is the trick. The whole point of this book is to provide you with an engaging way to learn how the software works. The software can be a little difficult at first, and at times you may be frustrated. The good news is that with a little effort, practice, and patience, you'll quickly learn all you need to know to start creating amazing digital sculptures and compositions. With many 3D packages, it seems like there is no end to the amount of information you need to absorb before you can create anything. With ZBrush, once you get a handle on the interface, you can get to work immediately; there's only so much you need to learn. And just like riding a bike—once you figure out how not to fall over, you can spend your time enjoying yourself.

ZBrush has introduced a unique approach to creating models on the computer. In fact, it is the first program to replace the concept of digital modeling with digital sculpting. This means that instead of the more tedious approach to modeling—where polygons are extruded, split, and sewn together—creating forms in ZBrush feels more like sculpting virtual clay. ZBrush began as a 2.5-dimensional paint program, but it quickly evolved into a 3D sculpting tool. Many of the 2.5-dimensional paint features were adapted for use on 3D models, and thus a digital sculpting tool was born.

Along with sculpting, ZBrush offers an excellent way to paint colors and textures directly on a 3D model. The models and textures can be imported and exported from ZBrush for use in other 3D animation programs. This makes ZBrush extremely easy to incorporate into any digital modeling production pipeline.

ZBrush is not an animation tool, which is part of why there's only so much you need to learn. Among the most common uses for ZBrush are creating digital characters and creatures for use in animation programs, enhancing digital models created in other animation programs, creating digital maquettes for conceptual development in production, and creating illustrations and digital compositions.

Who Can Benefit from This Book

This book is for beginners. It assumes a certain amount of proficiency using computers, but you don't need any prior experience with 3D animation packages or digital paint programs. For the most part, this book does not require that you have other digital art software installed on your machine. Only Chapter 9 discusses using ZBrush with other software packages. The first chapter introduces basic computer graphic (CG) concepts that will help you understand the terminology used throughout the book. If you've never used a 3D modeling program before, you may have a slight advantage over those who have. ZBrush's interface is very different from typical 3D programs, and this has been known to throw experienced modelers off. Either way, try to approach learning ZBrush with an open mind and see how far you can go.

If you are an experienced CG artist looking to incorporate ZBrush into your production pipeline, you will find that this book covers every essential aspect of working with ZBrush, including tips on how to use ZBrush with other 3D programs and with plug-ins that are designed to improve ZBrush's compatibility in a production environment.

About This Book

This book was written in conjunction with Scott Spencer's *ZBrush Character Creation: Advanced Digital Sculpting* (Sybex, 2008). Scott's book is about the art of sculpting on the computer, and this book is an in-depth guide to how ZBrush works. The two books are meant to work together to provide the reader with a complete understanding of how to become a digital sculptor using ZBrush. Although this book is introductory, it is not meant to replace the ZBrush documentation. You are encouraged to use the free documentation as well as this book to gain a complete understanding of ZBrush. However, I recommend using the search feature on the documentation rather than trying to read through every section.

Each chapter of this book provides an overview of how the various aspects of ZBrush work together and then demonstrates their use in a series of exercises. Some exercises are short and some span several chapters. The key to mastering ZBrush is practice, and that is why this book takes a hands-on approach to learning ZBrush.

The chapters work together to build a foundation of understanding; they are grouped together in the most logical way possible. Chapters 1 and 2 cover digital art terminology and the ZBrush interface. If you are an experienced digital artist, you may want to skim Chapter 1, but please read Chapter 2 carefully. The ZBrush interface is unique: without taking the time to understand how it works, you'll find yourself quickly lost and frustrated. Chapters 3 and 4 cover 2.5-dimensional digital painting. If you're primarily interested in digital sculpting, you may want to skip Chapters 3 and 4 and skip ahead to Chapter 5. However, to gain a complete understanding of all the tools available in ZBrush, you'll want to go through Chapters 3 and 4 eventually.

Chapters 5, 6, and 7 are the core of the book. They cover digital sculpting, which is the most popular use for ZBrush. The approach taken in these chapters is as simplified as possible, but they are still meant to be a challenge. The methods I use are not the only methods possible or available, but they are, I believe, the most suited for beginners. Chapters 5, 6, and 7 should be read in order to achieve the best results.

Chapter 8 covers rendering, lighting, and materials in ZBrush. It is a self-contained chapter. Chapter 9 covers using ZBrush with other software programs. Maya is used as an example since it is the most commonly used 3D application; however, ZBrush can be used with any 3D application that can import models and textures. Chapter 9 also covers using ZBrush with Curious Labs Poser.

Finally, Chapter 10 covers some of the more useful ZBrush plug-ins and includes a brief introduction to ZScripts. ZScripting is covered in detail in *ZBrush Character Creation: Advanced Digital Sculpting*. If you find that ZScripting is something that interests you, check out Scott's book.

As you go through the exercises in this book, take the time to practice the concepts before moving on to the next section, otherwise you may feel overwhelmed rather quickly. Practice is the key to mastering any art form, including art created on a computer. A fast processor is no substitute for experience.

The Companion DVD

This book is actually more of a learning kit than a book. There are so many files that accompany the lessons that a CD could not provide enough space. The DVD has the entire example scene files as well as files at various stages in each project. You can use the files to pick up a lesson at almost any point. You can also use them to compare your results with the examples in the lesson. To get the most out of this book, the student is encouraged to take advantage of these files.

The DVD also contains movies of many of the lessons in the book, recorded straight from the ZBrush interface. These movies show as much as possible of the actual sculpting process used. Sculpting is not a step-by-step process; the thousands of strokes used to create a sculpture would make for some dry reading if they were described in the text. At the same time, it's important to see how you can work in ZBrush, so please, watch the movies that come with each chapter. You may get the best results if you watch them before *and* after completing each lesson. Chapters 3, 4, and 5 come with macros. Macros are sessions that are recorded and played back within ZBrush—like an old-style player piano, the macro takes control of the entire interface so that you can see a ZBrush session performed right before your eyes. Macros work well for short sessions, while movies work better for longer sessions because they can be paused and rewound. This is why movies are used for the later chapters. Loading and playing macros in ZBrush is described in Chapter 3.

ZBrushCentral.com

ZBrushCentral.com is the heart of the ZBrush community. You are encouraged to visit this site often for inspiration, learning materials, software updates, news, advice from users, and most importantly, the opportunity to upload your own ZBrush artwork for praise and critique. The ZBrush community is full of great artists and great people with more enthusiasm for ZBrush than should be legally allowed. Without ZBrushCentral.com, the software is incomplete!

Mouse vs. Tablet

Using a mouse as an input device while working in ZBrush is possible, but it's a lot like sculpting clay while wearing ski gloves. ZBrush is really designed to be used with a digital tablet input device like those created by Wacom (www.wacom.com). Sculpting and painting brushes in ZBrush are meant to take advantage of a tablet's pressure sensitivity, and many controls, such as the Transpose handle, are specifically designed to work with a tablet. Plus, using a mouse to create the thousands of strokes necessary for digital sculpture could lead to repetitive wrist strain injuries. Therefore, if you don't have a digital tablet, you should seriously consider purchasing one to use with ZBrush. You don't need the largest or most expensive tablet model; as long as it has a pressure-sensitivity feature and works with your computer, you should be fine.

Throughout the book the term *click* is used when referring to activating buttons in the ZBrush interface. Typically, *click* refers to clicking a mouse button while holding the cursor over a button in the interface. When you use a tablet, tapping the pen on the tablet while the cursor is over the interface button performs the same action. When you see the phrase "click on the button" in an exercise, understand that tapping the pen on the tablet can perform the same action.

Apple Macintosh vs. Windows

At the time of this writing, the Macintosh version of ZBrush 3.1 is not available. However, it will likely release before this book is published. This book is written for the PC version, which can be run on Intel-based Macs that use Windows as an alternate operating system.

When the Macintosh version is released, give special consideration to the hotkeys used in the book. The Command key replaces the Ctrl key modifier in most Macintosh applications. Most likely this will be the case with the Macintosh version of ZBrush.

Whether you are using a PC with Windows or an Apple Macintosh running Windows as an alternative OS, please pay attention to Pixologic's recommended software and hardware requirements when running ZBrush. The system requirements for running the software are described in this book's appendix. For the most up-to-date information, check www.pixologic.com/zbrush/system.

Preferences and Interface Customization

The ZBrush interface is fully customizable. As you first start learning ZBrush, you may want to stick with the standard layout until you are comfortable with what all the tools, settings, and controls do. Keep in mind that the entire interface can be rearranged to suit your own needs. When you've gained confidence working with ZBrush, feel free to experiment with your own customization. This section offers a few tips; more details on customization can be found in the ZBrush documentation.

Hotkeys ZBrush, like many software programs, uses hotkey shortcuts for many commands. A single key or a combination of keys is reserved to quickly enact frequently used commands. A list of these is found at the end of Chapter 1.

You can also quickly create your own hotkey by following these steps:

1. Simply press and hold the Ctrl key, then click the button or command you'd like to assign a hotkey to.

2. Release the Ctrl key and then press the key or key combination you want assigned to that command.

3. Upon leaving ZBrush, you'll be asked if you want the hotkeys saved for future ZBrush sessions.

Custom Colors The ZBrush interface colors can be changed at any time to suit your needs. The Preferences palette's Colors subpalette contains buttons that will allow you to change the color of each and every type of button, control, and menu. You can also change the opacity of the menus. In the upper-right corner of the title bar, you'll find a pair of buttons that store a number of preconfigured interface color schemes. You can cycle through the combinations by pressing on these buttons.

You can save your own color configuration using the controls in the Preferences palette. To make ZBrush start up with a particular configuration, click the Store Config button in the Preferences palette.

Layout Presets ZBrush has a number of layout presets available to suit your own working style. You can cycle through these layouts using the buttons in the upper-right corner of the title bar. To save a configuration as the default, click the Save UI button in the Preferences palette.

Quick Info To learn more about a particular button or control in ZBrush, you can hold the cursor over the button in question while pressing the Ctrl key. A brief explanation will appear in a pop-up window. The settings for the quick info pop-up display are found in the Preferences palette.

Customize UI You can customize the interface by dragging buttons and controls to other parts of the interface or to your own custom menus. To do this, you must first activate the Enable Customize button in the Custom UI subpalette of the Preferences palette. Then you can hold the Ctrl key down while dragging a button to a new position on the interface. The Customize UI subpalette also has controls for creating your own menu.

Memory and Performance ZBrush periodically compacts memory. This means it will store data to a file in order to free up available RAM. The compact memory slider in the Mem subpalette of the Preferences palette allows you to set the number of megabytes of RAM used before ZBrush executes a compacting memory routine. The Mem subpalette also contains settings for the number of undos available for both the document and tools as well as the maximum number of polygons ZBrush will allow for a polymesh tool.

The Performance subpalette contains settings for multithreading. You can test the multi-threading capabilities of your machine by clicking the Test Multithreading button. ZBrush will execute a number of commands designed to test your system. It will then adjust the multithreading settings based on the results of this test.

Tablet Settings The Tablet subpalette has controls for adjusting the sensitivity of your tablet input device. If you're using a mouse with ZBrush, disable the Use Tablet button. Otherwise, use these controls to adjust how the pressure sensitivity feature of the tablet will affect the brushes within ZBrush.

There are a number of other settings and controls available in the Preferences palette. Take a look at the documentation for more information on setting preferences. Most importantly, understand that if you don't like a particular interface feature, you have the power to change it!

CHAPTER 1

Pixels, Pixols, Polygons, and the Basics of Creating Digital Art

Any experienced artist knows that the composition of the tools they use—the chemistry of the paint, the ingredients of the clay—affects the quality of a finished work of art. When you are learning to become an artist, you spend a great deal of time studying how the tools behave. It is the same with digital art. This chapter reviews the fundamentals of digital art. Just as an oil painter learns how the mixture of pigments and oils works with the canvas, a digital artist needs to learn how color depth, channels, file formats, and other elements factor into the quality of a digital masterpiece.

This chapter includes the following topics:

- An introduction to ZBrush
- Understanding digital images
- Understanding 3D space
- Being a digital artist

An Introduction to ZBrush

Imagine walking into a fully stocked artist's studio. Inside you find cabinets and drawers full of paints and brushes, a large canvas, a closet full of every type of sculpting medium imaginable, a lighting rig, a camera, a projector, a kiln, armatures for maquettes, and a seemingly infinite array of carving and cutting tools. On top of this, everything has been neatly arranged for optimal use while working. This is ZBrush, a self-contained studio where you can digitally create paintings and sculptures—and even combinations of the two. Furthermore, you are not limited to what you find in ZBrush. Digital 3D models and 2D textures can easily be imported from other applications and used as tools within ZBrush. ZBrush can function as a self-contained digital art workspace and it can be integrated into a production pipeline for the purpose of creating and editing digital models for animation.

The most common use of ZBrush is for creating and editing digital models that are then animated and rendered in other 3D packages, such as Autodesk's Maya and 3ds Max, and Softimage XSI. Artists choose to create and edit models in ZBrush to use in another package because the unique technology behind ZBrush allows them to work with very dense models (literally millions of polygons) to create a stunningly rich level of detail on organic surfaces in a way that traditional 3D packages just can't. Fine wrinkles, fleshy folds, pores, bumps, scales, scars, and scratches can be easily sculpted into the model and then exported either as part of the geometry or as bump and displacement textures that can enhance the geometry of a model when the model is rendered in another package. The result is often an amazing level of detail and realism built into a virtual object (see Figure 1.1). Color texture maps can also be painted directly on the model in ZBrush in an intuitive fashion and then exported for use in shaders applied to the same model in other 3D packages. Production pipelines at studios such as ILM, Weta, and Sony Imageworks have used ZBrush in this way to create many of the characters, monsters, and set pieces seen in such films as *The Lord of the Rings*, *Pirates of the Caribbean*, and *Sky Captain and the World of Tomorrow*.

ZBrush is also the software of choice for creating digital maquettes. Before the advent of ZBrush, a maquette was often created by hand-sculpting clay, Plasticine, latex foam, and other real-world materials. A studio would hire sculptors to build the maquettes based on concept drawings provided by the art department (see Figure 1.2). This allowed the director to see the concept for the creature or character in actual 3D space. The maquettes could be scanned using laser devices and then brought into a 3D animation package such as Maya. After some of the data is cleaned up, the model could be rigged and then animated. Because ZBrush's intuitive artistic interface allows for the creation of models that are every bit as detailed as clay models, it has recently started to eliminate the need for an actual clay maquette. The artists can now start their work directly in the computer, and the director can make changes in the model's design as it is developed. With the introduction of 3D printers and rapid prototyping technology, an actual physical model can now be fabricated from the ZBrush digital sculpt. ZBrush sculptors are now finding their way into the production pipeline for toy and collectable figure markets.

Figure 1.1

A highly detailed ZBrush model

ZBrush can also be used as an illustration tool: the program has digital sculpting and painting tools as well as its own unique rendering technology. With ZBrush, artists can create custom materials, which can be procedurally designed or captured from digital images. These materials can be applied to an artistic composition and, when rendered, react to virtual lights and shadows. Many artists have taken advantage of the flexible workspace and powerful tools to create amazing compositions entirely within ZBrush. In addition, ZBrush works very well with other 2D paint programs such as Photoshop and Painter. Digital 3D models and 2D images can be exported and imported freely between these programs, so there is no limit to what can be achieved when ZBrush is incorporated into the digital artist's toolbox.

Figure 1.2

Clay maquette sculptures are often created by the art department of a visual effects studio during the production of a film. This sculpture was created by John Brown for his maquette sculpting training DVD series produced by the Gnomon Workshop.

Understanding Digital Images

Now let's take a brief look at how computers actually create images that are displayed on the screen, on a printed page, or in an animated movie. There are actually several ways a computer can create digital imagery. The two most common technologies use pixels and vectors.

Anatomy of a Pixel

A pixel is a colored square that appears on the screen at a specified position—pretty simple, at least to begin with. A raster graphic refers to an image made up of thousands of pixels. A pixel is imbued with a certain amount of color and position information that is stored in memory. If you load a rasterized graphic into a digital viewing program and then scale the image up (or zoom in), you can actually see how the image is composed of these pixels (see Figure 1.3).

A digital image file stores the positional information of these pixels in terms of x- and y-coordinates. The y-coordinate is the vertical position and the x-coordinate is the horizontal position. It may seem obvious, but it's important to note that when you zoom in or scroll around on a digital image in the software, the position and size of each pixel changes relative to the screen. However, the software still needs to remember the position and size of each pixel relative to the digital image that is being viewed. You should be aware of this fact, but don't spend too much time thinking about it now; that's your computer's job.

The amount of random access memory (RAM) your computer hardware has will affect how much information it can keep track of at one time and thus the performance of the software as you move all this information around on the screen.

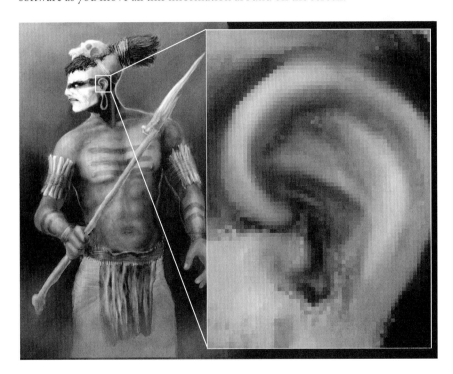

Figure 1.3

A digital painting created in Corel's Painter. The region around the figure's ear is enlarged to show how the picture is composed of thousands of tiny squares called pixels.

Taking the Edge off with Anti-Aliasing

Aliasing refers to the situation in which a curving line or shape displayed on a computer screen appears jagged. This is because the image is composed of tiny squares. In order to correct this problem, graphic software employs *anti-aliasing*, which smoothes the edges of curving shapes by blending pixels along the edge with other pixels of similar hue but varying degrees of lightness or opacity. This fools the eye into perceiving the edge as being smooth.

In Figure 1.4, the edge of the letters in the word *jagged* appear jagged because the square pixels are visible along the curving edges of the letters; this image is *aliased*. The edges of the letters in the word *smooth* appear smooth because of the blending technique that mixes pixels of varying lightness along the curving edge of the letter. The image is *anti-aliased*.

Figure 1.4

The edges of the letters in the word *jagged* are aliased. The edges of the letters in the word *smooth* are anti-aliased.

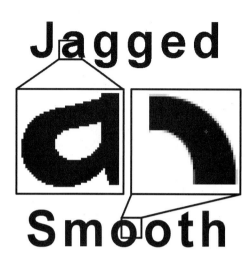

Channels and Color Depth

Along with positional data, the pixel stores information about how to display colors. A computer screen creates color by mixing red, green, and blue light. If a pixel is 100 percent red mixed with 0 percent blue and 0 percent green, it looks red. If a pixel is composed of 50 percent red with 50 percent blue and 0 percent green values, the pixel will look purple. When all three values are 0 percent, the pixel is black, and when all three are 100 percent, the pixel is white.

Color depth refers to how much color information is stored for each pixel in the image. A grayscale image discards all color information except for black, white, and the range of gray in between; this usually comes out to 256 shades of gray. The result is a black-and-white image, like the images in this chapter. Since color information is limited to the 256 shades of gray, the file has less information that needs to be stored.

If you have studied painting you may have learned that the primary colors are red, yellow, and blue. The secondary color green, for example, is created when blue is mixed with yellow. This is true for paint but not so for colors created by a lighted computer screen. As far as computers are concerned, red, green, and blue are the primary colors. Red and green mixed together produce the secondary color yellow.

An RGB image stores red, green, and blue information. The information is divided into three channels (red, green, and blue) and each channel stores the values (or percentage) of red, green, and blue for each pixel. To see a demonstration of how this works, follow these instructions to open up the system palette on your computer.

1. Start up ZBrush; on the opening screen, choose Other (see Figure 1.5).

2. Click Color on the menu bar to open up the Color menu/palette.

3. Click the button labeled SysPalette to open the System palette (see Figure 1.6).

Figure 1.5
When ZBrush opens, choose the Other option on the startup screen.

Figure 1.6
Click SysPalette to open the System palette.

4. In the System palette, move the picker around in the color area and observe the values in the Red, Green, and Blue fields. These values change depending on the mixture required to create the selected color. Notice that the highest value possible for each channel is 255 and the lowest is 0 (see Figure 1.7).

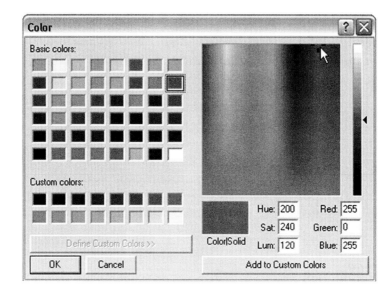

5. Type in values in the Red, Green, and Blue fields. Set Red to 255, Green to 0, and Blue to 255. The resulting color is a bright fuchsia.

An image in an RGBA format has an additional, fourth channel known as the alpha channel. The alpha channel stores information on the opacity of individual pixels. This allows for an image to have regions of transparency. The left side of Figure 1.8 shows a basic scene rendered in a 3D program; the floating spheres are transparent. The right side of Figure 1.8 shows the alpha channel. White areas are 100 percent opaque and black areas are 100 percent transparent. The gray areas show the amount of transparency.

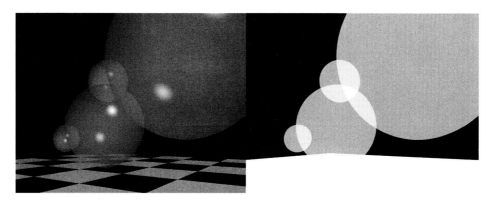

ZBrush can use an alpha channel as a filter, which it applies to a sculpting brush as a modifier or to the canvas as a stencil. In general practice, the term "alpha" refers to an additional channel of information that is stored in an image file.

Color depth refers to how much information is used for each of these color channels. Computers use bits to store information. A bit is a series of 1s and 0s (known as binary because there are only two options, 1 and 0). A 24-bit RGB image uses 8 bits of information for each channel ($3 \times 8 = 24$). Each 8-bit channel stores a range of 256 shades of color, allowing for an image to have a total of 16 million colors. A 32-bit RGBA image uses an additional 8 bits for the alpha channel.

The more bits you have, the more information you can store, and with more bits, the image can be displayed using a wider range of color. More memory is required to store and work with higher-bit images. An image that uses 16 bits per channel (48 bits total for an RGB image, 64 bits for RGBA) can be confusingly referred to as a 16-bit image (as in a 16-bit TIFF or 16-bit SGI).

Beware; this is not the same as a 16-bit or high color image that uses about 5 bits for each channel. Welcome to the confusing world of computer terminology. You will get used to these kinds of naming conflicts with some experience. Although computers are strictly logical, the humans that create and use them are not always so! If you are working as an artist in television or film production, you will be using 16-bit (per channel) images much more often than 16-bit (5 bits per channel) high color images.

Image Formats

A digital image can be stored in a number of ways, known as formats. A format is simply the arrangement of information in a file. Typical image formats include Tagged Image File Format (TIFF), Joint Photographic Experts Group (JPEG), and Graphics Interchange Format (GIF).

Many programs have their own native document format. Photoshop can read many file formats but also has its own Photoshop Document (PSD) format. Likewise, Corel's Painter stores special information in a format called Resource Interchange File Format (RIFF). ZBrush has its own ZBR document format.

An image format can be compressed to conserve storage space. Some image formats have compression built in (such as JPEG and GIF), and some can exist with or without compression (such as SGI, or Silicon Graphics Image). Compression usually affects the quality of the image. If you look closely at a JPEG image from a typical website using a browser, you may notice that it is blurry or grainy or that the colors are not quite right. Image quality has been sacrificed to allow faster download when viewing images over the Internet.

When the quality of an image is diminished by the compression, it is said to be a *lossy* compression format. There are also *lossless* compressions that can reduce the size of an image without significantly affecting quality. These formats, such as Portable Network

Graphics (PNG), result in file sizes that are larger than those for which lossy compression is used. Compression applied to sequences of images is also used for video.

In Figure 1.9, the image on the left is uncompressed and the image on the right is compressed. Look closely and you can see the distortion, known as *artifacts,* in the image on the right. This distortion is especially apparent in the squirrel's fur and on the edges of the fence posts.

Understanding file formats and compression will become important as you work with computer graphics, not only with respect to images you create and share in ZBrush, but also with textures and alphas created in ZBrush and used on 3D models in other programs. Some 3D applications and rendering engines will prefer some formats more than others. This will be covered in more depth later in this book.

Figure 1.9

The image on the left is uncompressed; the image on the right is compressed.

Vector Images

As stated earlier, computers can also use vectors to create digital images. A vector graphic is created from formulas and mathematical calculations performed by the computer and its software. The results of these calculations are smooth lines and shapes that are often filled with colors. Vector graphics are continually drawn and updated when the image is scaled, moved, or rotated, so the graphic is always of the same quality no matter what its size and position.

Adobe Illustrator and Adobe Flash are popular vector graphic programs. Vectors are used in a modeling interface to represent 3D objects in 3D packages such as Maya and 3d Studio Max, and these packages have special rendering engines that can create vector graphics as final output as well. Vector graphics are not used very much in ZBrush, so I'll end the discussion of vectors for now.

Understanding Resolution

It is hard to overstate the importance of understanding resolution when working with ZBrush. Unfortunately, computer resolution is kind of a tricky concept. There's a lot of confusing terminology as well as different ways to measure and calculate resolution and different types of resolution. This is a topic that I will revisit often throughout this book, so don't panic if you haven't mastered complete understanding of resolution by the end of this section.

Simply put, resolution refers to the density of information within a given area. Most often in computer graphics, resolution is applied to the number of pixels that occupy a given area of the screen or a document. However, it can also refer to the number of polygons or vertices in a given part of the surface of a 3D model. The resolution of your computer screen can determine how the resolution of your images is displayed and created. In addition, when you apply a 2D image texture to a 3D model, the pixel resolution of the 2D image and the polygon resolution of the 3D model must be taken into account or the results achieved may be somewhat disappointing. You do this kind of work a lot in ZBrush, thus resolution is something you must always keep in mind.

Screen Resolution

Let's start with screen resolution. The computer you use to create your ZBrush images and models no doubt has a computer monitor attached to it (if not, your career in computer graphics may be getting off to a rocky start). The monitor displays text and images on the screen. Screen resolution refers to the number of square-sized pixels that appear on the screen, and this is measured horizontally and vertically. The physical size of the screen itself is usually described in diagonal terms. A 22-inch monitor refers to a screen size that measures 22 inches from one corner diagonally to the opposite corner.

Your particular screen should be able to display text and images in a number of different resolutions. The current resolution is set in the operating system's control panel or system preferences. Screen resolution is described in the number of pixels available horizontally times the number of pixels available vertically. Some typical resolutions include 640×480, which used to be the common standard in the old days when monitors were smaller; 720×486, which is the standard for broadcast television in the United States; and 1920×1080, which is used for high-definition television (HDTV). The iMac I am using to write this book is currently set to a resolution of 1440×990.

Screen resolution will affect how ZBrush looks on your screen. When you have your screen set to a low resolution, less space is available to display both the ZBrush interface and the documents. This is why computer graphics artists will invest a great deal of money on the largest computer monitor they can afford.

Document Resolution

Next, let's look at document resolution. In an earlier discussion on pixels, I mentioned that when you zoom in on a digital image using a graphics program, you can see the individual pixels that make up the image. Now, the actual pixels that display the image on the screen do not get any larger or smaller, and you do not affect the resolution settings in your computer's hardware. Rather, the graphics program allows you to see a visual representation of the image at a higher magnification than the document's native resolution.

If you take a document that is 320×240 in size and set the magnification to 200 percent, the document is now shown at 640×480 and each pixel on the document is using twice as many computer monitor pixels. Thus it looks blocky. Likewise, when you zoom out, or shrink the document, half the number of pixels is displayed. Zooming in and out of a document is a useful feature for graphics programs. It can allow you to work on the fine details of an image. But of course, here is where things get tricky: Because of the ability of computer software to zoom in and out of an image, document resolution can be different than screen resolution. When working with computer images, you must always keep in mind the resolution of your document regardless of how it appears on the screen.

Dots per inch (DPI) is typically used to describe document resolution (sometimes referred to as PPI, or pixels per inch), even in countries such as France that have long used the metric system. An image that is displayed on a computer monitor at 100 percent of its resolution is usually 72dpi. An image destined for the printed page needs to be at a higher resolution, usually 300dpi.

3D Resolution

When speaking with 3D texture artists, you'll often hear terms like *2K texture map* thrown around. What they mean is an image that is 2048 pixels × 2048 pixels. The term *2K* means two thousand to normal people, but to computer graphics artists, 2K = 2048. This is because most texture images are set to a resolution that is a multiple of 12. Thus 1K = 1024, 4K= 4096, and 512 means, well, 512×512.

Images of these sizes are always square, as long as you're talking to texture artists. However, if you walk into a production facility and they ask you to render an animation at 2K and you give them a square 2048×2048 image sequence, they may quickly toss you out the door. Why? Because to production people, 2K actually means 2048 pixels × 1556 pixels, which is not really 2K at all (or even square for that matter). In this context, 2K is shorthand for *2K Academy*, which is a standardized resolution for film. I told you humans were not logical!

Since this book is focused on ZBrush, I'll be talking the language of texture artists. So 2K means 2048×2048. If and when you move to animation software such as Maya, you may need to be aware that 2K means different things to different people, depending on the context. The safest bet is to get the people you're talking with to be specific about what they want. Geeks love jargon, but it's more often a hindrance than a help.

> Some computer professionals use *K* as shorthand for kilobyte or Kb, which refers to the actual storage size of a file on disk! Yet another level of confusion!

Aspect Ratio in 3D

Aspect ratio refers to the dimensions of the image size as a ratio. When you create an image at 320×240 or 640×480, the aspect ratio is 4:3. If the aspect ratio is 16:9 or 1.85:1, the image size is widescreen. A typical 16:9 resolution is 1280×720. This is something you may be more concerned with when rendering an animation for final output from an animation package such as Maya. In ZBrush, aspect ratio may only enter the conversation when you're creating a composition that could be used as a matte painting in an animation or for another purpose.

Polygon Resolution

Finally, resolution can also be used to describe the number or points or polygons that make up a 3D model. I'll discuss polygons in more detail later on in this chapter, but for now you should understand that the surface of a 3D model is composed of geometric shapes defined by three or more points (polygons in ZBrush are restricted to three or four points, but in other modeling programs they can have more). A model can be subdivided, which increases its smooth appearance and allows for a higher level of detail to be sculpted into the surface.

In ZBrush, a model can consist of millions and millions of polygons, as you can see in Figure 1.10. Because of the special way ZBrush handles memory, these high-resolution models can easily be edited with much less of a performance slowdown than would be experienced using other 3D applications. Furthermore, ZBrush stores many levels of sub-division resolution within a single model file, so you can raise and lower the resolution of the 3D geometry while you are working as well as export the same model at several different resolutions for use in another 3D animation package.

This ends our introduction to the concept of resolution. Rest assured that this topic will be popping up again throughout this book!

Figure 1.10

A high resolution model in ZBrush. The lines on the surface show how the model consists of millions of square polygons.

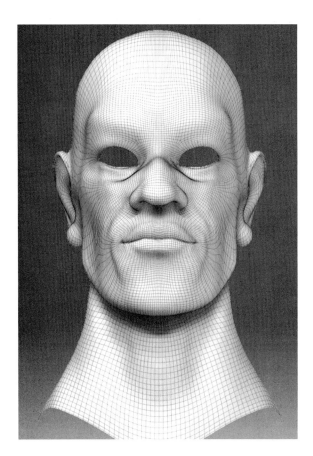

Understanding 3D Space

In a typical 3D software package such as Maya, 3D space is defined in terms of x-, y-, and z-coordinates. The horizontal dimension is usually described by the x-axis, vertical space is usually defined by the y-coordinates, and depth is usually defined by the z-coordinates (some packages reverse the meaning of the y- and z-axes). In Maya, the virtual world contains a grid. It's also crucial to understand that a point in 3D space, such as an individual vertex on a piece of 3D geometry, has an absolute position in the 3D world. This is known as its world space coordinates. It also has a position relative to the object it is part of; this is known as its local, or object, space coordinates.

Think of it this way: You are wearing a pointy party hat. The point at the very tip of the hat exists in the world at the top of your head; the world space Y coordinates of this point is very high relative to the points that make up the rest of you. At the same time, the object space Y coordinates of the tip of the hat are also very high relative to the rest of you. However, if you decided to hang upside down while wearing the party hat, the world space coordinates of the tip of the hat would now be lower than the world space coordinates that make up the rest of you. Yet, in terms of object space, we understand that the tip of the hat is still the very top of the object, even when the hat is upside down. This is based on how we understand the object and its purpose in the world. If you were to model that hat using 3D modeling software, you would understand that the tip of the hat is the top, even when you rotate the hat upside down. The 3D software also keeps track of these ideas using the two sets of coordinates—world and object (see Figure 1.11).

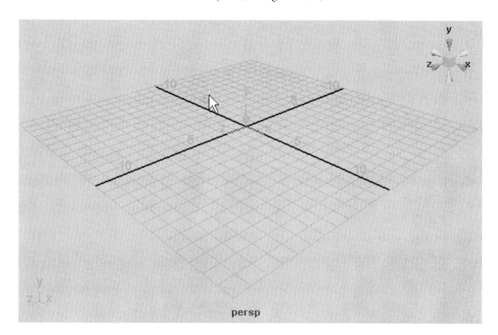

Figure 1.11

A typical 3D model-ing environment: the grid and the 3D compass help the artist keep track of x-, y-, and z-coordi-nates in virtual 3D space.

You have no doubt noticed that our software of choice for this book is called ZBrush. The reason the software is named with a *Z* explains much about how the interface works within ZBrush. Unlike in typical 3D software, the artwork you create in ZBrush does not exist on a 3D grid within a 3D world. Rather, it is painted on a canvas that contains depth information along the z-axis.

For many 3D artists who are accustomed to programs such as Maya, in which model-ing and animation take place in a 3D world, the concept of working on a canvas can be a little disconcerting at first. However, once you understand how space in ZBrush works, you often find that focusing on sculpting a 3D model is much easier. Think of ZBrush as a virtual workshop with a sculpting stand that can rotate along every axis.

Anatomy of a Polygon

There really is no such thing as a 3D object in computer graphics. Unless you are working with rapid prototyping machines that can fabricate a physical object based on data stored in a virtual 3D file, you will always be working with two-dimensional representations of three-dimensional objects on a computer screen. (Subsequent editions of this book will no doubt have to deal with rapid prototyping as the technology becomes cheaper and more accessible to artists. For now it's safe to say you'll mostly be dealing with what you see on a 2D screen.)

When we speak of 3D we are using shorthand that assumes we are talking about a 3D virtual object that exists on a 2D screen. A typical digital painting program such as Photoshop plots pixels horizontally and vertically, along the x- and y-axis respectively. A 3D program stores information with additional coordinates along the z-axis, which gives the virtual image depth. A virtual object existing in the 3D space of the software is made of polygons. The polygons give the object a surface which can be deformed, translated, and animated.

A polygon is a geometric shape defined by 3 or more points (points are also referred to as vertices); examples of polygons are shown in Figure 1.12.

Figure 1.12

An image of a 3-point, 4-point, and *n*-sided polygon as displayed in Autodesk's Maya.

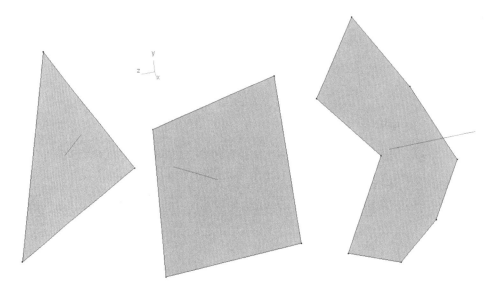

ZBrush restricts the polygons to 3 or 4 points, but other software packages can have polygons with any number of vertices. This is important to remember when importing objects from another package into ZBrush. ZBrush will automatically convert an *n*-sided (more than 4-point) polygon into a 4-point polygon (or quadrilateral) when it is imported.

In other programs you may encounter other types of 3D geometry, such as NURBS and subdivision surfaces. These are converted at render time to triangle-shaped polygons by the rendering engine, thus polygons are the standard currency of 3D software. When it comes to 3D models, ZBrush works only with polygon geometry.

As was discussed in the section titled "Understanding Resolution," the number of polygons an object has with affect how smooth the surface appears and how much detail can be modeled into that surface. The resolution of a 3D object is also referred to as its *density*. ZBrush is programmed in such a way that a 3D object can have millions of polygons and an astonishing level of detail while still maintaining a high level of response on the computer during the sculpting and editing process. This is what allows the ZBrush artist to feel as if they are sculpting digital clay in a very intuitive and artistic fashion.

ZBrush does not actually use the Open Graphics Library (OpenGL) specification when it displays 3D objects on the screen. Pixologic has developed its own protocols for 2 and 3D images based on the pixol. This means that ZBrush is free from the polygon limits imposed by the OpenGL standard.

A polygon appears in ZBrush as a shaded shape with three or four vertices. A virtual 3D object is made up of adjacent polygons that form the surface. (In ZBrush, the term *3D tool* is used to refer to a 3D object; the reason for this is explained in Chapter 2.) The surface of a polygon has an inside and an outside. The information regarding which side of a polygon faces out and which side faces in is known as the polygon's normal. A 3D tool made up of millions of polygons has millions of normals that describe how the surface appears when it reacts to virtual light and shadow (see Figure 1.13).

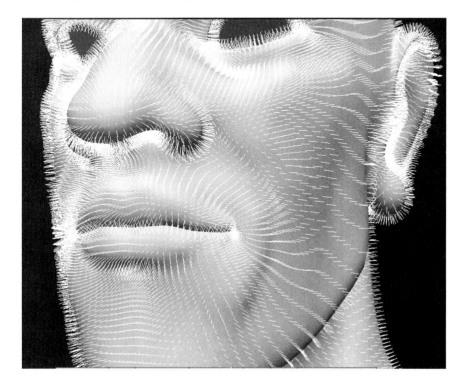

Figure 1.13

An image of a model in ZBrush with its normals visible. The normal is displayed as a line that shows which side of the polygon is pointing "out."

Normals are an important aspect of working with polygon geometry. Information about the direction of normals on a dense object can be stored in a special texture known as a normal map. Rendering engines for 3D software and video games can use these maps to make a lower-density version of the same model appear to have more detail than its geometry will allow by using a normal map to help shade the object. ZBrush is an extremely popular tool in the gaming industry because of the ease with which normal maps can be created and exported from the software.

Pixols versus Pixels

As was stated earlier, an image created in a typical digital painting program is usually composed of thousands of pixels. A pixel is a square that contains information about color, transparency, and its location along the x- and y-axis. The unique innovation of ZBrush is the pixol, which is like a pixel with added information about its location along the z-axis. In other words, a pixol contains depth information as well as color, transparency, and x and y positional data (see Figure 1.14). Furthermore, the Pixol also stores information on the material applied to it. This means each Pixol knows how to react to the lighting, shading, and the environment of a ZBrush composition when it is rendered.

Figure 1.14

The left side of the diagram shows how standard pixels work using X and Y information; the right side shows how pixols also store Z-depth information.

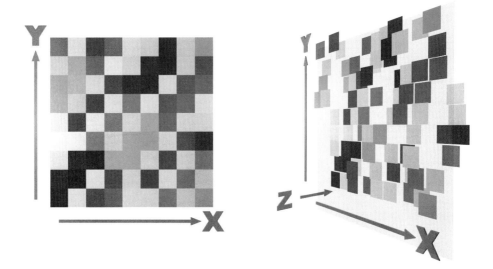

When Pixologic first introduced ZBrush, it began as a paint program that could create images in two and a half dimensions (known as 2.5D). A brush stroke in ZBrush is painted on the canvas and then can be rotated, scaled, and positioned anywhere on the canvas. This explains why the ZBrush interface does not use the typical 3D world with a grid that you find in other 3D programs. Everything exists on a canvas. ZBrush added 3D objects that could be incorporated into 2.5 dimensional compositions as well as materials and lights that added shadow, reflections, and occlusion. Subsequent versions of ZBrush refined the sculpting tools and improved the portability of 3D objects with animation projects that led to the overwhelming popularity of ZBrush as a digital sculpting program.

Pixols are a big part of ZBrush, especially if an artist is interested in creating 2.5D compositions entirely in ZBrush. If your primary interest in ZBrush is as a polygonal sculpting tool, then you may not need to delve into pixol technology too deeply; however, it certainly is a fun area to explore. Painting with pixols will be explored deeper in chapters 3 and 4 of this book. If you are eager to get right into sculpting with 3D tools, read chapter 2 and then feel free to skip to Chapters 5, 6, and 7.

Being a Digital Artist

It is almost as easy to create bad art on a computer as it is to create good art. There is nothing inherent in the computer or the software that will turn you into a great artist. Becoming a good artist still must be achieved the old-fashioned way—through hard work, practice, and study. Nine times out of ten, when you see some jaw-dropping, amazing piece of digital art in an Internet forum or as part of a film, the artist who created it has spent a fair amount of time studying traditional art. Even if the artist has never held a real paintbrush, they still have studied what it takes to make a great work.

This book is concerned with making you feel comfortable using ZBrush. There will not be much discussion on the fundamentals of art or sculpting. That said, you should understand that composition, balance, positive and negative space, lighting, form, and silhouette are just a few of the concepts a real artist (digital or traditional) must master. The student is strongly encouraged to step away from the computer monitor, pick up a pencil or a brush, and attend some life drawing classes. Likewise, working with digital clay is much more meaningful if you've spent time sculpting with actual clay. Your digital artwork will reveal much about who you are as well as how much time you have taken to study and explore traditional art techniques as well as the natural world.

Resources

This book is just the beginning. While working through the exercises in this book on your way to mastering the ZBrush interface and its tools, you should also take the time to explore more using the resources on this list. In addition, *ZBrush Character Creation: Advanced Digital Sculpting* by Scott Spencer (Sybex, 2008), which is now being written, will pick up where this book leaves off. His book will incorporate a deep level of understanding of the art of digital sculpture and the concepts behind creating great artwork into more advanced ZBrush topics and lessons.

Websites

- www.pixologic.com
- www.zbrushcentral.com
- www.highend3d.com

- www.cgchannel.com
- www.gnomon3d.com
- www.gnomononline.com
- www.digitaltutors.com
- www.3d.sk
- www.conceptart.org

Books

- *ZBrush Character Creation: Advanced Digital Sculpting* by Scott Spencer (Sybex, 2008)
- *The Artist's Complete Guide to Facial Expressions* by Gary Faigin (Watson-Guptill, 1990)
- *Constructive Anatomy* by George Bridgman (Dover, 1973)
- *Bridgman's Life Drawing* by George Bridgman (Dover, 1971)
- *Artistic Anatomy* by Dr. Paul Richer (Winston-Guptill, 1971)
- *Anatomy for the Artist* by Sarah Simblet (DK Publishing, 2001)

DVDs

- The Gnomon workshop has a large number of DVDs devoted to ZBrush as well as an excellent series of maquette sculpture DVDs by John Brown. These can be ordered online at www.thegnomonworkshop.com.
- Digital Tutors has a large selection of ZBrush DVDs available at www.digitaltutors.com.

CHAPTER 2

Facing the ZBrush Interface

From the moment the ZBrush interface appears, its creative potential is obvious. Few other digital art packages boast such an elegant working environment. The ZBrush interface may seem a little intimidating, but once you grasp the philosophy behind the design, you'll find that it is a comfortable place for digital sculpting and painting.

This chapter walks you through the ZBrush interface; it's much like a tour of an artist's studio. If, on a real studio tour, an artist pointed out various objects and tools without an explanation, you might get pretty frustrated. On the other hand, the artist could never adequately explain every tool in a short amount of time.

The situation is the same with this chapter. There's a lot to cover in the interface and only so much space to do it. In this interface tour, I will try to strike a balance between explaining where the ZBrush tools are and explaining what they do. The rest of the book will provide deeper explanations about the tools and interface features. To get the most out of this chapter you may want to have ZBrush at the ready. There are a few exercises to help you make sense of all the information.

This chapter includes the following topics:

- The Zen of ZBrush
- Using the transformation gyro in Paint mode
- Tools in Edit mode
- Palettes and trays
- The title bar
- Hotkeys

The Zen of ZBrush

If you've never done any 3D modeling or animation, you might actually be able to approach ZBrush with a slight advantage over someone who has spent a lot of time in programs such as Maya, 3ds Max, or XSI. This is because the tools in ZBrush are very different from the typical 3D modeling and animation tools. If you are an experienced 3D modeler, you may panic a little bit at the fact that ZBrush lacks a grid, a 3D compass, and any of the standard modeling tools. Either way, the best thing to do when you first open ZBrush is to shed your preconceived ideas of how a 3D program is supposed to work. In fact, don't think of ZBrush as a 3D modeling program, a paint program, or even a texturing program. Instead, step back for a moment and accept the "isness" of what ZBrush actually is. It is a digital sculpting and painting workshop.

While in ZBrush, you don't have to juggle animation, modeling, dynamics, and render modes. There are only two modes you truly need to be aware of when you are working: Draw and Edit. When you draw a stroke on the canvas using a ZBrush tool, you bring it into being, place it on the three-dimensional canvas, then position, scale, and rotate it.

When you edit a tool, the canvas becomes a virtual workspace. You suspend work on all other strokes that may exist on the canvas so that you can focus and refine that one particular object (known as a "3D Tool" in ZBrush parlance) until you are satisfied. Then you can export that particular 3D tool as a 3D model or use the 3D tool as a brush to paint copies of itself on the canvas for use in a composition. The same workspace is used in both cases. Some settings and controls work differently in Edit mode than they do in Draw mode, some settings are only available in one mode or the other, and some settings are universal. This tour will explain how the ZBrush controls work in either mode.

All objects are tools. A brush is a tool and so is a model of a dragon. In fact, you can think of a model of a dragon as a tool for painting dragon-shaped brush strokes. These tools are always within easy reach during a ZBrush session. We'll delve into these concepts more deeply as we go forward. For now, this explanation should provide you with enough background to understand why the interface is set up as it is.

The ZBrush Canvas

Open up ZBrush and the start page will present you with a number of options. You can work with some of the preset tools that ship with ZBrush or you can start with a blank document. Choose the Other option from the list to open a blank document (hotkey = Esc) to start with.

Figure 2.1 shows the ZBrush interface in its full glory. It seems like a lot to take in, but remember, this is a digital workshop. Just as when you first enter an artist's studio, you are taken aback by all the tools, paints, armatures, lights, shelves, and half-finished works. It's not long before you realize that an artist uses only a small number of the objects and tools in the studio at any one time. ZBrush is the same way. There's a lot there but you won't be using all of it all of the time. Furthermore, ZBrush helps you keep your studio neat by allowing you to put the tools you need most within easy reach.

Let's start with the center of the interface and work our way outward. Breaking the interface down like this will help to make it more accessible. The best place to start is with the canvas.

left shelf   menus/palettes   top shelf

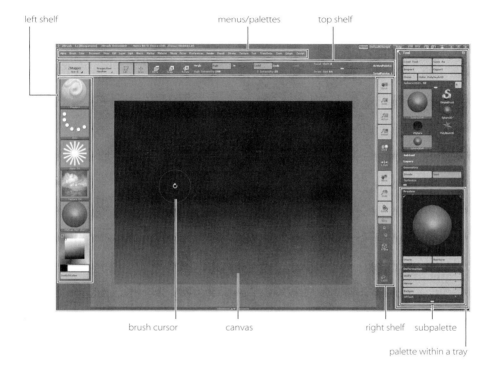

brush cursor   canvas   right shelf   subpalette

palette within a tray

Figure 2.1

The ZBrush interface

ZBrush ships with a number of interface configurations, and you can create custom interface layouts. This guided tour of the interface will show you the standard interface setup. To follow along properly, make sure you have this configuration loaded: click on the Preferences palette at the top of the page, expand the Config submenu, and click the Restore Standard UI button. You may also want to initialize ZBrush by clicking on the Init ZBrush button. This will clear all custom tools and settings from the palette. The colors of the interface have been changed in the figures to make the images more legible in print. Don't be alarmed if the images don't match exactly.

You see a ZBrush document on the canvas. The canvas is the square that dominates the center of the program, and it has some special properties that are part of what makes ZBrush so different. It's quite obvious from the outset that the canvas has height and width, which we refer to as the y- and x-axes. The ZBrush canvas also has depth axis, or a z-axis. Hence the name, ZBrush. When you use a tool to paint a brush stroke on the canvas, you can move it backward and forward in space, placing it in front of or behind other brush strokes. The default gradient you see on the canvas is meant to suggest the depth dimension in the canvas.

There are two ways to look at the canvas. If you are interested in using ZBrush as a self-contained painting and sculpting program, the canvas is the place where your artwork will be created, rendered, and saved for the world to see. What you place on the canvas is your art in progress. However, if you intend to use ZBrush as a modeling workshop where you create, edit, and texture 3D models to be used in scenes in another modeling and animation program, then think of the canvas as a sculpture stand. When you draw your model as a 3D tool onto the canvas and switch to *Edit* mode, you can mold your sculptures, push and pull their parts, and carve and tweak and even add additional parts until you are ready to export. Furthermore, you can continually switch and swap tools on the canvas while you work. You can use the canvas to record simple movies of your work in progress as well as turntable animations to show off your sculptures on a demo reel.

The ZBrush Shelves

On the top and either side of the canvas are shelves that hold the ZBrush buttons and controls (see Figure 2.2). We'll explore these shelves by moving from left to right around the canvas.

Figure 2.2

Shelves with various buttons and settings surround the ZBrush canvas on the left, top, and right.

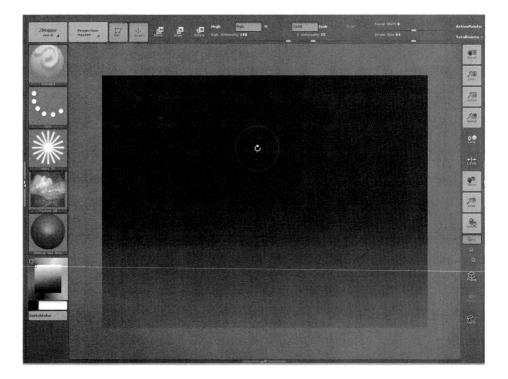

If you forget what a button or control in ZBrush does, you can hold the Ctrl key down while your mouse cursor hovers over the button in question. A little text box will appear with some explanatory notes about what the button does.

The Shelf on the Left

The left shelf holds several items that you will access often in a typical ZBrush editing session. These items include the current brush at the top, the brush stroke mode, the current alpha (if any), the current texture (if any), and the current material. Below these items is the all-important color picker.

The brushes are a used for sculpting 3D tools in Edit mode. If a 3D tool is not in Edit mode the icon is grayed out and the brushes are unavailable (Edit mode is explained in detail later in this chapter). Holding the cursor over the Brush icon causes it to appear enlarged and with more details about the current brush. Clicking on the icon reveals the inventory of available brushes. The Stroke icon below the brushes shows how the current brush will apply its stroke to the 3D tool you are editing. Clicking on the Stroke icon opens up an inventory palette of stroke types that can be used with the brushes.

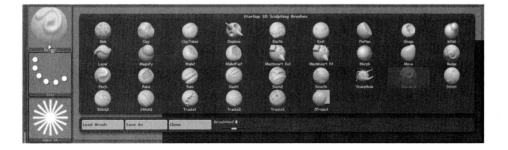

Figure 2.3

The inventory of 3D sculpting brushes

The Alpha, Texture, and Material icons provide easy access to the standard inventory of ZBrush alphas, textures, and materials that load when you start ZBrush as well as any custom alphas, textures, and materials you may make along the way or import from your own custom library (see Figure 2.4). Alphas, textures, and materials are each big topics that will be explored more deeply in Chapter 7 and Chapter 8.

The color picker has one square within another. You select the value and saturation of the current color from the inner square and you select the current hue with the outer square. Below the picker are two swatches for holding colors in memory.

You can select any color on the screen or applied to the 3D tool by dragging the mouse from the center square to any spot on the screen within the ZBrush interface. The picker will not select the colors of shadows on strokes or tools on the canvas, just the color applied to the stroke or tool.

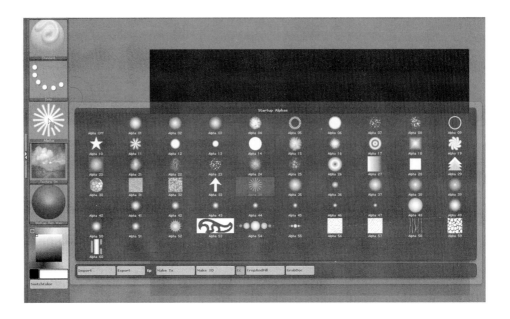

The Shelf at the Top

The top shelf has a number of buttons and sliders devoted to manipulating tools and brushes within ZBrush. At the far left are buttons that allow you to access two commonly used ZBrush plug-ins: ZMapper and Projection Master (see Figure 2.5). ZMapper allows you to create and edit normal maps; Projection Master is an advanced texturing environment you can use for your tools. Explanations of these plug-ins can be found in Chapter 10.

Next to the ZMapper and Projection Master buttons on the top shelf, there are a series of five important buttons. The first two are crucial. Understanding the purpose of the Edit and Draw buttons is key to unlocking the mysteries of the ZBrush environment. So let's begin our discussion by stepping back a few thousand years…

Human beings are tool users. Once we as a species started using and creating tools, we separated ourselves from the rest of the animals. Everything humans use to communicate, socialize, and survive is a tool, including language, culture, and microwave ovens. Likewise, you use tools to draw strokes on the canvas. A brush stroke is a tool. A model of a centaur is also a tool, or rather, it's a centaur-shaped tool that draws copies of itself on the canvas.

The Draw button puts you in Draw mode, which allows you to draw a stroke on the canvas using a tool (tools are found in the Tool palette; this will be discussed more in the section "Trays and Palettes" later in this chapter), thus calling it into existence within the frame of your artwork. This is just as true for simple 2.5-dimensional brush strokes as it is for complex 3D centaur models or a model of a head, as shown in Figure 2.6. That's the essence of working in Draw mode.

You use the Edit mode to edit a 3D tool. When you use a 3D tool to draw a stroke on the canvas and switch to Edit mode, it places the tool into a temporary state where the 3D tool can be edited. So when you draw your centaur tool on the canvas and then turn on the Edit button, you can modify the geometry of the centaur, paint texture maps and displacement maps, and add additional subtools to the centaur. When you are done editing the tool, you can either export it for use in another 3D modeling and animation program as a model or drop it on to the canvas for use in a composition. Or use the centaur tool to paint copies of the newly edited centaur all over the canvas; that's the quickest way ever to call up an army of centaurs! Chapter 5 will explore editing 3D tools in greater detail. As you edit a 3D tool, a version of the tool is updated in the tool inventory. As long as the ZBrush session is in progress the changes you make to a 3D tool will be stored in the tool inventory. The icon in the inventory will update to reflect the changes.

Switching between Draw and Edit mode in ZBrush often causes a great deal of stress for new ZBrush users. It may seem awkward at first but try and relax as you practice and experiment. You'll find that it becomes second nature fairly quickly.

Figure 2.6

The DemoHead 3D tool paints copies of the DemoHead.

The next three buttons on the top shelf are the Move, Scale, and Rotate buttons. They will behave differently depending on the status of the Edit and Draw buttons. When you draw a tool on the canvas, these three buttons will allow you to position the tool as a whole on the canvas using the special gyro manipulator. However, if you draw a tool on the canvas and then turn on the Edit button, these buttons will allow you to use the special Transpose handle to move, scale, and rotate either the whole tool or unmasked parts of the tool. Okay, that's a lot to fit into your head. Let's continue the interface tour and we'll revisit the concepts in the upcoming exercise, "Using the Transformation Gyro in Draw Mode."

The next section of the top shelf is a series of buttons and sliders. The buttons are labeled Mrgb, Rgb, and M. The *M* stands for *material* and the *Rgb* stands for *red green blue*, which to a computer is the same thing as saying *color*. So these buttons choose between painting modes. You can paint material and color (Mrgb), just color (Rgb), or just material (M). The slider below controls the intensity of the color contribution of the current brush. If none of these buttons are activated, the brush will affect the canvas only according to the settings applied by the next set of buttons.

A similar triad of buttons follows. These buttons are labeled *ZAdd*, *ZSub*, and *ZCut*, and they control whether or not a sculpting brush raises the surface of a 3D tool (ZAdd), pushes it down (ZSub), or cuts into it (ZCut). The Z intensity slider controls how much each stroke of the brush raises, lowers, or cuts into the surface of the 3D tool. If none of these buttons are activated, the brush may simply be set to paint color, material, or both without changing the 3D tool.

Finishing off the top shelf are the sliders that control the focal shift and the size of the brush. The brush appears on the canvas as a circle within a circle (Figure 2.7). The Size slider controls the diameter of both circles as a group, which in turn controls how much of the canvas or tool is affected by the brush. The focal shift controls the softness or the falloff of the edge of the brush. Moving this slider back and forth will cause the inner circle to grow and shrink. If both circles are the same size, the brush will have a hard edge; if there is a large gap between the size of the outer circle and the inner circle, there will be a sizable falloff from the center to the edge of the area affected by the brush.

The Shelf on the Right

The right shelf contains controls that are meant to help you navigate the canvas (see Figure 2.8). The Scroll and Zoom controls move the canvas around. When you use the Zoom tool to move into the canvas, you'll see the edges of the strokes on the canvas become jagged. It's just like zooming into an image in a paint program such as Photoshop.

The Actual and AAHalf buttons will snap the canvas to 100 percent and 50 percent in size, respectively. By reducing the canvas to 50 percent, you increase the anti-aliasing quality of the image on the canvas. If you're creating a composition in ZBrush, you may want to work at double size and then export at 50 percent so that the edges look smoother than they otherwise might. Anti-aliasing is discussed in Chapter 1.

focal shift

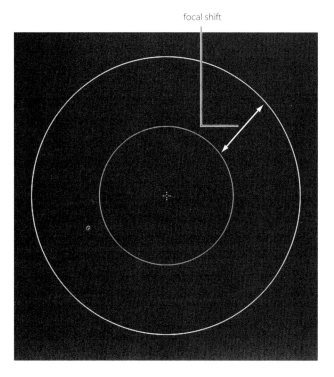

Figure 2.7
The distance between the concentric circles of the cursor represents the focal shift, or the falloff of the brush.

The top four controls on the right shelf are used mostly when you are creating a composition in ZBrush as if it were a painting program. The rest of the controls in this shelf are used most often when a tool is in Edit mode, in particular, 3D tools.

The Local pivot button will make the last area of an edited 3D tool become the center of rotation during editing. This is a very useful function and helps keep you from getting lost on your 3D tool as you spin it around. The L.Sym button is used when editing a 3D tool comprising many subtools. L.Sym causes sculpting and editing brushes to operate symmetrically in local space rather than global space. This ensures that symmetry is preserved when you're editing subtools.

The Move, Scale, and Rotate buttons on the right shelf can be a bit confusing at first because there are also Move, Scale, and Rotate buttons on the top shelf. They do not do the same thing. The buttons on the right shelf are for use on 3D tools in Edit mode. They help you manipulate a 3D tool while working. Think of them as controls for manipulating the sculpture stand that is the ZBrush canvas.

The Frame button turns on a wireframe display on the current 3Dtool. This is combined with whatever material is applied to the 3D tool, which will affect how the wireframe looks. When the Frame button is activated, you can get a better idea of the topology of the tool as well as see how the tool is grouped into various parts.

Figure 2.8
The right shelf contains canvas navigation buttons as well controls used while editing 3D tools.

The three buttons labeled XYZ, Y, and Z set the axis of rotation for the Rotate button on the right shelf. The Transp button allows you to make subtools transparent while working, and the final button activates lasso selection, which is helpful when selecting the individual polygons of a 3D tool in Edit mode.

Using the Transformation Gyro in Draw Mode

Okay, so all those tools on the shelves were a lot to take in and we're just getting started. Before we continue the interface tour, let's take a moment to test out some of these controls so the descriptions become clearer. To do this, we'll play with one of the models that ships with ZBrush.

1. If ZBrush is not loaded on your computer, go ahead and load it now. On the opening splash screen, choose the DemoHead. If ZBrush is open, you can activate the startup screen by clicking the DefaultZScript button at the very upper right of the screen next to the Help button. Once the startup page loads, choose the DemoHead (see Figure 2.9).

Figure 2.9

The startup screen offers a number of 3D polymesh tools that are useful for practice.

2. The DemoHead appears centered on the canvas. Take a look at the top shelf; notice that the Edit button is on, indicating that we are already in Edit mode. Notice that the Draw button is also activated. Turn the Edit button off and start dragging on the canvas; you'll see copies of the DemoHead appear wherever you drag. You are essentially drawing on the canvas using the DemoHead tool. Think of it as a brush that stamps copies of a head sculpture, as shown in Figure 2.10.

Figure 2.10

The DemoHead tool used as a brush

3. Draw copies of the head on top of the original DemoHead. Notice that each copied head aligns itself relative to the surface of the original head. It does this based on the normals (the direction in which the surface faces) of the surface already on the canvas.

4. Now click the Move button on the top shelf. The Draw button becomes inactive; the modes these buttons control are mutually exclusive. You'll see a manipulator appear that looks like a series of 3D circles. This is the gyro tool, which you can use to position a stroke in 3D (see Figure 2.11).

   It is important to understand that this controller works for only the most recent stroke. You can't use it to change the position of any of the strokes created up to the most recent ones. Those strokes—the DemoHead copies in this case—have been dropped on the canvas. To change them, you'll have to undo a number of times and redraw them. This concept tends to make first-time users of ZBrush a little nervous. Once you get used to working in ZBrush, you'll find that there are many ways to change a composition as you go; you're never really stuck with anything that you create.

Figure 2.11

The gyro transformation control lets you reposition the most recent stroke placed on the canvas.

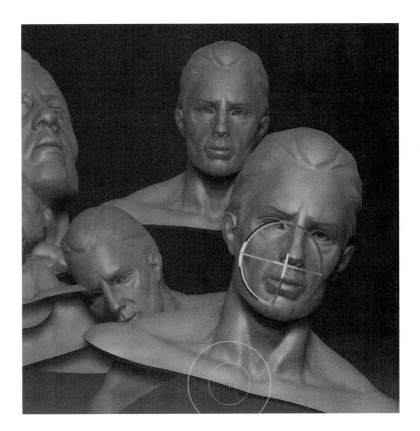

5. With the Move button still active, try dragging on various parts of the gyro manipulator. Try moving the active head stroke on top of the pile of heads and drag up and down somewhere on a blank spot on the canvas. Here's what you'll see when you play with the gyro while in Move mode:

   • The stroke you are transforming will move differently depending on what part of the gyro your mouse cursor is over when moving.

   • Dragging on one of the gray parts of the gyro ring will move a stroke parallel to the canvas.

   • Dragging on one of the colored ring intersections will restrict the movement of the stroke to the direction perpendicular to that intersection. That sounds complicated, but try dragging on one of these intersections and the meaning will become apparent.

   • Dragging within the area defined by the gyro, but not on one of the rings, will align the tool either parallel to the canvas or to the surface normal of any strokes below the current stroke. Play with this for a while to get a sense of what this means (see Figure 2.12).

- Dragging up and down on a blank spot on the canvas with the Gyro activated will cause the current stroke to move back and forth along the Z axis. Note that the tool will not appear any smaller as it recedes in the distance or larger as it moves forward but the depth positioning of the stroke is changing. This is most obvious when the stroke is on top of another tool/stroke.

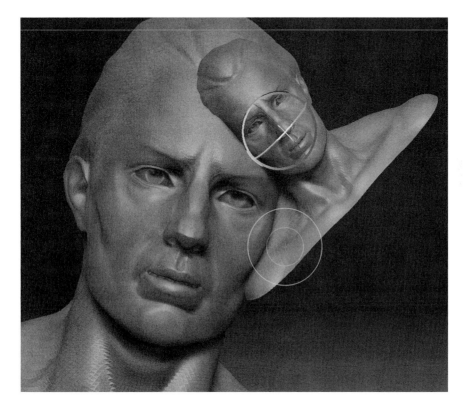

Figure 2.12

Selecting the gyro within the spherical area of the tool causes the stroke to align itself per-pendicular to the normal of the sur-face below it.

6. Switch the mode of the gyro to Rotate and Scale and continue experimenting. In Rotate mode, the gray ring rotates the 3D tool parallel to the canvas; the colored rings restrict the rotation to the axis indicated by the ring, and dragging within the area defined by the gyro allows for freeform rotation.

7. In Scale mode, the intersections of the rings restrict the scaling to the axis indicated by the intersection; uniform scaling is accomplished by dragging within the area defined by the gyro. Dragging on the rings has no effect.

8. The hotkeys for the gyro's Move, Rotate, and Scale modes are w, e, and r respectively.

Play with drawing more copies of the head on the canvas and use the gyro to position them. Working in this way is what Draw mode is all about in ZBrush. These are the basics of how you create a composition in ZBrush, and if your goal is to use ZBrush as an illus-tration tool, then you'll find yourself working like this quite often. If you're more interested in using ZBrush for digital sculpting, you may not find yourself using the gyro all that much. It's still a good tool to become familiar with.

> For new users, the gyro is often a stumbling block. It takes some patience and practice to master. Undo (Ctrl+z) does not work while the gyro is active. Undo will work once you are finished using the gyro but it will undo all the changes you've made while the gyro was active. All transformations performed while the gyro is active are considered a single action. This will drive you crazy for a while, especially if you are used to typical transformation manipulators in other 3D applications. Don't give up, it will make sense after some practice. Understand that there are other ways to transform 3D tools!

Using Tools in Edit Mode

Now it's time to see what Edit mode is all about. If you are keen on digital sculpting, Edit mode will quickly become your home in ZBrush. While in Edit mode you can constantly change your 3D tool without worrying about dropping it on the canvas. The transformation gyro is not used; instead, you'll use the move, scale, and rotate buttons on the right shelf to position the 3D tool while sculpting.

While in Edit mode, the transformation buttons on the top shelf will access the transpose handle instead of the transformation gyro. As you become quicker in ZBrush, you'll find that using the hotkeys becomes second nature and worrying about which Move button does what will become less of a concern. But before you get to that point, you'll need to practice. Let's return to the DemoHead for further experimentation.

1. If your document with a big pile of heads is still open, activate the Draw button, drag on the canvas so that another DemoHead appears, turn on the Edit button (hotkey = t), and press Ctrl+n to clear the canvas of all the dropped tools.

   If you're in a different ZBrush scene, click the DefaultZScript button at the very top line of commands in ZBrush and choose DemoHead from the startup screen. The DemoHead will already be in Edit mode when ZBrush loads. If ZBrush is not open at all, start it and choose the DemoHead scene from the options on the startup screen.

2. Drag the cursor on an area of the canvas outside of the 3D tool. The 3D tool will rotate around its pivot. This is how you can access different parts of a 3D tool while editing. If you click and drag on the Rotate button on the right shelf, you get the same result.

3. Click and drag on the Move button on the right shelf and you'll see the 3D tool move about the canvas. Now hold the Alt key while dragging on a blank spot and you get the same behavior.

4. Click and drag on the Scale button. The head gets bigger and smaller. Now hold the Alt key down, press down on the canvas with the brush, release the Alt key, and drag. The 3D tool scales just as it does with the button. This last action takes a little practice.

5. Try scaling, moving, and rotating the 3D tool. Use the hotkey combinations as much as possible; you will become a faster sculptor using hotkeys than if you rely on the buttons. You'll find these actions work very well when using a digital tablet.

6. You can center the 3D tool on the canvas by holding the Alt key and clicking on the canvas, or simply click one of the Move, Scale, or Rotate buttons on the right shelf.

7. Hold the Shift key down while rotating the 3D tool. You'll see the 3D tool snap into the closest orthographic view.

It's also useful to think of the scale function in Edit mode as actually more like a zoom function when you're editing a 3D tool. You can use it when you want to zoom in and focus on refining a specific area of a 3D tool.

8. Make sure the Draw button on the top shelf is activated and start moving the cursor over the surface of the 3D tool. The 3D tool bulges and distorts! You are now actually doing some digital sculpting (see Figure 2.13).

   The sculpting brushes are available when both the Draw and Edit buttons are activated. Dragging on the canvas no longer draws copies of the head all over the place. You may also notice that by default your sculpted strokes are mirrored onto the other side of the model. Symmetry is on by default in the DemoHead scene. We'll be working with symmetry in Chapter 5.

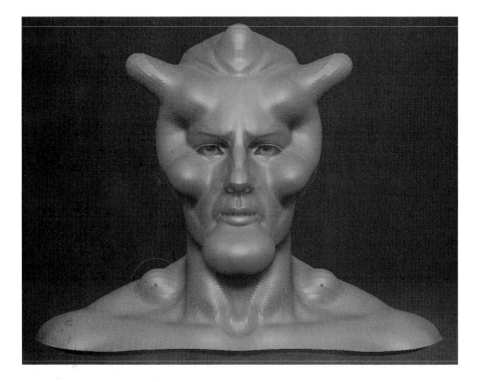

Figure 2.13

Activating the Draw button on the top shelf while in Edit mode lets you sculpt the 3D tool.

9. Take a look at the Brush icon at the top of the left shelf. It is no longer grayed out, meaning that it is active in Edit mode. If you hover your cursor over the Brush icon, you'll see the icon enlarged with details about the current brush. The Standard brush is active by default.

   If you click on the icon, you'll see a selection of brushes appear in the expanding inventory palette. Now is a good time to try out these brushes; see how badly you can mess up the DemoHead's face. We'll get into detailed descriptions of many of these brushes in Chapters 5 and 6. If you hold the Ctrl key while positioning the brush cursor over one of the brush icons in the brush inventory, a pop-up window will appear with a description of how the brush works.

10. Try activating the Move, Scale, and Rotate buttons on the top shelf. When any of these buttons are active while editing a 3D tool, you'll see a triad of circles connected by a line appear in the canvas (Figure 2.14). If you drag the inner circles around, the tool will distort. Dragging the outer circles repositions the tool.

    While in Edit mode, the Move, Scale, and Rotate buttons on the top shelf activate the Transpose handle. This is an advanced set of controls that is most often used for posing 3D tools. It's a rather large topic, so we'll leave the discussion of the Transpose handle for Chapter 6. Feel free to play with them a bit, but don't worry if they don't seem to make sense immediately.

Figure 2.14

The Transpose handle appears as a triad of concentric circles connected by a line.

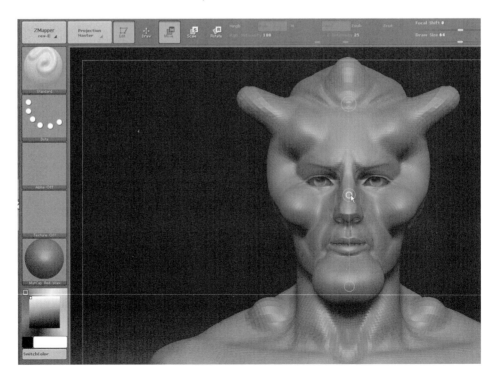

11. Deactivate the Edit mode button and draw on the canvas. You'll see copies of the head appear again, but now they reflect the changes you've made to the 3D tool (Figure 2.15). A copy of the 3D tool with all the most recent changes is stored in the tool inventory as you work. You can save these copies to your local disk as your own custom 3D tools (see the section on the Tool palette later on in this chapter).

Figure 2.15

Painting on the canvas results in copies of the edited 3D tool.

12. Before moving on to the next part of the interface, take some time to play around with the settings we've discussed. Try changing the brush size and focal shift of the brush. Play around while the Move, Scale, and Rotate buttons on the top and right shelves are activated until they start to make some sense. Change colors, materials, brushes, and stroke types. Sculpt the 3D tool with the brushes and try changing the ZAdd, ZSub, and ZCut buttons. Once you feel as if you have a general idea on how these things work, move on to the next section, which will take us to the area of the interface beyond the shelves.

Trays and Palettes

We'll continue working our way outward from the canvas with another level. This takes us to the trays. On the right side of the canvas you'll see a section labeled *Tools* within a large gray area. The Tool menu is also known as the Tool palette. The large gray area is a tray. If you click on the gray triangles nestled in the divider between the left shelf and the tray, the tray collapses, expanding the work area. Click on them again and it reappears. The tray is analogous to a drawer in an artist's toolbox. A tray exists on the right and the left sides of the canvas as well as below the canvas. You'll fill the trays with tools so that you've always got your favorite tools and settings close at hand. The tools that will fill these trays are located in the palettes, Figure 2.16 shows the tool palette stored in a tray.

The palettes exist normally as menus at the top of the screen. You can see the alphabetized list of menus starting with the Alpha menu at the upper left and ending with the ZScript menu on the upper right. If you click on the Alpha menu, you'll see the Alpha palette expand (see Figure 2.17). Here's where you'll find all the settings related to working with alphas. The palette is divided into several sections, or groups of settings, called subpalettes. This is true for all of the palettes.

Take a look at the Tool palette in the right tray. Click on the large tool icon in the upper left of the palette to expand the tool inventory. Choose a 3D tool such as the Gear tool. The Tool palette has a really large number of subpalettes, which are groups of controls within the rounded boxes, depending on what has been chosen as the current tool; some are collapsed by default to keep the palette from getting too long. You can expand them—try clicking on the word *Preview* in the Tool palette and you'll see the Preview settings expand in their own subpalette (see Figure 2.18).

If you expand a number of subpalettes, you'll see that the Tool palette gets so long that all of its contents can't fit on the screen. No problem; you can click on the side of the Tool palette and drag up and down. The palette scrolls up and down, giving you access to all the different settings. When the palette is not in a tray, it drops down like a menu in a more typical software package. To close a palette that has dropped down, move your brush off of the palette interface. It closes automatically.

You'll find that some palettes are accessed constantly during a ZBrush session, and some you use only once in a while. This is where the trays come in. In the right tray, click on the circular icon at the upper-right corner of the Tool palette. The palette disappears from the tray. Click on the word *Tool* in the top menu bar. It expands here as a menu. Click on the circular icon again and it pops over to the right tray. Try opening and closing the tray. The tools stay there right where you need them even when the tray is closed. You can also move the tray up and down by dragging up and down on the side of the tray. To remove the palette from the tray, click on the circular icon in the upper-right corner of the palette. Clicking on the title bar of a palette while it's in the tray will collapse the palette, freeing more room in the tray while at the same time keeping the palette available in the tray.

Make sure the Tool palette is in the tray and expand the Transform palette. Click on its circular icon in the upper right. The Transform palette pops over to the right tray above the Tool palette. You can load the tray with all of your favorite palettes and remove them by clicking on their circular icons. This action becomes very quick and natural after a little practice.

The palettes load up the tray from top to bottom in the order in which you add them. You'll also notice that palettes have a default tray that they like to go to when you click on their circular icon. Some go to the right tray by default; some go to the left. If you decide you prefer a palette to be in the tray on the opposite side, you can grab the handle with your cursor and drag the entire palette to your preferred tray position. The cursor will turn into a crosshair when it's over the handle, indicating that you can drag the palette by the handle.

Figure 2.16

The Tool palette as it looks while in a tray

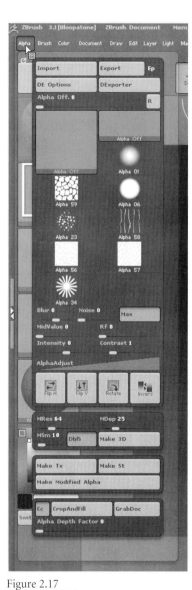

Figure 2.17

The palettes expand like a menu when not stowed in a tray.

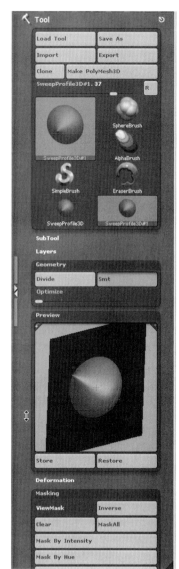

Figure 2.18

The palette contains subpalettes that can expand and collapse.

You can also drag palettes to different locations on the tray to rearrange them. It's easiest to do this by dragging from the top menu to a blank spot below the last palette in a tray. To remove a palette from a tray, drag its circular handle icon off the tray or click on it. Notice that a palette temporarily disappears from a tray when you click on its label in the top menu. This keeps you from being able to load multiple copies of the palette into a tray, which would be confusing for both you and ZBrush.

Many of the palettes contain sliders that allow you to adjust the settings applied to a tool or control. You can change the value of the slider by grabbing the handle with the cursor and moving it back and forth. You can also click on the numeric indicator that is paired with the slider and type in a value on your keyboard. This is the best method for ensuring that the value is accurate.

Now that you have some idea of how palettes and trays work, let's take a brief look at the settings available in each palette. Complete descriptions of each palette can be found in the ZBrush documentation under the Palette Reference section. We'll get a chance to explore each one throughout the book as well.

Alpha

The Alpha palette contains settings for adjusting the current alpha texture, a dialogue for importing and exporting alphas to and from your hard drive, and access to the Displacement Exporter plug-in options and interface. The Alpha palette is related to the alpha inventory icon on the left shelf, but in the Alpha palette you have more controls for refining the current alpha, including access to the alpha adjustment curve.

In ZBrush, you'll use alphas to adjust the shape of brushes, as stencils for applying texture and colors to limited areas, and as displacement maps, which can be exported from this palette. Alphas are covered in detail in Chapter 7. Clicking on the large Alpha icon gives you access to the startup alpha inventory, just like the button on the left shelf (see Figure 2.19).

Brush

The Brush palette offers access to the 3D sculpting brush startup inventory just like the brush icon on the left shelf. It also has a large number of controls, which you can use to customize the current 3D sculpting brush. One of the most interesting settings is the gravity button; when this is activated your the changes you make with the brush behave as if gravity is pulling on the surface of the 3D tool. The sculpting brushes are available only when a 3D tool is in Edit mode. You can load brushes saved to disk from this palette or save your customized brushes. Sculpting brushes are covered in detail in Chapter 5.

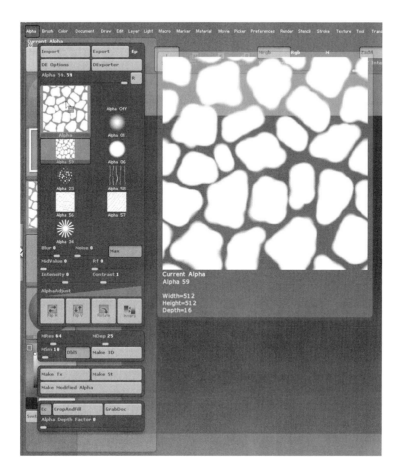

Figure 2.19
The Alpha palette contains controls and settings for the alpha textures. Hovering the cursor over an icon in the palette will cause an enlarged view of the alpha to appear on the canvas.

Color

The Color palette has a copy of the color picker you see on the left shelf. It also has numerous additional pickers and controls found in the Modifiers subpalette.

Document

The Document palette is where you load and save ZBrush documents. You can also import Photoshop files and other supported formats (BMP, JPEG, TIFF). You may be tempted to save an edited 3D model using the save function on this palette, but that won't work the way you might expect. As stated before, a 3D model in ZBrush is a tool, and to save a tool, use the Tool palette. The save function here is for compositions you create in ZBrush. ZBrush warns you if you try to save a tool in Edit mode using the controls on the Document palette (see Figure 2.20).

CONTROL CURVES

Many palettes come with a Curve Editor that allows you to fine-tune the settings applied to a tool. The Curve Editor is a visual control that uses a graph to indicate how the settings are applied. You can edit the graph by moving control points up and down, which changes the shape of the graph. To understand better how this works, try out the following steps:

1. Expand the Alpha palette.

2. Click the Alpha icon and choose Alpha 01 from the menu. It's a fuzzy white dot.

3. Click on the box labeled Alpha Adjust to expand the graph.

4. You'll see a line graph with a diagonal moving up to the right. The graph represents the intensity of values applied to the alpha. Intense areas are light or white; less intense areas are dark. In the case of Alpha 01, the alpha is most intense at the white center of the circle and less intense toward the edges. Outside of the fuzzy white dot, the intensity is zero.

5. The left side of the graph is where the alpha intensity is zero; the right side is where the intensity is 1.

6. Click on the graph to add a control point. Move it up and down, left and right; note the difference in the Alpha icon.

7. To remove a control point, drag it all the way up to the top of the graph and outside the graph box.

8. To make the in and out points of a particular control point straight, drag the control point up and off the graph and then back down on to the graph. Doing this repeatedly will alternate between straight and curved in and out points.

9. You can shift the entire graph left or right without moving the control points using the Focal Shift slider.

10. You can offset the graph, add noise, reset, copy, save, and load the graph using the buttons below the graph. Copied curves can be pasted into other control curves in other palettes.

11. To collapse the graph, click on the Close bar below the graph. The graph will still be active, but it will be collapsed to save space on the palette.

12. If you change alphas, the settings will be applied to the new alpha. The settings may not be reflected in the large icon that appears when you hover the cursor over an Alpha icon, but they will be applied to that alpha. The smaller icon on the palette is a more accurate representation of how the alpha will be applied.

Control curves like this one are present in many of the palettes and affect a variety of settings. To find out how a control curve affects a setting or tool, press the Ctrl key and hover your mouse cursor over the graph.

The Document palette also has controls for setting the background gradient colors, the border colors, and, most important, the size of the document. The Pro button constrains the proportions of the document, maintaining the current aspect ratio. Set the document size when you are first starting a document. You can't resize the image while in the midst of creating a composition without dropping all the tools onto the canvas.

The StoreDepthHistory and DeleteDepthHistory buttons deal with the ZDepth of a composition. This feature is used in conjunction with the Projection Master plug-in.

Draw

The Draw palette has controls that duplicate the brush controls in the top shelf. These are size, focal shift, and the material and color settings as well as the brush depth controls (ZAdd, ZSub, and ZCut). Below these controls is a subpalette that offers a preview of the brush stroke as well as more advanced controls. This subpalette is used for the 2.5D brush strokes created in Draw mode and not so much the brushes used to alter a 3D model in Edit mode.

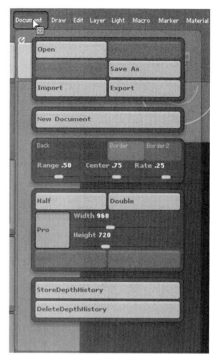

Figure 2.20

The Document Palette has controls for setting the size of the canvas.

The preview shows how the tip of the brush looks to the ZBrush canvas. You can rotate the image around to see a 3D view. The width, height, and depth of the brush tip can be adjusted as well how the brush stroke is embedded into previously existing strokes on the canvas. These settings will affect all of the brushes you use in a ZBrush session; they are global controls for how the strokes are drawn on the canvas.

The Draw palette also has a Perspective toggle and a Focal Length slider. This allows you to switch the camera, normally in orthographic mode, to a camera with perspective distortion. Adding perspective to the scene can make a 3D tool look more natural and increase the drama of the composition.

When you create strokes using a 3D tool, the 3D tool will appear transparent if the RGB slider is lower than 100 percent. Your brush strokes will appear translucent. Adjusting the refraction and the blur will affect the quality of the transparency seen on the tool (see Figure 2.21).

Edit

This palette offers access to the Undo and Redo buttons as well as a running tab of how many undos are available in the cue. The undo hotkeys, like many programs, are Ctrl+z for undo and Ctrl+Shift+z for redo.

Figure 2.21

The Refract and Blur
sliders in the Draw
palette modify the
look of the trans-
parency by adding
refraction and
refraction blur.

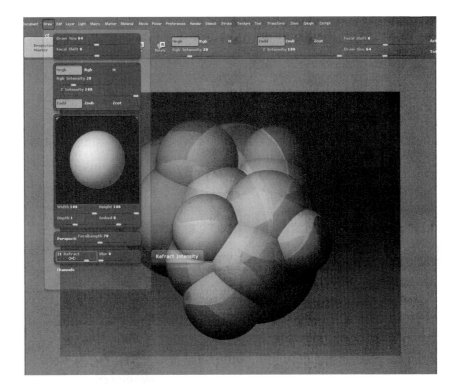

Layer

ZBrush can create layers in a document, similar to layers in a paint program such as Photoshop. However, remember that ZBrush has depth, so unlike layers in a typical 2D paint
program where one layer will obscure all layers below it, ZBrush layers respect the depth
of all strokes in all the layers equally.

It might be easier to think of a ZBrush layer as a group. You can create a layer, fill it
with a number of 2.5D and 3D strokes, create another layer, and fill it with even more
2.5D and 3D strokes. The strokes in both layers will interact with each other because they
exist in the same space. However, you can use the layer controls to hide the strokes on one
layer while you refine the strokes in the other; you can also delete a layer or merge its contents with another. This gives you another level of editing power beyond just undo and
redo. ZBrush allows up to 16 layers in a single document.

In the Layer palette (Figure 2.22), the active layer is outlined in white. Holding the cursor over the layer icon will reveal an enlarged silhouette preview of the layer. To show or
hide a layer, make the layer active, click on it to toggle its visibility, then click on another
layer. Shift+clicking on a layer icon will make all layers visible. Holding the tilde key (~)
while clicking on a stroke on the canvas will cause the associated layer to become the
active layer. There is always at least one layer in a ZBrush document.

You need to keep in mind that creating and switching layers will cause all strokes to be dropped to the canvas. You may not use the Layer palette much if you are creating digital sculpts for animation, but if you use ZBrush for creating compositions and illustrations, layers will quickly become your best friend. The palette includes controls for duplicating, flipping, and offsetting layers in all three dimensions. You can bake in lighting and rendering for the strokes currently on the layer. This can save time and processing later on if you want to render a complex scene in ZBrush. The Wrap mode will cause strokes moved off one side of the screen to appear on the other, making it very easy to create seamless textures in ZBrush. Layers are explored more in Chapter 3.

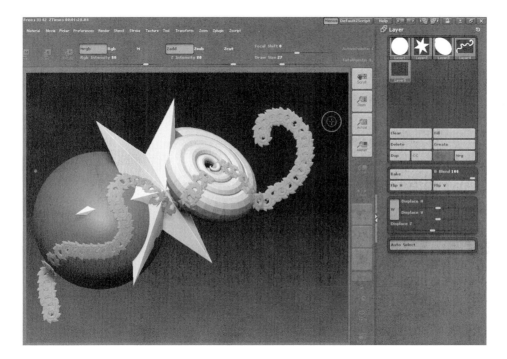

Figure 2.22

The Layer palette allows you to control the order and positioning of the layers.

Be careful not to confuse the layers in the Layer palette with the 3D layers in the Tool palette. The Tool palette layers are completely different and relate only to 3D tools in Edit mode.

Light

In traditional art, rendering light is quite difficult. Attention must be paid to relative intensity, the consistency of the light's direction, how the shadows reveal form, and how they behave based on perspective, specular highlights, and reflective properties. In ZBrush, much of that work is taken care of with virtual lights.

The Light palette is where you adjust the settings for the current light, create additional lights, and adjust shadows and shadow type (see Figure 2.23). Of course, any time computer software takes the difficulty out of a particular aspect of artistic technique, the danger of becoming a lazy artist emerges. Just because ZBrush can put shadows in your scene automatically doesn't mean you don't need to study lighting. The only way to keep computer-generated art from looking computer generated is to study the fundamentals of art and always have them in mind regardless of the medium in which you are presently working.

Lights and their settings will be explored more in Chapter 8. You can reposition a light by dragging the cursor over the material preview sphere. The sphere will update to show the lighting position in the scene. The ability to easily change the lighting while you work in ZBrush is an important feature. Sculptors in the real world continually change the angle of the light while they work on a sculpture. Seeing the sculpture in a new light can reveal problems or open up areas of artistic exploration.

> MatCap materials, such as the default Red Wax material, have lighting baked in so they will not react to a change in lighting position. Choose a standard material from the lower portion of the material inventory, such as a Fast Shader, before changing the light position. Then the preview sphere will react properly.

Macro

The Macro palette offers controls for recording and loading macros. A macro is simply a list of commands that tell ZBrush to do something. Let's say you find yourself constantly resetting the document size to a specific resolution. You can record a macro that performs this specific action and then it will appear in the Macro palette as a button. Click the button and everything you did while recording the macro will happen again; your document will be resized to your stored specifications. Let's try a quick example so you can see how this works.

1. In the Macro palette, click the New Macro button. Your macro is now recording; everything you do from this point on will be part of the macro.

2. Open the Document palette.

3. Turn off the Pro button.

4. Set Width to 1440 and press Enter.

5. Set Height to 810 and press Enter.

6. Click the Resize button and accept the warning in the pop-up box that says this action is undoable.

7. Open the Macro palette and click the End Macros button. The Save dialog box appears. You should be in the `Pixologic\ZBrush3\Startup\Macros` folder. If not, navigate to this location.

8. Save your macro in the Misc folder. Notice that it is just a regular TXT file; it's really just a list of ZScript commands. Make sure the name you give the macro is at least eight characters long, otherwise it will not appear in the Macro palette. Name it resizeTo16by9.txt and save it.

Figure 2.23

The Light palette allows you to adjust and add lighting to a ZBrush composition.

Figure 2.24

Custom macros are saved under the Misc heading. A custom folder labeled Erix has been created as well. The macros in this folder appear on the Macro palette.

9. In the Macro palette, click the Reload All Macros button. You'll see your macro appear as a button under the MISC subpalette along with a few macros that come with ZBrush.

10. Start a new document set to the default size and then test your macro by clicking the button in the Macros menu.

> If you create a new folder in Pixologic\ZBrush3\Startup\Macros directory and save your macros there, the name of this folder will appear in the palette with your custom macros loaded (see Figure 2.24).

Marker

Markers are a way to store information about a 3D tool's position on the canvas before it has been dropped. This way you can redraw the tool if you need to recall it later on after changes have been made to the composition. The buttons on the palette determine what information is to be stored on the canvas. The markers themselves are hot spots on the canvas. Using the Multi-marker tool you can create groups of 3D tools that can be stored as a single tool. However, the introduction of subtools in ZBrush 3 has replaced some of the usefulness of this feature.

Material

In ZBrush, *materials* refers to the quality of a surface and how it reacts to light, shadow, and other strokes in the scene. Materials come in two main types, *MatCap*, which are materials created using the material capture tool, and standard materials. Creating and using materials in ZBrush is a pretty big topic that will be fully explored in Chapter 8. For now it's enough to say that the Material palette is where you can edit, load, save, and clone the materials you use in a scene.

As with the Alpha palette, there is a large icon that you can click on to show the material inventory, which has all the materials available in the scene (see Figure 2.25). The Material icon on the left shelf allows access to the same inventory. If you expand the Modifiers subpalette, you'll see that there are a lot of settings to adjust when modifying a material. The number of settings will vary with the type of material used.

Movie

You can record your ZBrush sessions using the controls in this palette. In fact, the movies that appear on the DVD that accompanies this book were recorded in ZBrush requiring no additional software. This is a great way to share your ideas with other ZBrush users, create tutorials, or show off your work in a demo reel. The Movie palette has controls for how you can record the movies as well as for loading and saving movies.

Figure 2.25

The Material palette and material inventory show the many materials that can be applied to ZBrush strokes. The settings in the Material palette allow you to create and save your own custom materials.

Picker

The Picker palette is very useful when you're creating an illustration in ZBrush using 3D tools. It allows you to determine how a 3D tool will be drawn on the canvas in relation to the canvas itself and other strokes that may already exist (see Figure 2.26). There are also controls for determining each stroke's color and material attributes. Try the following:

1. Click on the Default ZScript button in the upper right of the screen to start a new ZBrush session.

2. Choose the Dog model from the startup screen. You can also use the Load Tool button on the tool palette to load the dog tool. The tool is located in the Program Files\Pixologic\ZBrush3\ZTools folder.

3. When the dog appears on the canvas, click the Edit icon on the top shelf to deactivate Edit mode. You want to be in Draw mode to see how the Picker palette works.

4. Click and drag on the Dog model; you'll see copies of the dog appear wherever you drag. Note the orientation of each pooch as it appears on the screen.

5. In the picker palette, rotate the pencil icon by dragging the cursor in the preview box. Then draw some more strokes on top of the other dog strokes. Notice that the new dogs match the orientation of the pencil icon when they first appear on the screen. Of course, you can rotate the current dog stroke around as long as your brush is active. Right now the pencil icon shows the initial orientation as they are drawn on the screen.

6. On the left shelf, change the stroke type from dragRect to Freehand.

Figure 2.26

The Pencil preview window shows the orientation of the brush stroke as it will be created on the canvas. You can move the pencil around to change the orientation.

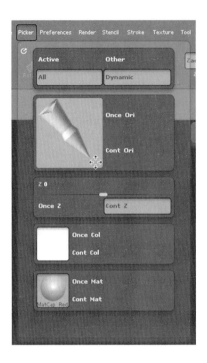

7. Paint some more on top of the dogs; now the dogs appear depending on where you paint. If you activate the Once Ori button and draw more dogs on top of the original dogs, the orientation of all of the new dogs in the stroke will be determined by the normal of the first surface you start the stroke on. If you turn on the Cont Ori button, the orientation of each new dog in the stroke will update based on the normals of the surface beneath it. In both cases, the orientation will be determined by the pencil icon on the Picker palette if you paint on a blank part of the canvas.

8. Likewise, the Color and Material subpalettes allow you to change the color of the 3D tool in the stroke based on the colors and materials of the strokes below.

9. The ZSlider sets the overall ZDepth of the 3D tools in the stroke relative to the 3D tools under the current stroke. Just as with the orientation, color, and material, you can have the ZDepth determined by the first 3D tool in the stroke (once Z) or have it continually update (cont Z).

As you first start using ZBrush, you may not use the Picker palette often. The tools here have a subtle power that you will appreciate as you become more experienced.

Preferences

The Preferences palette is where you set the overall behavior of ZBrush. It contains settings for everything from customizing the interface to how 3D models behave when they are imported.

Render

The Render palette is where you access the controls for the lighting, shading, anti-aliasing, and other qualities of your ZBrush composition. The controls in this palette are used in conjunction with the controls in the Light and Material palettes when you're creating a composition. Rendering in ZBrush occurs right on the canvas; depending on the settings, it can take anywhere from a few seconds to a few minutes. You can choose between several render quality settings (see Figure 2.27).

- Preview is the default quality of ZBrush. It shows basic color and texture information with simple real-time shadows.

- Fast quality removes material and shadow information from the scene to improve performance.

- Flat render quality displays only the color of the pixols on the screen.

- Best quality is the most computationally expensive. A number of settings in the Render palette affect how Best quality is calculated. Best quality renders the lighting, texturing, shadow, and materials of the strokes on the canvas and takes into account how they interact with each other in terms of reflection and light occlusion.

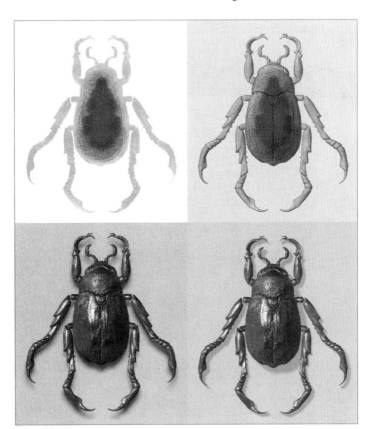

Figure 2.27

A 3D tool stroke rendered in the four different render qualities—Flat, Fast, Preview, and Best (from left to right)—using the Reflected Map material.

You will want to render at Best quality when you are finishing a ZBrush composition. None of these render settings will affect a model exported from ZBrush. The settings on the Render palette will be discussed further in Chapter 8.

Stencil

The Stencil palette is related to the controls in the Alpha palette. A stencil masks out areas on the canvas where paint strokes will appear. A stencil can be created from an alpha and then moved about the screen as you work, allowing for some interesting texturing possibilities. The stencil is manipulated with its own floating control interface called the coin controller. Let's take a quick look at some of the ways the stencil can be used.

1. Click on the DefaultZScript button in the upper right of the screen to start a new ZBrush session. Or open ZBrush if it isn't already running.

2. Choose the DemoHead tool from the startup screen.

3. Make sure you stay in Edit mode; it should be on by default in this scene. Take a look at the top shelf to make sure.

4. Open the Alpha palette by clicking on the Alpha menu on the top toolbar.

5. Click the large Alpha icon, and from the pop-up alpha inventory, choose alpha number 10—the star.

6. In the Alpha palette, click the Make St button toward the bottom of the palette (see Figure 2.28); this will turn the current alpha into a stencil.

Figure 2.28

Making a stencil from an alpha

7. The screen should turn grayish except for a star surrounded by a red square. This is the stencil; most likely it is positioned somewhere randomly on the screen. It can be repositioned using the coin controller (see Figure 2.29).

8. Hold down the spacebar; you'll see the coin controller appear beneath the position of the brush.

9. Click on the bottom of the controller on the letters MOV and drag the stencils on top of the model. Place the star stencil on the DemoHead's forehead.

10. Paint some brush strokes over the stencil. The current sculpting brush is the Standard brush. It will cause a star shape area to rise from the surface of the DemoHead (see Figure 2.30).

11. The coin controller changes its behavior depending on where you click it. You can use the coin controller to rotate, scale, and position the stencil. By dragging on the area labeled MOV ROT, the stencil will be positioned based on the normal of the surface.

Figure 2.29
The stencil can be moved around using the coin controller.

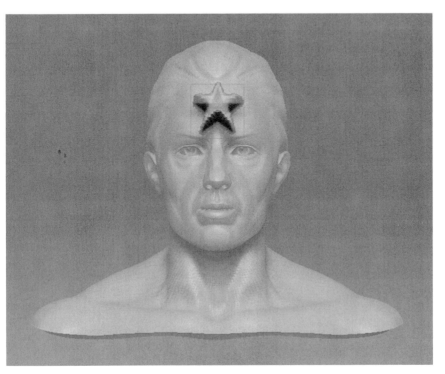

Figure 2.30

Painting over the model using a sculpting brush with the stencil activated changes the model's surface only in the area defined by the stencil.

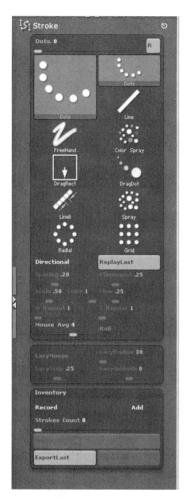

Figure 2.31

The Stroke palette settings control how brush strokes behave on the canvas. These settings affect both the tools and the sculpting brushes.

The Stencil palette offers some more controls for adjusting the stencil. The RGB and Elev buttons at the bottom of the palette control how the stencil is displayed; they don't affect the functionality of the stencil.

Stroke

The Stroke palette allows access to the stroke inventory as well as a variety of settings for customizing the strokes (see Figure 2.31). Strokes affect how a brush stroke draws on the canvas. For example, the Freehand stroke causes the brush to paint like a normal paintbrush would. If the Freehand stroke is used with a 3D model tool, the copies of the model will flow out of the brush in a line. Other stroke types such as Drag Rect will allow for precise positioning of a stroke on the canvas. As you drag, the stroke will appear, scale, and rotate depending on how you move the cursor before releasing pressure on the digital tablet or letting go of the left mouse button.

The Stroke palette also allows you to record and play back brush strokes.

The LazyMouse settings control how closely the stroke follows the cursor when you draw on the canvas. This feature can help you achieve steadier and straighter brush strokes as you paint over the surface of the model. Try this short exercise to get the feel of the LazyMouse settings:

1. Start a new ZBrush document. Click on the DefaultZScript button in the upper left of the screen to display the startup page.

2. From the startup page, choose the PolySphere tool.

3. The PolySphere tool will load up already in Edit mode. Choose the Standard brush from the brush inventory on the left shelf. Set the stroke type to dots.

4. Paint a few strokes across the surface of the PolySphere.

5. Open the Strokes palette and activate LazyMouse.

6. Paint some more strokes on the surface of the PolySphere. You'll see a red line appear between the cursor and the actual stroke (see Figure 2.32). Make some curving arcs and notice how the stroke behaves.

7. Try wiggling the stroke as you paint across the PolySphere. You'll notice that the stroke is less sensitive to small movements with LazyMouse on; this allows you to paint straighter lines.

8. Try adjusting the settings in the LazyMouse subpalette and notice the difference in the strokes. Higher LazyStep settings will cause the stroke to break up into discrete steps. LazyRadius increases the length of the Lazy-Mouse line (think of the line as defining the radius of a circle: the edge is your cursor; the center is the actual stroke). LazySmooth will adjust the strength of the LazyMouse effect.

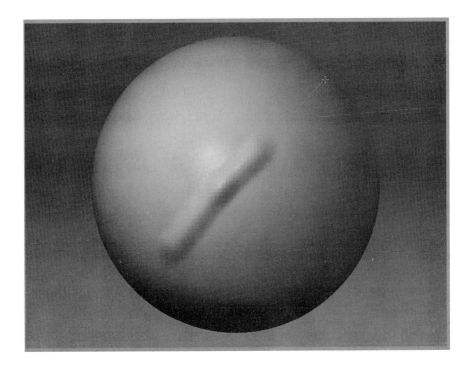

Figure 2.32

The LazyMouse feature creates a delay between the brush and the actual stroke; this is displayed by a red line.

Texture

The Texture palette is similar to the Alpha and Material palettes in that the controls here allow you to load, save, and adjust textures. Textures are 2D images, which can be created in ZBrush or in other paint programs and used for a variety of purposes (see Figure 2.33). Textures can be used to paint 3D tools. You can also create a texture based on the colors applied to a painted 3D tool. The texture can be exported for use in a 3D animation and rendering program as a texture map in a shader. Textures are discussed in detail in Chapter 7.

In addition to loading and saving textures, the controls in the Texture palette allow you to do the following:

- Flip a texture horizontally and vertically.
- Invert the colors of a texture.
- Adjust the colors using a gradient based on the main and secondary color buttons.
- Resize and clone a texture.
- Make an alpha based on a texture.
- Fill the background using a texture.
- Create a texture based on the current state of the canvas.

Figure 2.33
The Texture palette has an inventory of 2D texture images that can be applied to strokes and 3D tools.

Tool

The Tool palette is the most used palette in ZBrush; it is at the heart of digital sculpting. Everything you draw onto the canvas is a tool, and this is where you find them. All 3D tools are here as well as 2.5-dimensional paint and editing tools (see Figure 2.34). You'll most likely want to keep this palette in a tray so that it's always handy. In fact, the standard user interface configuration loads with this palette already in the right-side tray.

Figure 2.34
The Tool palette contains an inventory of 2.5-dimensional and 3-dimensional tool types as well as a wide array of subpalettes.

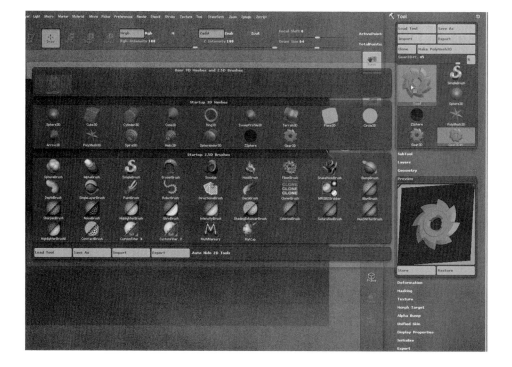

Everything in this palette will be touched on throughout this book. Once again, it's difficult to explain the settings for displacement maps or ZSpheres before explaining what a displacement map or a ZSphere is. Rather than dissect every setting in this tour, let's try a few quick exercises so you can get a feel for how the palette works. This way you'll be comfortable using it when we delve deeper in future chapters. The inventory of tools in the Tool palette is divided between 3D model tools at the top and 2.5D tools on the bottom.

Working with 2.5D Tools

1. Load a blank scene into ZBrush and place the Tool palette in one of the trays.

2. Click on the large tool icon to open up the tool tray (see Figure 2.35). Choose the SphereBrush and paint some strokes on the canvas. Make sure you are using the SphereBrush (located in the lower portion of the inventory with the 2.5D brushes and tools) and not the 3DSphere tool. Set the stroke type to Freehand.

3. In the upper shelf, click the Move button to activate the gyro. Your stroke may disappear; it's actually just gone back along the z-axis a little too far. Drag down on the canvas a few times to bring the stroke forward; it should appear after a few drags.

4. Switch the gyro to Rotate and try rotating the stroke (see Figure 2.36).

5. Switch back to Draw mode and paint some more strokes; note how the new strokes interact with the stroke you rotated.

6. In the Tool palette, select the AlphaBrush.

3D tools

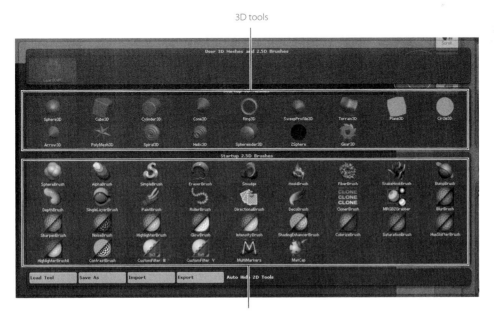

2.5D tools

Figure 2.35

The Tool palette's inventory is divided between 3D tools and 2.5D tools.

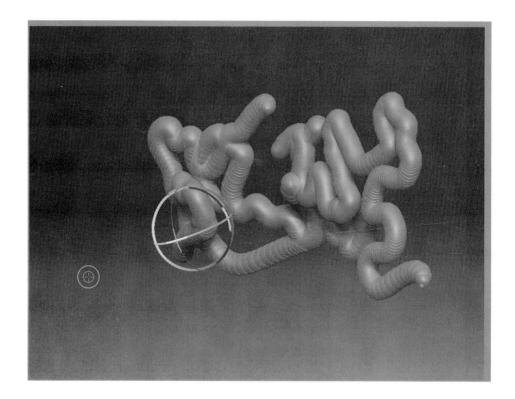

7. Click the Alpha icon on the left shelf and choose an alpha; alpha 33 is a good one to try. Paint some strokes on the canvas. Try switching to the gyro by clicking Move, Rotate, or Scale and play with repositioning the last stroke (see Figure 2.37). Notice that you cannot switch to Edit mode while using the 2.5D brushes.

8. As you switch between the SphereBrush and AlphaBrush, note that there is a Modifier subpalette in the Tool palette. With these brushes, there aren't too many options.

Working with 3D Primitive Tools

1. Press Ctrl+n to clear the canvas.

2. Click the Tool icon and choose the Gear tool from the upper set of tools; this is where all the 3D model tools reside.

3. Draw the gear on the canvas and press Ctrl+t to enter Edit mode (see Figure 2.38).

4. Rotate the gear around by dragging on the canvas.

5. In the Tool palette, scroll down and expand the subpalette labeled Initialize (see Figure 2.39).

Figure 2.37
The AlphaBrush is used to paint a stroke based on the current alpha.

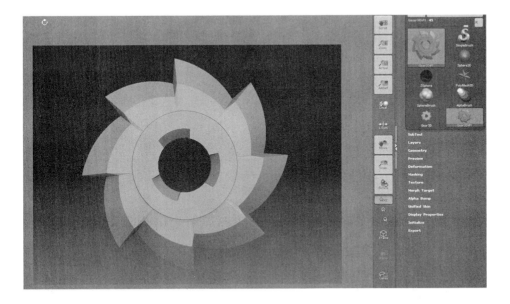

Figure 2.38
The Gear tool is drawn on the canvas.

Figure 2.39

The Initialize sub-palette on the Tool palette has settings for the 3D parametric primitives.

6. Try changing the Width, IRadius, profile curves, and whatever other settings look interesting. Note the changes to the gear model.

7. Try using one of the sculpting brushes on the left shelf to edit the model. You get a warning that says, "To enable sculpting, please convert this 3D-Primitive to a PolyMesh3D by pressing the 'Make PolyMesh3D' button in the Tool palette." Sounds like good advice, but what does it mean? Well, the 3D primitives found in the standard inventory are parametric 3D tools. Polymesh objects can be created from the parametric primitives or imported from other programs. Polymesh 3D tools are edited directly using the sculpting brushes. The DemoHead model and the Dog tools are good examples of polymesh 3D tools you've already used in this chapter. The parametric primitives differ from the polymesh 3D tools in that they are procedural tools that can be changed using the settings in the Initialize subpalette (see Figure 2.40). You can tweak these for quite a while and create your own interesting 3D tools. The parametric tools such as the Gear 3D are great for less organic shapes and details.

8. Before converting this tool, take a look at the icons in the Tool palette. Now there are two gears. Click on the first gear icon and the original gear 3D tool appears. Click on the second and your edited version appears. As you continue to make changes in Edit mode, this version of the tool will update. You can save these tools as your own custom parametric primitives.

9. On the Tool palette, click the Save As button. Save the tool on your local disk. Now you can import this into future ZBrush sessions.

10. Click the MakePolymesh3D button at the top of the Tool palette. Notice that a new icon is added to the tools; it looks just like the parametric 3D tool. Holding your mouse cursor over the tool reveals its name as well as details about the tool itself. If you look in the settings in the Tool palette, you'll notice that the Initialize subpalette is not available for your converted polymesh gear. It is no longer a procedural model and can be edited directly using only the sculpting brushes and transpose handle (see Figure 2.41).

11. Select a sculpting brush from the left shelf and paint over the tool; now you can edit this 3D tool like a sculptor.

12. In the Tool palette, expand the Geometry tab and click the Divide button. This increases the polygon resolution of the tool, subdividing the model into a denser mesh (see Figure 2.42). This allows for more detailed modeling using the sculpting brushes. The SDiv slider becomes available, allowing you to move up and down between levels of

subdivision. You can sculpt at any subdivision level and the higher and lower levels will update accordingly. This is one of the most powerful and useful features of ZBrush. The ease at which you can do this is what separates ZBrush from other modeling programs.

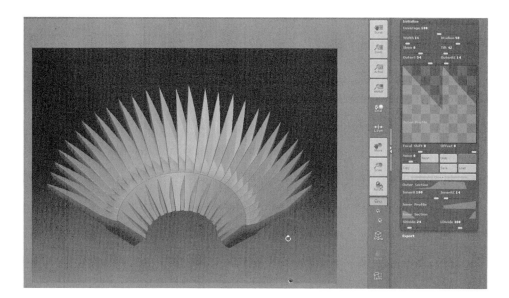

Figure 2.40
The gear primitive has been edited using the settings in the Initialize subpalette.

Figure 2.41
The gear primitive has been converted to a polymesh and can now be edited using the sculpting brushes.

Figure 2.42

The gear polymesh tool is subdivided several times, making the model smoother and allowing a finer level of detail for sculpting.

We'll look at this in great detail in future chapters, but let's test a few more features of the Tool palette before continuing our tour of the palettes.

Importing Tools

1. Click the Load Tool button.

2. Use the dialog box to navigate to the `pixologic\ZBrush3\ZTools` directory.

3. Choose the DemoSoldier tool and load it.

4. He'll probably show up on the screen close to the camera. Make sure Edit mode is on, press the Alt button, and tap on the screen (or tap on the Move button on the right shelf—sometimes this works better with a mouse click than a Wacom tablet, depending on how sensitive your tablet settings are) so that he becomes centered on the screen.

5. On the Tool palette under the Geometry subpalette, you'll notice that the demo soldier has been saved with several levels of subdivisions. This is true for any tool that you save from the Tool palette.

6. Expand the SubTool palette; you'll see that the 3D tool is divided up into several subtools for the soldier's body, clothing, and possessions. Each subtool can have its own independent subdivision settings as well (see Figure 2.43).

7. Select one of the subtools in the SubTool subpalette. Notice that all the other parts are darker than the selected subtool.

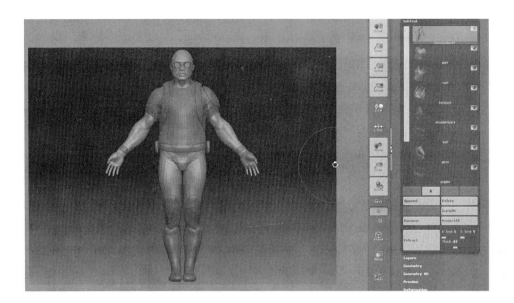

Figure 2.43

The DemoSoldier has been split up into subtools; these can be found in the SubTool subpalette on the Tool palette.

8. Try painting on the subtool using a sculpting brush. You'll see that only the selected subtool is affected; all the others are masked off.

9. Expand the Layers subpalette (the Layers subpalette exists within the Tool palette and is not the same as the Layer palette found in the menu bar). Click the New button to add a new layer (see Figure 2.44).

10. Make some more edits to the subtool using the sculpting brush.

11. Click on the layer's eyeball icon to hide the layer; the changes disappear.

12. Click on the icon again to bring the changes back. Try changing the Intensity slider. The edits made on this layer can be decreased or increased based on the Intensity slider. Each subtool can have multiple edit layers, making for a nearly endless amount of editing choices.

13. Click the Delete button in the Layers subpalette. The changes made on the layer will now be passed on to the model based on the intensity settings.

14. You can save this tool in its current state under a different name. The subtools and layers will be saved with the tool.

This is just a very brief look at the settings in the Tool palette. We did not even discuss masking, deformations, extracting geometry, or creating UVs and textures from the model. The Tool palette will play a starring role in several of the upcoming chapters as we explore more of its functionality and potential.

Figure 2.44

The Layers subpalette allows for multiple levels of editing for 3D tools.

Notice that we used the Load and Save buttons on the Tool palette to save the model and not the Load and Save buttons on the Document palette. This is an important distinction. Saving from the Document palette will not save your tool and its settings; it will drop the tool onto the canvas and you'll lose the edits to the tool. Always save your tool using the buttons on the Tool palette. You can also export your tool as an OBJ format file from the Export sub-palette at the bottom of the Tool palette.

Figure 2.45

The Transform palette contains the symmetry settings.

Transform

The Transform palette contains a number of buttons that exist on the shelves as well. These include the Draw and Edit buttons, the Move, Rotate, and Scale buttons found on the top shelf, and the buttons located on the right shelf. You may decide to design a custom interface that has no shelves. In that case, the Transform palette can be placed in a tray, giving you another way to access these controls. The Camera icon is a snapshot feature that allows you to drop a copy of a 3D tool on the canvas in its current position while keeping the original tool in Edit mode.

The most important feature of the Transform palette is the symmetry settings (see Figure 2.45). The symmetry feature is used when editing 3D tools. It can be used to speed up the sculpting process by allowing you to work on both sides of a 3D tool at the same time. To work with symmetry, you need to have the Activate Symmetry button on. You'll see the brush appear on each side of the model based on which axis is activated. The M button next to the axis choices ensures that the symmetry is mirrored.

If you're sculpting a symmetrical 3D tool such as a face or skull, mirroring symmetry while you work across an axis means that any changes you make to one side of the face will also occur on the other. If the symmetry is not mirrored, then pulling points toward the left of the canvas on one side of the 3D tool will cause the corresponding points on the other side of the 3D tool to move left as well. To see this in action, load the DemoHead scene, which has symmetry activated by default.

You are not confined to symmetry on just one access though. You can click more than one axis button at a time and have the symmetry mirrored across multiple axes. The (R) button activates radial symmetry, allowing you to edit a 3D tool at many locations at the same time. Try these steps to see how this works:

1. Start a blank scene in ZBrush.

2. From the Tool palette, choose the 3D Ring tool, draw it on the canvas, and turn on Edit mode.

3. Rotate the ring so that it is parallel to the canvas. This means the local Z axis of the 3D tool is aligned with the Z axis of the camera.

4. In the Tool palette, activate the MakePolymesh3D button.

5. In the Transform palette, click the Activate Symmetry button so that symmetry is on. Click the M button so that the symmetry is mirrored. It should be activated by default.

6. Click the Z button to make sure symmetry is on for the Z axis. Turn off the X and Y axis buttons.

7. Click the (R) button to activate radial symmetry. Set the Radial Count slider to 8.

8. Paint on the 3D tool. You'll see eight bumps rise up in symmetrical fashion (Figure 2.46).

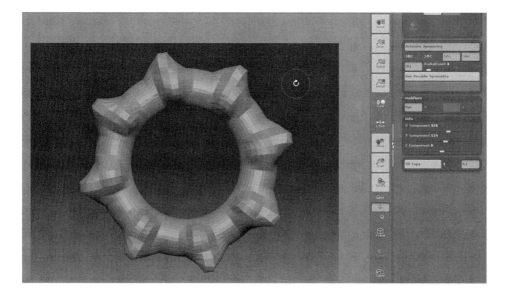

Figure 2.46

The radial symmetry setting allows for several brush strokes at once.

The Transform palette also has settings at the bottom to allow you to restrict your edits to a single axis or pair of axes. The XYZ button is on by default, which allows edits to occur in any direction.

The Info subpalette gives information on the coordinates of the brush. This can be very handy when you're trying to determine the depth of a 3D tool or stroke on the 2.5D canvas.

The 3D copy button and modifiers allow you to copy a texture placed in the background onto a 3D tool.

Figure 2.47
The Zoom palette has two mini preview windows that can be used to examine the canvas closely without having to zoom in on the whole thing.

Zoom

The Zoom palette has controls that offer various ways to zoom in on the canvas. It also has a couple of mini windows that give you an alternate view at a higher magnification. This means you can zero in on fine details without having to change the magnification of the entire canvas. The mini windows follow the position of the brush. To change the magnification within a mini window, you can click in the window (see Figure 2.47).

ZPlugin

The ZPlugin palette is where you can access plug-ins for ZBrush as well as links to important ZBrush-related sites. There is also an access point for editing your ZBrush license as well as a link to the help files.

Two major plug-ins that ship with ZBrush are Projection Master and ZMapper. We'll take a closer look at these in Chapter 10.

ZScript

ZBrush has a built-in scripting language called ZScript. ZScripts can be simple macros such as the Canvas Resizing macro we created earlier in this chapter, or they can be functional plug-ins with their own interface. ZScripts can be recorded through the interface using the controls on this palette or by typing commands into a text file.

The Title Bar

The final stop on our interface tour is the title bar. Here you will find useful bits of information on the upper-left side of the screen. These include the title of the document, the name of the person or company to whom this copy of ZBrush has been registered, information regarding memory usage, and the time spent in this current ZBrush session.

On the right side of the title bar are some useful buttons. Moving from left to right, the first button, labeled Menus, is a toggle for hiding the menus. The second button is the default ZScript button; you've already used this button to launch the startup screen. The Help button launches the online documentation. The two arrow buttons allow you to quickly choose between interface color presets. Likewise, with the next two buttons you can browse through saved user interface configurations. These buttons are a convenient way to quickly switch layouts without having to go to the Preferences palette. Finally, the last buttons are the standard minimize and maximize buttons common to most software.

Hotkeys

To wrap up the tour, here is a list of the ZBrush hotkeys you'll be using a lot. Take some time to practice using them; you'll find that they speed up work in the program quite a bit. A complete list of all hotkeys can be found in the ZBrush documentation. As you work through exercises, you'll be reminded of these hotkeys and encouraged to use them so that by the end of the book you'll be sculpting like a pro!

To create your own hotkey, hold the Ctrl key while pressing a button. Then press the hotkey or combination you'd like to assign for the button.

- Undo: Ctrl+z
- Redo: Shift+Ctrl+z

Interface Actions and Help

These hotkeys relate to the built-in help messages and interface customization.

- Show item description (when Popup Info is switched on): Ctrl+cursor over item
- Move item to custom interface position: Ctrl+drag (when Enable Customize is switched on)
- Remove item from custom interface position: Ctrl+drag to canvas (when Enable Customize is on)
- Actual size: 0 [zero]
- Anti-aliased half size: Ctrl+0
- Zoom in: + [plus sign]
- Zoom out: - [minus sign]

Transforming 3D Tools and Strokes

These hotkeys are used when transforming 3D tools in Edit Mode and the gyro manipulator in Draw mode.

- Move: w
- Scale: e
- Rotate: r
- Edit: t
- Free rotate: Click and drag background
- Move: Alt+click and drag background
- Constrain to 90-degree rotation: Click+drag, press Shift

- Scale: Alt+click, release Alt, drag background
- Rotate around Z axis: Shift, click, release Shift, drag

Working with Document Layers

These hotkeys are used when working with document layers.

- Clear layer: Ctrl+n
- Fill layer: Ctrl+f
- On layer thumbnail, toggle all layers on/off: Shift+click
- Select layer on which clicked pixol resides: ~+click canvas (U.S.) @+click canvas (U.K.)
- Move layer contents up/down/sideways (X and Y): ~+drag (U.S.) @+drag (U.K.)
- Move layer contents forward/backward (Z): ~+Alt+drag (U.S.) @+Alt+drag (U.K.)

Working with 3D Tools

These hotkeys are used when working with 3D tools in Edit mode.

- Save tool: Shift+Ctrl+t
- Divide: Ctrl+d
- Lower res: Shift+d
- Higher res: d
- Toggle ZAdd and ZSub: Alt (hold down)
- Edge loop: Ctrl+e (partially hidden mesh)
- Show mesh portion: Shift+Ctrl+click and drag
- Hide mesh portion: Shift+Ctrl+click, release Shift, drag
- Show entire mesh: Shift+Ctrl+click background
- Show only selected polygroup (on fully visible mesh): Shift+Ctrl+click
- Hide selected polygroup (on fully visible mesh): Shift+Ctrl+click
- Reverse visibility: Shift+Ctrl+click and drag background
- Center mesh in canvas (when in Edit mode): f
- Draw polyframe: Shift+f
- Point selection mode: Shift+Ctrl+p
- Set pivot point: Ctrl+ p
- Clear pivot point: Shift+p
- Snapshot: Shift+s

Masking and Stencils

These hotkeys are used when working with masks and stencils.

- View mask: Ctrl+h
- Invert mask: Ctrl+i
- Clear mask: Shift+Ctrl+a
- Mask all: Ctrl+a
- Paint mask on tool (alphas/strokes can be used): Ctrl (hold down)
- Delete or paint reverse mask: Ctrl+Alt (hold down)
- Reverse mask: Ctrl+click background
- Clear Mask: Ctrl+click+drag background
- Constant intensity mask: Ctrl+click, release Ctrl, drag (starting off mesh)
- Alpha intensity mask: Ctrl+click and drag (starting off mesh, Lasso off)
- Blur mask: Ctrl+click on mesh
- Stencil on: Alt+h
- Hide/show stencil: Ctrl+h
- Coin controller: spacebar

Rendering

These hotkeys are used when rendering.

- Render all: Shift+Ctrl+r
- Cursor selective render: Ctrl+r

Strokes

These hotkeys are used when working with strokes.

- LazyMouse: l
- Replay last stroke: Ctrl+1
- CropAndFill: Shift+Ctrl+f
- Grab texture from document: Shift+Ctrl+g

Working with ZSpheres

These hotkeys are used when working with ZSpheres.

- Preview adaptive skin: a
- Activate symmetry: x
- Draw pointer: q

Summary

In this chapter, I took you on a quick tour of the ZBrush interface. The goal of this tour was to get you comfortable enough with locating tools and settings in ZBrush so that you can easily work through the exercises in the rest of the book. Complete descriptions of all the tools and palettes can be found in the ZBrush documentation. The palettes are described in detail in the Palette Reference. The following list includes some things you should understand after completing this chapter:

- How to load the startup page using the DefaultZScript button
- How the ZBrush 2.5-dimensional canvas works
- What tools and settings are located on the shelves
- How to open up an inventory quick palette
- The difference between Draw and Edit mode
- How to expand and collapse the trays
- How to move a palette from a menu to a tray
- What tools and settings are located in each palette
- How to work with subpalettes
- The basics of working with 2.5D brushes and 3D tools
- How to work with layers
- How to work with 3D parametric primitives and polymeshes
- The more common hotkeys

CHAPTER 3

Painting with Pixols, Part 1

In this chapter and Chapter 4, you'll get some hands-on experience with a variety of ZBrush tools and techniques as you create a simple composition. You'll explore ZBrush's painting and illustration capabilities as well as some simple sculpting. The exercises in this chapter will give you a taste of how to work with ZBrush using both 2.5D brushes and 3D primitive tools.

This chapter includes the following topics:

- Setting up the document
- Document layers
- 3D parametric primitive tools
- Using macros
- Assigning materials

Setting Up the Document

Fewer artistic endeavors are more daunting than facing a blank canvas. Even when you have an image crystal clear in your mind, transforming it into a visual reality is not always a straightforward path. To start the exploration of ZBrush as an illustration tool, you'll begin by roughing out the composition as a sketch and then you'll add elements (2.5-dimensional strokes and 3-dimensional tools), gradually refining the image and the elements as you go. It's always important to work the entire canvas as the image is created rather than focusing on perfecting one small piece in a corner before moving on to the next. This ensures that the composition remains strong all the way to its completion.

Many of the exercises in this chapter will demonstrate the creation of a composition in different stages. The final image will be a simple underwater scene depicting a cartoonish, futuristic submerged sea lab and some deep-sea volcanic vents. Whether or not you replicate this scene exactly is not as important as gaining proficiency with the ZBrush toolset and workflow. You should come out of the chapter with plenty of your own ideas on how to approach the creation of a composition in ZBrush. We'll start by creating a new document.

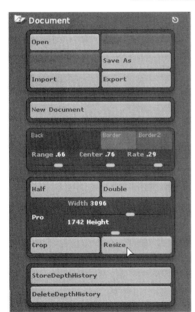

Figure 3.1

Set the size of the canvas and the background gradient colors in the Document palette.

1. Start ZBrush, and on the startup page, choose Other to begin a blank composition.

2. You will need to set the resolution of the document at the very beginning.

    If the document is enlarged after pixols have been painted onto the canvas, the pixols will stretch and document quality will suffer. This is why it's best to start large and scale down later on if necessary. In the Document palette, turn the Pro button off (the Pro button constrains the proportions of the document) and set the document size to a large value.

    The example image in this scene is 3096 by 1742. Enter these values in the Width and Height numeric fields; remember to press the Enter key after inputting each value (see Figure 3.1). Click the Resize button in the Document palette to commit to this change.

3. Most likely the canvas no longer fits on the screen. Drag your cursor over the Zoom button on the right shelf, or use the + and - hotkeys to zoom in or out on the canvas until the whole image fits in the ZBrush interface.

4. Since this is an underwater scene, it's probably a good idea to change the background color to something more aquatic. In the color picker on the left shelf, set the color to blue. Then click the Back button on the Document palette. This sets the background gradient to the current color in the color picker. You can adjust the look of the gradient using the Range, Center, and Rate sliders.

5. Save your blank document by clicking the Save As button so that these settings will be preserved in the future as you continue to work through this chapter. Name the file underwaterScene_v1.zbr.

Creating a Plane for a Quick Background Sketch

Now you'll create a plane that will provide a surface for a quick, rough sketch. The sketch will serve as a guide to make it easier to place the 2.5D strokes and 3D tools that will populate the scene.

1. Place the Tool palette in one of the trays if it's not there already. You'll be accessing it a lot during this chapter.

2. From the tool inventory, choose the Plane 3D tool and draw it on the canvas.

3. Activate the Move button on the top shelf (hotkey = w) to put the Plane 3D tool in Transform mode, as shown in Figure 3.2. Use the transform gyro to position the plane at the center of the screen.

Figure 3.2

Activating the Move button on the top shelf puts the 3D tool in Transform mode.

Before you continue, let's quickly review how the buttons on the top shelf affect the state of a 3D tool. When a 3D tool is selected as the current brush, it can be in any one of several modes. Using buttons on the top shelf determines the mode of the 3D tool:

- If only the Draw button is activated, then the 3D tool will draw copies of itself wherever you paint on the canvas. The tool is considered to be in Draw mode. Each previous copy is converted to pixols as you draw a new copy on the canvas. Pixols are discussed in Chapter 1 in the section "Pixels versus Pixols."

- If the Edit button is active, the 3D tool's actual shape can be changed; the tool is considered to be in Edit mode.

- When both the Edit and Draw buttons are active, you can use the sculpting brushes to change the tool's shape (accessed through the brush inventory on the left shelf or through the Brush palette).

- When Edit and the Move, Scale, or Rotate buttons are active then the Transpose control is available. The Transpose control is primarily used for posing 3D figures; this control is explored in Chapter 6.

- When the Move, Scale, or Rotate buttons are active and the Edit button is deactivated, then the 3D tool is in Transform mode. The transformation gyro is available, allowing you to reposition or scale the 3D tool. The transformation gyro is discussed in Chapter 2 in the section "Using the Transformation Gyro in Draw Mode."

- If another tool is selected or if you switch to a different document layer, the current 3D tool will be dropped to the canvas. This means that the polygons that make up the tool will be converted to pixols. The tool will look exactly the same but you will not be able to edit or transform it as a 3D tool. It is now a 2.5-dimensional brush stroke on the canvas. You'll see this workflow in action as you create the underwater scene in this chapter.

GYRO TIPS

The gyro is often the bane of many ZBrush users. It has some unique properties, which can cause some frustration until you get used to it. Here are a few tips that should help you keep your composure while using the gyro to position 3D tools in Transformation mode. Patience and practice will pay off in the end.

- When using the gyro in Move mode, resist the temptation to click in the area defined by the outer circle if you want to move the tool to a different location on the screen. Clicking here will realign the tool based on the normals of the object behind the active tool. This will drive you crazy very quickly, especially if you've spent time rotating the tool into the position you want. To position the object, click carefully on the silver or colored rims of the gyro and drag the object into place using that. This will take practice.

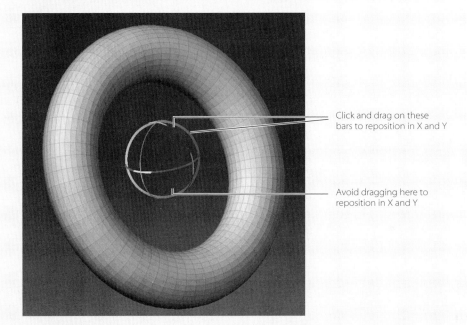

Click and drag on these bars to reposition in X and Y

Avoid dragging here to reposition in X and Y

- You cannot undo transformations to a tool made with the gyro. The reasoning behind this is that the gyro is not actually transforming the tool: it is transforming a 3D stroke made by it. If you look in the Preview window of the Tool palette, the tool itself remains unchanged even when you scale a tool on the canvas nonproportionally using the gyro. Once you finish the transformations and convert the tool to pixols by leaving Transform/ Edit mode, the tool will be dropped to the canvas. Pressing Ctrl+z to perform an undo will undo the 3D stroke made on the canvas and the tool will disappear. You'll have to redraw the tool on the canvas and use the gyro to reposition it all over again. This can also drive new users crazy.

- If using the gyro is not your cup of tea, you can use the Size, Offset, and Rotation sliders in the Deformation subpalette of the Tool palette. To restrict the scale, rotation, and transformation of the sliders to particular axes, click the X, Y, and Z buttons to the right of the sliders. The big advantage these sliders have over the gyro is that undo does work. The disadvantage is that the changes you make with deformations do alter the shape of the original 3D tool.

STEPS TO TAKE WHEN A TOOL DROPS TO THE CANVAS

Working with the gyro can take a little practice at first; don't get discouraged if it doesn't immediately behave they way you would like it to. If you find that you accidentally drop the plane to the canvas (thus converting it to pixols), take the following steps:

1. Clear the canvas (Ctrl+n) and click on the Draw button on the top shelf.

2. Redraw the plane.

3. Switch to the Transform mode to activate the gyro.

4. Try positioning it again.

A tool will be dropped to the canvas whenever you select a new tool from the Tool palette, switch layers, save the document, or activate the Draw button on the top shelf while not in Edit mode.

4. Click the Rotate button on the top shelf to switch the gyro to Rotate mode (hotkey = r) and rotate the plane so that it is perpendicular to the camera if it is not already. Holding the Shift key down as you drag the gyro will snap the 3D tool into an orthographic position (see Figure 3.3).

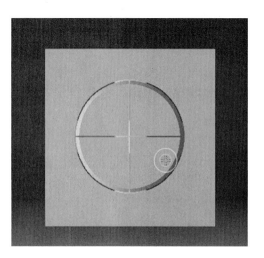

Figure 3.3

Activate the Rotate button on the top shelf and drag within the area defined by the gyro to freely rotate the 3D tool.

5. While positioning and rotating, you may find that the plane disappears. This is because it has been pushed back along the z-axis, behind the back edge of the canvas. To bring it back you can switch to the Move tool on the top shelf and repeatedly drag the mouse downward on a blank part of the canvas until it reappears.

6. Click the Scale button on the top shelf to switch the gyro to Scale mode (hotkey = e) and drag on the top crossbar of the gyro (the colored section of the gyro where the two circles cross at the top) to scale the plane vertically. Drag on the colored cross bar on the side to scale the plane horizontally so that it covers the entire canvas (see Figure 3.4). Sometimes a tool will temporarily switch to a wireframe display while you are transforming it with the gyro; this is just a way to improve performance in ZBrush. Once you are finished transforming the tool, it should return to a shaded view.

Figure 3.4

Activate the Scale button on the top shelf and drag on the cross on the side of the gyro to scale the plane horizontally.

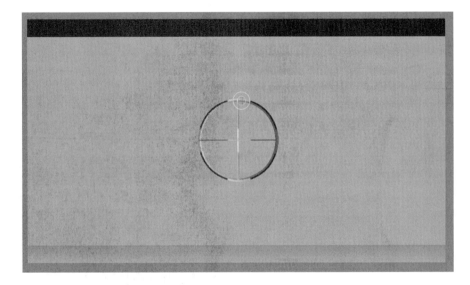

7. Once the plane is roughly in place, switch to Move mode and open the Transform palette. In the Transform palette there is an Info subpalette with sliders that can help you position the plane numerically (see Figure 3.5).

This subpalette is especially helpful for setting the position of the plane along the Z coordinates because visually it's hard to tell where the plane actually is. You want the plane to be as far back as possible before it disappears behind the canvas.

8. Use the slider or input a value using the numeric keypad. Adjust the slider so that the plane is placed in Z just before it disappears behind the canvas. This may take a few tries moving the slider back and forth.

Don't fret about the exact position at this point. You just need it to be in the background; it can be readjusted using the Layer controls later on if necessary. Lower values (including negative numbers) bring a stroke or 3D tool closer to the viewer; higher values push the stroke or tool deeper into the canvas.

9. Click the Rotate button on the top shelf to switch the gyro to Rotate mode and observe the values in the Transform palette's Info subpalette (see Figure 3.6). Now they display the rotation in each axis. Set the rotation to 0 in X, 0 in Y, and 90 in Z.

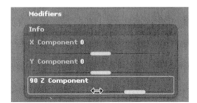

Figure 3.6

Switching the gyro to Rotate changes the function of the sliders in the Info subpalette.

10. If you switch the gyro to Scale mode and look at these values, they show the size of the tool in pixols.

11. Once the plane has been positioned, click the Material icon on the left shelf to bring up the material inventory. Set the current material to Flat Color, as shown in Figure 3.7. The plane should turn white.

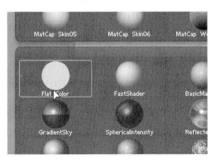

Figure 3.7

Choose the Flat color material from the material inventory.

Figure 3.5

The Info subpalette is at the bottom of the Transform palette.

12. In the color picker, set the color to a bluish gray (see Figure 3.8). The bright white is a little harsh for painting. It's usually best to start with a midtone so that you can paint values that are both darker and lighter than the background.

13. In the Tool palette, open the inventory and choose the Paintbrush from the 2.5D tool section.

    Switching tools will cause the plane to be converted to pixols and dropped to the canvas. You'll see a message that reads, "Would you like to exit Edit/Transform mode and switch tools?" Click on the Switch button to switch to an exit Edit/Transform mode and switch tools. The polygons that make up the plane are now pixols on the canvas. This distinction is important to understand when creating a composition in ZBrush. Polygons and pixols are discussed in detail in Chapter 1.

14. Save the document.

Figure 3.8

Choose a light bluish gray color in the color picker.

Sketching the Composition on the Background Plane

Painting a rough sketch is a good way to plan out the composition. You really only need to spend a few minutes doing this, and it needs to be detailed only enough so that you have an idea of where the compositional elements will be placed.

1. Make sure you have the Paintbrush tool selected from the Inventory on the Tool palette.

2. Set the color picker to a dark gray.

3. In the top shelf, turn the ZAdd button off. Turn on the RGB button, and set the RGB intensity to 30. Setting a lower intensity will allow you to build the strokes up in opacity as you go.

4. Set a thick Draw size—70 should work well—and try painting some strokes on the plane, just to block in the major forms.

5. Start sketching out your own version of the underwater scene. Figure 3.9 shows the sketch created for this exercise.

6. As you continue to make passes roughing in the forms, you can dial the size of the brush down and the intensity up as the drawing becomes more detailed. Also try choosing a light-blue color to paint in some simple highlights on the dome. Once again, this is just for reference; no need to try and make it a Rembrandt.

7. To erase strokes, don't switch to the Erase tool in the tool inventory! That will actually erase the pixols of the background plane as well as the sketch. To erase parts of the sketch you don't like, drag from the color picker to a blank spot on the plane. This will set the plane's color to the current paintbrush color. Set the intensity of the Paintbrush to 100 and paint over the strokes you don't like.

Figure 3.9

The Paintbrush tool is used to sketch the composition quickly on the background plane.

8. Additionally, you can erase large areas by setting the stroke type of the Paintbrush to DragRect and the current color to the plane's color and dragging over the sections of the sketch you don't like. This works best when the alpha is set to None.

9. When you are happy with the sketch, save the document. You may get a warning message asking if you want to save the tool or the document; save the document.

Drawing in ZBrush using this method is only one way to get a sketch on your canvas. You may prefer to draw on actual paper and scan the image in using a program such as Photoshop, or you may prefer Photoshop or Painter's drawing tools for sketching. Either way, an alternative to this method would be to import a file in BMP, PSD, TIFF, or JPEG format and use it as the guide for the composition. To do this, make sure the file you import is the same size/resolution as the ZBrush document, and use the Import button on the Document palette to import the image. If you import a Photoshop document that has multiple layers, ZBrush will flatten the layers.

> There's a free plug-in for ZBrush called Zketchpad which makes sketching in ZBrush very similar to sketching in Photoshop or Painter. The plug-in can be downloaded from www.zbrushcentral .com/zbc/showthread.php?t=029621. The tutorial in this chapter does not use this plug-in, a work-flow using Zketchpad may be significantly different from the steps described here.

Working with Document Layers

At this stage, you can start to block in the major forms of the composition. You'll start by creating the undersea lab using 3D primitive tools. You'll use layers to keep compositional elements on the background, midground, and foreground separate.

1. Open the Layer palette and create a new layer by clicking the Create button.

   ZBrush layers are not like layers in other programs, such as Photoshop. Objects on one layer do not necessarily obscure objects in the layer below. In fact, there is no *above* or *below* since all objects on the layers can exist anywhere in Z space. It might be easier to think of a layer as a way to group elements. You can even adjust the position of all of the strokes on a layer using the offset controls in the Layer palette.

> Working with a layer's visibility can be tricky. If a layer is active, you'll see it outlined on the Layer palette. To hide a layer, click on its icon in the Layer palette to make it active and then click on the icon of the second layer to deactivate the first. To make a nonactive layer visible, click on its icon twice so that a gray border appears around it, then click on the second layer. The first layer should be nonactive but still visible. Practice this a few times so that you get the hang of it.

It's important to remember while working that if you have a 3D tool in Edit mode on one layer and you switch to another layer, the 3D tool will be dropped to the canvas and you will no longer be able to use it as a 3D tool; it will be converted to pixols. If this happens, you can clear the layer with the dropped 3D tool (Ctrl+n), select the 3D tool in the Tool palette, redraw it on the canvas, and switch to Edit mode. Once again, this takes a little getting used to.

2. Make sure you're on a new layer and the sketch layer is still visible in the background. In the Tool palette, select the Cylinder3D object and draw it on the canvas.

3. Click the Material button on the left shelf to open the material inventory. Switch the material to the Fast Shader and set the color picker to white.

4. Once you have the cylinder on the canvas, press the r key to switch to the gyro in Rotate mode, and then rotate the cylinder so that you can see the top and sides (see Figure 3.10). Don't switch to another tool at this point or the cylinder will be dropped to canvas; keep the cylinder in Transform mode (where the gyro is visible) for the next few sections of this tutorial.

Figure 3.10

The 3D Cylinder tool is drawn on the canvas and the gyro tool positions the cylinder.

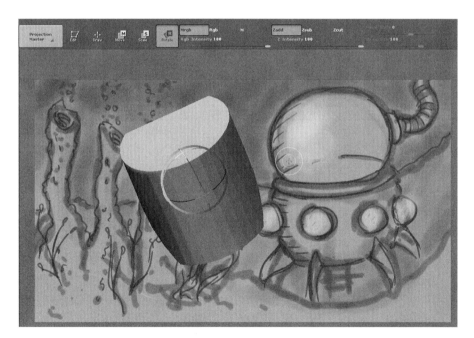

5. Press the w key to switch the gyro to Move mode; drag down repeatedly on the canvas to move the cylinder forward in Z space, otherwise it will be partially obscured by the sketch plane on the first layer. You can open the Transform palette and use the sliders in the Info subpalette to numerically enter a z-coordinate value. A value of 3600 should work well enough.

By default, 3D tools in ZBrush are drawn on the canvas without perspective distortion, as if being seen through an orthographic view. This can help when you're sculpting an object, but you're when creating a composition, it makes things look a little unnatural, or at the very least, less dramatic. You can turn perspective on using the controls in the Draw palette.

6. Open the Draw palette and click the Perspective button to activate it, as shown in Figure 3.11. You can adjust the focal length if you wish to exaggerate or diminish the perspective distortion. For this composition, a setting of 70 works just fine. The Perspective button is off by default; before dropping 3D brush strokes to the canvas, remember to double-check that this button is on if you want the strokes created with the 3D tools to look consistent.

Once a 3D tool has been dropped onto the canvas, changing the perspective on that layer will no longer have any visual effect.

Figure 3.11

Activating the Perspective button on the Draw palette enables perspective distortion.

Working with Parametric Primitive 3D Tools

ZBrush actually has three kinds of 3D tools: parametric meshes, polymeshes, and ZSpheres. All of the 3D startup tools in the inventory, except for ZSphere and the Polymesh star, are parametric meshes (see Figure 3.12). Parametric meshes are edited using the numeric sliders in the Initialize subpalette of the Tool palette. Different settings are available depending on which parametric mesh you are editing. Polymesh tools are edited using the sculpting brushes. A parametric mesh can be converted to a polymesh at any time; however, polymeshes cannot be converted to parametric meshes. Parametric meshes are great for nonorganic objects. ZSpheres are a special 3D tool which will be discussed in Chapter 4. In this section, we'll block out the undersea lab using a parametric cylinder.

Figure 3.12

Parametric 3D primitives make up the standard 3D tools in the tool inventory.

1. Your cylinder should still be in Transform mode and the gyro should still be visible. Use the gyro to roughly position the cylinder over the sketch of the undersea lab. If it has been dropped to the canvas, don't panic; you can clear the layer by pressing Ctrl+n. The cylinder should still be the active tool; draw the cylinder on the canvas again and then switch to Transform mode by activating the Move button (hotkey = w).

> The fear of accidentally dropping a tool to the canvas while working often stresses out new users. Don't forget that the changes you make to a tool are stored in the tool palette while you work so if a tool gets dropped to the canvas, all is not lost! You can always clear the layer and redraw the tool. It's just like learning how to ski, you fall down a lot but before you know it you're zooming down the black diamond trails. With patience and practice you'll get the hang of working with 3D tools in Draw mode.

2. Rotate the cylinder so that the top is visible (hotkey = r).

3. Use the Info subpalette on the Transform palette to verify that the z-coordinate of the cylinder is still a positive number (lower and negative values are closer to the viewer). You want the cylinder to exist in front of the sketch plane, but not too far forward; you'll need some space in the foreground to fit in the volcanic vents. A value of 3600 should work well.

4. Expand the Initialize subpalette in the Tool palette. Move the TaperTop slider so that one end of the cylinder shrinks down, as shown in Figure 3.13. It's possible that the cylinder has been rotated so that the top shrinks; if this is the case, switch the gyro to Rotate mode and rotate the cylinder so that the bottom is tapered.

5. Adjust the Inner Radius value so that the cylinder becomes more of a hollow tube. A setting of 80 should be good. The inside of the cylinder is where the undersea explorers make their home.

6. In the Transform palette, deactivate the Quick button; this will remove the faceted look of the cylinder geometry. The edges of the cylinder may become too rounded. To fix this, you can increase the VDivide value in the tool's Initialize subpalette.

7. Continue to work on positioning, rotating, and scaling the cylinder until you're satisfied that it matches the sketch.

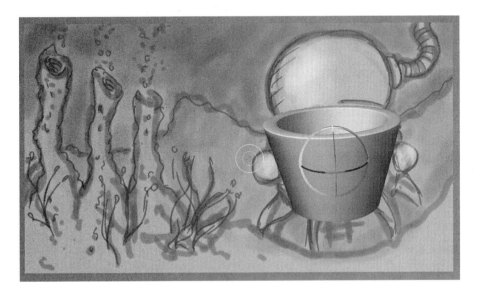

Figure 3.13

Adjusting the settings on the Initialize subpalette turns the solid cylinder into a tapered tube.

Creating Snapshots

A snapshot is a way drop a copy of the current 3D tool on the canvas. Snapshots provide for an easy way to add details to the elements of a composition.

1. Switch the gyro to Move mode.

2. Open the Transform palette and click the Snapshot button (it looks like a camera) or press Shift+s (see Figure 3.14). An exact duplicate of the current stroke (the cylinder in this case) has been created in the same position and orientation as the current stroke and dropped to the canvas; you can't see it until you move the original 3D tool using the gyro.

3. Drag upward on the colored cross of the gyro to move the cylinder up.

4. Switch the gyro to Scale mode (hotkey = e). Drag upward within the perimeter of the gyro but not on one of the handles to perform a uniform scale of the cylinder.

5. Drag downward on the top of the Gyro to shorten the cylinder; alternatively you can go to the Initialize subpalette of the Tool palette and reduce the Z Size value.

Figure 3.14

The Snapshot button makes a copy of the active 3D tool and drops it to the canvas.

6. Reduce the value of the TaperTop slider in the Initialize subpalette.

7. Position the snapshot on top of the original cylinder so that it looks as if a reinforced girdle of steel is laid on top of the dropped cylinder.

8. Continue scaling and moving until you're happy with the placement. Use Figure 3.15 as a reference.

Figure 3.15

Use the transform gyro to scale and position the cylinder over the dropped copy.

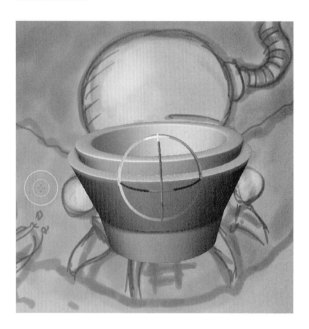

Using ZCut Mode

Next you'll cut holes into the cylinder for windows. To do this, you'll use the 3D Sphere tool in ZCut mode. Both the ZCut and ZSub modes are subtractive, meaning that they cut into pixols rather than build onto them. The difference between ZCut and ZSub is that ZCut creates a hole or a tunnel through the pixols and ZSub scoops the pixols out. The difference can be subtle; the best way to figure out which mode is best is to experiment switching between the two modes.

1. In the Tool palette inventory, select the Sphere3D from the 3D tools. By selecting a new tool, you will cause the cylinders to be converted to pixols and dropped to the canvas. This is okay; the cylinders are in the right place now.

2. Drag on the canvas to draw a sphere.

3. Switch to Scale mode (hotkey = e) and scale the sphere stroke down by dragging your brush within the area defined by the circles of the gyro control.

4. Switch to Move mode (hotkey = w) and move the sphere on top of the cylinder. If you drag the gyro within the perimeter of the handles, but not on top of the handles

themselves, the sphere stroke will align itself with the surface of the cylinder. This makes it easy to position the sphere on the surface of the cylinder (Figure 3.16).

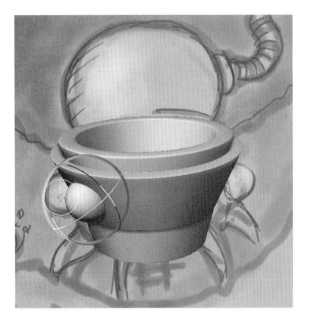

Figure 3.16

Use the transform gyro to position a 3D sphere on the surface of the cylinder.

5. On the top shelf, click the ZCut button. Now the sphere actually digs a spherical hole into the dropped cylinder, as shown in Figure 3.17.

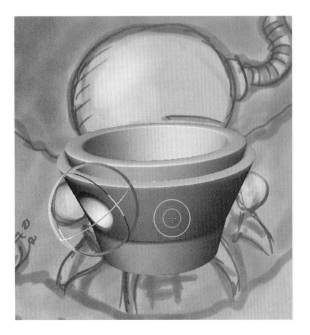

Figure 3.17

Activating the ZCut button causes the sphere to cut into the surface of the dropped cylinder.

6. Position the Sphere3D tool on top of the steel girdle that surrounds the original cylinder; move it to the left side. Position it so that it looks like a hole for a window. When you are happy, click the Snapshot button to make a copy (hotkey = Shift+s). Move the snapshot to the right to make another window. Repeat this technique so that you have four windows around the girdle of the cylinder (see Figure 3.18).

Figure 3.18

Use Snapshot to make copies of the Sphere3D tool and arrange them to form holes for the windows.

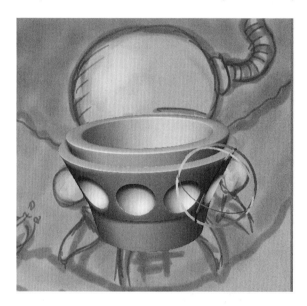

Add a Ring

You'll use the Ring 3D tool to add a little more detail to the sea lab. The ring is another parametric object, in the shape of a torus.

1. From the Tool palette, select the 3D Ring tool.

2. In the Draw palette, make sure the Perspective button is active.

3. Draw the ring on the canvas.

4. Switch the mode to move (hotkey = w) and move the ring on top of the original cylinder.

5. In the Initialize palette, reduce the ring's SRadius so that the ring becomes fairly thin. An SRadius of 9 works well (see Figure 3.19).

Figure 3.19

Adjust the SRadius slider in the Tool's Initialize subpalette to make the ring thin.

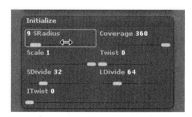

6. Move, scale, and rotate the ring so that it sits on top of the cylinder.

7. Save the document as underSeaScene_v2.ZBR. You'll get a warning that asks if you want to save the document or the tool. Save the document.

Loading Tutorial Macros

A macro is a recording of the actions performed during a ZBrush setting. After recording a macro you can play it back in ZBrush and see every action repeated just as it was performed. When the macro is finished playing, you have all the tools available that were created during the session, available in your ZBrush palette. The DVD that comes with this book has macros of many of the exercises created for the book. Right now, you'll take a break from this tutorial so that you can see how to load a recorded ZBrush session. The macro you'll load will play through the creation of the sea lab cylinder so far.

1. Minimize ZBrush and find the Pixologic folder in your program files directory using Windows (Some versions of Microsoft Windows label the program files directory as "Program Files(x86)").

2. In the ZBrush3\ZStartup\Macros folder, create a new folder called introducingZBrush_c03 (see Figure 3.20).

Figure 3.20

Creating a new folder in the Macros directory

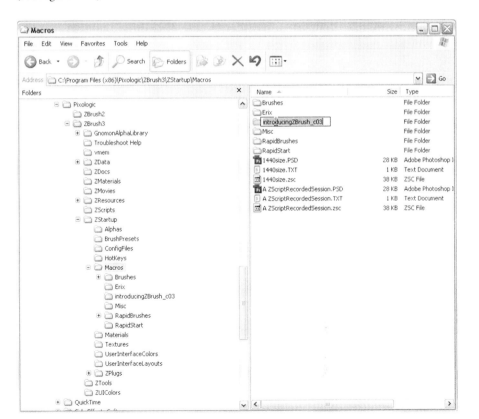

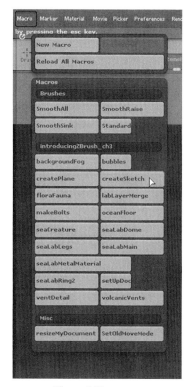

Figure 3.21

Buttons to launch custom macros become available when you restart ZBrush or click the Reload All Macros button.

3. Open the Chapter 3 folder on the DVD and find the macros directory.

4. Select all of the TXT files and copy them.

5. Return to ZBrush3\ZStartup\Macros\introducingZBrush_c03 and paste these files.

6. These macros will become available when you either quit and restart ZBrush or click on the Reload All Macros buttons on the Macro palette.

7. Save your document to your local disk using the Save As button in the Document palette.

8. In the Preferences palette, click the Initialize ZBrush button; this will clear the document and the Tool palette of all custom tools.

   The macros in this chapter have been recorded in a specific order that follows the various exercises. Before playing a macro, you should initialize ZBrush and load the document that corresponds with each button. You'll be told, as you go through the exercises, which documents need to be loaded and when.

9. From the Chapter 3 folder on the DVD, load the underwaterScene_v1.zbr file into ZBrush. This scene has the background sketch already created.

10. Use the button on the right shelf to zoom out so that the entire sketch is visible.

11. Expand the Macro palette; you should see a new section called introducingZbrush_ch3. In this section are a series of buttons; each one will launch a macro recorded for this chapter (see Figure 3.21).

12. Click on the seaLabMain button and watch as ZBrush takes over and performs the steps described in the sections of this chapter called "Working with Document Layers," "Working with Parametric Primitive 3D Tools," "Creating Snapshots," "Using ZCut Mode," and "Add a Ring."

13. It's a good idea to initialize ZBrush (Preferences → Initialize) before opening up a document and running the macro. If you run a macro in the middle of a session, the results may be slightly different from what you would expect due to the state of various ZBrush settings at the time you launch the macro. Initialize will clear the Tool palette of any custom tools and close the current document, so be sure to save before initializing. The macro will position objects according to the document dimensions used when the macro was originally created. If the current document size is different, you may see the macro positioning objects outside of the current canvas.

14. When the macro has completed, you can either continue with this document or reload the version of the scene you were working on. You can stop a macro at any time by pressing on the Esc hotkey.

15. Notice that the new introducingZbrush_ch3 macros section has macros for setting up the document and background plane as well as one for painting the background sketch.

Now that you understand how to load macros, you can watch the exercises in this book in action; it's a great way to share knowledge with other ZBrush users. If you decide at some point you want to remove the macros from the palette, simply go to Windows Explorer and remove the `introducingZbrush_c03` directory from the `ZBrush3\ZStartup\Macros` folder.

Working with Deformations and Materials

Deformers are another way to edit 3D tools. Deformers are applied to a 3D tool using the wide array of sliders in the Deformation subpalette, which is found in the Tool palette. You can apply deformations to the entire tool or to unmasked portions of the tool. Using the deformers, you can create a nearly infinite number of variations of your 3D tools.

Materials in ZBrush define how a surface will look when rendered. When you assign a material to a 3D tool or to pixols that have been dropped to the canvas, you can then adjust how shiny, bumpy, reflective, coarse, or smooth the surface will be and many other surface qualities that define how an object looks when rendered. This section provides a brief overview of how to work with materials, Chapter 8 has a more in-depth discussion of how to create materials.

Creating the Legs

To create the legs that keep the undersea lab steady on the ocean floor, you'll use the Ring 3D tool and some deformations.

1. In the Tool palette, open up the inventory and select the 3D Ring tool.

2. In the Draw palette, make sure the Perspective button is activated.

3. Draw the Ring tool on the canvas and switch to Transform mode by clicking the Move button on the top shelf (hotkey = w).

4. Open up the Initialize subpalette on the Tool palette and set the coverage to 100. Now you just have a section of the ring.

    Next you'll use one of the deformers in the Deformation subpalette to flatten the ring, making it look more like a machined piece of steel.

    In some cases, deformations work better on a polymesh 3D tool than with a parametric 3D mesh. Sometimes the deformation will conflict with the initialize settings and the results can be unpredictable. With some experience and experimentation you'll learn when you need to convert a parametric tool to a polymesh before using a deformer.

5. Click the Edit button on the top shelf to switch to Edit mode (hotkey = t). Then click on the Make Polymesh3D button on the Tool palette (see Figure 3.22).

When you switch to Edit mode before converting to a polymesh, the 3D mesh will not be dropped to the canvas and the parametric object will be replaced by the polymesh version while the tool is still active. If you convert the parametric object to a polymesh without switching to Edit mode first, the active parametric object will be dropped to the canvas. You'll then have to select the polymesh version from the Tool palette, draw it on the canvas, and then erase the original parametric version. This involves too many steps and is confusing; it's best to switch to Edit mode before converting a parametric object to a polymesh.

6. Turn off the Edit mode button and click on the Rotate button to switch to Transform mode (hotkey = r). Use the gyro to rotate the 3D ring section so that you can see the edge.

7. In the Tool palette, expand the Deformation subpalette (see Figure 3.23).

Figure 3.22

Click the Make Polymesh3D button to convert the parametric 3D primitive to a polymesh.

The Deformation subpalette consists of a large number of sliders. Each slider will perform a deformation on the current stroke as long as it has not been dropped to the canvas. The sliders control the amount of deformation. Moving a slider to the right creates a positive deformation—in the case of the inflate deformer, this inflates the object outward. Moving the slider to the left causes a negative deformation—in the case of the inflate deformer, this will inflate the object inward as if the object is being crushed.

The sliders are additive, meaning that when you move the slider one direction or the other, it adds the result to the current shape. So repeatedly moving the slider in one direction compounds the effect of the deformation. The sliders are also sensitive; it takes some practice to get used to how they behave. You can select the value itself and enter it numerically if you prefer. The Undo button (Ctrl+z) will come in handy when applying deformers. Hold the Ctrl key while the cursor is over the name of a deformer to get a short description of how each deformer works.

You'll notice that to the far right of each slider are the letters *X*, *Y*, and *Z*. These determine the axis of the deformation. You can click on the letters to toggle them on or off. You can use any combination of the three axes in your deformation. The axis is determined by object space, not world space coordinates (object space is discussed in Chapter 1).

8. In the Deformation subpalette, find the RFlatten (radial flatten) slider. Make sure the axis toggle has Z activated and X and Y deactivated. Push the slider to the right a couple times, just a little bit; this will flatten the top and sides of the Ring tool, making it look more mechanical (see Figure 3.24).

9. When you are happy with the look of the leg, switch the tool to Transform mode by activating the Scale button (hotkey = e). Scale the object inward along the z-axis by dragging on the yellow cross on the gyro. This will make the leg thinner (Figure 3.25).

10. In the Transform palette, make sure the Quick button is off so the leg appears smooth.

11. In the Draw palette, make sure the Perspective button is activated so that the leg matches the perspective of the rest of the undersea lab.

Positioning the Legs

You'll use the gyro and the Snapshot function to position and duplicate the legs just as you created the holes for the windows.

1. Switch to Transform mode by clicking the Move button on the top shelf (hotkey = w) and move the leg toward the sea lab.

2. Use the gyro to scale, position, and rotate the leg into place so that it matches the sketch.

3. When the first leg is in position, click the Snapshot button in the Transform palette (Shift+s) to make a copy. Position this leg as well.

Figure 3.23

The Deformation subpalette has a large number of deformers that can be applied to the current 3D tool.

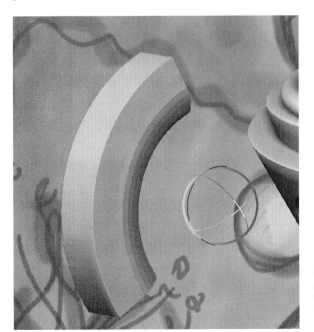

Figure 3.24

Applying the RFlatten deformer makes the pipe look like a piece of machined steel.

4. Create two more copies for a total of four legs (see Figure 3.26).

5. To see a macro that runs through the leg creation steps, initialize ZBrush, load the underWaterScene_v2.ZBR document into ZBrush, then click the button labeled seaLabLegs in the Macro palette.

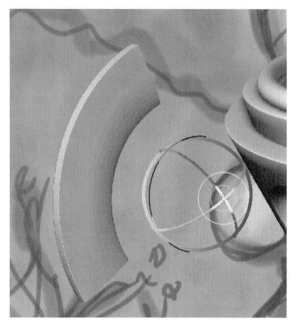

Figure 3.25

The deformed pipe is made thinner using the gyro in Scale mode.

Figure 3.26

The legs are copied using the Snapshot function and positioned with the transform gyro.

Assigning a Material to the Undersea Lab

At this point it's a good idea to assign a single material and color to the undersea lab. The ZBrush default render mode is Preview, which can give you an idea of how the materials look. However, you won't see every aspect of a material until you render with Best quality.

Materials determine the surface quality of the pixols painted on the canvas as well as 3D tools. A surface can be shiny, reflective, translucent, bumpy, and so on. Some materials contain a color component which can affect the colors applied to pixols, some do not. Materials consist of one or more shaders. A shader is a group of settings that determine the surface quality of the material. If a material has more than one shader, the shader settings are combined to create the final look of the material. Shader settings are accessed by clicking on the S1, S2, S3, and S4 buttons at the top of the material palette's modifier subpalette (see Figure 3.29).

ZBrush has two main types of materials: standard and MatCap. In the material inventory, they are divided into two sections, with MatCap materials on the top and standard materials on the bottom, as shown in Figure 3.27. Standard materials are adjusted by tuning the multitude of settings each standard material has in its palette. MatCap materials are created using the Material Capture tool. Chapter 8 of this book goes into detail on how to work with both types of materials. For this chapter, you'll work with only the standard materials and on a fairly basic level.

Figure 3.27

MatCap materials are in the upper section of the material inventory and standard materials are in the lower section. Materials altered during a ZBrush session move to the very top row.

There are a few ways to apply materials in ZBrush. If a tool is in Edit or Transform mode and you select a material from the material inventory, it will automatically be applied to the tool. You can select a material before painting a stroke and it will be applied to the stroke when you paint on the canvas. You can paint a material onto pixols with a brush if the M or Mrgb button is activated on the top shelf. With the M button activated, only the material selected in the inventory will be painted. Mrgb paints both the selected material and the current color in the color picker.

At any time during the process of working on a composition, you can open the settings for these materials in the Material palette and make changes. Every stroke or tool on the canvas that has that material applied to it will update automatically. If you adjust the settings on a material, that material will move to the User Materials section of the material inventory.

Furthermore, the changes you make to materials are saved with the document. You can save your own custom materials to disk for use in other projects. Finally, you can copy a material from the inventory and paste it over of a user material at the top of the materials inventory. All pixols with the previous material applied will now have the pasted material applied to them. For now you'll apply one material to the sea lab structure and then tweak its settings later on after the rest of the composition has been created.

1. Open the underwaterScene_v3.ZBR scene from the Chapter 3 folder on the DVD.

2. From the material inventory, select the Textured Metal material (see Figure 3.28).

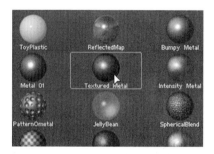

3. In the Tool palette, select the PaintBrush tool.

4. Set the stroke to Drag Rect.

5. Set Alpha to off.

6. In the top shelf, make sure ZAdd, ZSub, and ZCut are deactivated.

7. Turn the M button on; this will cause the brush to apply just the material and not the color.

8. Make sure the layer with the sea lab is activated in the Layer palette before painting.

9. Drag a stroke over the sea lab so that the entire lab is covered with the material; you can use multiple strokes if you need to.

10. Open the Material palette and expand the Modifiers subpalette. Click the S2 button at the top of the modifiers to switch to the material's second group of shader settings, and adjust the diffuse quality of the material to make it lighter: a setting of 80 should work. Notice that this material is now moved to the user defined section (see Figure 3.29).

11. Save the document.

    For now, leave the material the way it is. After we have the rest of the scene together, you'll adjust more settings on this material.

12. To see a macro of the texture application, initialize ZBrush, open the underwaterScene_v3.ZBR file from the Chapter 3 folder on the DVD, and run the seaLabMetal material macro from the Macro palette.

Adding the Dome and Windows

In this next section we'll add the bubble dome and windows so the undersea explorers can hang out in their lab comfortably.

1. In the Material palette, select the JellyBean material (see Figure 3.30).

2. In the Tool palette, select the Sphere 3D tool.

3. In the top shelf, set the RGB intensity to 5. This will cause the tool to be semitransparent when drawn (see Figure 3.31).

4. In the Draw palette, make sure Perspective is activated. Set Refract to 60. This will make the transparency of the sphere appear refracted.

5. In the Transform palette, make sure the Quick button is off so the sphere appears nice and smooth.

6. Draw the sphere on the canvas.

7. Activate the Move button on the top shelf (hotkey = w) and use the gyro to position the globe on top of the sea lab.

8. Use the gyro to rotate, scale, and position the sphere so that it matches the sketch, as shown in Figure 3.32.

9. When you are satisfied with the sphere's position, use the Snapshot tool in the Transform palette to make a copy.

10. Move the copy down to the lower part of the lab, set the gyro to Scale mode (hotkey = e), scale the sphere copy down, and position it in the window hole on the left side of the lab.

11. Use the Snapshot tool to make copies of the smaller sphere and position these in the other window holes. These bubble windows should be slightly smaller than the holes they occupy (see Figure 3.33).

12. To see a macro that runs through the material application and dome creation steps, initialize ZBrush, load the underWaterScene_v4.ZBR document into ZBrush, then click the button labeled seaLabDome in the Macro palette.

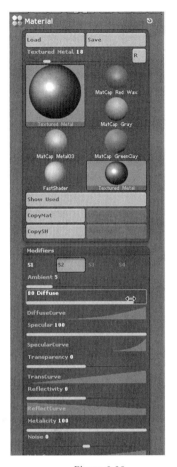

Figure 3.29

Adjust the Diffuse setting under the S2 button in the Modifiers subpalette to make the material lighter.

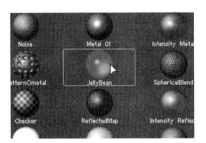

Figure 3.30

The JellyBean material in the Standard section of the Material palette

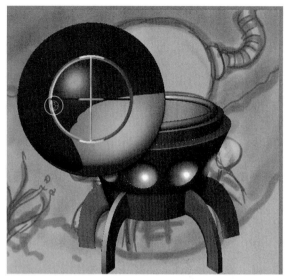

Figure 3.31

With a low RGB setting, the 3D sphere is semitransparent when drawn. The Refraction slider on the Draw palette adds a refraction effect.

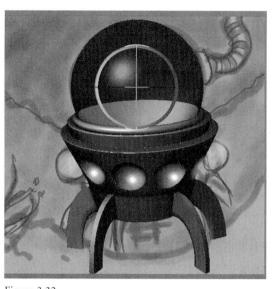

Figure 3.32

Use the transform gyro to position the dome on the undersea lab to match the sketch.

Figure 3.33

Copies of the dome sphere create the bubble windows around the undersea lab.

Detailing the Sea Lab

At this point, you can add some excitement to the sea lab by adding details. You'll start by adding some bolts to the structure.

1. In the Tool palette, select the Sphereinder 3D tool (see Figure 3.34).

Figure 3.34

The Sphereinder 3D tool can be used to create bolts on the sea lab structure.

2. In the Layer palette, create a new layer.

3. Open the Picker palette, and make sure that the Cont Ori button is activated. This ensures that when 3D objects are drawn onto pixols, the orientation of the stroke continuously updates based on the surface direction of the pixols below it.

4. In the Initialize subpalette of the Sphereinder 3D tool, set the Z size to 30.

5. In the Draw palette, make sure Perspective is still activated.

6. Set the stroke type to DragDot; set the draw size to 20.

7. In the Material palette, select the Textured Metal material from the user materials at the top.

8. Use the Zoom button on the right shelf to zoom in on the sea lab.

9. Drag the brush across the surface of the sea lab; the Sphereinder 3D tool will follow wherever you drag until you release the brush; then it will be dropped to the canvas (see Figure 3.35).

Figure 3.35

The DragDot stroke type makes it easy to position bolts on the surface of the lab.

Do you really need to go through all of these settings every time you change tools? Well, as you gain experience, changing brush and tool settings will become second nature. It seems rather tedious when you are learning but this is because you're going through an exercise, duplicating something that has been created by someone else. When you start doing your own artwork you'll find yourself experimenting more and you'll know what to expect and it won't seem like such a chore. Actually, it will be a lot of fun!

10. Use the Sphereinder 3D tool to create bolts on the surface of the sea lab. You can use Figure 3.35 as a guide or just experiment with your own style of bolting.

11. From the Tool palette, select the Cube3D tool. Make sure you're still on the bolts layer.

12. Activate the ZSub button on the top shelf.

13. Set the Z size of the cube to 10.

14. Use the cube to cut small panels into the lower part of the sea lab (see Figure 3.36).

15. To create a pipe that leads to the surface, switch to the SphereBrush (not the Sphere 3D tool!).

16. Set the draw size to 45.

17. On a blank part of the canvas to the right of the sea lab, slowly draw a snaking pipe that curves upward; it does not have to connect. The SphereBrush will create a smooth stroke if you draw slowly.

18. Activate the Move button to put the sphere stroke in Transform mode. The stroke may disappear, but it's just hidden behind the canvas. Drag down on the canvas repeatedly until the stroke appears.

19. Use the gyro to move and rotate the sphere stroke into place (see Figure 3.37); it should look like it's coming out of the dome. When you are happy with the position, switch to the SimpleBrush.

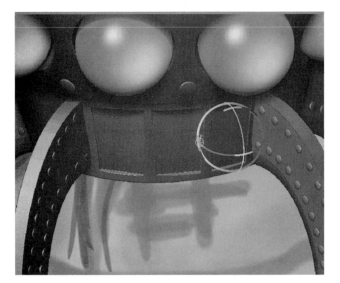

Figure 3.36

The 3D Cube tool in subtract mode cuts panels into the structure.

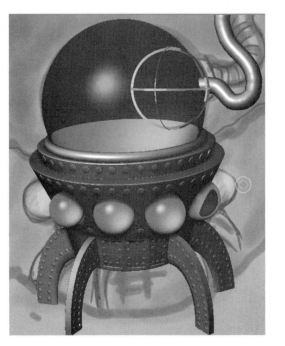

Figure 3.37

The stroke created with the Sphere-Brush is positioned using the Gyro.

20. Activate the ZSub button on the top shelf, deactivate the M, Rgb, and Mrgb buttons.

21. Set the alpha to a fuzzy dot: alpha 36 should work well.

22. Set the draw size fairly low, between 5 and 7, and the intensity to 5.

23. Use the SimpleBrush with these settings to carve lines into the hose that goes to the surface; use Figure 3.38 as a reference.

Figure 3.38

Lines are cut into the hose using the SimpleBrush in Subtract mode.

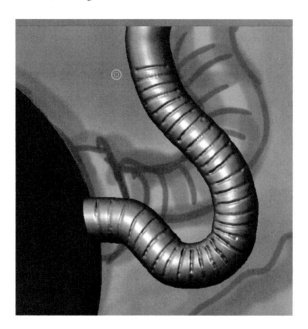

Introducing Masks

Masks are a way to restrict edits to a 3D tool to only certain parts of the surface. There are a large number of ways to apply masks to 3D tools. In this section you'll see how using a mask with a parametric 3D object can allow you to create some interesting shapes.

1. Create a new layer in the document.

2. From the material inventory, select the Fast Shader; set the color picker to white.

3. From the Tool palette, select the Ring3D tool and draw it on the canvas.

4. Click the Move button (hotkey = w) to put the tool in Transform mode.

5. Expand the Initialize subpalette in the Tool palette.

6. Set the SRadius to 10. Set the LDivide value for the ring to 120; set SDivide to 20. This increases the rows and columns of polygons that make up the Ring3D tool (see Figure 3.39).

7. Expand the Masking subpalette of the Tool palette. There are a lot of buttons here; for now you'll just focus on the buttons that work with 3D parametric objects. Click the MaskAll button (see Figure 3.40).

8. Set the Sel slider to 10. Set Skp to 0. Click the Row button.

   You'll see bands of alternating white and gray running around the ring. By clicking the Row button, you've unmasked areas of the ring based on the Sel slider. The mask is applied to 10 rows of polygons and then unmasked for another 10. Since the ring has 20 rows of polygons, the mask divides the ring evenly in half (see Figure 3.41).

9. Click the Inverse button to reverse the mask.

10. Set the Sel slider to 4 and the Skp slider to 8.

11. Click the Col button. Now the unmasked area includes rows of polygons. Every four columns of polygons are unmasked; then eight columns are skipped before another four are unmasked (see Figure 3.42)

12. Click the Inverse button again.

13. Expand the Deformation subpalette.

14. Move the Inflate slider a couple times to the right. The unmasked portions of the ring are pushed outward (see Figure 3.43).

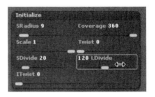

Figure 3.39

Adjusting the settings in the Initialize subpalette of the Ring3D tool

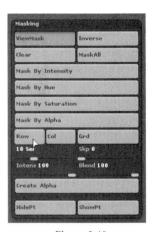

Figure 3.40

The Masking subpalette

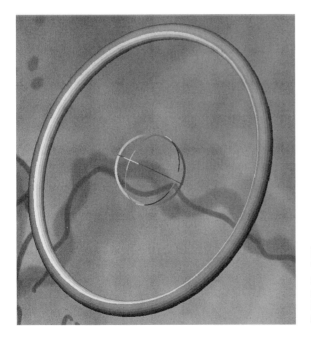

Figure 3.41

The Row button unmasks rows of polygons based on the setting of the Sel button in the Masking subpalette.

Figure 3.42
The Col button unmasks rows of polygons on the Ring 3D tool.

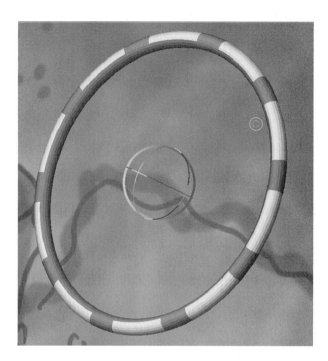

Figure 3.43
The inflate deformer creates bulges in the unmasked portions of the ring.

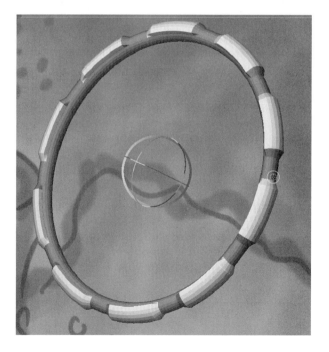

15. Click the Clear button in the Masking subpalette to clear the mask.

16. From the material inventory, select the Textured Metal material from the very top of the Material palette.

17. From the Transform palette, deactivate the Quick button to smooth the appearance of the ring.

18. In the Draw palette, click the Perspective button.

19. Use the gyro to position the ring just below the dome on the sea lab, as shown in Figure 3.44.

20. Save the document.

21. To see a macro that demonstrates how to apply masks to the ring, initialize ZBrush, load the underwaterScene_v6.ZBR document, and click the sealabRing2 button in the Macro palette.

Figure 3.44

The edited ring is positioned on the lab.

Summary

This chapter has covered a lot of ground, but it is just the beginning. The popularity of ZBrush for creating digital sculptures has overshadowed its powerful drawing and painting tools. In this chapter, you were introduced to ways in which document layers, 3D parametric objects, polymesh tools, masks, and materials can be used to create fantastic illustrations. The techniques we used are well known to experienced ZBrush users. At this point, you should be able to develop your own ways of accomplishing the task of illustrating in ZBrush.

Chapter 4 continues with this same project, introducing even more tools, such as ZSpheres, fiber brushes, alpha brushes, and 2.5-dimensional painting tools. If you found illustrating in ZBrush difficult to get used to, don't fret too much. It's a very different approach than in programs such as Photoshop. There are powerful illustration tools and lots of techniques to explore in ZBrush and they take time and practice to master. You may find that you enjoy sculpting objects in ZBrush more than creating illustrations. If this is the case, try skipping ahead to Chapter 5 and Chapter 6. You can always come back to Chapter 4 later on!

Painting with Pixols, Part 2

In Chapter 3 you learned the basics of how to create a composition in ZBrush. In this chapter, you'll continue with the same project. New tools will be introduced, including the versatile ZSphere. Basic sculpting will be explored and you'll spend more time working with your tools in Edit mode. This project is designed to introduce the basics of ZBrush painting tools. After completing these exercises, you'll be ready to explore more advanced features, including digital sculpting and rendering.

This chapter includes the following topics:

- Working with ZSpheres
- Fog effects and background elements
- Painting with the Fiber brush
- Creating new 3D tools using alphas

Introducing ZSpheres

You'll start this chapter with some more organic sculpting methods. In the foreground of the composition, you'll create some deep sea volcanic vents. To do this you'll use ZBrush's unique ZSphere tool.

A ZSphere is a very special 3D tool unlike anything you may have encountered in other 3D programs. ZSpheres allow you to sketch out a simple skeleton made of spheres, like drawing a stick figure on a piece of paper. You can then instantly skin a polymesh membrane over the ZSphere skeleton with the click of a button. ZSpheres are great for creating figures and organic forms, but you can use them for anything. We'll start out with some simple undersea volcanic vents.

1. Open the underWaterScene_v7.ZBR from the Chapter 4\ZDocs folder on the DVD or continue with your current version. In the Layer palette, click the Create button to make a new layer. Make sure the new layer is the active layer and that the other layers are still visible.

2. Set the material to Fast Shader.

3. From the Tool palette, select the ZSphere tool (Figure 4.1).

Figure 4.1

Choose the ZSphere tool from the Tool palette's inventory.

4. Draw a ZSphere on the canvas and switch to Edit mode by clicking the Edit button on the top shelf (hotkey = t), shown in Figure 4.2.

Figure 4.2

Activate Edit mode by clicking the Edit button in the top shelf.

Here's a quick review of how to work with a 3D tool in Edit mode:

- To rotate, scale, or move a 3D tool, you can use the buttons on the right shelf.

- Alternatively, to rotate the 3D tool you can drag around on the canvas, to move the 3D tool you hold the Alt key while dragging on the canvas, and to scale the 3D tool you release the Alt key while dragging.

- The Local button on the right shelf sets the pivot point of the 3D tool to the last area edited. This can help you keep from getting lost as you constantly rotate the 3D tool (Figure 4.3).

Now that you have a ZSphere on the canvas in Edit mode, let's see how you can work with this unique tool. An underwater volcanic vent is really just a thin tube that spews bubbles and volcanic ash out the top. Creating a volcanic vent using ZSphere should be pretty simple, but the same techniques will apply when you decide to create something more complex like a person or a monster. These techniques will be explored in Chapter 6.

5. Make sure both the Draw and Edit buttons are activated on the top shelf.

6. Hold the brush over the ZSphere but don't press down. You'll notice that a red circle appears (top image in Figure 4.4) with a line connected to the center of the ZSphere. This is a guide that will help you to place more ZSpheres as you add them to the original.

7. Notice that the circle turns green when the brush is over certain parts of the original ZSphere. Although you can add a ZSphere to the original at any point, the ideal location is indicated by the green circle. The center image in Figure 4.4 shows an example of this optimal placement.

8. When you find the spot where the circle turns green, press down on the tablet (or click the mouse button if you are using a mouse) and drag. You'll see that a new ZSphere is drawn connected to the original. As you drag on the canvas, the new ZSphere scales up, as shown in the bottom image of Figure 4.4.

9. Hold the brush over the newly added ZSphere and find another green circle. This time, hold the Shift key down as you click on the ZSphere at the position of the green circle. A third ZSphere appears; this one is already scaled to match the previous ZSphere.

   Holding the Shift key adds a copy of the previous ZSphere to the ZSphere chain. This can come in handy when you want to speed up your work flow (see Figure 4.5).

Positioning ZSpheres

The power of ZSpheres becomes evident when you start to add and position them. In this section you'll learn how to move ZSpheres around to block out a ZSphere skeleton.

1. Rotate the ZSphere chain around so that you can see the opposite side of the first ZSphere. Find the green circle by holding the brush over the ZSphere and then use the Shift+click method to add a fourth ZSphere to the chain. Adding another ZSphere on the opposite side of the chain helps the skinning process remain stable when the ZSpheres are converted to a polymesh (Figure 4.6).

Figure 4.3

The Local button continually repositions the pivot point of a 3D tool in Edit mode.

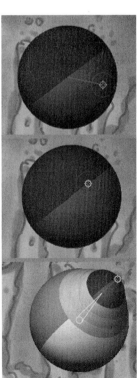

Figure 4.4

The circles on the ZSphere indicate where the next ZSphere will be drawn. Clicking on the ZSphere while the Draw button is active causes a new ZSphere to be added to the first.

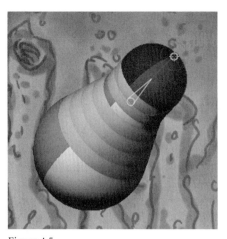

Figure 4.5

Clicking on the ZSphere while holding the Shift key adds a copy of the previous ZSphere to the ZSphere chain.

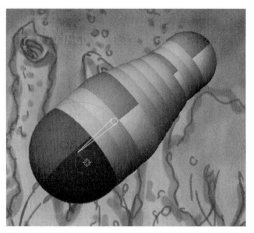

Figure 4.6

Add a new ZSphere to the other side of the chain by clicking on the first ZSphere.

2. Press the *a* hotkey. You'll see the ZSphere turn into a polymesh. Press the a key again to return to ZSpheres (Figure 4.7).

   The a hotkey allows you to preview what the ZSpheres will look like when you are ready to convert them into a polymesh.

   It's important to remember not to try to sculpt or edit the preview polymesh or the results will be unpredictable. As you work with ZSpheres, you'll want to continually switch between adaptive preview mode (hotkey = a) and the ZSphere mode as you go. This will help you to position the ZSpheres before committing to the polymesh version.

Figure 4.7

Pressing the a hotkey lets you see a preview of the skinned ZSpheres.

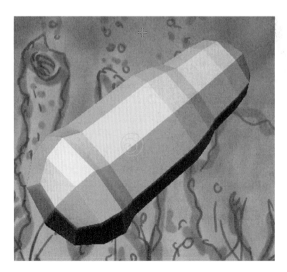

When you press the a key to see a preview, you may notice that one end of the mesh appears twisted; you can fix this by switching back to the ZSphere mode and rotating the twisted ZSphere. Fixing this problem is discussed in the upcoming section on skinning ZSpheres.

3. Click the Move button on the top shelf (hotkey = w). Notice that the gyro does not appear. While you're editing ZSpheres, the Move, Rotate, and Scale buttons on the top shelf behave differently than they do while you're transforming a tool.

4. With the Move button activated, click on a ZSphere on the end and drag it outward. Notice how a chain of gray ZSpheres connects the shaded ZSpheres. The Shaded ZSpheres act as joints while the plain gray ZSpheres act as connectors between the joints.

5. Click on any of the other shaded ZSpheres and try moving them. The number of gray ZSpheres changes depending on the distance between the joint ZSpheres. When you move a shaded ZSphere, it moves independently of the others in the ZSphere chain. As you move the ZSpheres, you'll see a triangle drawn on top of the ZSphere chain. The triangle resembles the depiction of a joint in other 3D animation applications. The thick part of the triangle is on the parent sphere and the pointed end points toward the child ZSphere (top of Figure 4.8).

6. Try moving a gray connecting ZSphere; when you move a gray ZSphere, all of the child ZSpheres downstream move as well. However, the upstream shaded ZSphere acts as the pivot for the chain.

7. Activate the Scale key and try scaling one of the shaded ZSpheres (center of Figure 4.8). If you scale one of the gray, connector ZSpheres, all of the ZSpheres downstream will scale uniformly. The shaded ZSphere above the connector you're scaling from acts as the pivot point for the scaling operation.

8. Activate the Rotate button on the top shelf (hotkey = r). Try rotating a shaded ZSphere. The shaded ZSpheres rotate independently (bottom of Figure 4.8). Rotating a gray connector ZSphere changes the orientation of all the downstream child ZSpheres in the chain.

9. Click the Draw button on the top shelf and then click on a gray connecting ZSphere. This converts a connecting ZSphere to a joint ZSphere (Figure 4.9).

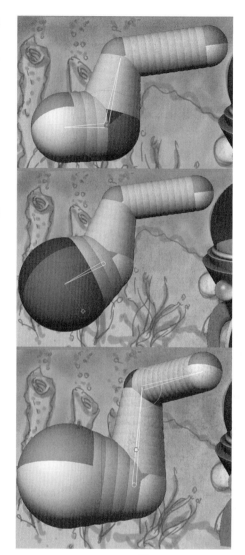

Figure 4.8

Activating the Move, Scale, and Rotate buttons on the top shelf allows you to reposition, scale, and rotate the ZSpheres in the chain. The triangle indicators point from the parent ZSphere toward the child ZSpheres.

Figure 4.9

Clicking on a gray
connecting sphere
with the Draw but-
ton activated con-
verts the gray
connector to a
shaded joint
ZSphere.

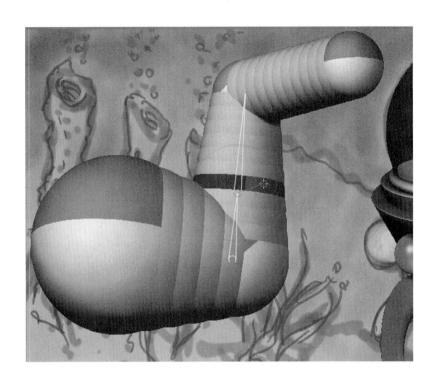

Figure 4.9

Clicking on a gray connecting sphere with the Draw button activated converts the gray connector to a shaded joint ZSphere.

Figure 4.10

The Tool palette has controls for converting a ZSphere chain into either a unified or adaptive skin.

Skinning ZSpheres

There are two ways to skin a ZSphere chain. You can create a unified skin or an adaptive skin. A unified skin creates a mesh that envelops the ZSphere skeleton with a uniform number of polygons. Actually, any 3D tool can be converted to a unified skin (Figure 4.10).

The adaptive skinning method allows you to set parameters that will control how the skin is stretched over the ZSpheres. When you click on the Preview button (hotkey = a), you actually see the ZSpheres temporarily converted into a preview of the adaptive skin. Changing the parameters in the Adaptive Skin subpalette determines how the skinning procedure will behave. Adaptive skinning is generally preferred over unified skinning when converting ZSpheres into a polymesh. It's more efficient and the controls in the subpalette allow you to fine-tune the polymesh before actually converting the ZSpheres.

1. With the ZSphere chain still in Edit mode, open the Tool palette and expand the Adaptive Skin subpalette.

2. Press the a hotkey to toggle a preview of the ZSphere chain.

3. The skin may look twisted at one end, as shown in Figure 4.11. If this is the case, switch back to ZSpheres by pressing the a hotkey, activate the Rotate button, and rotate the ZSphere that's causing the twisting. You may need to toggle back and forth between the ZSphere and preview modes until you get the rotation correct and the twisting is eliminated (Figures 4.11 and 4.12).

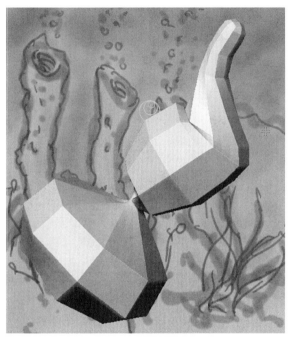

Figure 4.11

The ZSphere on one end of the chain is rotated incorrectly, causing the skin to be twisted in the adaptive skin preview.

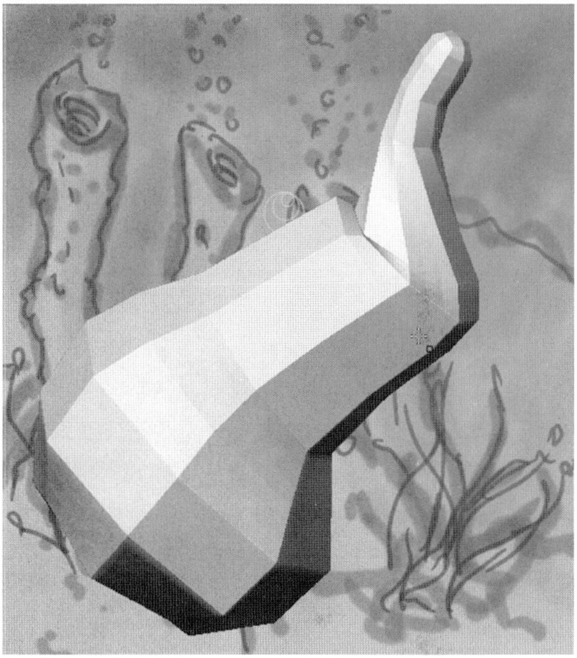

Figure 4.12

After the rotation of the ZSphere is corrected, the twisting has been eliminated in the adaptive skin preview.

4. Try adjusting the Density slider. This controls the density of the mesh that will be created when the ZSpheres are converted to a polymesh (Figure 4.13). Usually you can leave the Density at a low value and then subdivide the adaptive skin after you commit to the adaptive skin.

5. The IRes slider controls the intersection resolution. The effects of this slider are more obvious when it is set to 1 and the density is low.

An adaptive skin creates areas of high and low resolution that adapt to the position, scale, and rotation of the ZSpheres at the time of conversion to a polymesh (i.e., when the ZSpheres are *skinned*). The IRes slider sets a threshold value to determine which

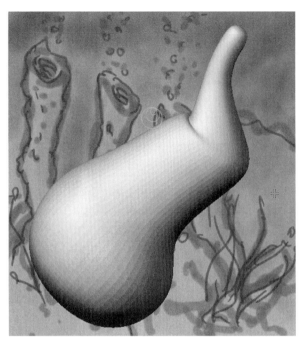

Figure 4.13

The Density slider adjusts the number of subdivisions in the adaptive skin.

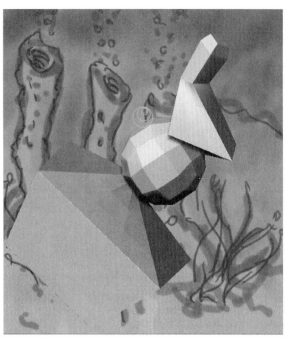

Figure 4.14

The effect of the IRes control is more obvious when the density of the adaptive skin is low.

areas of the mesh will be high or low resolution based on the number of ZSpheres in a given area of the mesh. IRes is an advanced control used for fine-tuning a ZSphere skeleton that is not converting to polymesh correctly. For our simple volcanic vent model, the default value of 6 should be fine (Figure 4.14).

6. The Mbr button controls the membrane curvature. The membrane refers to the polymesh skin that can be thought of as being stretched over the ZSphere skeleton. Adjusting this value allows you to fine-tune the smoothness of this stretching. A higher value results in a looser skin (top of Figure 4.15); a lower value thins out the areas between the ZSpheres (bottom of Figure 4.15). For your vents, the default value of 0 should work fine.

    The MC and MP buttons are the Minimal Skin to Child and Minimal Skin to Parent controls, respectively. They control the resolution of the mesh between child and parent spheres. In the case of a simple vent, these controls are not really necessary.

7. Use the a hotkey to toggle off the adaptive skin preview and switch back to the ZSpheres.

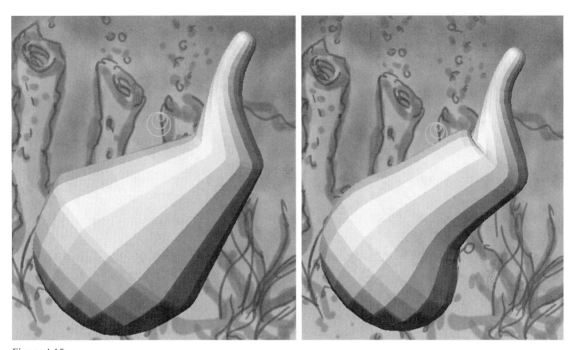

Figure 4.15

The membrane curvature of this skin has been set to 100 in the left image. The membrane curvature of this skin has been set to 0 in the right image.

Creating the Vent

With a few more tweaks to the ZSphere chain you'll be ready to convert it into a polymesh and sculpt the simple tube into a volcanic vent.

1. Arrange the ZSpheres so that they form a straight line. It should not be perfectly straight; you want the vent to look organic and chaotic.

2. Make sure there are five shaded joint ZSpheres in the chain.

3. Scale the ZSpheres on one end of the chain up, making each ZSphere joint a little smaller as you move along the chain from one end to the other. This will create the conical shape of the volcanic vent, as shown in the top of Figure 4.16.

4. Move the ZSpheres in the middle of the chain slightly off center so that the resulting shape is more organic. Feel free to use the a hotkey to preview the polymesh as you work.

5. Switch to Draw mode and add one more ZSphere at the small end of the chain (center of Figure 4.16).

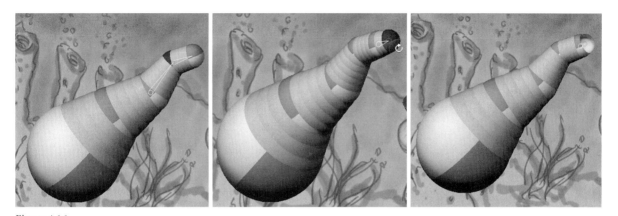

Figure 4.16

The ZSpheres are arranged in a semi-straight line. The size of the ZSpheres decreases as the spheres move from left to right. An additional ZSphere is added to the end of the chain and is moved back into the previous ZSphere causing it to have a negative, or subtractive, effect.

6. Activate the Scale button on the top shelf and scale this last ZSphere down so that it is smaller than the preceding ZSphere.

7. Activate the Move button on the top shelf and move this last ZSphere back toward the center of the chain. At a certain point it should turn gray and the shading will reverse. This last ZSphere now has a negative function; it will subtract from the polymesh rather than add to it. Use the a hotkey to toggle the adaptive skin preview. You should see a crater forming at the small end of the mesh (bottom of Figure 4.16).

8. Press the a hotkey to switch back to ZSphere mode and continue to fine-tune the position of this last ZSphere; toggle back and forth between ZSphere and adaptive skin preview modes while you position this last sphere. You want to make a crater that looks like an opening at the end of the vent.

9. When you are satisfied with the position of this last ZSphere, click the Make Adaptive Skin button on the Tool palette's Adaptive Skin subpalette to convert the ZSphere chain (Figure 4.17).

10. Once you convert the ZSphere chain to an adaptive skin, you'll notice that nothing happens to the ZSphere model. Open the Tool palette inventory and select the new tool labeled Skin_ZSphere#1. The ZSphere chain will be replaced by the new polymesh. The original ZSphere version still exists in the inventory while this ZBrush session is still active (Figure 4.18). If you want to save it for future ZBrush sessions, use the Save As button in the Tool palette and save the tool to your local hard disk. The converted ZSphere skin will be listed in the Tool palette with the prefix *Skin* appended to the name. This indicates that it is a polymesh skin, which can no longer be edited as a ZSphere.

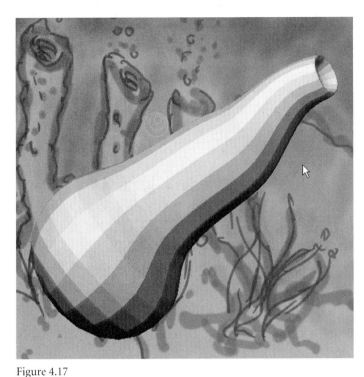

Figure 4.17

The subtractive ZSphere creates a crater at the thin end of the adaptive skin.

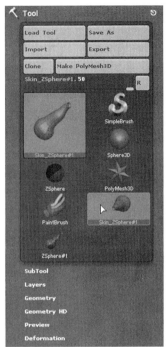

Figure 4.18

Once the ZSphere chain has been converted to an adaptive skin, it is available as a polymesh object in the Tool palette.

Sculpting the Vent

Now you have a nice piece of geometry that you can refine even further.

1. In the top shelf, turn off Edit mode and activate the Move button to switch to Transform mode.

2. Use the gyro to position the vent so that it matches the background sketch. The vent should be in the foreground. Open the Transform palette, and in the Info subpalette, make sure the Z value is between 0 and 100. You can verify the position of the vent by dragging it in front of the sea lab temporarily. Make sure it does not intersect with the sea lab's pixols.

3. Click the Rotate button on the top shelf (hotkey = r) and orient the vent so that the thin end with the crater is at the top (Figure 4.19).

4. Once you have the vent positioned to match the sketch, reactivate the Edit button on the top shelf (hotkey = t).

Figure 4.19

The volcanic vent mesh is positioned in the foreground to match to sketch.

5. In the Tool palette, expand the Geometry subpalette. Click the Divide button until the vent has five levels of subdivisions (SDiv). At the highest subdivision level, the vent should have 8,704 polys and 8,706 points. You can verify this by holding the brush cursor over its icon in the Tool palette; the pop-up window will show the point statistics in the corner.

6. In the Tool palette, expand the Display Properties subpalette and set the DSmooth value to 1. This will eliminate the faceted look of the vent. (See Figure 4.20.)

Figure 4.20

The DSmooth slider controls how smooth polymesh objects appear on the canvas.

Now the real fun begins. With the vent still in Edit mode, you can begin to actually sculpt it using the 3D sculpting brushes to add rocky details.

7. Click the 3D Sculpting brush icon on the left shelf to open the brush inventory. Choose the Elastic brush.

8. Set the Brush Size slider on the top shelf to around 60 and the Z intensity to 80.

9. Start painting on the vent geometry. Don't be too careful; this is a blobby rocky vent made of lava on the ocean floor. Have fun with making bumps and indentations. Alternate sculpting with the Alt key on and off to toggle between adding and subtracting strokes (Figure 4.21).

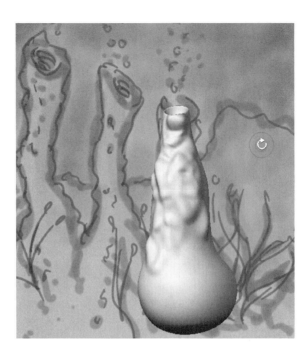

Figure 4.21

Detail is added to the vent tool using the Elastic sculpting brush.

10. Hold the Shift key down as you paint to activate the Smooth brush and continue to work the surface over.

11. Experiment with the Inflate, Standard, Clay, and Blob brushes. (Note that in ZBrush 3.1, the inflate button is actually labeled *Inflat*).

12. Try using various alphas from the Alpha palette in conjunction with the sculpting brushes.

13. Use the Move brush to pull the surface of the vent. See if you can stretch the edges of the top of the vent to make the crater more pronounced. Chapter 5 will explore these brushes in depth. For now feel free to experiment and see what you can create.

14. When you are happy with the look of the vent, you can reposition it on the canvas to match the sketch.

15. Turn off the Edit button and activate the Move button on the top shelf to switch to Transform mode. In the Transform palette, use the Snapshot button to create a copy (hotkey = Shift+s). The copy will be converted to pixols and dropped on the canvas, but the original vent should still be a polymesh object in Transform mode. Move the original vent over to the left of the first vent.

16. Scale the second vent up to match the sketch.

17. Switch to Edit mode and use the brushes to sculpt the vent. You want it to look different from the first (Figure 4.22).

18. Make one more copy of the vent using the Snapshot tool, move it to the left, scale it up, and sculpt it so that it looks different from the other two.

19. Save the document.

20. To see a macro that runs through the creation of the vents, initialize ZBrush, load the underWaterScene_v7.ZBR document into ZBrush, then click the button labeled Volcanic Vents in the Macro palette.

Figure 4.22

The Snapshot tool is used to duplicate the vent. The duplicate is edited using the sculpting brushes to distinguish it from the first vent.

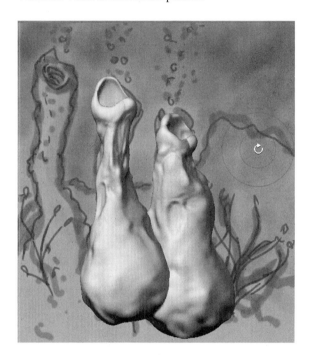

Adding a Material to the Vents

Just as with the sea lab in Chapter 3, you'll assign a material to the vents. The material can be tweaked later on once all the other elements of the composition are in place.

1. Check the Layer palette to make sure you are using the layer that contains the vents.

2. In the tool inventory, select the PaintBrush tool. You may get a warning message letting you know that switching tools while in Edit mode will cause the current tool to be dropped to the canvas. Click Switch to accept this warning.

3. In the top shelf, turn on the M button so that the PaintBrush only paints a material.

4. Turn off ZAdd (and ZSub and ZCut if they are on). This will ensure that the Paint-Brush does not alter the pixols that have been dropped to the canvas.

5. Set the stroke type to Drag Rect and the alpha to Alpha Off.

6. In the Material palette, choose the Noise Pattern1 material. Drag over the vents to apply the material to these objects (Figure 4.23).

7. Save the document.

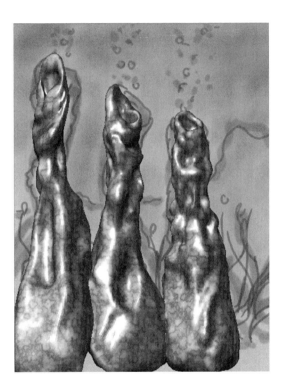

Figure 4.23
The Noise material has been painted onto the vents.

Creating the Ocean Floor

According to the sketch, there are two parts to the ocean floor that still need to be created: a small hill in the foreground that supports the volcanic vents and a rocky area beneath the sea lab. This rocky area will recede into the background where it forms some distant underwater terrain. Start by creating the hill in the foreground.

1. In the Layer palette, click the Create button to make a new layer.

2. Set the material to Fast Shader.

3. From the Tool palette, select the Sphere3D tool.

4. In the Draw palette, make sure the Perspective button is activated.

5. Draw the sphere on the canvas.

6. Activate the Scale button on the top shelf to turn on the gyro (hotkey = e). Scale the sphere up so that it's large.

7. Switch to Move mode and position the sphere in the foreground beneath the vents. Allow the sphere to intersect with the base of the vents (Figure 4.24).

8. On the top shelf, activate both the Edit and Draw buttons.

9. In the Tool palette, click the Make Polymesh button.

10. In the Tool palette, expand the Geometry subpalette, and click on Divide button to increase the resolution of the sphere. Do this twice.

11. Click the Sculpting Brush icon on the left shelf to open the brush inventory, and select the Elastic brush. Set the Draw Size to 60. Experiment with using an alpha on the Elastic brush; try selecting Alpha 23 from the alpha inventory.

12. Use the brush to sculpt the surface of the sphere, making it nice and rocky (bottom of Figure 4.24).

13. Try switching between the Elastic, Standard, Inflate, and Blob brushes, making the surface nice and rough. Try to push areas up around the base of the vents so that it looks as if the vents formed from the sphere. Vary the Draw Size and the intensity as you go (remember, you can hold the button on your pen as you press on your tablet, or right-click with the mouse, to bring up the drawing controls menu; this will save you from having to constantly revisit the top shelf buttons).

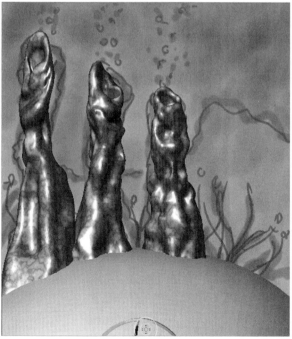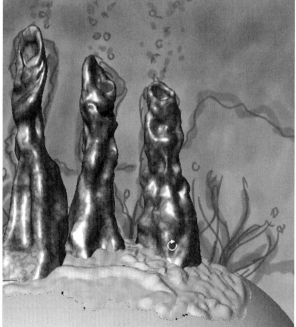

Figure 4.24

The sphere is positioned below the vents and then sculpted using the Elastic sculpting brush.

14. In the Display Properties subpalette on the Tool palette, set the DSmooth value to 1 to eliminate the faceted look of the sphere. Turn off the Quick button in the Transform palette. In some cases, you may see artifacts on the surface of the sphere as you paint; if this happens, you can adjust the position of the sphere slightly and they should disappear.

15. When you are satisfied with the shape of the sphere, use the paintbrush to apply the Noise Pattern1 material to the sphere just as you did for the vents in the section "Adding a Material to the Vents." You may see a warning letting you know that switching tools will cause the current tool to be dropped to the canvas. That's fine; switch tools and continue.

16. Create another layer in the Layer palette.

17. Select the Fast Shader from the material inventory.

18. From the Tool palette, choose the Terrain 3D tool.

19. Draw it on the canvas.

20. Use the gyro to scale the terrain up, flatten it out a bit, and position it behind the vents and underneath the sea lab (Figure 4.25).

21. Positioning the terrain can be a little tricky. It's okay if the ground overlaps the legs on the sea lab. Remember that you can more precisely position the terrain using the Z slider in the Info subpalette of the Transform palette.

22. Switch to Edit mode (hotkey = t). In the Tool palette, click the Make Polymesh button. Don't forget to activate the Perspective button in the Draw palette.

Figure 4.25

The 3D terrain object is positioned using the gyro.

Figure 4.26

The Noise Pattern1 material is applied to the ocean floor.

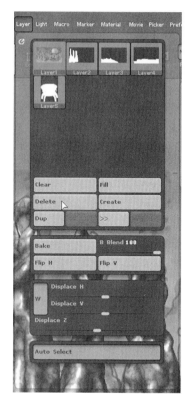

Figure 4.27

The sketch layer is selected in the Layer palette and deleted.

23. In the Tool palette, expand the Geometry subpalette, and divide the terrain three times.

24. While still in Edit mode, use the sculpting brushes to add detail to the terrain.

25. Use the Move brush to pull up some hills out of the terrain in the distant background.

26. From the material inventory, select the Noise Pattern1 material. If the sea floor is still in Edit mode, the material will be automatically applied to the tool (Figure 4.26).

27. Save the document.

28. To see a macro that runs through the material application and ocean floor creation steps, initialize ZBrush, load the underWaterScene_v8.ZBR document from the Chapter 4 folder on the DVD, and then click the button labeled Ocean Floor in the Macro palette.

Removing the Sketch

Now that all the major elements of the composition are in place, you can get rid of the background sketch and start focusing on adding details to the scene.

1. Open the Layer palette and select the sketch layer.

2. Click the Delete button in the Layer palette to eliminate this layer and its contents (Figure 4.27).

Adding Fog and Distant Background Elements

Adding fog to a scene increases the sense of depth. Considering that this particular scene takes place underwater, the fog is particularly helpful in making the viewer feel that they are at the very depths of the ocean. You can adjust your fog settings and then turn the fog on or off as you work.

1. You create the distant background mountains using techniques similar to those described in the section "Creating the Ocean Floor." Place the distant background on its own layer and push the 3D Terrain tool as far back in Z as possible, just before it disappears behind the canvas (see Figure 4.28).

Figure 4.28

Terrain in the distant background is added.

2. After you sculpt the distant background, apply the Noise material.

3. The fog settings are accessed through the Render palette. You may want to place the Render palette in a tray while you adjust these settings. To activate the fog, press the Fog button in the Render palette. The scene should suddenly turn very white (see Figure 4.29).

4. To fine-tune the fog, expand the Fog Modifiers subpalette. You can tone down the fog by decreasing the intensity; try a setting of 75.

5. Below the Intensity slider are two settings: Depth1 and Depth2. These determine where the intensity of the fog begins and ends. Pixols with a Z position lower than Depth1 (remember, lower numbers are closer to the front of the canvas) are not affected by the fog. Pixols with a Z position higher than Depth2 get the full intensity of the fog.

Figure 4.29

**Pressing the Fog
button in the Render
palette turns the
scene white.**

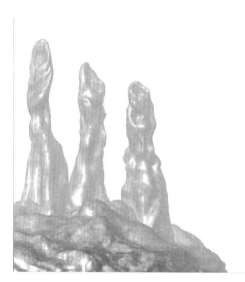

You can tweak these numbers to get a look that you like, or you can set them inter-actively. To set Depth1 interactively, select the Depth1 slider so that a border appears around it and drag to a point on the canvas. In this case, drag to one of the volcanic vents in the near foreground. Set Depth2 by dragging from the slider to the terrain in the distant background. You can continue to tweak these values numerically if you need to.

6. The two color swatches below the Depth sliders determine the start and end color of the fog. In the color picker, choose a light blue color and then click on the first color swatch on the far left. This sets the color of the fog closest to the front of the canvas. Set the color picker to a deep green and click on the color swatch on the far right; this sets the color of the fog furthest from the viewer.

   • Between the two color swatches in the Fog Modifiers subpalette are two blank swatches. The one on the left applies a texture to the fog. You can click this but-ton and select a texture from the Texture inventory. This texture will override the colors set by the swatches. If you find that all of the textures in the inventory are grayed out, or unavailable, switch your current tool to one that can use textures (such as the 3D Sphere). Even though the fog settings have nothing to do with the current tool, there is a bug/feature in ZBrush that may keep you from access-ing fog textures depending on which tool is currently active.

   • The Fog Alpha button on the middle right applies a texture to the fog from the texture inventory but applies the colors in the two swatches to the texture.

7. The Curve Editor at the bottom of the Fog Modifiers subpalette allows you to fine-tune the intensity of the fog (see Figure 4.30). Curve Editors are discussed in detail in Chapter 2 in the sidebar "Control Curves."

    The value on the left side of the Curve Editor corresponds with the front of the canvas; the value on the right corresponds to the pixols at the furthest depth of the canvas. Since this is an underwater scene, you may want to adjust the curve so that areas close to the viewer are clear but then quickly become foggy around the position of the undersea lab. The distant background should be barely visible. Figure 4.31 shows the scene with the fog settings applied.

8. To see a macro that adds fog to the scene, initialize ZBrush, load the underWaterScene_v10.ZBR document from the Chapter 4 folder on the DVD, and then click the button labeled BackgroundFog in the Macro palette.

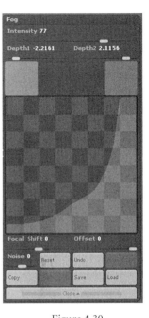

Figure 4.30

The Curve Editor allows you to fine-tune the fog.

Detailing the Vents

The vents could use a little detail to make them look more like volcanic rock. Using the 2.5D brushes, you can continue to edit and sculpt the pixols that have been dropped to the canvas.

1. Load underWaterScene_v11.ZBR from the Chapter 4 folder of the DVD or continue with your current version of the scene. Set the layer in the Layer palette to the vents layer.

2. In the Tool subpalette, select the BumpBrush from the 2.5D brushes (Figure 4.32).

3. Set the stroke type to Spray.

Figure 4.31

Adding fog increases the drama and the sense of depth in the scene.

Figure 4.32

Select the Bump-
Brush from the tool
inventory.

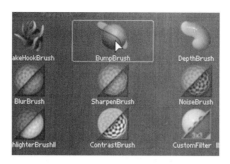

4. Set the Draw size to 60 and the Z intensity to 5; select Alpha 13 from the alpha inventory.

5. Make sure that the M, Rgb, and Mrgb buttons are off, and turn on ZAdd.

6. Paint over the vents to add bumpy details. The bumps will be restricted to the pixols on this layer; however, if you paint on the blank canvas behind the mountains in the background, you'll get raised bumps, so be careful when painting the tops of the vents. The blank part of the canvas is editable in each layer; it's a little hard to get your head around at first, but each layer is like a separate ZBrush document that shares the same canvas with the others, so blank parts of the canvas are not a separate layer. If you do accidentally paint on the background, you can erase the changes using the Erase brush (Figure 4.33).

The vents should start to look nice and lumpy.

Figure 4.33

The BumpBrush
adds detail to
the vents.

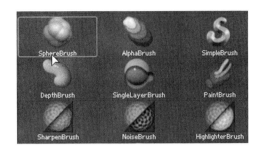

Figure 4.34

Select the Sphere brush from the 2.5D brushes.

7. Switch to the SphereBrush in the Startup 2.5D brush section (not the Sphere 3D tool!). See Figure 4.34.

8. Set the Draw size to 35.

9. Turn the M button on, and set the material to the Noise Pattern1 material.

USING M, MRGB, AND RGB

Activating the M button causes the paintbrush to paint just the material on the pixols. In the instructions for detailing the vents, the material is Noise Pattern1. Materials control surface qualities such as shininess, reflectivity, transparency, and even additional bumpiness.

The Rgb button causes the paintbrush to paint only with the color selected in the color picker. Mrgb paints with both material and color combined. You can paint an object using just the material (M) button and then go back later and add color (Rgb) however you'd like. This is one advantage to painting with only the material (M) button activated on the first pass. Materials are covered in more detail in Chapter 8.

10. Turn on ZAdd, and set the Z intensity to 5.

11. Set the stroke to Spray.

12. This brush will paint on all of the pixols regardless of the layer they are on. Try to restrict your strokes to just a few clumps of bubbly lava on the front of the vents. Try switching the brush to ZSub or ZCut to add bubbly holes.

13. Switch to the DecoBrush.

14. Turn off M, Rgb, and Mrgb on the top shelf, and turn on ZCut.

15. Set the Z intensity to 100 and the draw size to 4.

16. Drag some curving cracks across the surface of the vent.

17. Switch to the Blur Brush in the 2.5D brushes (Figure 4.35).

18. Turn off Rgb and turn on ZAdd.

19. Turn Z Intensity to 70.

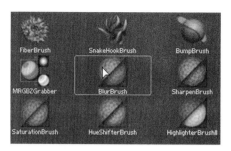

20. Set Draw Size to 80.

21. Paint over the vents to blend the details you've created. The Blur brush does a great job of blending the details together to make the rock look more like lava. Try to avoid painting over the edges of the vents; the pixols will blend with the background and distort the shape of the vents (see Figure 4.36).

22. Switch to the layer that contains the rock supporting the vents and use the same techniques to add detail. You can also experiment with the ocean floor beneath the sea lab and the hills in the background (see Figure 4.37).

23. To see a macro that adds detail to the ocean floor, initialize ZBrush, load the underWaterScene_v11.ZBR document from the Chapter 4 folder on the DVD, and then click the button labeled ventDetail in the Macro palette.

Figure 4.36

The BlurBrush helps blend the details together.

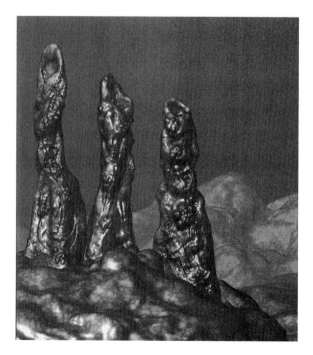

Figure 4.37

Details are added to the scenery using the 2.5D brushes.

Adding Undersea Flora and Fauna

The vents are looking a little naked right now. In reality, undersea volcanic vents often attract a wild array of strange plant and animal life. You can add some additional elements to make the vents look a bit more exciting.

1. Open the underWaterScene_v12.ZBR document or continue with your current version. In the Tool palette, select the Fiber brush and open up the Modifiers subpalette for this brush.

2. Set Density to 1. This controls how dense the patch of fibers are when you paint them on a surface.

3. Set Gravity to -30.

4. Set Grooming to 0. Grooming causes the fibers to follow the direction of the brush stroke.

5. Set Turbulence to 80; this will make the fibers look as if the current is pushing them around somewhat randomly.

6. In the color picker, choose a light bluish green. Click on the secondary color swatch beneath the picker and set the background color to a dark greenish blue. In the Modifiers subpalette for the Fiber brush, make sure the C button is activated. This causes the brush to color the fibers with a gradient. The gradient uses the secondary color at the base and the foreground color for the tips.

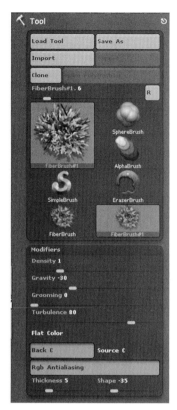

Figure 4.38

The settings for the Fiber brush

7. Turn on Rgb Antialiasing, and set the Thickness of the fibers to 5 and the shape to -35. Numbers below 0 cause the fibers to be long and thin, while numbers above 0 cause the fibers to be short and thick. The Thickness slider and the draw size of the brush can also affect the thickness and length (see Figure 4.38).

8. From the Material palette, choose the Fibers1 material.

9. Create a new layer in the Layer palette.

10. Set the draw size to 70 and paint clumps of undersea grass on the ground beneath the vents and the sea floor beneath the sea lab. Feel free to vary the draw size of the brush and the Shape setting in the Fiber Brush subpalette to add variation to the grass. (See Figure 4.39.)

11. From the Tool palette, choose the Alpha brush.

12. Set the stroke type to Color Spray. The Color Spray stroke varies the color of each instance of the sprayed stroke.

13. In the Stroke palette, set the flow to .09. This will help space out the instances of the brush stroke created by the spray.

14. Set the color picker to a blue color.

15. In the Alpha palette, choose alpha number 52. Set the material in the material inventory to Noise Bump.

16. Paint some strokes on the rocky areas where you painted the fibers. Place clumps of these sea-urchin-like objects throughout scene, and even paint a few on the legs of the sea lab. Experiment with Alphas 10, 11, 19, and 24 as well.

Figure 4.39

Sea grass is added to the scene using the Fiber brush.

17. Choose Alpha 11 and click the Make 3D button on the Alpha palette. The alpha has now been skinned and turned into a 3D tool.

18. From the Tool palette, choose the new star-shaped polymesh 3D tool.

19. Set the stroke type to Drag Dot. Drag some of these new objects on the canvas. The strokes created with this tool align themselves with the surfaces they are painted on, just as when you created the bolts on the sea lab. You can also edit these tools just like any other 3D tool. You can try turning a simple star shape into a detailed starfish. Figure 4.40 shows the volcanic vents and the ocean floor covered in plant life.

20. To see a macro that adds plant life to the scene, initialize ZBrush, load the `underWaterScene_v12.ZBR` document from the Chapter 4 folder on the DVD, and then click the button labeled floraFauna in the Macro palette.

Figure 4.40

Additional plant life is added to the scene using the Alpha brush.

Adding Bubbles to the Vents

One last element to add before rendering: the volcanic vents need to spew out some bubble. You can use the Sphere3D tool in combination with the spray stroke type; however, you'll have a tough time positioning the stroke precisely in Z space. You can set the Z position of strokes by adjusting the Z slider in the picker palette, but an even better way to precisely position paint strokes in Z space is to use the following trick using document layers.

1. Open the `underWaterScene_v13.ZBR` document or continue with your current version of the scene. Create a new layer in the Layer palette.

2. From the Tool palette, select the Cone 3D tool and draw it on the canvas.

3. Use the gyro to position the cone with the pointed side stuck in the top of one of the volcanic vents (Figure 4.41).

4. Scale the cone so that it is long and thin; position the cone so that the wide part goes off the top of the screen.

5. Use the Snapshot tool in the Transform palette to duplicate the cone twice. Position the duplicates so that they emanate from the other two volcanic vents.

Figure 4.41

The Cone3D tool is used to place cones at the top of each vent.

6. Create another new layer.

7. From the Material palette, pick the Reflection Gel shader.

8. In the Tool palette, select the Sphere 3D tool.

9. Set the stroke type to Spray.

10. In the Stroke palette, set the flow to .02.

11. Set the draw size to 30, and set the Rgb intensity to 5.

12. Use the Sphere 3D tool to cover each of the cones with spheres.

13. When you are satisfied, go to the Layer palette and delete the layer containing the cones.

14. You may want to use a similar technique to add additional bubbles throughout the scene.

15. To see a macro that adds bubbles to the vents, initialize ZBrush, load the underWaterScene_v13.ZBR document from the Chapter 4 folder on the DVD, and then click the button labeled Bubbles in the Macro palette. Figure 4.42 shows the bubbles added to the vents.

Figure 4.42

Bubbles are painted above the volcanic vents.

Creating a Sea Creature with 3D Tools

To finish the composition, we'll add a simple sea creature that swims around the vents. The deep sea is host to all kinds of strange-looking beasties. ZBrush's sculpting tools are particularly suited to the task of making wonderful and weird organic shapes. You'll take advantage of this as you populate the vents with some of your own deep-sea monsters.

1. Save your document if you haven't already.

2. In the Document palette, start a new document; the default size is fine.

3. In the Tool palette, select the Spiral3D tool. Draw it on the canvas and switch to Edit mode (hotkey = t).

4. Expand the Initialize subpalette and enter the following settings (as shown in Figure 4.43; if a setting is not listed, you can leave it at the default):

    • Coverage = 950

    • S.Thick (Start Thickness) = 20

    • E.Thick (End Thickness) = 0

- S.Radi (Start Radius) = 55
- E.Radi (End Radius) = 5
- S.Disp (Start Displacement) = -2.75
- E.Disp (End Displacement) = -2.84
- SDivide (Subdivision) = 40
- LDivide (Subdivision) = 200

Figure 4.43

These settings in the Initialize subpalette of the Spiral3D tool are a good start for a sea creature.

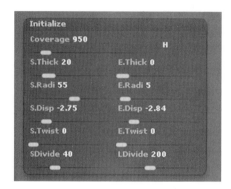

5. Once you have a nice squiggly shape, click the Make Polymesh button to convert the parametric object into a polymesh (see Figure 4.44).

Figure 4.44

The Spiral3D tool is converted into a polymesh.

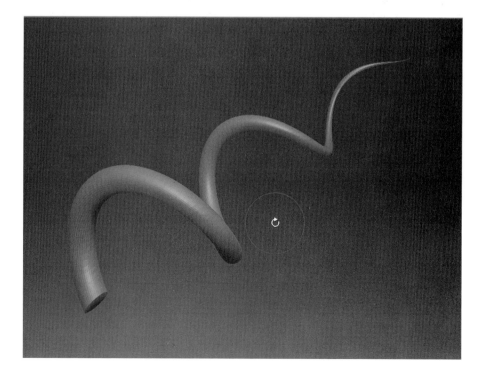

6. Expand the Geometry subpalette and click the Divide button to increase the subdivisions.

7. In the brush inventory on the left shelf, select the Inflate brush. (Note that in ZBrush 3.1, this brush is labeled *Inflat.*)

8. Inflate the large end of the spiral to give the creature a head, hold the Shift key, and paint across the surface to smooth your changes. Remember to activate the Local button on the right shelf as you edit the 3D spiral. This will reset the tool's pivot to center around the most recently edited points, which helps keep you from getting lost as you sculpt the sea creature.

9. Use the Inflate tool to create bulges that go down the length of the spiral.

10. From the brush inventory, choose the SnakeHook brush.

11. Use the brush to pull out the area around the opening of the head to create a creepy mouth.

12. Pull out some spikes from the bulges along the spiral.

13. Use the Smooth brush to smooth the changes.

14. Use the Gouge brush to enlarge the mouth opening.

15. Increase the draw size and use the Move brush to create variations along the length of the monster. The monster will be fairly small in the final scene, so don't overdo the detail (see Figure 4.45).

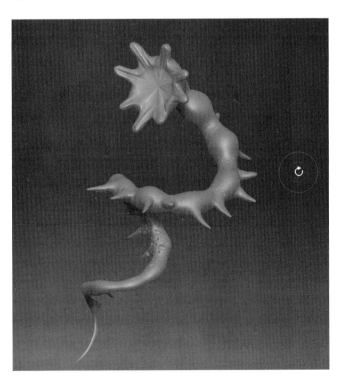

Figure 4.45

The sculpting brushes are used to add detail to the sea creature.

16. Once you are happy, use the Save As button in the Tool palette to save your creature to your local disk. Save the file as seaMonster.ZTL.

17. To see a macro that creates the creature, initialize ZBrush, and in the new blank document, open the Macro palette and click the seaCreature button.

18. Experiment with these techniques and the other parametric tools to create more of your own creatures, save these to disk.

Adding the Sea Creature

As the final touch for this stage of the composition, you'll load your sea monsters and add them to the scene.

1. Open the underWaterScene_v14.ZBR document.

2. In the Tool palette, click the Load Tool button.

3. Browse your computer to the directory where you saved the seaCreature.ZTL file and load it into ZBrush. Or open the Tools directory in the Chapter 4 folder on the DVD and load the seaCreature.ZTL file.

4. Choose the Noise Pattern5 material from the Material palette.

5. Turn the Perspective button on in the Draw palette.

6. Create a new layer in the Layer palette.

7. Draw your monster on the canvas (see Figure 4.46).

8. Use the Snapshot tool and the transform gyro to position copies of your monster throughout the scene (see Figure 4.47).

Figure 4.46

The sea creature brush is used to add a beastie to the scene.

Figure 4.47

Copies of the sea creature are positioned throughout the scene.

Merging Layers and Final Changes

The painting looks pretty good, but you may want to tweak the position of an object after dropping it to the canvas. The advantage of using document layers is that you can reposition the layer itself, which allows you to fix minor problems. In the case of the undersea lab, the top of the dome is very close to the top of the canvas, creating a somewhat claustrophobic feeling. To fix this you can merge the layers that make up the lab and reposition the merged layer.

1. Open the underwater_v15.ZBR document from the Chapter 4 folder of the DVD.

2. In the Layer palette, select Layer 9; this layer contains the basic structure of the lab.

3. Click the Mrg button in the Layer palette to merge Layer 9 with Layer 8—the layer that contains the ring detail (see Figure 4.48).

4. Layer 9 and Layer 8 have now been merged into one layer called Layer 8.

5. Click the Mrg button again to merge Layer 8 with Layer 7—the layer that contains the lab bolts. Now you have a new Layer 7 that contains everything that makes up the lab. The Mrg button will merge one layer at a time, and it will always merge the layer with the layer below it (in the Layer palette, icons to the left indicate layers below the icons on the right). You can use >> and << to rearrange the order of the layers before merging them.

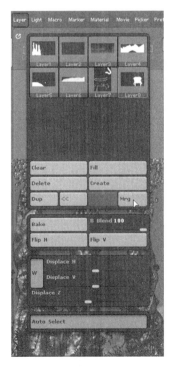

Figure 4.48

The Mrg button merges document layers.

6. To move the lab down a bit, nudge the Displace V slider in the Layer palette to the right a few times, as shown in Figure 4.49. You'll see the lab sink into the ocean floor. You'll also see the bottom of the legs appear at the top of the screen. This is because the layer's wrap mode is on, indicated by the W button.

Wrap mode tiles the layer so that when the layer is displaced vertically and pixols are moved off the bottom of the canvas, the same pixols appear at the top of the canvas. This also works when the layer is displaced horizontally. If Wrap mode is off, the pixols that are moved off the canvas are deleted, so if you displace the layer again, a piece of the image will be gone. It's a good idea to keep Wrap mode on while you adjust the position of a layer.

Figure 4.49

The Displace V slider moves the entire layer up or down.

7. From the Tool palette, select the Eraser brush and set the Draw Size to 40. Use the Eraser brush to remove the parts of the leg that are sticking out at the top of the screen.

8. The hose that connects the lab to the surface has been cut off. To fix this, select the Cloner brush from the Tool palette. Leave the Draw Size at 40. Ctrl+click on the middle of the hose just below where it is cut off; this sets the source for the clone.

9. Paint in the blank area above the hose to fill in the gap (Figure 4.50).

Figure 4.50

The Cloner brush fills in the gap at the top of the screen.

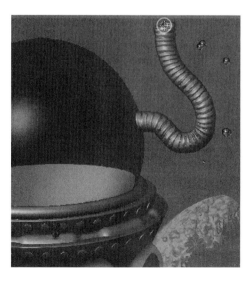

10. In the Render palette, turn on fibers, shadows, softZ, and soft RGB, click on Best to create a high-quality render. The final image is shown in Figure 4.51. For more information on rendering, refer to Chapter 8.

Figure 4.51
The final image is rendered at Best quality.

Summary

In this chapter you learned how to work with parametric 3D primitives and ZSpheres. Basic sculpting techniques were introduced as well as working with 2.5-dimensional brushes.

Although this chapter covered quite a bit of ground, it really only scratched the surface of how to paint in 2.5 dimensions, and that is just a small part of what you can do in ZBrush! Take a look at Chapter 8 to delve more deeply into lighting, rendering, and materials. Take what you've learned from these exercises and see how far you can go.

ZBrush Artists Gallery

On the following pages, you will find a gallery of images created using ZBrush 3. Students of Scott Spencer at the Gnomon School of Visual Effects as well as professional artists created these images. Some of these artists have been using ZBrush for only a short time. Most of the images have been rendered in ZBrush. There are also color versions of a couple of the example scenes from the exercises in the book.

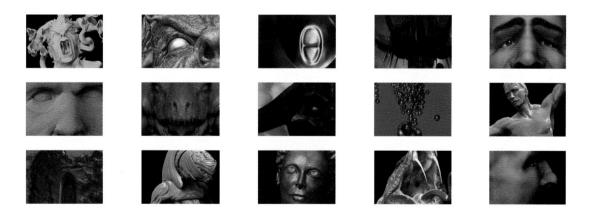

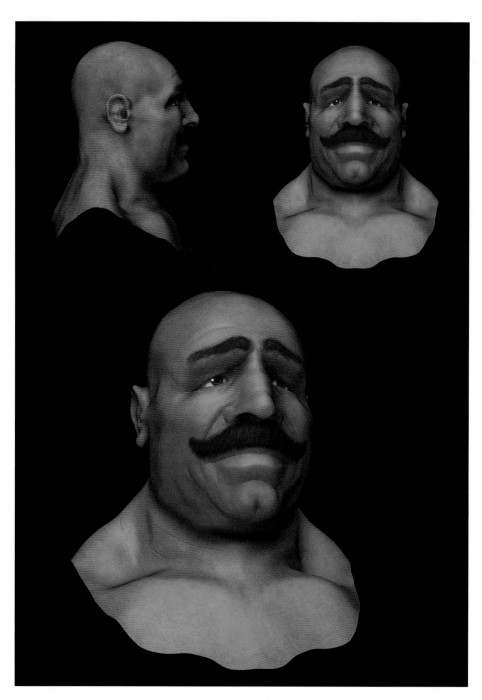

Portrait of the Iron Sheik by Ari Bilow

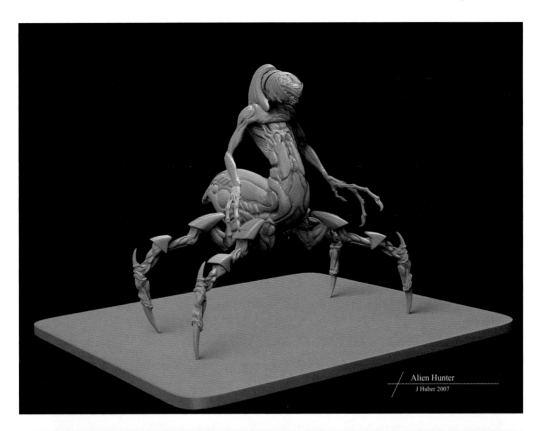

Alien Hunter
J Huber 2007

ABOVE: Alien Hunter maquette by Johannes Huber
BELOW: Dinosaur model by Kyle Mulqueen

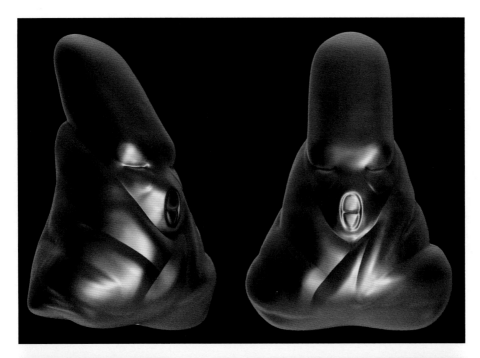

ABOVE: Sage by Ara Kermanikian
BELOW: The Guards of Achernar by John Stifter

ABOVE: Stone Cathedral by John Stifter
BELOW: Male dancer study by Johannes Huber

Copyright Johannes Huber 2007

Female dancer study by Johannes Huber

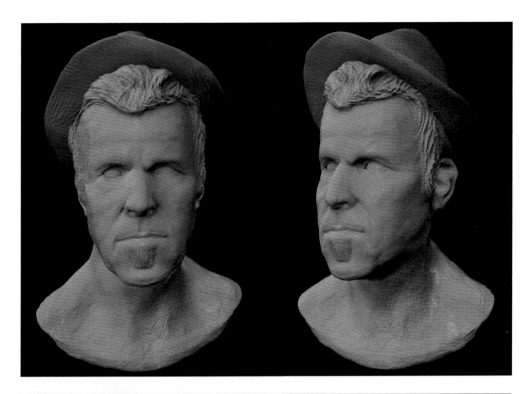

ABOVE: Portrait study by Eric Keller
BELOW: The underwater scene from Chapters 3 and 4 is rendered at Best quality.

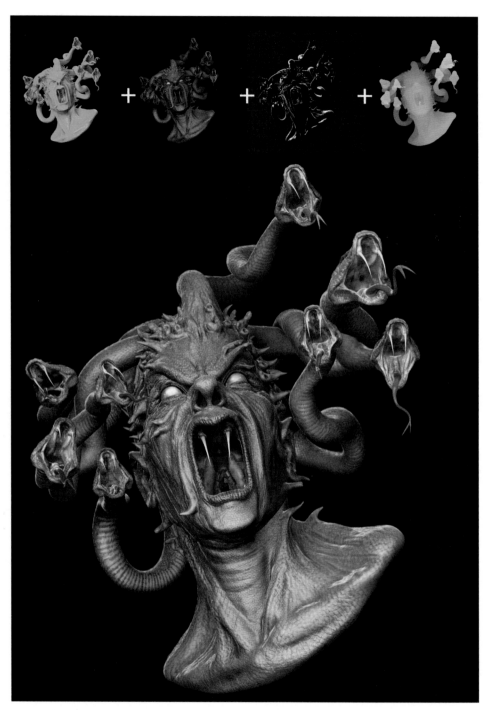

The Medusa maquette from Chapters 6 and 7 is painted and rendered. The final image was created by compositing several renders of the Medusa at Best quality and then compositing the exported images in Photoshop. Minimal touch-up was added using Photoshop in the final composite. The various render passes are shown at the top of the image.

CHAPTER 5

Digital Sculpting

The popularity of ZBrush as a modeling program stems from its powerful sculpting tools. Working with geometry in ZBrush feels just like working with digital clay. ZBrush 3 introduces a wide variety of sculpting brushes that allow you to easily add an astonishing level of detail in your models. In this chapter, you'll be introduced to a basic sculpting workflow as you learn how to build a human skull.

This chapter includes the following topics:

- Subtools
- The reference plane
- Sculpting Brushes
- Basic modeling with symmetry

Subdivision Levels

A 3D tool in ZBrush can be thought of as a paintbrush that paints copies of itself on the canvas (as was demonstrated in Chapter 3 and Chapter 4), and it can also be thought of as a digital model. This model can be sculpted, posed, and textured while in Edit mode and even exported for use in other 3D programs. The lessons in this chapter will focus on sculpting geometry in Edit mode. The following exercise demonstrates some basic concepts for sculpting in ZBrush.

1. Start ZBrush. From the startup window, choose the PolySphere object (Figure 5.1). If ZBrush is already open you can click the DefaultZScript button in the upper-right portion of the title bar. If it does not appear on the screen you can choose Open Model and select it from the `Program Files\Pixologic\ZBrush3\ZTools` folder.

Figure 5.1

Choose the Poly-Sphere tool from the ZBrush 3 startup screen.

2. The PolySphere will appear on the canvas in Edit mode. Drag on a blank spot of the canvas and you'll see the sphere rotate.

3. On the right menu, click the Frame button (hotkey = Shift+F). A wireframe display will be visible on the tool (Figure 5.2). This shows how the polygons that make up the sphere are arranged.

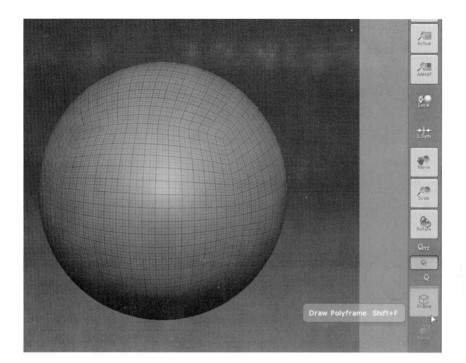

Figure 5.2

The Frame button draws a wireframe on the tool; this shows how the polygons that make up the tool are arranged.

4. Place the Tool palette in the tray if it's not already there. Expand the Geometry subpalette. The SDiv slider is at 3. Move it down to 1 and you'll see the subdivisions in the tool decrease; the polygon resolution of the tool is lowered. Move the slider back up and you'll see the resolution increase. The hotkey for setting the slider to a lower subdivision (SDiv) level is Shift+D; to move to a higher level, the hotkey is D.

    The ability to move freely between levels of subdivisions makes the task of modeling much easier. At lower subdivisions, you can rough out the major forms of a model; at higher levels, you can create fine detail (Figure 5.3). At any point during the sculpting process you can move back down to a lower subdivision level, make changes, and the details at the higher subdivision levels will still be there. The Smt button causes the tool to be smoothed as it is divided.

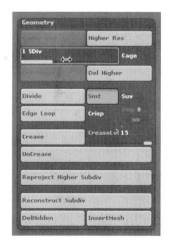

Figure 5.3

The SDiv slider allows you to move between lower and higher subdivision levels.

5. Move the SDiv slider to 3 and click the Divide button. It may not be obvious with a smooth sphere, but you've just added another level of subdivision to the tool.

6. Move the slider down to 1 and hold the brush over the polysphere icon in the Tool palette. A larger icon will appear, and in the corner you'll see some statistics informing you of the number of points and polygons that make up the tool. At the lowest SDiv level, the polysphere is made up of 1,536 polygons and 1,538 points (Figure 5.4).

Figure 5.4

A pop-up menu
shows point and
polygon statistics.

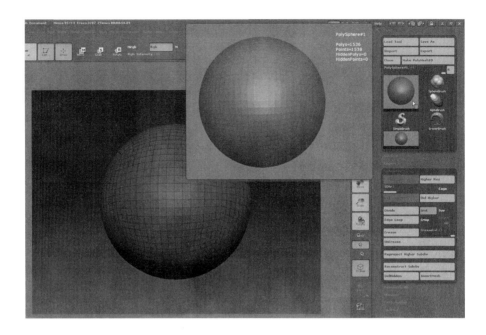

7. Move the SDiv slider to 4 and you'll see that the polysphere now has 98,304 polygons
    and 98,306 points. Depending on the speed of your computer and the amount of RAM
    available, ZBrush can handle a 3D tool with millions of polygons. These levels of sub-
    division are stored with your tool when you save it using the Save As button in the
    Tool palette.

    It's usually a good idea to save a 3D tool at the lowest level of subdivision because it
    takes up less space on your hard disk than if you save at a higher SDiv level. In the
    preferences palette you can adjust the max number of polygons each mesh (or
    subtool) can have using the MaxPolyPerMesh slider in the Mem subpalette. This
    limit is specified in millions of polygons per mesh (a limit of 12 means 12 million
    polygons). At a certain point a model with millions and millions of polygons will
    start to slow down the performance of the software, but understand that ZBrush's
    unique programming allows it to handle many more polygons per mesh than
    another 3D application would be able to on the same machine!

The PolySphere tool is actually different than the Sphere 3D tool. The Sphere 3D tool is a
parametric object, meaning that it is edited using the settings in its Initialize subpalette. The
PolySphere is a polymesh object, meaning that it is edited using the sculpting brushes. More
importantly, even though the two tools look identical at higher levels of subdivision, their
topology is different. *Topology* refers to how the polygons are arranged on the surface of the
model. This affects the flow of the geometry, which in turn affects how easily the tool can be
sculpted into various shapes.

8. Move the SDiv level of the PolySphere down to 1 and then choose the Sphere 3D tool from the Tool palette. With the Frame button activated, you can see the difference in the topology between the two tools (Figure 5.5).

   The Sphere 3D tool has poles, or regions, at either end where all the polygons come together at a point, like the longitude lines on a globe. The PolySphere has six sides, or sheets, of square polygons. The sheets meet at eight corners. The PolySphere is really a rounded cube. It can be easier to model shapes such as the human head from the PolySphere tool than from the Sphere 3D tool. The poles of the sphere can to bunch up and distort while modeling.

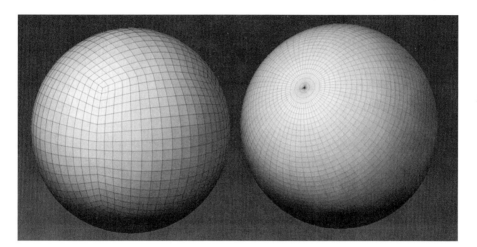

Figure 5.5

When the Wireframe button is activated, you can see the difference in topology between the Poly-Sphere (on the left) and the Sphere 3D tool (on the right).

9. Select the PolySphere tool in the Tool palette. Move the SDiv slider down to 1. Click the reconstruct subdivision button (Figure 5.6). This button causes ZBrush to create lower levels of subdivision. This feature works better with some models than others because ZBrush has to guess how to reduce the number of polygons in the tool. If ZBrush cannot reconstruct a lower subdivision level, no change in the model will occur. The tool's SDiv level 1 is now replaced with this new lower subdivision setting and all the previous levels are moved up, so now the tool has five levels of subdivision. Click the reconstruct subdivision button to give the tool six levels of subdivision. Move the SDiv slider up and down to see the change.

10. Save the PolySphere to your local drive in your own project directory for future use.

    To save the PolySphere, use the Save As button in the Tool palette, not the Document palette. Remember that saving a document saves only what is drawn on the canvas; it will not save a custom tool and all of the tool's settings. Name the tool myPolySphere.ZTL. You might want to create your own custom tool folder on your hard drive so that you can differentiate your own tools from those that come with ZBrush 3.

Figure 5.6

The Reconstruct Subdiv button adds a lower level of sub-division to the tool. The PolySphere now has a lower number of polygons at sub-division level 1.

Figure 5.6

The Reconstruct Subdiv button adds a lower level of sub-division to the tool. The PolySphere now has a lower number of polygons at sub-division level 1.

Sculpting Brushes

Most of the actual process of sculpting in ZBrush is done while a tool is in Edit mode, using the sculpting brushes available on the left shelf. This exercise will show some ways to use some of these brushes. A description of how each brush works is revealed in the interface when you hold the Ctrl key down and hover the cursor over the brush icon in the inventory (Figure 5.7). As you gain experience as a ZBrush artist, you'll find that you have your own favorite brushes that you use all the time, a few you use only for special cases, and some brushes you may almost never use.

1. If you have started a new ZBrush session, use the Load Tool button in the Tool palette to load the PolySphere.ZTL tool. The PolySphere.ZTL tool is located in the ZTools folder in the `Program Files\Pixologic\ZBrush3\ZTools` subdirectory. You can also use the PolySphere tool you saved from the previous exercise.

   If you are continuing from the previous section, select the PolySphere tool from the top row of the tool inventory in the Tool palette. Draw the PolySphere.ZTL tool on the canvas and switch to Edit mode.

Figure 5.7

Hold the Ctrl key and hover the cursor over an icon in the brush inventory for a brief description.

2. Make sure the SDiv slider in the Geometry subpalette of the Tool palette is at the highest SDiv level.

3. Move the Brush palette to a tray and expand the modifiers. There are a number of settings in here, some of which only work with certain brushes or when alphas are applied to a brush. These settings will be described as you follow this exercise.

4. From the brush inventory, choose the Standard brush; this is usually the default brush when you enter Edit mode (Figure 5.8). Paint across the surface of the 3D tool; you'll see bulges appear on either side. Notice that in the top shelf, the ZAdd button is activated. Hold the Alt key down and paint a few more strokes. Instead of bulges, you should see a depression in the surface of the 3D tool (Figure 5.9).

   The Alt key activates Subtract mode. The buttons on the top shelf do not reflect this, but if you activate the ZSub button, you'll notice that the Alt key's function is reversed.

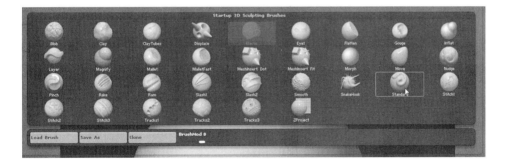

Figure 5.8

The Standard brush in the brush inventory

5. Hold the Shift key down as you paint some strokes. The Shift key activates the Smooth brush temporarily; note that the brush cursor turns blue (Figure 5.10).

   Painting on a surface while holding the Shift key activates the secondary brush. By default the Smooth brush is assigned as the secondary brush because ZBrush assumes that you will use the Smooth brush frequently. You can change the secondary brush by holding Shift while selecting any brush from the brush inventory. Then whatever brush you have chosen will be assigned as the secondary brush. For this exercise, leave the Smooth brush as the secondary (Shift key) brush.

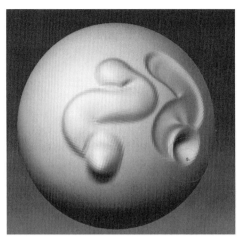

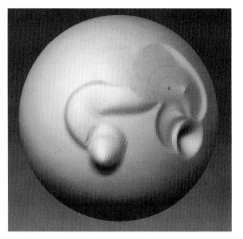

Figure 5.9

Painting on the surface of the polysphere with the standard brush causes the surface to rise. Holding the Alt key while painting creates a depression.

Figure 5.10

Holding the Shift key while painting on the surface activates the Smooth brush.

6. The Z Intensity slider on the top shelf determines the strength of the current brush's effect on the surface of the tool. The Smooth brush has a default setting of 100 that can obliterate your sculpting strokes very quickly. To change this, select the Smooth brush form the inventory, change the Z Intensity slider to 20, and then switch back to the Standard brush. Now when you hold the Shift key down while sculpting on the surface, the smoothing action will not be as drastic.

> The draw size of the Smooth brush can affect how intense the smoothing effect will be. This is because smoothing actually averages the displacement of vertices within the area of the brush. More vertices within a given area affect how the displacement is calculated. This also means that the effect of the smoothing brush within the same area of the tool's geometry will seem less drastic at higher subdivision levels than lower subdivision levels. You may want to get in the habit of setting the Smooth brush's Z Intensity to 20 (or less) every time you start a sculpting session in ZBrush. You can save a version of the Smooth brush with your own custom settings to the `Program Files\Pixologic\ZBrush 3\StartUp\BrushPresets` folder. It will appear in the Brush Inventory the next time you start ZBrush.

7. Rotate the PolySphere tool to a blank spot by dragging on the canvas. Paint some strokes on the surface with the Standard brush with the ZAdd button activated. The Standard brush pulls the surface out in the direction of the surface normals at the center of the stroke (surface normals are discussed in Chapter 1).

8. In the Brush palette, set the BrushMod slider to 25 and paint some strokes (Figure 5.11). The BrushMod slider adds a secondary pinching action to the Standard

brush (Figure 5.12). The intensity of this pinching is determined by the setting on the BrushMod slider. Negative values cause an inflation effect to be added to the Standard brush. The BrushMod slider acts this way only for the Standard brush. For other brushes, it determines a value to be added to the elevation of the sculpting effect, and for still others, it is not available at all. It's probably a good idea to use this slider sparingly when you are first learning sculpting in ZBrush. Once you have a firm grasp on how all the brushes work, you may want to experiment with using the BrushMod feature; for now its affect on the brushes may add an unnecessary level of confusion.

Figure 5.11

The BrushMod slider in the Brush palette adds a pinching effect to the Standard brush.

9. Use the Load Tool button in the Tool palette to reload the PolySphere tool. This will remove all the brush strokes you've made so far. Reset the Brush-Mod slider and paint some strokes with the Standard brush on a blank part of the object. Make sure the ZAdd button is active on the top shelf. Switch to the Inflate brush, set the Z Intensity to 25, paint some strokes, then switch to the Magnify brush and paint some strokes.

These brushes are similar except that, where the Standard brush raises the surface based on the surface normals below the brush, like pulling up a mountain, the inflate brush raises the surface based on the normals of each individual vertex, so you get an expanding action as if the surface is billowing out. The magnify brush is just slightly different from the inflate brush. The magnify brush pushes the vertices outward away from the center of the brush while at the same time elevating the surface of the brush. The difference between inflate and magnify is a little subtle in terms of theory, but in practice you can see how the effect is different. The Blob brush is another variation on the magnify brush; the effect has been slightly altered to make the Blob brush more suited for organic sculpting. As you work, experiment with these brushes and make a note of which ones you prefer for certain sculpting tasks (Figure 5.13).

10. Use the Load button in the Tool palette to reload the PolySphere tool. Select the Move brush from the inventory and paint across the surface. Wiggle the brush a little as you paint and notice how the vertices follow the motion. This brush pulls vertices in the direction of the stroke (Figure 5.14).

If you've worked in other 3D programs, this brush will probably remind you of pulling and pushing vertices on a polygon object. If you reduce the draw size on the top shelf to a value of 1, the brush will pull single vertices. Setting the Z Intensity slider to 100 will cause the brush to have a stronger hold on the vertices within the area selected by the brush. If you hold the Alt key and drag left or right while using the Move brush, the surface of the tool will move in or out based on the normal direction of the surface just below the tip of the brush.

The Transpose handle (discussed in Chapter 6) has a similar behavior to the Move brush. However, posing a model with the Move brush, while not impossible, is certainly challenging.

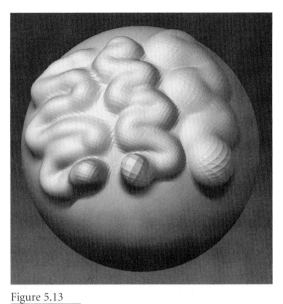

Figure 5.12

Both strokes in this image were created with the Standard brush: the stroke on the right had a BrushMod setting of 25, which adds a pinching effect.

Figure 5.13

The Standard, Inflate, and Magnify brushes have slightly different ways of altering the surface of a polymesh tool.

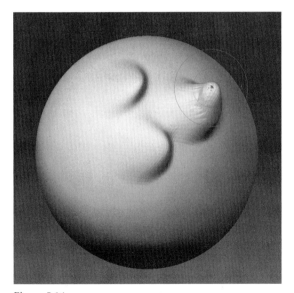

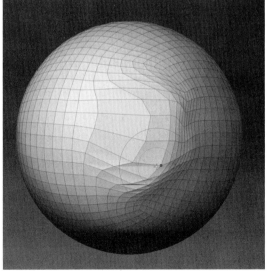

Figure 5.14

The Move brush pulls vertices from the surface of the polymesh tool.

Figure 5.15

The Nudge brush pushes vertices across the surface of a polymesh tool.

11. Use the Load button in the Tool palette to reload the PolySphere tool. Switch to the Nudge brush and move across the surface (Figure 5.15). This also moves vertices in the direction of the brush, similar to the Move brush. However, the result is more of a pushing action than a pulling. This brush is great for fine-tuning details.

12. Use the Load button in the Tool palette to reload the PolySphere tool. Increase the subdivisions on the current 3D tool. Select the Flatten brush. Paint some strokes on the surface. The Flatten brush flattens areas of the model just like pushing a spatula across the surface of clay (Figure 5.16).

The Flatten, Rake, Clay, and Clay tubes brushes all work best with tools that have a high number of vertices. These brushes are very good at simulating the feel of real clay. They will fill in recessed areas before raising the rest of the surface much like adding soft clay to a real sculpture. The Rake Brush in ZSub mode carves away at the surface just like a rake tool in real life but without the bits of clay sticking to the floor.

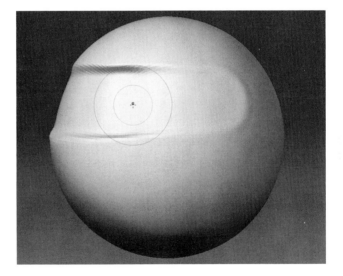

Figure 5.16

The Flatten brush acts like a spatula on the surface of clay.

Brushing with Alphas

You can use an alpha from the alpha inventory to modify the sculpting brushes. An alpha is a grayscale image applied as a filter to a brush: the brush is masked in such a way that its shape is determined by the light areas of the alpha. Controls in the Brush palette influence how the alpha is applied.

1. From the Tool palette, choose the Plane 3D tool. It should appear on the canvas; if it doesn't, turn off Edit mode and draw it on the canvas. Turn Edit mode back on and press Ctrl+n to clear everything else from the current layer.

2. Click the Make Polymesh button in the Tool palette. If the plane disappears, it may just be that the Double button is off (the Double button allows you to see both sides of a 3D tool) and you are looking at the back of the plane. In the Tool palette's Display Properties subpalette, turn Double on (Figure 5.17). Normally Double is off to save memory resources and improve performance in ZBrush.

Figure 5.17

Activating the Double button allows you to see both sides of a 3D tool.

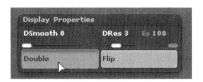

3. Click the Divide button a few times, create five levels of subdivisions, and keep the plane at level 5.

4. Choose the Clay brush from the brush inventory.

5. Set Stroke Type to dots.

6. Choose the arrow alpha (Alpha 33) from the alpha inventory (Figure 5.18).

Figure 5.18

The arrow alpha in the alpha inventory

7. Paint some strokes on the plane. The surface rises in the shape of the alpha (Figure 5.19).

   The Clay brush is similar to the Standard brush and the Flatten brush. It raises the surface and adds a flattening effect. It fills in recessed areas as it raises the surface. It works particularly well with tools at a high polygon resolution.

8. Paint some curving lines on the plane; notice how the arrow flows in the direction of your stroke. Increase the AlignToPath slider in the Brush palette— set it to 25 (Figure 5.20 inset). This causes the alpha's following action to be slightly looser (Figure 5.20). Experiment with different settings as you paint on the plane, then set the slider back to 4.

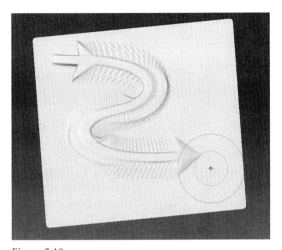

Figure 5.19
The stroke appears in the shape of the alpha. Notice that the arrow alpha rotates to point itself in the direction of the stroke.

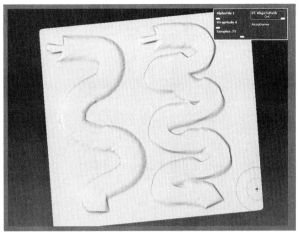

Figure 5.20
The AlignToPath slider (upper-right inset) in the Brush palette controls how loosely the alpha's orientation follows the path of the stroke. The stroke on the left has an AlignToPath value of 4; the stroke on the right has an AlignToPath value of 25.

9. Set AlphaTile to 3 and paint some strokes. Now there are three arrow alphas applied to the stroke (Figure 5.21).

10. Set AlphaTile to 1 and WrapMode to 2. This creates multiple copies of the stroke in a grid across the surface of the plane. Increasing this value increases the frequency of the grid copies on the surface (Figure 5.22).

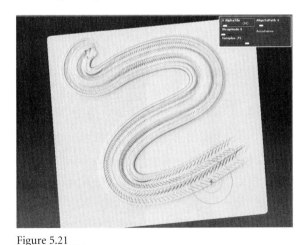

Figure 5.21
The AlphaTile slider (upper-right inset) increases the repetition of the alpha across the width of the brush stroke. With the AlphaTile setting at 3, there are now three arrows painted with each stroke.

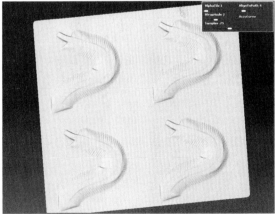

Figure 5.22
The WrapMode slider (upper-right inset) repeats the stroke across the surface in a grid. The WrapMode set to 2 allows you to paint multiple copies of the stroke.

You can use the controls in the Alpha palette to change the initial orientation of the alpha as well as its intensity and a large number of other attributes. You can also import your own alphas. This is particularly helpful when creating skin details such as wrinkles and pores. Brushing with alphas will be explored some more in Chapter 7. The changes you make to these settings apply to the currently selected brush and will continue to apply to that brush throughout the ZBrush session. If you change brushes, the new brush will use its default settings.

Additional Brush Settings

There are a few more settings for the brushes that are worth looking at before moving on to other tools.

1. Use the Load button in the Tool palette to reload the PolySphere tool.

2. In the Brush palette, reset AlphaTile to 1 and the Wrap mode to 0. Choose the Standard brush, and in the Brush palette, move the Gravity Strength slider to 100.

3. Paint across the surface. You'll see that the bulges created by the stroke are pulled downward as if gravity is affecting the digital clay (Figure 5.23).

4. You can change the direction of the gravity by rotating the pointer in the preview window next to the gravity slider. When sculpting, you may want to work with a less-extreme value such as 10 or 15.

5. From the Tool palette, select the Cube 3D tool. Make sure the tool is in Edit mode. In the Tool palette, click the Make Polymesh button to convert the cube into a polymesh.

Figure 5.23
The Gravity slider makes the strokes droop as if gravity is pulling the clay downward as you sculpt. The Sphere tool in this image was rotated as the strokes were applied. The pointer next to the Gravity Strength slider (upper-right inset) determines the direction of the gravitational pull.

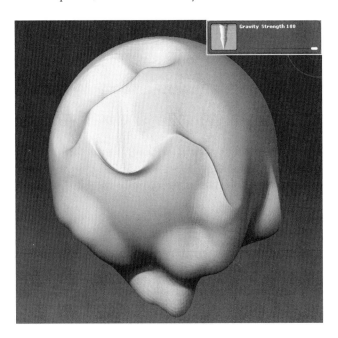

6. From the brush inventory, choose the MeshInsert Dot brush.

7. In the Brush palette, click on the MeshInsert preview window, and from the tool inventory that pops up here, choose the Gear3D tool (Figure 5.24).

8. As you draw on the cube, instances of the Gear3D tool are created on the cube's surface. The cube is still in Edit mode, so you can rotate it around while painting. Changing the alpha or the stroke type has no effect on how the gear instances are drawn (Figure 5.25). You can switch sculpting brushes and edit the cube and gear instances as a single sculpture.

9. Load the PolySphere tool, and set it to SDiv level 3 if it is not already. Use the Standard brush to sculpt some hills and valleys on its surface (Figure 5.26).

10. From the brush inventory, select the Standard brush. In the Brush palette, turn on the CavityMask button and paint on the surface.

    With CavityMask activated, the effect of the brush is not as strong in the deep crevices in the surface of the tool (Figure 5.27). You can fine-tune the cavity mask's strength using the intensity slider and the Curve Editor below the cavity masking settings. Holding the Alt button while painting with CavityMask reverses the effect so that only areas inside crevices are affected, but the brush's default behavior is also reversed. If you want to reverse the cavity masking but not the action of the brush, set the cavity masking intensity slider to a negative number.

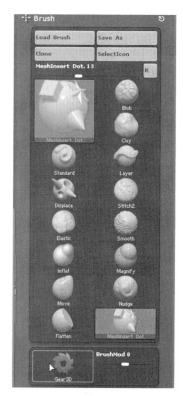

Figure 5.24

The MeshInsert preview window allows you to choose the 3D tool that will be inserted with the MeshInsert Dot brush.

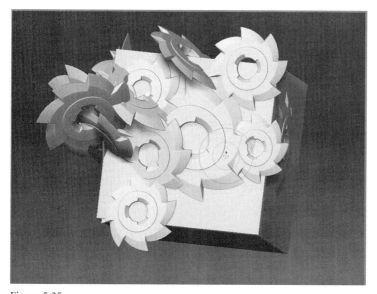

Figure 5.25

The MeshInsert Dot brush creates copies of a selected mesh on the surface of a 3D tool.

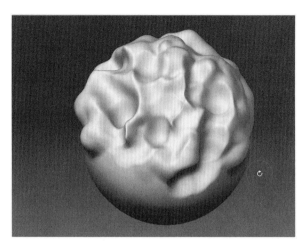

Figure 5.26

Create some hills and valleys on the PolySphere tool using the Standard brush.

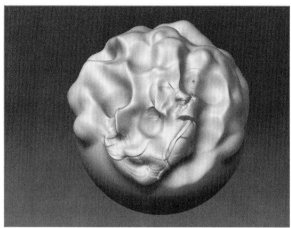

Figure 5.27

With CavityMask enabled, the effect of the sculpting brush is not as strong in the crevices of the 3D tool.

The ColorMask feature and CavityMask work in a similar way; however, the masking effects are determined by colors painted on the surface of the tool.

The BackfaceMask button and settings mask off areas of a tool that are facing away from you as you sculpt. This can be useful when working on thin parts of a tool.

11. The Edit curve is a master control that adjusts the falloff of the current sculpting brush's effect on the model. This curve is an excellent way to customize your brush. Deactivate cavity, color, and backface masking if they are currently on. Make sure you have the Standard brush selected with no alpha applied. Make changes in the Edit curve and paint on the surface of the tool (Figure 5.28).

12. Save your own custom brushes by clicking the Save button in the Brush palette. All the settings in the Brush palette as well as the current alpha will be saved with the brush. If you'd like your custom brushes to appear in the Brush inventory, save them to the `Program Files\Pixologic\ZBrush3\ZStarup\BrushPresets` folder directory. To create a custom icon, create a 96 x 96 pixel image file, save it as a .BMP, .TIF, .JPEG, or .PSD format to the same folder and then select the file using the SelectIcon button in the Brush palette.

The Smoothing curve and settings give you a way to customize the secondary smoothing brush that is invoked when holding the Shift key. The Alt Brush Size slider allows you to change the size of the Shift key brush so that you can have two different brush sizes—one for your normal sculpting brush and another for the secondary brush assigned to the Shift key (which is the Smooth brush by default).

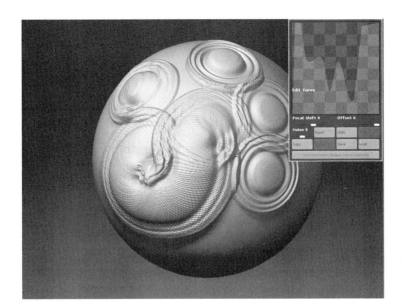

Figure 5.28
Change the shape of the Edit curve to customize the brush. You can use the Edit curve to create your own custom brushes.

Creating Reference Planes

Now that you have learned the basics of working with a 3D tool in Edit mode, it's time to actually create a digital sculpture. The remaining exercises in this chapter will take you through the process of creating a human skull tool. You'll expand on what you have learned so far and learn about some new tools and techniques in the process. The skull is a great introductory subject as its structure is fundamental to understanding how to create believable humanoid heads. This tutorial updates the skull-modeling lesson that is part of the Sculptor's Workshop that comes with the ZBrush documentation.

Before jumping into modeling, a few words of advice for those who are just beginning their study of digital sculpting. You should own at least one or two anatomy books and keep them nearby as you work. Chapter 1 has some suggestions for good anatomy books for the artist. Also, if you can afford it, a plastic, life-size human skull model is one of the best purchases you can make. Anatomy books are excellent, but nothing beats being able to hold a 3D reference in your hand as you work.

At the end of this chapter are some suggestions as to where you can get a plastic skull model. If all else fails, a quick image search on the Internet for "human skull" should turn up a variety of useful reference images. Creating a folder on your computer with as many skull images as you can find will help immensely with this exercise. Of course, you can also use the 3D skull tools in the Chapter 5 directory of the DVD as well (see Figure 5.29).

Figure 5.29

Anatomy books are essential references for the artist. A plastic replica of the human skull is one of the most helpful tools you can buy.

Loading an Image into ZBrush

There are a several ways to load reference images into ZBrush. You can import images directly into the document and place them on a background document layer or you can use 3D reference planes with the reference image mapped on as a texture. These planes can be loaded as subtools so that they move with the object as you sculpt. Subtools are introduced in Chapter 2. Working with document layers is discussed in Chapter 3. You may find that you prefer reference planes to background layers when editing a 3D tool. ZBrush has both a reference plane object and a reference cube object. The following steps show you how to set them up.

1. Initialize ZBrush and start a new session.

2. In the Tool palette, click the Load Tool button and then browse the file system and find the `imagPlaneX.ZTL` tool in the `C:\Program Files\Pixologic\ZBrush3\ZTools` directory.

3. Draw the object on the canvas and switch to Edit mode.

4. Rotate the object by dragging on the canvas. You may notice that parts disappear as you rotate. This is because the object is single sided. Click the Double button in the display options so that all sides of the model are visible.

5. From the material inventory, choose the Fast Shader material and set the color to white (Figure 5.30).

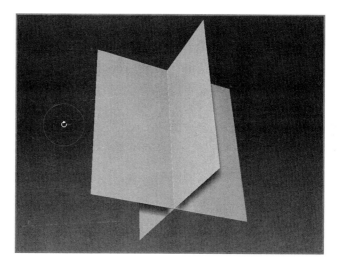

Figure 5.30

The imagePlaneX 3D tool is a pair of image reference planes that can simplify modeling based on an image.

6. Open the texture inventory and click the Import Textures button. Browse to the C:\Program Files\Pixologic\ZBrush3\ZTools directory and choose the imagePlaneX.PSD texture.

7. The texture is mapped onto the planes (see Figure 5.31). The text displays which is the front and which is the side. This particular texture can work as a guide for creating your own reference texture.

   If you open this texture in a paint program such as Photoshop, you can add a new layer and replace the *Front* and *Side* text with your reference drawing or photos. Make sure you place the reference drawings carefully so that they match up correctly when mapped to the planes.

8. In the Texture palette, click the Load button and browse to the Chapter 5 directory on the DVD. Load the skullReference image. Choose the skullReference texture in the texture inventory, and the front and side texture will be replaced with the simple skull drawing. Your own reference images can be as simple or as detailed as you like, but it's a little easier to model using a simple sketch with bold lines (Figure 5.32).

9. From the Tool palette, load the PolySphere tool. If you get a warning message about the size of the texture, you can safely ignore it.

Figure 5.31
Load the image-
PlaneX.PSD texture
into the material
inventory.

Figure 5.32
The image on the
reference plane tool
is replaced with the
skullReference
image when it's
loaded into the Tex-
ture palette.

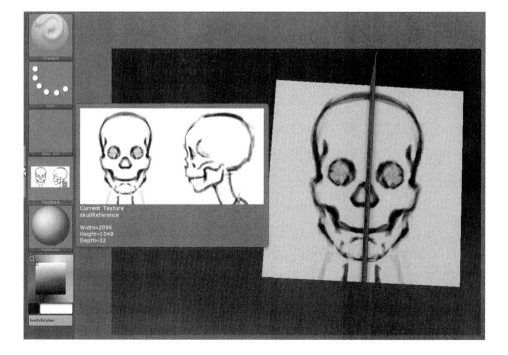

10. In the Tool palette, select the imagePlaneX tool; it should appear on the canvas in Edit mode. In the Tool palette, expand the Subtools subpalette. Click the Append button at the bottom and choose the PolySphere tool to add it as a subtool.

11. Immediately you'll notice several problems—the PolySphere tool and the reference plane tool may not be aligned properly, and the skull drawing is applied to both objects (Figure 5.33). Materials and textures applied to a tool will also be applied to all of its subtools, but this can be changed. To fix the alignment problem, select the PolySphere subtool in the Subtool subpalette, expand the Deformation subpalette, and click the Unify button. This will cause both subtools to have the same pivot, orientation, and size (Figure 5.34). Make sure the X, Y, and Z toggles are activated on the Unify button when you click on it.

12. In the Subtools palette, select the reference plane subtool. Click on the Eyeball icon next to the PolySphere object to hide the polysphere.

13. Expand the Geometry subpalette. Deactivate the Smt button and click the Divide button four times to give the tool a total of five subdivision levels (Figure 5.35).

    Turning off Smt will prevent the planes from being smoothed as the subdivisions are increased. Subdividing the planes will not affect the PolySphere subtool. SDiv levels for each subtool are independent of other subtools.

    Subdividing the reference plane is important because you will be converting the texture applied to the plane into a color. Colors are mapped to the vertices of 3D tools. Therefore, the higher the number of vertices/polygons, the higher the resolution of the color applied. By subdividing the planes, you ensure that the skull reference images will be clear.

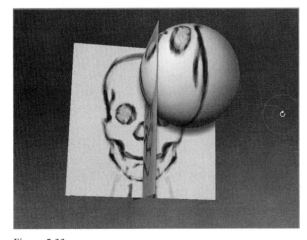

Figure 5.33

When the PolySphere tool is appended to the imagePlaneX tool, the alignment of the two tools may be off.

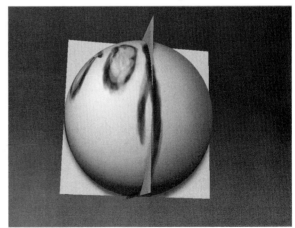

Figure 5.34

The Unify button in the Deformation subpalette will fix the alignment problem.

Figure 5.35

Subdividing the planes with the Smt button deactivated will prevent the planes from being smoothed as they are divided.

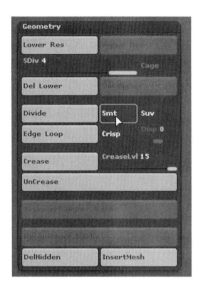

Subtools share the same texture but they can have different colors. By converting the skull image from a texture to a color, you can prevent the skull texture from being applied to both the planes and the polysphere. The difference between applying a color and applying a texture to a 3D tool may be confusing at first. A texture is an image file, like a PSD or a TIFF, that is mapped to the surface of a 3D tool. The resolution of the texture (number of pixels) is independent of the resolution (number of vertices) of the 3D tool. A color is simply an RGB value applied to each vertex of the 3D tool, so the resolution of a color painted onto a 3D tool is determined by the number of vertices in the tool. If you convert a high-resolution (lots of pixels) texture that has been applied to a low-resolution (few vertices) 3D tool into a color, the image will become blocky when it is mapped to the vertices of the 3D tool.

14. Open the Texture subpalette of the Tool palette (not the Texture palette from the menu bar). Click the Txr>Col button (Figure 5.36). The skull texture is converted to a color and applied to the planes. The texture no longer appears on the polysphere.

Figure 5.36

The Txr>Col button turns the texture into a color mapped to the vertices of the image planes.

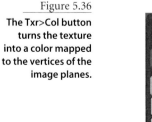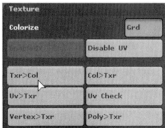

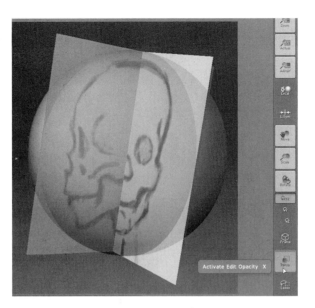

Figure 5.37

The Transp button on the right shelf makes the subtool semitransparent.

15. The reference image is now obscured by the PolySphere subtool. To fix this, activate the Transp button on the right shelf. The currently selected subtool will become partially transparent, allowing you to see the image on the reference plane (Figure 5.37).

16. Use the rename button to name the reference plane subtool "reference plane," and the PolySphere subtool "skull."

Applying Different Materials to Subtools

By default, all the subtools that make up a single 3D tool share the same material; however, you can easily change this behavior.

1. Select the PolySphere subtool in the Subtool subpalette.

2. On the top shelf, activate the M (materials) button.

3. Choose the Red Wax material from the Material palette.

4. In the Color palette, click the FillObject button (Figure 5.38). This fills the current object with the current material. The current color is not applied since only the M (material) button is activated on the top shelf.

5. You'll notice no difference. This is because the Red Wax material is still applied to the reference planes as well. Select the Reference Plane subtool in the Subtool subpalette. Set the material in the Material palette to the Fast Shader. Now the reference planes have one material and the polysphere has another (Figure 5.39).

6. Save this tool as skull_v1.ZTL using the Save As button in the Tool palette.

Figure 5.38

The FillObject button on the Color palette fills the current tool or subtool with the selected color or material.

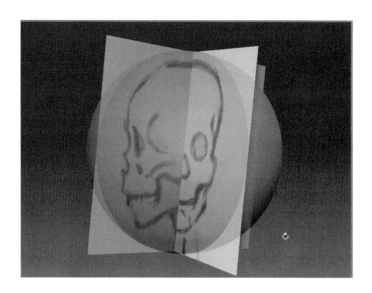

Using the Reference Cube

ZBrush also has a reference cube tool that works like the reference planes.

1. To use the reference cube, click the Load Tool button in the Tool palette and browse to the `C:\Program Files\Pixologic\ZBrush3\ZTools` directory. Load the imagePlaneCube.ZTL tool.

2. In the texture inventory, load the imagePlaneCube.PSD texture.

3. You'll see the cube labeled Front/Back, Side, Top/Bottom.

4. You can import the imagePlaneCube.PSD texture into a paint program such as Photoshop and replace the text with your own reference sketches or photographs. Follow the instructions in the previous segments, "Creating Reference Planes" and "Applying Different Materials to Subtools," to set the cube up as a modeling reference. In the case of the cube, the PolySphere would be inside the cube, giving you more views to work from if you need them (Figure 5.40).

Applying Symmetry Settings

The symmetry controls in the Transform palette can mirror the changes you make to one side of a 3D tool across an axis to the other side of the tool. For symmetrical objects such as the human skull, this essentially cuts your workload in half.

1. Load the skull_v1.ZTL tool into ZBrush using the Load Tool button on the Tool palette. You can use the version you saved or load the version that is in the Chapter 5 folder on the DVD.

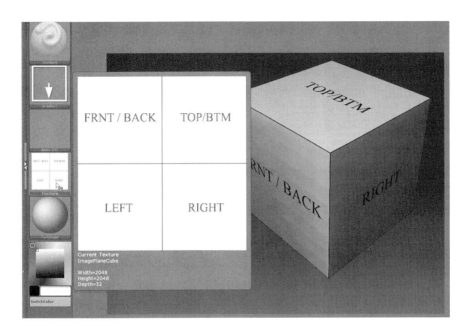

Figure 5.40
The image-
PlaneCube works
the same way the
imagePlaneX tool
works; however, it
gives you more
views to work from.

2. Select the Skull subtool from the Subtool subpalette in the Tool palette.

3. Click the Reconstruct Subdivisions button in the Tool palette twice to add two lower-resolution SDiv levels to the tool.

4. Make sure the Transp button on the right shelf is active.

5. In the Transform palette, click the Activate Symmetry button. Set the axis to >X<, and turn off >Y< and >Z< if they are on. The symmetry should be restricted to the x-axis. Make sure the >M< button is active so the changes are mirrored across the x-axis (Figure 5.41).

6. Set the SDiv slider in the Geometry subpalette to 1.

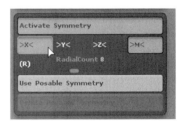

Figure 5.41
The symmetry settings in the Transform palette

Roughing Out the Forms of the Skull

The technique used in this lesson is one very basic way to sculpt a skull. The result will be a single unified mesh; that is, the jaw will not be a separate part. There are many ways to create a skull in ZBrush, and as you gain experience you will no doubt discover your own methods. The goal for this lesson is to make sure you are comfortable with a standard sculpting workflow in ZBrush. Remember that practice is key.

It's imperative that you have some form of anatomical reference as you work. The drawings on the reference plane provide a rough guideline to the overall form, but they lack the detail necessary to make an accurate sculpture. At the very least, do a search on the Internet for images of human skulls. A combination of photographs and illustrations from multiple views is best. If you can get an accurate plastic skull model, even better.

In the first stages of sculpting, it's best to keep the tool at the lower SDiv levels while you rough out the major forms. It's tempting to jump right into sculpting details at the higher SDiv levels, but doing so often leads to a poorly constructed sculpture. Try to stick to the lower three SDiv levels until the polysphere starts to resemble the shape of the sketch on the planes. In later stages of the process, you can hide the reference planes.

1. Load the skull_v1.ZTL tool from the Chapter 5 folder of the DVD or use the version you saved from the previous exercise. The Skull subtool should be at SDiv level 1. It should have 96 polys and 98 points at level 1—if it does not, then click the Reconstruct SubDiv button twice to add two lower-resolution SDiv levels.

2. Rotate the tool so that you can see the side view. As you rotate the tool by dragging on the canvas, hold the Shift key down to make the tool snap to the nearest orthographic view. Turn on the Frame button so that you can easily see the topology of the skull geometry as you work (see Figure 5.42).

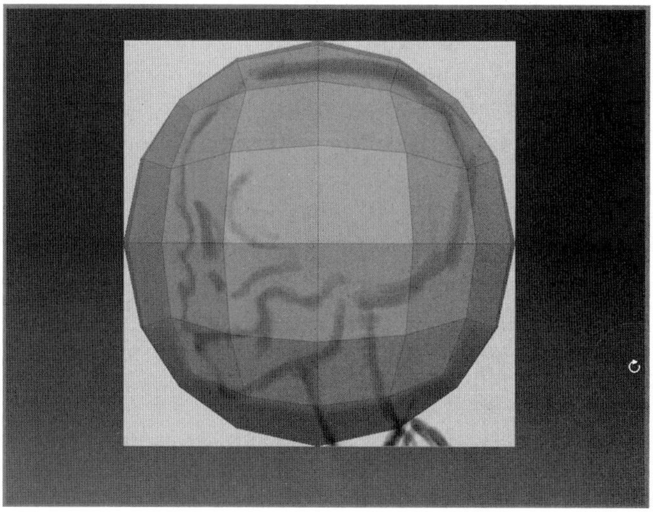

Figure 5.42

The skull subtool with reference planes. The skull subtool is at the lowest SDiv level.

3. Select the Skull subtool from the Subtool subpalette. Switch to the Move brush. Set the draw size fairly large, 50 to start with, and set the Z Intensity to 100. You'll see the center of the brush highlight the vertices of the tool as you move the brush over it. Use this as a guide to position your brush. Gently pull the vertices at the front of the Skull subtool toward the back so that they match the image on the reference plane (Figure 5.43). The vertices at the very center of the face may be a little tricky to select; you may need to rotate the tool to move these back properly. Make sure these vertices remain at the exact middle of the skull as you move them back.

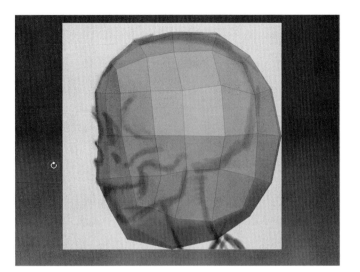

Figure 5.43

The vertices at the front of the skull are pulled back with the Move brush to match the sketch on the reference plane.

4. Pull the vertices at the back of the skull toward the front. Again, use the skull sketch as a guide.

5. Pull the bottom vertices up to match the bottom of the skull and the jawline. Try to match the lines of the wireframe geometry to the contours of the skull. At this subdivision level, they should form nearly straight lines across the surface; they should not zigzag up and down or move randomly. Take your time at this stage to lay the foundation for the sculpting correctly (Figure 5.44).

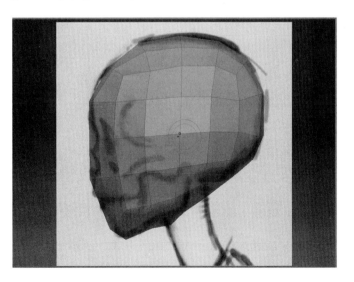

Figure 5.44

The Move brush moves the vertices at the back and bottom of the skull to match the sketch on the reference plane.

6. Switch to the front and continue to use the Move tool to bring the vertices close to the reference sketch (Figure 5.45).

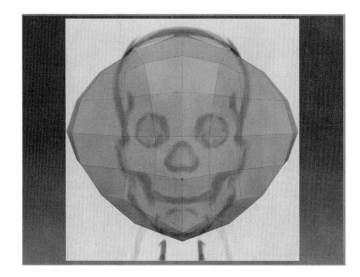

7. Draw the vertices on the front close together to approximate the shape of the nose, the eye sockets, and the cylinder that forms the teeth (Figure 5.46).

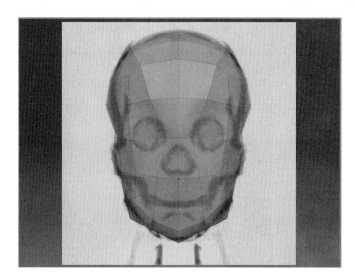

8. Rotate the tool and take a look at the vertices at the back of the skull. Use the Move tool to bring these in toward the center (Figure 5.47).

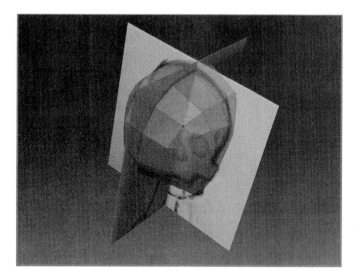

Figure 5.47

With the back of the skull visible, the vertices are pulled to the center to form the basic shape of the skull.

9. Pull the vertices at the bottom of the skull up inside (Figure 5.48).

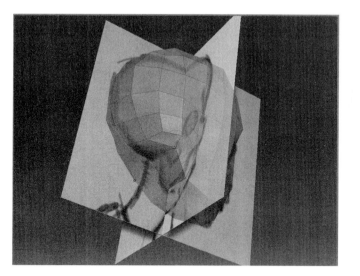

Figure 5.48

The vertices at the bottom of the skull are pulled upward and inside the skull.

10. Rotate to the top view. The top of the skull should look like a rounded wedge. The narrow part is at the front (Figure 5.49).

Figure 5.49

From the top view, the skull looks like a rounded wedge.

Skull Modeling Macros

Congratulations on completing the first stage of your skull model. If you'd like to see exactly how the model in these images was created, the DVD comes with a set of macros that will go through the process of modeling the skull one stage at a time. You can watch these macros after completing each of the stages in this chapter and compare your results. You can also use each tool included on the DVD as a starting place for each section. The following steps show you how to add the macros as buttons on the Macro palette.

1. In Windows Explorer, locate the Chapter 5 folder on the DVD. In the folder, copy the skull model directory.

2. In Windows Explorer, browse to the `C:\Program Files\Pixologic\ZBrush3\ZStartup\Macros` directory. Paste the skull model directory here.

3. Start up ZBrush, or if it's already open, click the Reload All Macros button on the Macro palette. You'll see a new section appear with buttons for each stage of the skull model.

4. Before running a macro, save any of the custom tools you want to keep, and initialize ZBrush.

5. Load the skull_v1.ZTL tool from the Chapter 5 folder of the DVD. It is important that you use the skull tools from the DVD with the macros, otherwise you'll get strange results.

6. *Do not* draw the tool on the canvas. Once the tool is loaded on the Tool palette, click the skullPart1 button on the Macro palette, sit back, and watch the modeling process in ZBrush.

THE FORMS OF THE SKULL

7. Each of the following sections has an associated macro you can run at the end of the section. Remember to initialize ZBrush and load the corresponding tool before running each macro.

Refining the Skull at Subdivision Level 2

If you are satisfied with the rough shape of the skull, you can move the SDiv slider up to level 2 and continue with the rough forms. Each step listed in the exercise describes how the skull in the example was made. Often each step describes changes that took many brush strokes to make. As you work through each section, the specific changes you make will most likely be slightly different than the changes described. The exercises illustrate a practical and disciplined approach to sculpting in ZBrush and should serve as a guide more than a literal step-by-step recipe.

1. Lower the draw size to 20, and continue to move the vertices with the Move brush. Make your changes slow and deliberate.

2. In the side view, push the vertices above the nose inward to form the bridge of the nose.

3. As you move the vertices around, be aware of how many vertices are in any given area. At the same time, try to keep the spacing of the vertices as even as possible. Keep two lines of horizontal vertices between the bottom of the nasal cavity and the line that divides the teeth (Figure 5.50).

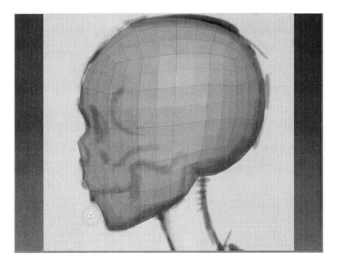

Figure 5.50

The area around the jaw is formed. There should be two rows of vertices between the nasal cavity and the line that separates the teeth.

4. Position the vertices around the eye sockets/orbital cavities so that they outline the shape of the eyes and the brow. Pull the vertices of the chin downward. Pay attention to the position of the vertices on the cheekbones (zygomatic bones). Remember to keep the lines of vertices as evenly spaced as possible (see Figure 5.51).

Figure 5.51

The area around the eye sockets is formed in the front view. The zygomatic bones are pulled out.

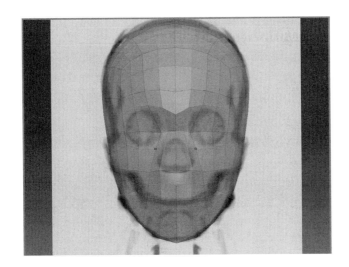

Figure 5.51

The area around the eye sockets is formed in the front view. The zygomatic bones are pulled out.

5. To see a macro of this stage, save your tool as skull_v2. Initialize ZBrush and load the skull_v2.ZTL tool from the Chapter 5 folder on the DVD (don't draw it on the canvas). Click the skullPart2 button in the Macro palette.

Defining Cheekbones at Subdivision Level 3

The basic skull shape is almost there. At this point you can start to use brushes other than the Move brush to add more detail.

1. Load the skull_v3.ZTL tool from the Chapter 5 folder of the DVD or continue with your model from the last section. Move the SDiv slider to 3 and inspect your model closely (Figure 5.52). Make sure the lines of vertices are even on the surface of the skull subtool. You can always move back down to level 2 to make corrections if you wish.

Figure 5.52

Increase the skull subtool's SDiv level to 3.

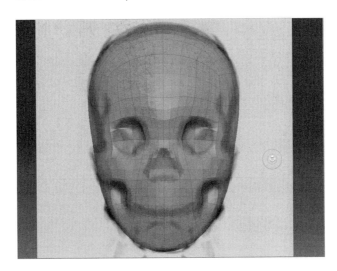

2. Switch to the Standard brush. Set the Z Intensity to around 20 and the draw size to 30. Hold the Alt hotkey down to set the Standard brush in Subtract mode. Create a depression over the eye socket. Don't get too extreme just yet. Alternate pushing and pulling with the Standard brush using the Alt hotkey. Pull out the vertices around the zygomatic bone. Push the vertices behind the zygomatic bone up into the skull. Create a depression for the nasal cavity.

3. At a certain point you should feel confident enough with the basic shape of the skull that you can turn the visibility of the reference planes off. Click the eye icon in the subtool palette for the reference plane subtool (see Figure 5.53).

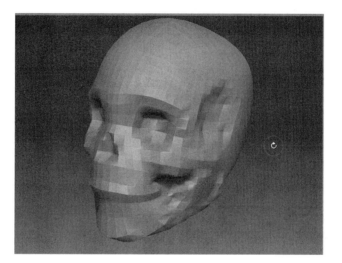

Figure 5.53

The reference planes are hidden to see the shape of the skull more easily.

4. Alternate using the Standard brush and the Move brush. Most skulls have somewhat of a slight overbite. To create this, push the row of vertices that make up the lower teeth back a little.

5. To see a macro of this stage, save your tool as skull_v3. Initialize ZBrush and load the skull_v3.ZTL tool from the Chapter 5 folder on the DVD (don't draw it on the canvas). Click the skullPart3 button in the Macro palette.

Building the Jaw at Subdivision Level 4

The tool should start to look a little more like a skull. It's time to start using different brushes. The work here becomes a bit more subjective as well.

1. Load the skull_v4.ZTL tool from the Chapter 5 folder of the DVD or continue with your model from the last section. Set the SDiv slider to 4.

2. Use the Standard brush to bring out the brow and the area around the nasal cavity. Bring out the back of the jaw and push in a bit more behind the zygomatic bone (Figure 5.54).

Figure 5.54

The vertices beneath
the zygomatic bone
are pushed up
and into the skull
to define this
shape more.

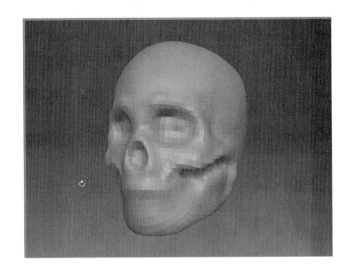

3. Rotate to the back of the skull and create a depression behind the back of the jaw. The back corners of the jaw are called the angle of the mandible.

4. By default, the Smooth brush is set to a Z Intensity of 100. When you hold the Shift hotkey to temporarily activate the Smooth brush, it tends to obliterate your work. Select the Smooth brush from the Brush palette. Set the Z Intensity slider on the top shelf to 20. Switch back to the Standard brush. Use the Shift hotkey toggle to switch to the secondary/Smooth brush and smooth out areas as you sculpt.

5. Rotate the tool so that you can see the bottom of the skull. Use the Standard brush to push the vertices at the bottom of the jaw up into the skull to create the horseshoe shape of the jaw (Figure 5.55).

Figure 5.55

The area beneath
the jaw is pushed
upward and into the
skull to define the
jawbone.

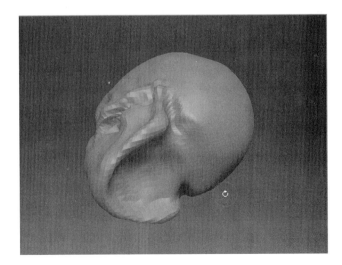

6. As the zygomatic bone joins the front of the face, it curves back around into the cavity it forms. You can carefully sculpt this in using the Standard brush, alternating between ZAdd and ZSub by holding the Alt hotkey as you sculpt (see Figure 5.56). Use the Smooth brush (hotkey = shift) to even out the areas as you sculpt.

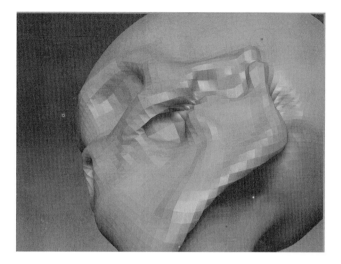

Figure 5.56

The area where the zygomatic bone meets the front of the face is refined using the Standard and Smooth brushes.

7. Define the area where the jaw meets the skull (this is the mandibular notch). Push the vertices around the temples in (this is the temporal fossa). Create the hollow behind the zygomatic bone by pushing those vertices down (Figure 5.57).

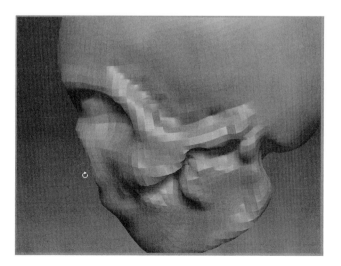

Figure 5.57

The area behind the zygomatic bone and the temple is refined. The back of the jaw is roughed in as well.

8. Make the separation between the teeth more obvious by pushing in with the Standard brush. You may want to try using the Nudge brush with a draw size of 15 to push the vertices of the lower teeth up behind the upper teeth (Figure 5.58).

The draw size of a brush remains constant regardless of how you scale/zoom in on a tool. You may need to experiment with the draw size on your brush to achieve the results shown in the figures.

Figure 5.58

The separation between the teeth is defined using the Nudge brush.

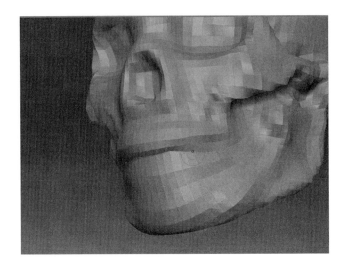

9. Switch to the side view. Use the Move and Standard brushes to form the curving shape at the bottom of the jaw. Continue to bring out the shapes that form the condyle, the mandibular notch, and the coronoid process. These shapes form the area where the jawbone meets the skull. You should always "sculpt in the round," meaning that you frequently rotate the tool working on various different parts while keeping an eye on the sculpture as a whole. Don't get stuck zoomed in on one part for too long—try to bring out all the parts of the sculpting at the same time as much as possible (Figure 5.59).

Figure 5.59

The jawbone is refined. The parts of the skull are all defined at the same time as much as possible.

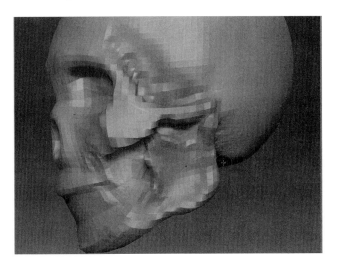

10. Rotate the skull so you can see the bottom. Use the Standard brush to form the hole where the skull sits on the spine, known as the foramen magnum (Figure 5.60).

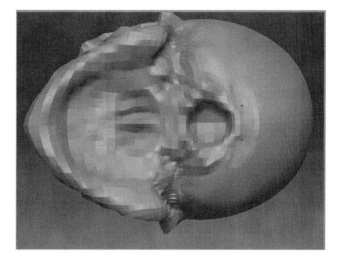

The opening where the skull sits on the spine is created.

11. At this point it's a good idea to double-check your work against the reference sketches. Parts of the tool start to move out of place as you sculpt. Click the eye icon on the reference plane subpalette to make the reference planes visible. Switch to the side view (see Figure 5.61).

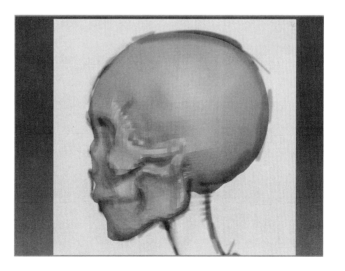

Figure 5.61

The visibility of the reference planes is restored to check the tool against the original sketches.

12. Use the Move tool with a large draw size to pull the skull back into its proper shape. You may want to move the SDiv slider down to 3 as you do this. You won't lose any changes made at the higher SDiv levels.

13. Switch to the Inflate brush. Set the draw size to 100 and the Z Intensity to 5. Sculpt lightly over the top of the skull to shape the cranium into more of a sphere.

14. Decrease the draw size and use the Inflate brush to form the bump of the mastoid process behind the jaw (see Figure 5.62).

Figure 5.62

The bump of the mastoid process behind the jaw is formed using the Inflate brush.

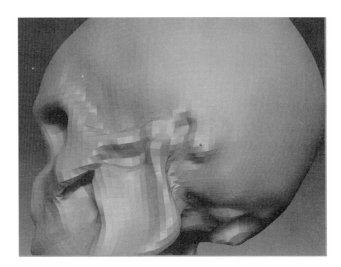

15. Rotate to the front and inflate the bone that runs along the outside of the orbital cavity. Continue to push in the vertices below the zygomatic bone. Bring out the line that runs from the coronoid process down the side of the jawbone beside the lower teeth. This is the oblique line (Figure 5.63).

Figure 5.63

The bone that forms the outside of the eye socket is refined along with the oblique line of the jaw.

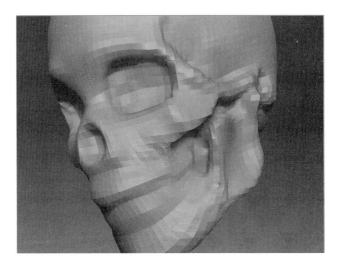

16. To see a macro of this stage, save your tool as skull_v4. Initialize ZBrush and load the skull_v4.ZTL tool from the Chapter 5 folder on the DVD (don't draw it on the canvas). Click the skullPart4 button in the Macro palette.

Adding Detail at Subdivision Level 5

Now the tool is ready for some detail. As the skull becomes more refined, you should feel free to use your own artistic sense while sculpting. The instructions in this exercise are guidelines; they do not describe each and every brush stroke you need to make.

1. Load the skull_v5.ZTL tool from the Chapter 5 folder of the DVD or continue with your model from the last section. Set the SDiv slider to 5.

2. Use the Pinch brush with a Z Intensity of 10 to bring together vertices on the edges of the bones and shapes (Figure 5.64).

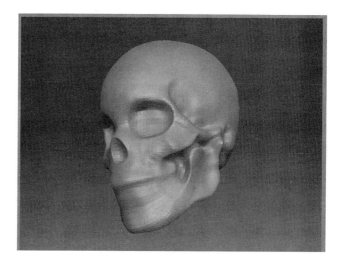

Figure 5.64

The Pinch brush refines areas around the eye sockets.

3. You can also use the Standard brush's BrushMod slider on the Brush palette to add a slight pinching as you sculpt. Don't raise this slider any higher than 20 or the Standard brush will behave more like the Pinch brush.

4. Use the Pinch brush to bring together the vertices along the divide between the upper and lower teeth (Figure 5.65).

5. Switch to the Flatten brush with a Z Intensity setting of 20. If the skull looks too rounded or "pillowy," you can use the Flatten brush to reshape the planes of the skull bones. Paint across the front and sides of the zygomatic bone as well as the areas on either side of the nose to define the planes of the skull. The chin and jaw could use a little flattening as well.

Figure 5.65
Figure 5.65

The line between the teeth is refined using the Pinch brush.

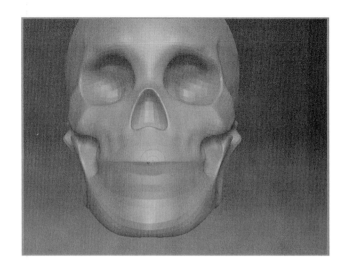

6. Pull up the bottom of the nasal cavity to form its upside-down heart shape (Figure 5.66).

Figure 5.66

The Flatten brush is used to define the planes of the skull. The nasal cavity is shaped.

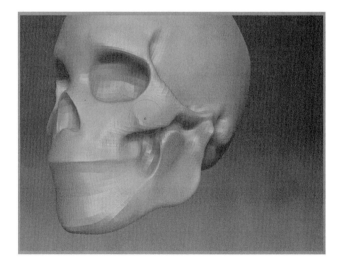

7. Remember to use the Smooth brush (hotkey = shift) as you go, and try to keep the vertices of the model as evenly spaced as possible.

8. Paint a line across the upper teeth while holding the Ctrl button; this will mask the upper teeth area. Use the Nudge brush to push the vertices of the lower teeth up and behind the upper teeth (see Figure 5.67).

9. To see a macro of this stage, save your tool as skull_v5. Initialize ZBrush, and load the skull_v5.ZTL tool from the Chapter 5 folder on the DVD (don't draw it on the canvas). Click the skullPart5 button in the Macro palette.

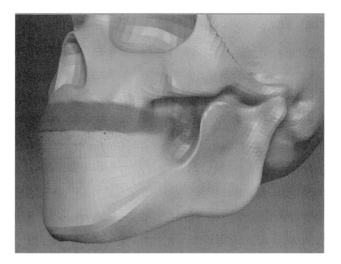

Figure 5.67

The upper teeth area is masked, and the Nudge brush pushes the vertices of the lower teeth underneath the upper teeth.

Refining Eyes and Teeth at Subdivision Level 6

At this point you can add another level of subdivision by clicking the Divide button. Refinement of the shapes continues.

1. Load the skull_v6.ZTL tool from the Chapter 5 folder of the DVD or continue with your model from the last section. Click the Divide button in the Geometry subpalette and set the SDiv slider to 6.

2. Use the Flatten and Pinch brushes to refine the planes of the skull and the areas around the orbital cavities (Figure 5.68).

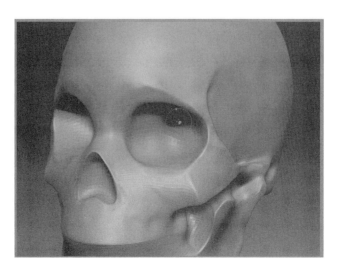

Figure 5.68

Use the Flatten and Pinch brushes to refine the Zygomatic bone and orbital cavities.

3. Form the bony line that separates the sides of the nasal cavity by using the Inflate, Standard, and Pinch brushes (Figure 5.69).

Figure 5.69

The bone that separates the sides of the nasal cavity is created using the Inflate brush.

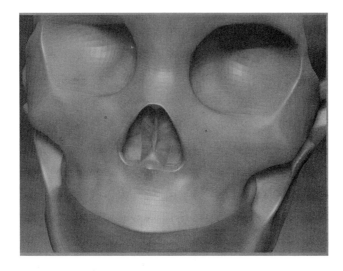

4. The skull in this example does not have enough space to create the teeth. Switch to the Move brush with a fairly large draw size and pull down on the areas of the lower skull to create more room (Figure 5.70). At this point it's okay to deviate somewhat from the sketch if the skull is not looking correct. The sketch is a guideline to help get you started.

Figure 5.70

Create more room between the nasal cavity and the upper teeth by using the Move brush.

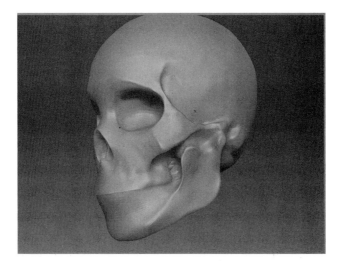

5. Hold the Ctrl key as you paint a line across the area where the front teeth will go. In the Masking subpalette, click the Invert key to reverse the mask so that the entire skull is masked except the front teeth (Figure 5.71).

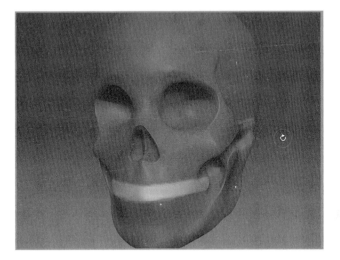

Figure 5.71

The entire skull, except for the front teeth, is masked.

6. Use the Inflate brush to rough in the upper teeth. Set the Z Intensity to 10.
7. Use the Pinch and Flatten brushes to improve the shape of the teeth (Figure 5.72).

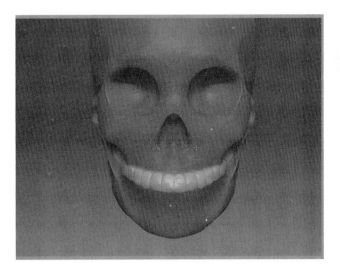

Figure 5.72

Use the Inflate brush to rough the upper teeth.

8. In the Masking subpalette, click the Inverse button to reverse the mask. The upper teeth are masked. Use the Inflate brush to rough in the lower teeth (see Figure 5.73).

Figure 5.73

The lower teeth are roughed in.

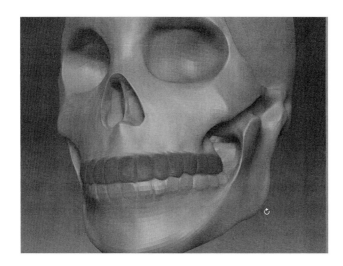

9. Use the Pinch, Nudge, and Flatten brushes to improve the shape of the lower teeth. The slight overbite has been lost in the process. To fix this, mask the upper teeth and use the Move tool to push the lower teeth back slightly (Figure 5.74). Creating the teeth takes a lot of time, so be patient with this part of the process. Remember to zoom out often while working on the teeth so that you can see them in context with the rest of the skull. You can also use the zoom palette to refine the teeth close up while the entire skull is visible on the canvas.

Figure 5.74

The overbite is restored by masking the upper teeth and pushing the lower teeth in slightly with the Move brush.

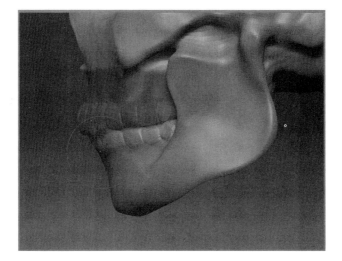

10. To see a macro of this stage, save your tool as skull_v6. Initialize ZBrush, and load the skull_v6.ZTL tool from the Chapter 5 folder on the DVD (don't draw it on the canvas). Click the skullPart6 button in the Macro palette.

Fine-Tuning in Subdivision Level 7

The skull is divided one more time so that a finer level of detail can be added.

1. Load the skull_v7.ZTL tool from the Chapter 5 folder of the DVD or continue with your model from the last section.

2. Click the Divide button in the Geometry subpalette to add another level of subdivision to the skull.

3. Use the Gouge brush with a draw size of 2 and an Z Intensity of 10 to refine the divisions between the teeth.

4. Smooth the cuts made by the Gouge brush by painting over them while holding the Shift key.

5. Use the Standard brush (with the Alt hot key) to push in the vertices in the hollow behind the upper teeth (Figure 5.75)

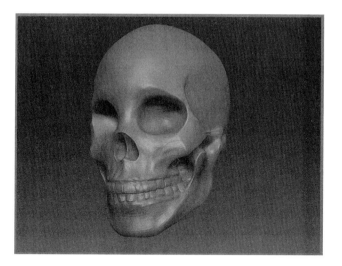

Figure 5.75

Create the hollow behind the upper teeth using the Standard brush.

6. Use the Inflate and Nudge brushes with small draw sizes to inflate and refine the area around the teeth and to indicate the bone behind the gum line known as the alveolar border (see Figure 5.76).

Figure 5.76

The area above and
below the teeth is
created with the
Inflate and Nudge
brushes.

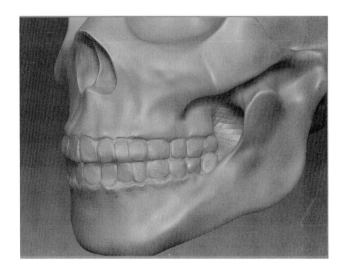

7. Create the hole for the ear (auditory hiatus) and refine the bones at the back of the
    jaw using the Standard, Smooth, and Inflate brushes (Figure 5.77).

Figure 5.77

The hole for the ear
and the jawbones
are refined.

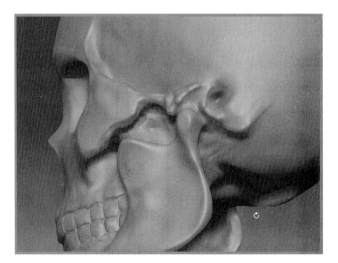

8. Switch to the Clay brush. Set the stroke type to Spray, and choose Alpha 7 from the
    alpha inventory. Set the draw size to 20 and the Z Intensity to 15. Make sure the RGB,
    M, and MRGB buttons on the top shelf are not activated—only ZAdd should be on.
    Lightly brush over the surface of the skull while holding the Alt key to create a porous
    texture on the surface of the bone (see Figure 5.78).

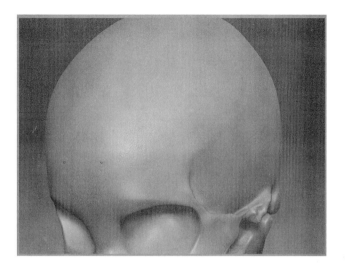

Figure 5.78

Use the Clay brush and an alpha to create a porous texture.

9. You can continue to add detail and make changes until you are happy. At this point though, you should have a decent skull model. Figure 5.79 shows the final skull.

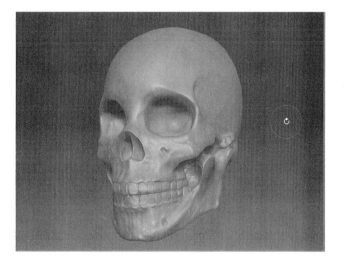

Figure 5.79

The final skull model from the front three-quarter view.

10. To see a macro of this stage, save your tool as skull_v7. Initialize ZBrush, and load the skull_v7.ZTL tool from the Chapter 5 folder on the DVD (don't draw it on the canvas). Click the skullPart7 button in the Macro palette.

Creating a Turntable Movie

Now that you have a decent model, you'll want to show it off to the world. One way to do this is to create a turntable move.

1. Load the skullFinal.ZTL tool from the Chapter 5 folder of the DVD or continue with your model from the last section. Set the SDiv slider to the highest level.

2. Rotate the tool so that you can see the front view, and use the Shift hotkey to snap the model into place as you rotate it.

3. In the Movie palette, activate the Doc button. This will restrict the recording to just the objects on the canvas. The rest of the ZBrush interface will be cropped out.

4. Click the Medium button to make the final movie size 50 percent of the canvas size.

5. Expand the Modifiers tab. If you'd like the motion of the movie to be smooth, increase the Recording FPS (frames per second) setting to 20. This will result in a larger file size for your final movie. Set the Playback FPS value to 20 as well so that the playback speed matches the recording.

6. Set the Spin Frames value to 40. This number determines how many frames it takes to rotate the model once. In this case, the record FPS is 20 and the there are 40 spin frames, so it will take two seconds for the skull to rotate once.

7. Set Spin Axis to Y so the skull rotates around the Y axis. Set Spin Cycles to 2 so that the skull spins twice.

8. Expand the Title Image tab at the bottom of the Movie palette. Click the Text 1 button to add some introductory text. Set the font size to large (see Figure 5.80).

9. You can set the FadeIn Time and the FadeOut Time values to adjust how long the text is on the screen before the turntable movie appears.

10. When you are ready to make the movie, click the Turntable button to record.

11. When the movie is finished recording, click the Play button in the Movie palette to play it back. If you are satisfied, you can save the movie using the Save As button. This will save it as a ZBrush movie, which can be played in ZBrush. To save as a QuickTime movie, use the Export button.

12. If you're not happy with the movie, use the Delete button to remove it from memory.

13. As long as you don't click the Delete button, any new movies you make will be added to the current one in memory.

14. To see a QuickTime movie of the skull turntable, open skull.mov.

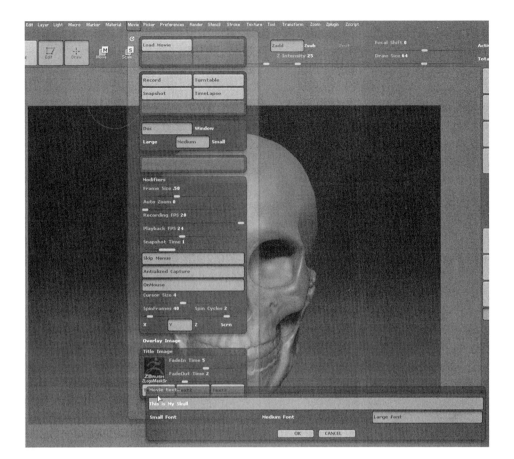

Figure 5.80

The Movie palette modifiers allow you to determine how the turntable movie will be recorded.

Summary

This chapter has given you your first taste of sculpting in ZBrush. Using a basic PolySphere object, you learned how to gradually refine the geometry of the tool into the shape of a skull using only the sculpting brushes. You also learned how to load an image onto reference planes for use as a guide while sculpting. Basic symmetry and masking tools were used to make the task of sculpting easier. The skills you learned while working through these exercises will improve with time and practice. They are the foundation skills that you will build upon as you continue to model in ZBrush. The next chapter explores more advanced sculpting techniques as you build a digital maquette of the Medusa's head.

The techniques used to create the skull sculpture represent one of many approaches. The sculpting brushes in ZBrush offer a wide variety of possibilities that this chapter only hints at. If you have a lot of experience sculpting clay you may find the technique of moving vertices around with the Move brush a little too technical. As an alternative to the techniques shown in this chapter, take a PolySphere, divide several times so that it has a lot of vertices, and try using the Rake brush in ZAdd and ZSub mode. Carve away at the surface the same way you would with real clay and see if it feels a little more natural. For more information on different sculpting approaches, read Scott Spencer's *ZBrush Character Creation: Advanced Digital Sculpting.*

Advanced Sculpting Techniques

The exercises in this chapter expand upon the basic sculpting techniques you learned in Chapter 5. If you felt that creating the skull tool in Chapter 5 was a real challenge, you may want to take some time to practice what you learned before tackling this chapter. Many more techniques will be introduced here as you sculpt the head of the Medusa maquette. QuickTime movies of the sculpting process have been included so that you follow every step of the sculpting process.

This chapter includes the following topics:

- Hiding geometry
- Polygroups
- Masking
- Edge loops
- The Transpose handle
- Combining subtools

Hiding Geometry

As you work in ZBrush, you will find it useful to hide parts of the geometry so that you can isolate regions for detail or masking. Hiding geometry also speeds up the performance of ZBrush on your computer because the hidden geometry frees up memory resources. This exercise takes you through the process of hiding selected polygons that make up the 3D tool.

Hiding parts of a tool is useful in several ways. If you just want to work on one part of a figure—such as the head—you can hide the rest of the body so it does not obstruct your view. Hiding geometry is also a way to organize a tool into polygroups as well as a necessary step when creating edge loops. Polygroups and edge loops are discussed later in this chapter.

1. Start ZBrush. From the startup screen, choose PolySphere to open a canvas that has this tool in Edit mode. Or choose "other" and use the Load Tool button in the tool palette to load the PolySphere.ZTL tool from the Program Files\ZBrush3\ZTools directory once ZBrush has started.

2. In the Transform palette, activate the Pt Sel and Frame buttons (see Figure 6.1).

> When the Pt Sel (Point Selection) button is off, polygons are selected based on the center of each polygon face. When this button is on, you can select the entire polygon by selecting any one of its vertices with the selection marquee. The Pt Sel button makes it easier to more precisely select specific polygons; you may find that you prefer to have this button activated whenever you are sculpting 3D tools.

3. Set the material to Fast Shader so it's easier to see what's going on.

4. Set the subdivision (SDiv) slider in the Geometry sub-palette to 1.

5. In the Display Properties subpalette on the Tool palette, make sure the Double button is activated so that both sides of the polygons are visible.

6. Rotate the tool to a side view, and hold the Shift button as you rotate to snap it into place.

7. Hold the Ctrl and Shift buttons down together. Starting at a blank part of the screen, drag downward diagonally to the right with the upper left portion of the 3D tool. You'll see a large green square appear (see Figure 6.2).

Figure 6.1
The Pt Sel button activates Point Selection mode.

This is the selection marquee. Drag the square so that some of the sphere's polygons are selected by the square. Once you are satisfied with your selection, release the pressure from the tablet or let go of the mouse button. All the polygons that were not within the green selection marquee should disappear. The polygons have not been deleted—they've been hidden.

8. To restore the visibility of these polygons, hold the Ctrl and Shift buttons down and tap with the brush or click the mouse button on a blank part of the canvas.

9. Repeat step 7 again to hide some polygons.

10. This time, Ctrl+Shift+click on the visible polygons. This action shows the inverse effect on the hidden geometry. The polygons that were not selected are now visible; those that were selected are now hidden.

    Alternatively you can Ctrl+Shift+drag and release on a blank part of the canvas to invert the visibility of the tool's polygons. Practice this a few times until you are comfortable with the process.

11. Ctrl+Shift+click or tap on a blank part of the screen to restore the visibility of the whole tool.

12. Now Ctrl+Shift+drag to bring up the selection marquee, and hold the marquee over some of the tool's polygons.

13. Before releasing the brush (by lifting the pen from the tablet or letting go of the mouse button), let go of the Shift key while the Ctrl key is still depressed. The marquee should turn red.

14. Now release the brush. The polygons contained in the red selection marquee are hidden. This is the reverse of the green marquee.

Practice hiding and showing polygons using the steps in this exercise. At first it may seem awkward, but once you get the hang of it you'll find it becomes second nature.

You can actually delete the polygons permanently using the DelHidden (Delete Hidden) button in the Geometry subpalette of the Tool palette (Figure 6.3). This will get rid of any hidden polygons permanently. Use this button with caution.

Figure 6.2

The selection marquee allows you to hide some of the polygons in the tool.

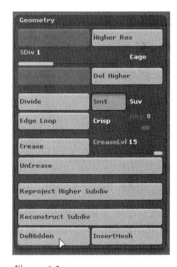

Figure 6.3

The DelHidden button permanently deletes all hidden polygons from the tool.

Creating Polygroups

ZBrush offers a way to organize 3D tools into groups of polygons. By organizing a poly-mesh tool using polygroups, you can make working with the tool easier when you are in a situation in which you are repeatedly hiding and unhiding the same piece of geometry. There are many ways to make polygroups. This exercise will show you how to create polygroups based on hiding parts of the tool.

1. Use the PolySphere object from the previous exercise. Ctrl+Shift+drag the green selection marquee around some of the polygons.

2. Release the marquee to hide the unselected polygons.

3. In the Polygroups subpalette of the Tool palette, click the Group Visible button (Figure 6.4). If the Frame button is activated in the Transform palette, you'll see the color of the polygons change.

4. Restore the visibility of the tool by Ctrl+Shift+clicking on a blank part of the canvas. The tool now has two polygroups, indicated by the colored areas as shown in Figure 6.5. If you turn the Frame button off, the original color returns. The grouped areas are only visible when the Frame button is on. The groups exist whether the Frame button is activated or not.

Figure 6.4

The Group Visible button creates a polygroup from any visible polygons.

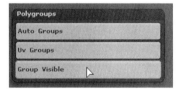

Figure 6.5

The colored portion of the polysphere indicates the grouped polygons. Groups can be easily hidden or isolated.

The colors of the groups are chosen randomly each time you create a group. When you organize a 3D polymesh into polygroups, the grouping will be saved as part of the polymesh tool when you click on the Save As button in the Tool palette.

5. Ctrl+Shift+click on any polygon within one of the groups. This will hide all other polygons in the tool outside of this group.

6. Ctrl+Shift+click again on the visible group. This will invert the visibility of the polygons.

7. Restore the visibility of the tool. Use the selection marquee to select some polygons that lie along the border of the two groups.

8. Click the Group Visible button to make a new group from these polygons.

9. Restore the visibility of the entire tool.

10. Now the tool has three groups, as shown in Figure 6.6. Creating the new group in the last step changed the membership of those polygons, so now they exist in a new group. Polygons can exist in only one group at a time.

11. Ctrl+Shift+click on a point that borders two of the groups. These two groups remain visible while the third is hidden (Figure 6.7). Ctrl+Shift+clicking in the same spot will invert the visibility of the polygons.

12. Restore the visibility of the entire tool. Click the Group Visible button in the Polygroups subpalette. This will replace all the groups in the tool with one group that contains all the polygons. This is one way to remove the polygroups from a tool.

Practice the steps in this exercise until you are comfortable with the process of creating polygroups.

Figure 6.6

The polysphere now has three polygroups.

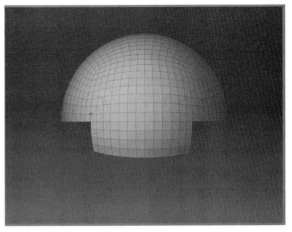

Figure 6.7

Ctrl+Shift+click on a point shared by both groups to hide all polygons that aren't in either group.

The Lasso button changes the selection marquee from a square to a freeform shape that you can draw on the canvas. Activate the Lasso button on the right shelf to switch to Lasso selection mode. The Lasso will be used for masks as well as hiding geometry. The hotkey for Lasso mode is Ctrl+Shift+M.

Masks and Polygroups

Masked areas of a 3D tool are impervious to changes made to the tool using deformers or sculpting brushes. In previous exercises, you learned that you can paint a mask directly on the surface of a 3D tool. Masks and polygroups work well together as a way to isolate parts of the tool for further refinement.

1. Using the same PolySphere tool from the previous exercise, create a polygroup from some of the polygons on the tool.

2. Hide all polygons of the tool except the new group you have created.

3. In the Masking subpalette of the Tool palette, click the MaskAll button (hotkey = Ctrl+a). The Visible polygons should become dark.

4. Ctrl+Shift+click on a blank part of the screen to restore the visibility of the entire tool. Note that now the polygons that make up the group are masked, while the rest of the tool is unmasked (Figure 6.8). It may be easier to see this if you turn off the Frame button in the Transform palette (or on the right shelf, hotkey = Shift+F).

5. Use the standard sculpting brush to paint across the surface of the tool, over the masked areas. Notice that only the unmasked portions are affected by the brush (Figure 6.9).

Figure 6.8

The area contained by the polygroup has been masked.

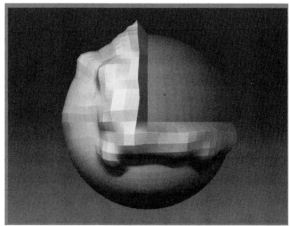

Figure 6.9

The masked area of the PolySphere is not affected by the sculpting brush.

6. Click the Inverse button in the Masking sub-palette. Now the polygons that were grouped are unmasked and the rest of the polygons in the tool are masked.

7. Click the Clear Mask button to remove the mask. Undo the last few actions until the PolySphere tool returns to its previous, unedited state.

8. Make sure the Draw and Edit buttons on the top shelf are still activated. Hold the Ctrl key down and paint some strokes on the surface of the tool to create a mask.

9. In the Masking subpalette, click the Hide Pt button. This will hide the unmasked areas of the tool.

10. In the Polygroups subpalette, click the Create Groups from the Group Visible button. This will create a group from the visible polygons (Figure 6.10). The polygroups are visible when the Frame button is activated (Shift+F).

11. Using steps 9 and 10, you can paint areas that you want to become polygroups.

Figure 6.10

A mask can be painted on a tool, isolated, and turned into a polygroup.

Deactivating the View Mask button will make the mask invisible. However, it is still functional, so the masked polygons are still impervious to edits. Occasionally you may find yourself unable to edit a tool; often it is because a mask is applied to the tool and the visibility of the mask is off. Make it a habit to check the View Mask button when strange things start to happen while sculpting.

Edge Loops and Creasing

You can use an edge loop to divide a part of the surface of a tool so that you have more geometry in a given area. The term *edge loop* refers to the circular arrangement of edges that define the divided area. For example, when you're adding an ear to a head tool made from a simple polysphere, you can use an edge loop to divide one polygon into a ring of polygons that can then be pulled from the head.

1. Use the Clear button in the Masking palette to remove the mask from the PolySphere.

2. Make sure the entire Polysphere is visible. Click on the Group Visible button to replace all the polygroups with a single polygroup.

3. In the Tool palette's Geometry subpalette, click the Reconstruct Subdivisions button twice to add two lower levels of subdivisions to the tool.

4. Set the SDiv slider to 1 so that you are on the lowest level of subdivisions.

5. Make sure the Double button in the Display Properties subpalette in the Tool palette is activated. Turn the Frame (Shift+F) button on in the Transform palette to make the wireframe visible. Make sure the Perspective button in the Draw palette is off.

6. Rotate the tool using the Shift key to snap it into an orthographic position.

7. Use the selection marquee to hide all of the polygons except the four that face the front of the canvas.

8. Rotate the tool to the side and hide the polygons on the opposite side (Figure 6.11). It's very easy to forget about the polygons on the opposite side of a symmetrical tool, especially if you don't have the Double button in the Display palette activated!

Figure 6.11

Hiding the polygons on the opposite side of the tool

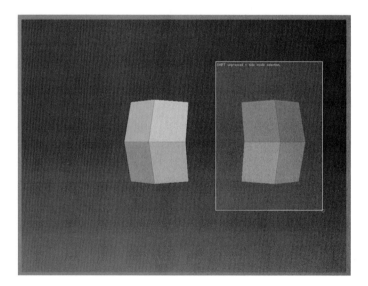

9. In the Geometry subpalette, click the Edge Loop tool. You'll see the four polygons divided so that a ring of new polygons now surrounds them. Also, polygroups have automatically been generated for the polygons at the center and for the new loop of polygons.

10. Shift+Ctrl+click on a blank part of the canvas to restore visibility to the tool. The tool is now divided into three sets of polygroups (Figure 6.12).

11. Note that you can create edge loops only when on the lowest subdivision level, but the newly created geometry and polygroups will exist in any higher SDiv level the tool may have or when you add higher levels of subdivision.

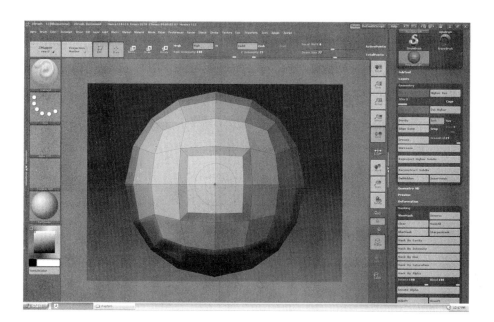

Figure 6.12

The Edge Loop button adds polygons to the tool and groups them at the same time.

12. Try creating another edge loop from part of the 3D PolySphere tool. Activate the Crisp button before clicking the Edge Loop button. This causes the border around the edge loop to be creased, giving it a harder edge when the tool is subdivided (Figure 6.13). The polygons that surround the edge loop are very thin, which causes the hard crease. This is helpful when creating nonorganic surfaces such as armor for a character.

13. Using the Crease button is another way to create a hard edge on a smooth surface (Figure 6.14). To crease an edge, hide all of the polygons of a tool that surround the edge you'd like to crease, and then click the Crease button. A dotted line will surround the creased polygons, as shown in Figure 6.15.

The Crease Level slider controls the hardness of the crease.

14. To remove a crease, click the Uncrease button.

Figure 6.13

The Crisp button causes the polygons of the edge loop to be thin and close to the border. This causes the edges to be harder at higher subdivision levels.

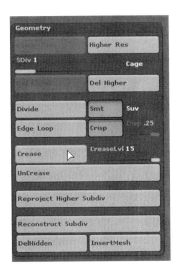

Figure 6.14

The Crease button in the Geometry palette

Figure 6.15

Creases create hard edges at higher levels of subdivision.

Transpose

The Transpose handle is a special mode of the Move, Scale, and Rotate buttons on the top shelf that are available only for 3D tools in Edit mode. This handle is designed to make posing figures easier. The following lesson shows how to use Transpose on a simple gingerbread man 3D tool.

1. Load the gingerbreadMan.ZTL tool from the Chapter 6 folder on the DVD. Draw him on the screen and make sure the tool is in Edit mode.

2. On the top shelf, activate the Move button (hotkey = w); the Edit button should remain on as well. When a 3D tool is in Edit mode, the Move, Scale, and Rotate buttons activate the Transpose handle (Figure 6.16).

3. In the Transform palette, make sure Activate Symmetry is off.

Figure 6.16

The Transpose handle is activated using the Move, Scale, and Rotate buttons on the top shelf.

4. Click at the center of the gingerbread man's head and drag straight down; hold the Shift key as you drag to make sure the line is straight.

   You'll see three circles connected by a line. This is the Transpose handle. It looks the same regardless of whether the Move, Scale, or Rotate button is active; however, the action is different for each button. The center line is the action line. The circles at the ends are its handles, as shown in Figure 6.17.

5. Hold the Ctrl key and drag from a blank part of the screen on the lower left of the gingerbread man: drag up toward the right to create a mask that covers the lower part of the gingerbread man. Essentially you want to create a mask where his pants would be.

6. Hold the brush over the circle at the center of the action line; a red circle will appear. Click and drag on this circle, and you'll see the unmasked portion of the gingerbread man move around as you drag this circle (see Figure 6.18).

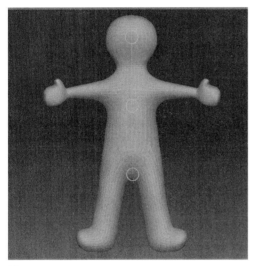

Figure 6.17

The Transpose handle consist of three circles joined by a line.

Figure 6.18

The unmasked part of the gingerbread man moves with the Transpose handle.

7. Click Undo (Ctrl + z) until the gingerbread man returns to his normal shape. Now hold the brush over the circle at the top of the action line, and click and drag on the red inner circle here. The unmasked portions of the gingerbread man become skewed (see Figure 6.19). The pivot of the skewing action is the circle at the opposite end of the action line.

8. Click Undo until the gingerbread man returns to his normal shape. To reposition the Transpose handle, drag the center circle by its edge or the action line itself. To reposition either end of the action line, click on the edge of the circles at the end. Experiment with this for a few moments.

Figure 6.19

Dragging the handle at the end of the Transpose handle skews the tool when the Move button is activated.

9. Click Undo until the gingerbread man returns to his normal shape. In the Masking palette, click the Blur Mask button two or three times to soften the mask. You can also Ctrl+click on the 3D tool to blur the mask.

10. Click the Rotate button on the top shelf (hotkey = r).

11. Reposition the action line so that it is at the center of the gingerbread man.

12. Click and drag upward on the white circle at the center of the middle circle. The unmasked portion of the gingerbread man pivots from the waist.

13. Drag on the center of the top circle and the unmasked portion rotates, using the circle at the opposite end as a pivot (see Figure 6.20).

Figure 6.20

The unmasked areas of the tool are bent when the Transpose handle is in Rotate mode.

14. Click on the outer edge of the bottom circle and drag upward to reposition it. Drag on the inner circle of the top control again; the unmasked portion rotates again but the pivot has been repositioned.

15. Click Undo until the gingerbread man returns to his normal shape. In the Masking subpalette, click Clear to remove the mask.

16. In the Transform palette, click the Activate Symmetry button.

17. Click the Draw button on the top shelf, and paint a mask that covers just the arms by holding the Ctrl key as you paint on the surface.

18. In the Masking subpalette, click the Inverse button to invert the mask so that only the arms are unmasked.

19. Ctrl+click on the gingerbread man tool once to blur the mask.

20. Activate the Rotate button on the top shelf (hotkey = r), and then click on the left shoulder and drag outward toward the hand; you'll see a line appear on the opposite arm representing the symmetrical copy of the transpose handle.

21. Make sure the Rotate button on the top shelf is active (hotkey = r). Experiment for a moment, rotating the arms around from the various points on the Transpose handle (see Figure 6.21).

    Note the difference when you drag on the center circle as opposed to the circles at the end. If you find that rotating by clicking on the center of the tool causes some of the polygons to distort, try rotating to a top view and reposition the ends of the Transpose handle just slightly. It may take a little practice.

22. Clear the mask, and make sure the Transpose handle is still active. Hold the Ctrl key and drag across the surface of the gingerbread man from the left shoulders out toward the hand. A mask appears based on how the Transpose handle is drawn. It automatically blurs itself when you let go. This is another way to mask the surface of a tool. The mask follows the topology of the 3D tool; it's called a "Topology Mask."

23. Experiment more with the Transpose tool. Click the Scale button (hotkey = e) on the top shelf and try scaling parts of the gingerbread man.

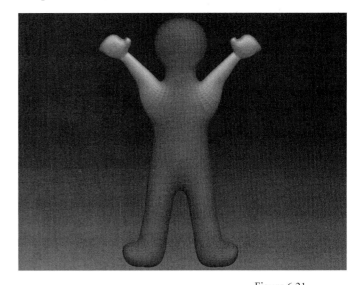

Figure 6.21

The arms are rotated up symmetrically.

Using the Transpose handle is a great way to pose arms and legs. It takes a little practice to get used to how it works. Remember that the handle works on whatever part of the tool is unmasked. If there is no mask at all, the Transpose handle acts on the entire tool. Using the Transpose handle on an unmasked subtool will allow you to reposition the subtool in relation to the main tool.

The Medusa Maquette

The remainder of this chapter contains a number of exercises that will take you through the process of sculpting a maquette of the Medusa's head. Maquettes are generally used as concept art. On a project such as a film or a TV show, they often serve as a means of artistic exploration, to help the director narrow down the look for a particular character or creature. Digital maquettes created in ZBrush can be used to fabricate actual sculptures using 3D printers.

This particular maquette will not be optimized for animation. To properly create a tool for animation, the topology of the surface needs to be created in a way that allows the geometry to be easily deformed by bone systems in other programs such as Maya, 3DsMax, and SoftImage XSI. ZBrush has tools for rearranging the topology of a 3D tool; these are often used to turn a sculpted maquette into a model suitable for animation. Using the ZBrush topology tools is an advanced topic that goes beyond the scope of this book. They are covered in Scott Spencer's *ZBrush Character Creation: Advanced Digital Sculpting* (Sybex, 2008).

To sculpt the Medusa's head, you'll begin by using the same polysphere and image plane setup described in the section "Creating Reference Planes" in Chapter 5. The main difference here is that the reference image itself is a quick sketch of a woman's head rather than a skull. To save time, the PolySphere tool and reference planes have been created for you. You'll use these to begin this exercise.

Chapter 6 Reference Movies

The process of sculpting requires thousands of strokes, decisions, and revisions. There's not enough room in this book to show everything that goes into making a tool. This is why QuickTime movies and 3D tools have been included on the DVD to demonstrate each step in the creation of the Medusa maquette. Watch each of the movies after reading the sections of the Medusa tutorial (or before if you prefer).

Creating the Neck

To add a neck to the head, you will use edge loops to add geometry. You will pull down the vertices to match the neck in the sketch.

1. Start ZBrush or create a new document by clicking the New Document button in the Document palette.

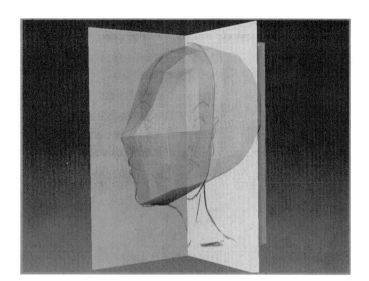

2. In the Tool palette, click the Load button and load the medusa_part1.ZTL tool from the Chapter 6 folder on the DVD.

3. Draw the tool on the canvas. You'll see the reference planes and PolySphere tool set up much like the skull in Chapter 5. The reference planes have a generic female head drawn on them (see Figure 6.22).

4. In the Subtool palette of the Tool palette, click on the eyeball icon to turn off the visibility of the reference planes. Make sure the Head subtool is selected in the SubTool palette.

5. Rotate the tool so that the bottom is visible; use the Shift hotkey to snap it into an orthographic view as you rotate.

6. In the Transform palette, make sure the Pt Sel, Local, Frame, and Activate Symmetry buttons are activated (the >X< and >M< buttons should be on as well). In the Display Properties subpalette of the Tool palette, make sure the Double button is activated.

7. In the Draw palette, turn the Perspective button off if it's not already.

8. Ctrl+Shift+drag a selection marquee starting from the upper left and select all of the polygons that form the side of the head geometry, as shown in Figure 6.23. Before letting go, release the Shift key so the marquee turns red. Release pressure from the tablet or let go of the mouse button to release the marquee. The polygons on the side of the head should disappear.

9. Use the selection marquee to hide all of the polygons on the tool except the six that make up the bottom of the head. Use Figure 6.24 as a reference. Remember to double-check and make sure the polygons on the top of the head have been hidden as well.

Figure 6.23

The selection mar-
quee is used to hide
all the polygons on
the side of the head.

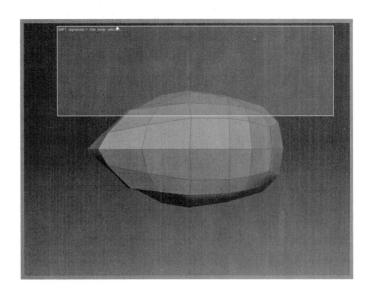

Figure 6.24

The six polygons at
the bottom of the
head are the only
ones that should be
visible.

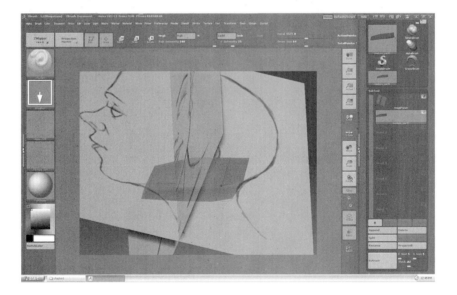

10. In the Geometry subpalette of the Tool palette, click the Edge Loop button to create an edge loop for this selection.

11. Crtl+Shift+click on one of the polygons on the edge to hide the newly created edge loop polygons.

12. Click the Edge Loop button again to make another edge loop.

13. Ctrl+Shift+click on a blank part of the canvas to unhide the entire head. The polygons at the bottom of the head should resemble Figure 6.25.

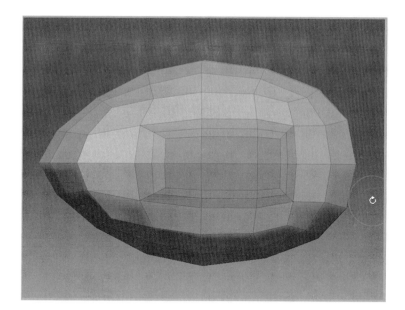

Figure 6.25

Two sets of edge loops have been created at the bottom of the head.

14. Ctrl+Shift+click on the polygons that form the rest of the head to hide the newly created neck polygons.

15. In the Masking subpalette of the Tool palette, click the Mask All button (Ctrl+a) to mask the head.

16. Ctrl+Shift+click on a blank part of the canvas to restore visibility to the entire head.

17. Select the Standard brush with a draw size of 100 and paint over the polygons of the neck; this will cause them to bulge out.

18. Use the Move brush with a draw size of 20 and a Z Intensity of 100 to pull the vertices of the neck downward. Turn the visibility of the Reference Plane subtool back on. Match the shape of the neck in the reference planes as best you can (Figure 6.26).

19. Click the Clear button in the Masking subpalette to remove the mask.

20. Rotate to the front, and pull out the vertices at the sides to form the shoulders. Try to make the arrangement of vertices follow the contours of the neck. The rows at the front should point in slightly to form a V shape that points toward the notch in the sternum. If the vertices are a little stubborn when you use the Move brush, try using the Standard brush to push them out.

> Hold the Alt key and drag left or right on the tool's surface while using the Move brush. This will cause the polygons to move inward or outward based on the normals of the surface below the tip of the brush.

Figure 6.26

The vertices of the neck have been pulled down to match the reference plane.

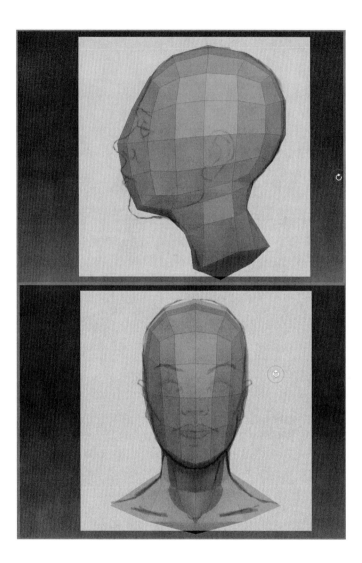

21. Rotate the tool so that the bottom is visible again. Turn off the visibility of the Reference Plane subtool.

22. Hide the entire tool except the polygons that make the bottom. Click the Edge Loop tool again to make another edge loop at the bottom of the neck. This will cause the bottom of the neck to shrink a little; you'll have to reposition the vertices at the bottom after making the new edge loop.

> When hiding and showing the tool's polygroups using the Ctrl+Shift hotkey, you may need to hide other subtools in the Subtool subpalette. Otherwise, ZBrush may switch the subtool when you click instead of hiding the polygroups you want hidden.

23. Save your tool to your local directory as medusa_v1.ZTL.

24. To watch a movie that demonstrates the steps involved in making the neck, use the Movie palette to load and play the medusa_part1.mov file from the Chapter 6 folder on the DVD.

RESTORING SYMMETRY

Every once in a while a 3D tool loses its symmetry and one side does not match the other. When this happens, you can use the Smart Resym button in the Deformation subpalette to copy changes on one side of the tool to the other. To do so, follow these steps:

1. Rotate the tool to a front view. Use the Shift key as you rotate to snap the tool to an orthographic view.

2. Turn off the Activate Symmetry button in the Draw palette.

3. Hold the Ctrl key as you drag a selection marquee over the side of the tool that you want to copy to the other.

4. In the Deformation subpalette, turn on the X toggle on the Smart Resym button and turn off Y and Z (this assumes you want symmetry across the x-axis; if you want symmetry across another axis, activate the appropriate toggle).

5. Click the Smart Resym Button. The two sides should now match.

6. Click Clear on the Masking subpalette to remove the mask.

7. In the Draw palette, turn the Activate Symmetry button back on.

Creating the Ears, Mouth, and Eyes

You will use edge looping to form the ears as well as the space for the eyes and mouth, much in the same way as you created the neck.

1. Continue with the tool from the previous section or load the medusa_v2.ZTL tool and draw it on the canvas.

2. Use the Move brush to pull the vertices in the front to match the nose in the reference plane, and move the chin out as well.

3. Rotate the tool to a side view. Ctrl+Shift+drag around the polygon closest to where the ear will be placed; use Figure 6.27 as a reference (you may need to hide the Reference Plane subtool for the selection marquee to work properly).

4. Release the brush to hide everything except this polygon and the matching polygon on the opposite side. If some of the surrounding polygons are still visible, use the selection marquee in Lasso mode (Ctrl+Shift+M) to hide these until just one polygon and its counterpart on the opposite side are visible.

Figure 6.27

**Ears are created
using edge loops.**

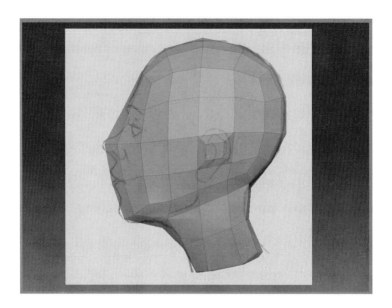

5. Click the Edge Loop button to make an edge loop for the ears. The ear on the opposite side should also have an edge loop now. See Figure 6.27.

6. In the Geometry palette, move the SDiv button up to level two. Turn the Reference Plane subtool's visibility back on if it is off.

7. Click the Delete Lower SDiv button to remove the lowest subdivision level. Now what was SDiv level 2 is SDiv level 1. This step is necessary so that edge loops can be created at a higher level of subdivision.

8. Use the Move brush to further refine the shape of the face so that it matches the reference in both the front and side view. Use Figure 6.28 as a guide for the arrangement of the vertices.

9. Hide all of the polygons except those at the front that encompass the lips. Double-check to make sure the polygons on the back of the head are hidden as well (Figure 6.29).

10. Click the Edge Loop button to create an edge loop for these polygons.

11. Do the same for the areas around the eyes (see Figure 6.30).

12. Use the Move and Standard brush to pull the vertices of the ears outward (Figure 6.30).

13. Save this tool as medusa_v2.ZTL.

14. To see a movie that runs through the process of creating the ears, mouth, and eyes, use the Movie palette to load and play the medusa_part2.mov file from the Chapter 6 folder on the DVD.

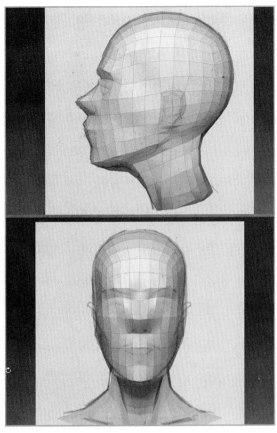

Figure 6.28
The face is shaped to match the reference.

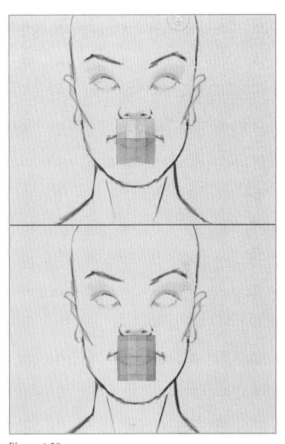

Figure 6.29
The polygons in front of the mouth are isolated; an edge loop is created.

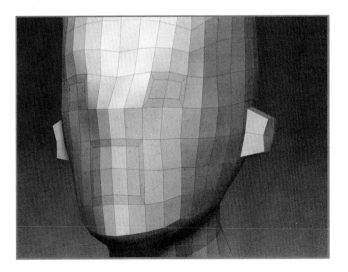

Figure 6.30
The ears are pulled out.

Shaping the Face

At this point you should have the geometry for the head nicely laid out. You may want to save this head as a generic starting place for future sculptures. As you continue to sculpt the Medusa, try to *sculpt in the round*, meaning that you should be constantly rotating the head, touching on all the parts of it as you go. With a few exceptions, you want to avoid getting stuck on one part of the tool for too long. Remember that as you increase the subdivision level of the tool to add more detail, you can also go back down to a lower subdivision level and continue to refine the basic form of the head; details made at higher subdivisions will remain intact even when you make changes at lower subdivision levels. As the sculpting process becomes more complex, it also becomes more subjective and the instruction becomes more general. Zoom out often so that you can assess how the forms of the face are working together and keep some reference images and anatomy books close at hand.

Remember, the head is not a cube, nor is it a sphere. The face does not lie on a flat surface; it wraps around the front of the skull, which is wedge shaped. Think of the skull as you shape the face—recall the forms of the skull you created in Chapter 5, particularly the cheekbones (zygomatic arches) and the horseshoe shape of the jaw.

Also, think of the character of the Medusa as you block in her forms. According to the poet Ovid, she was once a beautiful nymph who was cursed by Athena. She was given snakes for hair and made so ugly that the sight of her could turn a man into stone. It's quite possible that all of this has made Medusa somewhat upset. The concept behind the maquette in this chapter is one of an older Medusa. Her features are somewhat severe; behind them you can see traces of what once was a beautiful nymph. Along with hair consisting of snakes, she has worms and leeches growing from her skin. Her ugliness has tormented her to the point of insanity. The pose suggests she has been surprised and is poised for a counterattack. Figure 6.31 shows the final maquette.

Figure 6.31

The final maquette shows a very upset Medusa.

Blocking in the Ears, Eyes, and Mouth

The ears are an intimidating shape for beginners. It may be helpful to think of the function of the ears as you sculpt them. They are cups meant to capture sound and direct it into the ear canal. Think of the spiraling cartilage as a funnel for sound and the shape of the ear makes more sense.

At this level, just the basic shape is established. The ear has a large C shape on the outside and a secondary bent Y shape on the inside, as shown in Figure 6.32. Try not to cheat on the ear by hiding it behind hair (or in this case, snakes). Even if the ear is only partially seen, do your best to avoid sloppy modeling. The ear is often the true test of a modeler's skill.

1. Continue with the tool from the previous section or load the medusa_v3.ZTL tool and draw it on the canvas.

2. Set the draw size to 10. Choose the Move brush and set Z Intensity to 100.

3. Make sure symmetry is enabled and mirrored across the x-axis in the Draw palette.

4. Use the Move brush to position each vertex of the ear so that it forms a rough, backward, C shape, as shown in Figure 6.33. It may help to mask the head as you work on the ear.

5. Rotate to a side view. Push the vertices of the mouth inward. The Medusa will have an open mouth in the final version. Don't make the mouth wide open yet; just push the vertices inward as shown in Figure 6.34. You may need to rotate the tool and switch to the Standard brush to push them all in. They don't need to go back too far at the moment.

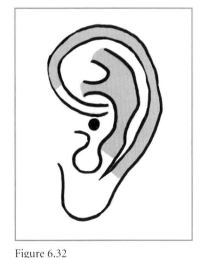

Figure 6.32

Diagram of the ear shapes. The backward C and Y shapes are shaded in.

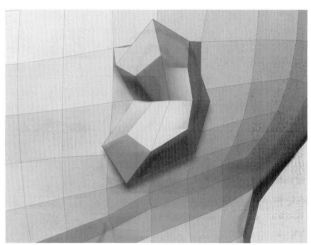

Figure 6.33

Create a rough backward C shape for the ear.

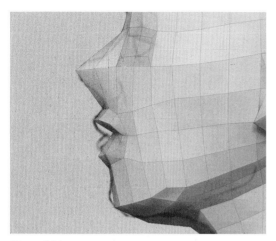

Figure 6.34

The vertices at the mouth are pushed back into the tool.

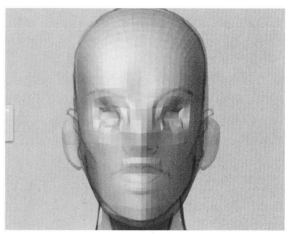

Figure 6.35

Make depressions at the position of the eyes.

6. Move the SDiv slider to level 2.

7. Make a depression in the position of the eye sockets using the Standard brush. Hold the Alt key while sculpting to push the vertices inward (see Figure 6.35).

8. Use the Standard brush with a draw size of 40 and a Z intensity of 10 to form the line of the jaw, the cheekbones (think of the shape of the skull!), and the brow. Lightly block them in.

9. Switch to the Smooth brush in the brush inventory. Set the Z intensity to 15 and switch back to the Standard brush. When you sculpt while holding the Shift button, you'll activate the secondary smoothing brush. If you lower the Z intensity, the smoothing will be easier to control.

10. When you use the Smooth brush, try lightly tapping on areas you want smoothed in very short, quick strokes.

Right-clicking on a blank part of the canvas will open a pop-up window with access to all the necessary brush controls. This can save you the trouble of having to constantly revisit the top shelf. And it can help you speed up the sculpting process.

Blocking in the Major Forms of the Head

A head should be forming from the polysphere. Keep rotating the tool, touching all the areas as you go. Constantly assess how the forms are working together. Feel free to start making your own artistic decisions as you go.

1. Use the Standard, Move, and Smooth brushes to pull lips out above and below the mouth.

2. Pull out the brow and cheekbones and refine the shape of the nose.

3. Think about how the zygomatic bone points back toward the ear as it wraps around the face. Create a slight indentation at the temples right behind the eye sockets. The temporalis is a large muscle that fills in the temple, so the indentation of the temples should not be as deep as it is on the skull.

4. Use the Standard brush to sculpt the strrernomastoid muscle that starts behind the ear at the base of the skull and wraps around to the front of the neck where it connects to the sternum.

   The sternomastoid is a very emotional muscle—it can become quite pronounced when a person is under stress (like our Medusa, for instance). Don't go too far just yet though; a few strokes to indicate its position should be adequate for now (see Figure 6.36).

5. Push the front of the ear back inside the cup of the ear, and shape the outside rim into the familiar C shape. Pull this rim out away from the skull somewhat.

6. When sculpting the neck, remember *not* to give the Medusa an Adam's apple; she is a lady after all! Take a look at Figure 6.36 to see some of these changes.

7. To see a movie that runs through the process described in the last two sections, use the Movie palette to load and play the medusa_part3.mov file from the Chapter 6 folder on the DVD.

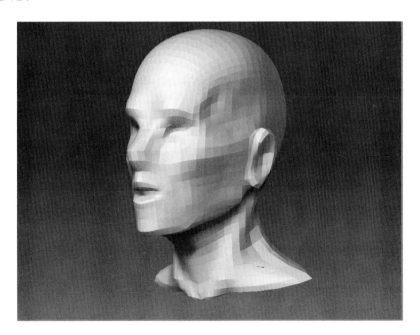

Figure 6.36
The head slowly takes shape as changes are made.

You may notice as you move up in subdivision levels that creases appear on the mesh. This is a result of the edge loops created earlier. It's not a big deal, and they can easily be removed using the Smooth brush. If you find that a few polygons have a different material applied, you can switch materials and click the Fill Object button in the Color palette to fix this. Make sure the M button is activated on the top shelf when you do this. It's a good idea to switch materials periodically as you sculpt. Different materials can reveal different things about the shape of a tool.

Shaping the Face

With the bone structure in place, you can move on to creating facial features. From here on you should feel more comfortable making your own decisions about specific brush settings such as draw size and Z intensity. Generally it's better to set the Z intensity to a low level, between 5 and 20 for any of the brushes, and use repeated strokes to make changes. Go slowly and make changes gradually.

The Ctrl+1 hotkey will repeat the last brush stroke. When defining a form, you can use the brush once and then hit the Ctrl+1 hotkey combination several times to repeat the exact same stroke again and again to bring the form out of the surface.

In addition to anatomy books, keep some photographic reference of women's faces close by. Use an Internet search engine to find images of faces. Try to find images of various facial expressions. Many digital artists and animators always keep a mirror near their computer so that they can test out facial expressions as they create them. The website 3D.sk has a huge library of human photographic references (be aware; there is a significant amount of nude references on this site). Fashion and photography magazines are a good source, especially for close-ups of the face. The steps in the following sections will be very hard to complete without some photographic references close by.

The movies included on the DVD in the Chapter 6 folder are meant to fill in the gaps that are not described in the text. You may want to watch the movies before and after each section to see how the sculpture was created.

1. Continue with the tool from the previous section or load the medusa_v4.ZTL tool and draw it on the canvas. You can watch the medusa_part4.mov movie to see how the example file was created for this section.

2. In the Geometry subpalette, set the SDiv slider to 3.

3. Smooth out any unsightly creases using the Smooth brush.

4. Use the Standard brush to shape the lips, and try not to make them stick out too far. The half-open mouth shape will probably look a little strange, as it's not a very natural expression. Shaping the mouth this way (as shown in Figure 6.37) will make it easier later on when you pull the jaw downward to make the mouth fully open. If you were to make a completely closed mouth, you might want to sculpt the lips together as one shape without any mouth cavity at all.

5. Choose the Inflate brush to form the lower lip, and set the Z intensity to 5. Lightly stroke across the center of the lower lip to create the bulge.

6. Use the Standard brush to sculpt the ear so that the front of the ear spirals in toward the center of the ear, as seen in Figure 6.37.

7. Hold the Ctrl key as you paint to create a mask that covers the upper lip. Use the Move or Nudge brush to bring the corners of the lower lip slightly inward toward the center of the mouth. Tuck them in below the corners of the upper lip ever so slightly.

Generally speaking from a sculptural point of view, lips are actually more defined by color than shape. The parts of the lips that are at the center, beneath the nose, tend to be fleshy bulges. However, the parts of the lips toward the corners actually transition into the skin on the face fairly smoothly. Avoid the temptation to sculpt a defined "lip liner" border that surrounds the entire shape of the lips.

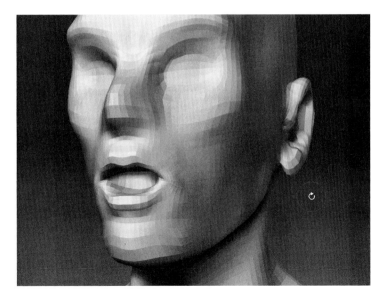

Figure 6.37
The lips are formed above and below the mouth.

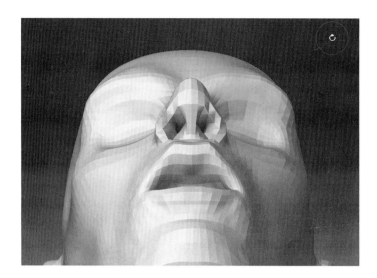

8. To form the nostrils, use the Standard brush to push in the holes (hold the Alt key as you paint with the brush). Be gentle as you paint. You can also use the Move brush to pull out the edges of the nostril. This is often easiest when the tool is rotated so that you can look up into the nose from the bottom, as in Figure 6.38.

9. Use the Inflate brush with a draw size of 100 and a Z intensity of around 40 to form the area below the neck into the top part of the chest. The Move brush will also be helpful. Use the Standard brush to roughly sculpt in the collarbones, the notch of the sternum, and the top part of the trapezius muscle in the back. See the two views in Figure 6.39.

   Figure 6.39 shows changes made to the jawline, nose, and ear. The tip of the nose is pulled up a little bit, giving it a more feminine quality. The shape recalls Medusa's original nymph-like features before Athena cursed her. However, you could give her a more pronounced and longer bridge if you wanted her to appear as more of a Greek or Mediterranean woman. The shape of the nose has an enormous impact on the overall look and personality of the character.

10. Use the Inflate brush with the Alt key to increase the size of the interior mouth cavity.

11. Also use the Inflate brush with the Alt key to push in a depression inside of the ear. Reduce the draw size and Z intensity when creating the ear details.

12. Use the Standard brush to form the crease of the nasolabial fold. Reduce the Z intensity to 15 and the draw size to 12. Brush lightly while holding the Alt key to make the crease, and then brush just above the crease without the Alt key to bring out the flesh above the crease. The crease starts just behind the nostril and moves down either side of the face. The end is just below the corners of the mouth, usually.

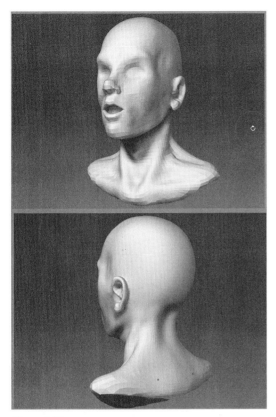

Figure 6.39

Extend the neck to form the upper part of the chest.

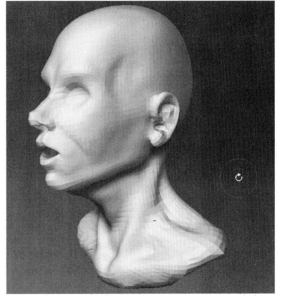

Figure 6.40

Use the Pinch brush to refine the creases in the face.

This crease adds a great deal of personality to the character. The size and depth varies a great deal from person to person. It tends to be more pronounced in men and older people or in certain facial expressions.

13. Use the Pinch brush with a Z intensity between 5 and 10 to refine the nasolabial fold and the areas behind the nostril.

14. Lightly brush along the outer rim of the ear with the Pinch brush as well. Figure 6.40 shows these changes.

15. Turn on the visibility of the Reference Plane subtool. Use the Move brush to make any changes you feel are necessary to make the head match the sketch on the planes. Ignore the mouth region; the open mouth does not need to be closed to match the sketch.

16. Save the tool as medusa_part4.ZTL on your local drive.

17. You can watch the medusa_part4.mov movie to see how the example file was created for this section.

When you save your tool to disk, all subtools are saved with it. However, you'll find that ZBrush will rename whatever subtool is selected in the Subtool palette after the filename you use. It's a good idea to get in the habit of selecting the main tool in the Subtool palette before saving the tool to disk—in this case it would be the Medusa's head.

Duplicating Subtools

To create the eyes, you will insert a sphere subtool into the ocular cavity and then mirror it across the x-axis. This technique will work for any subtool you need to mirror from one side to the other.

1. Continue with the tool from the previous section or load the medusa_v5.ZTL tool and draw it on the canvas. You can watch the `medusa_part5.mov` movie to see how the example file was created for this section.

2. In the Tool palette's tool inventory, select the Sphere 3D tool. The Medusa tool will be replaced by the Sphere 3D tool. Don't worry; nothing has happened to the Medusa tool. You've just switched tools.

3. In the Tool palette, click the Make Polymesh button to convert the sphere from a parametric object to a polymesh.

4. In the Tool palette's tool inventory, click on the Medusa to switch back to the Medusa tool.

5. In the Subtool palette, click the Append button. This will bring up the tool inventory. Select the Polymesh Sphere on the top row to append this tool to the Medusa tool.

6. In the Subtool subpalette, select the Sphere3D subtool. Click the Rename button at the bottom of the Subtool palette and rename the tool "eye."

7. Click the Scale button on the top shelf to activate the Transpose handle for the sphere.

8. Use the Transpose handle in scale mode to scale the sphere down to roughly eyeball size. Switch the Transpose handle to move mode and move the eye into position in the Medusa's left ocular cavity (see Figure 6.41).

9. Sculpt a bulge for the pupil using the Inflate brush. It doesn't have to be perfect at this point; you just need some kind of reference point so you know which direction the eye is looking. Later on you can replace this with a better version of the eye.

10. When you are happy with the size and position of the eye, click the Clone button at the top of the Tool palette. This copies the subtool, including its position and size. However, the cloned eye has not been appended to the Medusa.

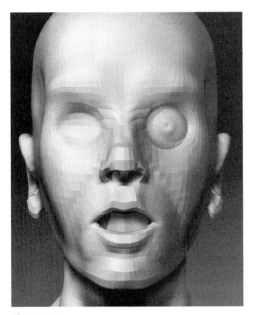

Figure 6.41

Position the eye on the Medusa's left side.

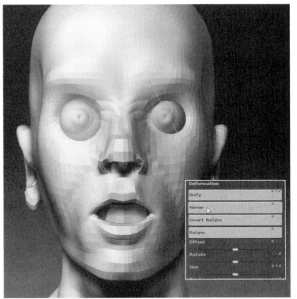

Figure 6.42

The Mirror deformer positions the clone of the eyeball on the opposite side of the face.

11. Click the Append button in the Subtool subpalette to add the cloned eyeball to the Medusa.

12. The copy of the eyeball appears at the same position as the original eyeball. To mirror it onto the opposite side, expand the Deformation subpalette. Make sure that only the X toggle on the Mirror button is activated and then click the Mirror button. The second eyeball should now appear in position on the other side of the head, as seen in Figure 6.42.

Creating the Eyelids

To form the eyelids, you sculpt the geometry of the face around the Eyeball subtools. The eye subtools act as guides for the sculpting process. The eyelids are tricky and take some practice. There are a number of creases and folds of flesh in the area that surrounds the eyes.

Facial features such as the area around the eyes, the nose, and the mouth vary from person to person, but their construction follows some general rules based on the structure of the skull and muscles beneath the face. For example, the inner corner of the eye is usually lower than the outside corner. The apparent difference between any two faces is more often a result of the sum of many minor differences in each face rather than a few large differences. Our brains are so finely tuned to pick up on these differences—out of the need to recognize family and friends over potential foes—that we often miss the truth that human beings really all look the same. Keep this in mind as you create your digital sculptures. Try to follow the same basic rules for facial structure in all your facial sculptures. To create different characters from generic features, try to create many small changes in these features rather than making just a few features wildly different.

1. Continue with the tool from the previous section or load the medusa_v6.ZTL tool and draw it on the canvas. You can watch the `medusa_part6.mov` movie to see how the example file was created for this section.

2. In the Subtool palette, select the Medusa head. Make sure the Transp button on the right shelf is active.

3. Select the Inflate brush and push the geometry from behind the eye subtools out forward. Use the eye subtools as guides to make two bulges that cover the eyes, as shown in Figure 6.43.

4. Use the Standard brush to create the flesh that hangs above the eye, bridging the space between the outer edge of the brow and the outside corner of the upper eyelid; see the top image in Figure 6.44. Create the crescent shape of the bags below the eyes as well.

Figure 6.43

Bulges are created over the eyes.

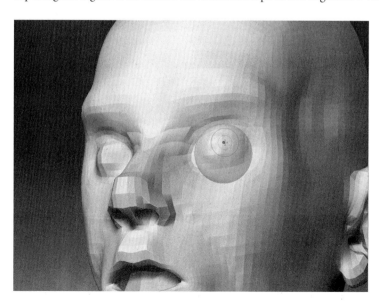

5. Carefully push in the geometry at the center of the eye bulge, leaving enough above and below for the eyelids. It may be easier to do this if the eyeball subtools are hidden.

6. Paint a mask over the outside edge (meaning the side of the eye opposite the nose) of the upper eyelids by holding the Ctrl key while painting; use the center image in Figure 6.44 as a reference.

The inside portion of the eye was created using an edge loop. You can take advantage of the fact that polygroups are automatically created with edge loops. You can use the polygroups to quickly mask hard-to-reach areas as was demonstrated in the section on polygroups and masks earlier in this chapter.

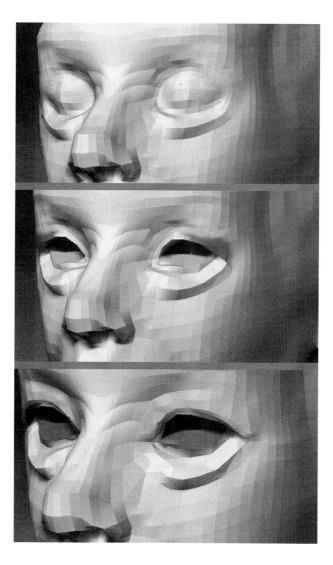

Figure 6.44

Flesh above and below the eyes is roughed in.

7. Use the Nudge brush to tuck the outside edge of the lower eyelid up and underneath the outside edge of the upper eyelid. The upper eyelid should hang over the lower lid—creases from this overhang often lead to crow's-feet wrinkles on older people. Since our Medusa is in her 50s (or seemingly in her 50s), she will probably have some wrinkles here in the final version. The bottom image in Figure 6.44 shows these changes.

8. Use the standard brush with a draw size of around 5 to pull up a row of vertices along the lower rim of the eyeball to form the lower eyelid. This will be easier to do with the visibility of the eyeball subtools restored.

9. Paint a mask along the edge of the upper eyelid, or create a mask from the eyelid's polygroup.

    To create a mask from the polygroup, Ctrl+Shift+click on the eyelid to isolate its visibility, mask all using Ctrl+a, and then Ctrl+Shift+click on a blank part of the canvas to restore visibility. Finally, invert the mask (Ctrl+i).

10. Use the Nudge brush to pull the flesh above the upper eyelid down slightly to form a crease that follows the shape of the upper eyelid, as shown in Figure 6.45.

11. The inside corner of the eye is generally lower than the outside corner of the eye. You can remove the mask and pull this area downward slightly. Use the Standard brush to form the triangle of the tear duct on the inside corner of the eye.

12. If your head sculpture looks slightly alien, it may be because the overall shape of the face has flattened out a bit. Remember the shape of the skull: the face wraps around the front of the head. To make Medusa slightly more human, rotate the head to a side view, and using the Move brush with a large draw size, pull back the outside edges of the eyes toward the ears (see Figure 6.45). The eyeball subtools may need some repositioning when this is done.

13. You may need to do some additional smoothing and pinching on the facial features to refine the overall look.

14. On either side of the nose, between the eye and the back of the nostril, are two pads of flesh covering a series of muscles. It is important to add a very slight padded bulge here. Often a computer-generated character will lack this padding and that omission can cause an otherwise well-sculpted model to look fake.

    This pad of flesh helps connect the form of the nose to the cheeks. It runs from the side of the nose down toward the cheeks just above the nasolabial fold. This bulge is often very slight and it can be more noticeable when it's not there than when it is. Use Figure 6.45 as a guide.

15. Save your tool as medusa_part6.ZTL.

You can watch the medusa_part6.mov movie to see how the example file was created for this section.

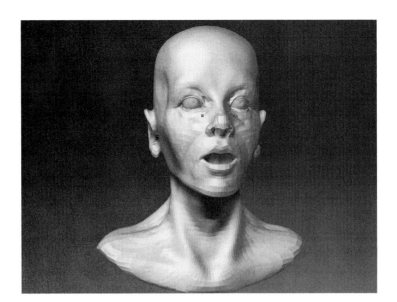

Figure 6.45

Add a small pad of
flesh to each side of
the nose.

Using LazyMouse

As the Medusa tool is further subdivided you'll see how the care you put into creating
well-proportioned and anatomically correct features starts to pay off. If the head looks
human at lower subdivision levels, then the task of sculpting details at higher levels is easier and more enjoyable. Of course, ZBrush allows you to move back and forth between
lower and higher subdivision levels at any time. The practice of working carefully at lower
subdivision levels before moving to higher levels is more an act of artistic discipline than
anything else.

The LazyMouse feature creates a delay between the end of the brush and the actual
change made to the surface of the geometry. This delay minimizes the effect of small
movements made while sculpting, making it easier to create straight lines as you sculpt.
This feature is particularly helpful when you create creases and wrinkles on the face. You
can use LazyMouse whenever you'd like; when you create faces, you may find it more useful at later stages in the sculpting process.

1. Continue with the tool from the previous section or load the medusa_v7.ZTL tool
   and draw it on the canvas. You can watch the medusa_part7.mov movie to see how the
   example file was created for this section.

2. Set the SDiv level on the tool to 4.

3. From the Brush palette, select the Standard brush.

4. In the Stroke palette, activate the LazyMouse button. Set LazyRadius to 8; this controls the maximum distance between the end of the brush and the actual stroke on the geometry. See Figure 6.46.

5. LazyMouse settings are applied to the current brush only. If you switch to another brush in the brush inventory, LazyMouse will be off. Switch back to the Standard brush and LazyMouse is on again. Each brush will remember its own LazyMouse settings as well.

6. In the Brush palette, set Brush Mod to 15. This causes a slight pinching effect to be added to the Standard brush as you use it to sculpt the geometry. This is can be helpful when creating details and wrinkles on the face.

7. Paint some test strokes along the cheek and adjust the LazyMouse and BrushMod settings until you're happy with how they work.

8. Set the Z intensity of the Standard brush to 10. Paint strokes just above the nasolabial fold to add some flesh to the cheeks, as shown in Figure 6.47.

9. Decrease the draw size to 5 and use the brush to refine the eyelids, as shown in Figure 6.48.

10. Increase the Z intensity of the brush to 15 and paint along the outside of the ear. Use the Standard and Inflate brushes to refine the structures on the interior of the ear as seen in Figure 6.49. Don't neglect the back of the ear.

11. Continue working with the face until you are satisfied that all the features look like the features of a female human being.

Figure 6.47

Add flesh to the face using the Standard brush.

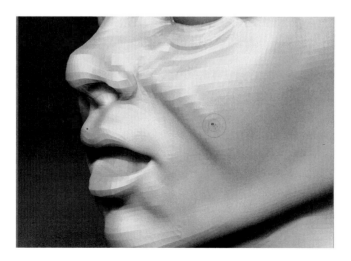

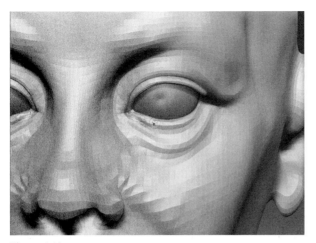

Figure 6.48

The eyelids are refined.

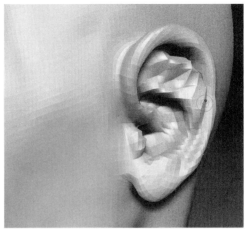

Figure 6.49

The interior structure of the ear is created.

Opening the Mouth

Now that you have created a convincing human face, it's time to give it some personality by adding a facial expression. The Medusa is about to strike. Her venomous fangs are out (well, they haven't been created yet, but they will be out in the final version), and her demeanor suggests that she is enraged. To open her mouth wide, you'll use the Transpose handle.

1. Continue with the tool from the previous section or load the medusa_v8.ZTL tool and draw it on the canvas. You can watch the medusa_part8.mov movie to see how the example file was created for this section.

2. Hold the Ctrl key and drag from a blank part of the canvas over portions of the head to mask it. Mask all of the head except for the jaw.

3. Paint on the tool while holding the Ctrl key to fill in any gaps and refine the area of the mask.

4. To erase parts of the mask, hold Ctrl and Alt while painting. Erase the areas of the mask around the outside corners of the upper lip.

5. Ctrl+click on the Medusa three times to soften the edge of the mask.

6. Rotate the tool to a side view.

7. On the top shelf, click the Rotate button.

8. Drag the Transpose handle from the corner of the jaw to a spot in front of the chin. Hold the Shift key as you drag the Transpose handle out past the chin onto a blank spot on the canvas. Use the top image in Figure 6.50 as a reference.

9. Use the Rotate Transpose handle to rotate the jaw to an open position. It's okay to overdo it just slightly; you want the expression to be somewhat exaggerated (see Figure 6.50).

10. Switch to the Move Transpose handle and push the jaw back in just a little bit. See the bottom image in Figure 6.50.

11. When you are satisfied, clear the mask by clicking the Clear button in the Masking subpalette.

12. Use the sculpting brushes to refine the shape of the mouth.

13. In the Geometry subpalette, click the Divide button to add another SDiv level to the tool.

14. Use Figure 6.51 as a reference for shaping the expression on the Medusa.

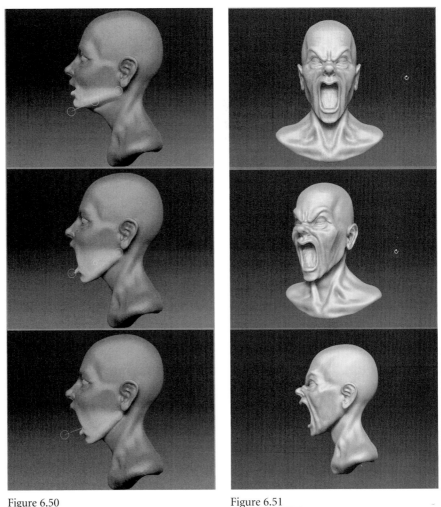

Figure 6.50

Use the Transpose handle to rotate the jaw and move it back a little.

Figure 6.51

The Medusa's face is sculpted to express rage as she attacks.

CREATING THE LOOK OF RAGE

There is no single method for creating a convincing expression. This is where reference photos help a lot. To make the Medusa look like she's about to attack a person as opposed to snacking on a 14-inch submarine sandwich, you must make a lot of major and minor adjustments. Sometimes the tiniest change can make the expression "click" into place. Use the following tips as a guideline:

- The overall shape of the lips should be more square than oval.

- Most of the time, if you open your mouth as wide as possible, it's more likely that the lip will curl inward towards the teeth. The stress of stretching the lips makes it very difficult to curl them upward and out, although it is not completely impossible.

- Flaring the nostrils will add to the impression of rage, but don't go too far. The outside edges of the nostrils should pull up and back.

Think about how the rest of the flesh on the face is reacting to the changes in the mouth and nose:

- The nasolabial fold should be deep and pronounced.

- The cheeks should bulge as the flesh is drawn back toward the ears.

- The skin on the nose should wrinkle and fold.

- The tip of the nose may point down ever so slightly.

- The ears may move back slightly.

- The bunching of the cheeks may cause the lower eyelids to move up and flatten out a bit. This also happens when you smile.

- The inside of the brows may point down and toward the bridge of the nose.

- If the brows are squished together in an expression of anger, the skin between them should bunch up as well.

- To increase the drama, pull the outside edges of the eyes and brows up and back and the inside edges of the eyes downward. This is more stylistic than realistic, but it augments the look of the enraged brow.

- The upper eyelids should pull up and back to make the eyes open wide.

Try experimenting with your own face in front of a mirror. Examine what happens to various parts of the face as you move it into extreme positions.

Don't allow the face to do anything that's not physically possible or at least plausible—some stylistic liberties may be taken, but don't excuse unrealistic or impossible muscle actions just because the Medusa is not completely human.

Posing the Head

The Medusa tool is looking pretty good, but it would be nice to increase the drama of the sculpture by posing the head and introducing some asymmetrical elements.

1. Continue with the tool from the previous section or load the medusa_v9.ZTL tool and draw it on the canvas. You can watch the medusa_part9.mov movie to see how the example file was created for this section.

2. Paint a mask on the surface of the Medusa tool that covers everything below the lower neck. Everything above should be unmasked as shown in Figure 6.52.

3. In the Transform palette, make sure Active Symmetry is turned off.

4. In the Subtool palette, turn off the visibility of the eyeball subtools.

5. Use the Transpose handle to pose the head. Rotate the head so that the Medusa is looking to her left (your right), and tilt it back and to the side a little. Use Figure 6.52 as a guide.

6. When you are happy with the position, click the Clear button in the Masking sub-palette to remove the mask.

7. Use the sculpting brushes to remove any creases or distortions that may have been created while posing the head.

8. Turn on the visibility of the eyeball subtools. Use the Transpose handle to position the eyeballs in place (see Figure 6.53). You may want to rotate them so they look at the viewer in a menacing way.

Figure 6.52

The Transpose handle is used to pose the head.

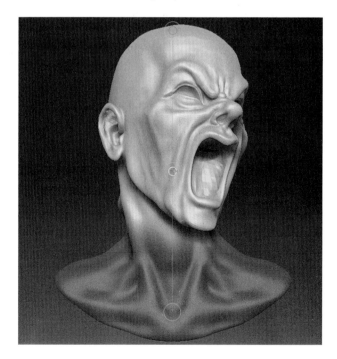

Figure 6.53

The Transpose handle is used to position the eyeballs back into the head.

There is a plug-in for ZBrush 3.1 called Transpose Master that allows you to pose subtools along with the main tool. It is discussed in Chapter 10.

Poseable Symmetry

If you decide you need to make a symmetrical change to the tool after posing the head, you can activate the Use Poseable Symmetry button, which will evaluate symmetry based on the tool's topology.

1. Remove any masks from the tool by clicking the Clear button in the Masking sub-palette.

2. In the Transform palette, click the Activate Symmetry button. Make sure both the >X< and the M buttons are on so that changes are mirrored across the x-axis.

3. Click the Use Poseable Symmetry button to activate poseable symmetry.

4. Try making changes to one side of the forehead; the other side will reflect the change (Figure 6.54).

Poseable symmetry can be activated only at the highest SDiv level. If you decide to subdivide the tool again, you will need to repeat these steps to rebuild poseable symmetry at the higher SDiv level.

Figure 6.54

Symmetrical
changes can still
be made on the
posed tool.

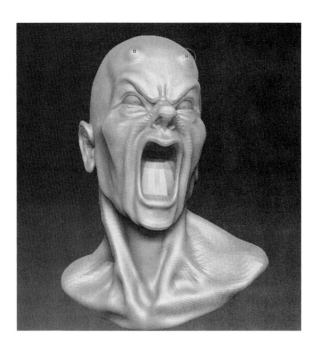

Creating Snakes

Medusa is looking gruesome now; however, she is missing her most defining characteristic—her hair made of snakes. This version of the Medusa will have many snakes of varying sizes. She'll have eight large snakes growing from her head, and around these large snakes she'll have smaller parasites and worms growing all over. First you'll create the large snakes using ZSpheres.

You will make the large snakes in two pieces to make sculpting easier. You will use a single ZSphere object to make the bodies of the eight large snakes and then you will make a single head as a separate tool. You can then copy and place the head at the end of each of the large snakes.

ZSphere basics were covered in Chapter 4. You may want to review this part of Chapter 4 if you are unfamiliar with how to use them.

1. Continue with the tool from the previous section or load the medusa_v10.ZTL tool and draw it on the canvas. You can watch the medusa_part10.mov movie to see how the example file was created for this section.

2. Click the Append button in the Subtool subpalette to append a ZSphere to the Medusa tool.

3. Select the ZSphere in the Subtool subpalette.

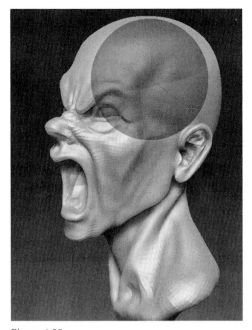

Figure 6.55

A ZSphere is appended to the Medusa tool and positioned inside the skull.

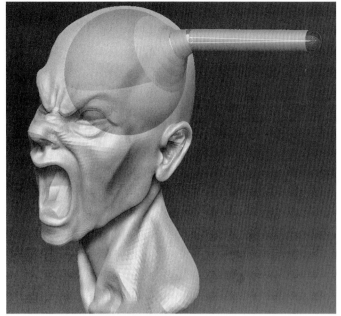

Figure 6.56

A ZSphere chain is added and extended from the center ZSphere.

4. Activate the Move button on the top shelf to position the ZSphere at the center of the head.

5. Activate the Scale button to scale the ZSphere so that it fits within the head, about where the brain should be. This part of the tool will not be visible in the finished sculpture, so you don't need to be overly precise about its position. (Figure 6.55).

6. Click the Draw button on the top shelf. Add a ZSphere to the center ZSphere. Position this on the side of the head. Scale it up so that it's a little larger than the eyeball subtools.

7. Add another ZSphere on top of this one, about the same size.

8. Add a third ZSphere on top of the second, about the same size.

9. Click the Move button on the top shelf, and move the third ZSphere out away from the head (Figure 6.56).

10. Click the Draw button on the top shelf. Click on one of the connector ZSpheres at the center of the chain. This will convert the connector ZSphere into an active ZSphere that can be repositioned.

11. Move the new ZSphere at the center of the chain so that an angle is formed in the ZSphere chain. Toggle on the Adaptive Skin Preview (hotkey = a) to see the polymesh that will eventually be created from the ZSpheres (Figure 6.57).

Remember, don't try to edit the Adaptive Skin Preview of the ZSphere polymesh! This will cause the polymesh to behave erratically when other ZSpheres are added.

Figure 6.57

An angle is created in the ZSphere chain by adding a ZSphere. The Adaptive Skin Preview shows what the mesh will look like with each change.

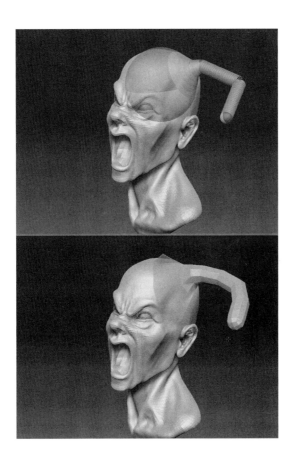

12. Toggle off the Adaptive Skin Preview mode (hotkey = a) to switch back to ZSpheres. Add more ZSpheres along the chain or at the end of the chain. Use the Move mode to position these ZSpheres so that the chain forms a twisty snake. Try to keep the ZSpheres as evenly spaced as possible along the chain, but don't get stressed out if they are not perfectly spaced.

13. Use the a hotkey to periodically preview the shape of the snake.

14. When you have a basic snake in place, start a new chain by adding a new ZSphere to the ZSphere at the center.

Occasionally while working with the ZSpheres, you may find that the entire tool suddenly shrinks or pops out of position. If this happens, don't panic. Press the a hotkey to go into polymesh Adaptive Skin Preview mode, and click the Move, Scale, or Rotate button on the left shelf (or Alt+click on a blank part of the canvas) to center the tool. Then click the a hotkey to convert back to ZSpheres. If this does not solve the problem, save your tool and restart ZBrush.

15. Repeat the process of creating and positioning snakes until you have eight large snakes coming from the top, back, and either side of the head. Be imaginative when you position the snakes. Have pairs of snakes twist around each other. Make a majority of the snakes face forward so that they appear to be attacking along with the Medusa (Figure 6.58).

    As you add new ZSpheres to the center ZSphere, don't worry about the exact position too much. The base of each snake will be hidden so the geometry need not be perfect.

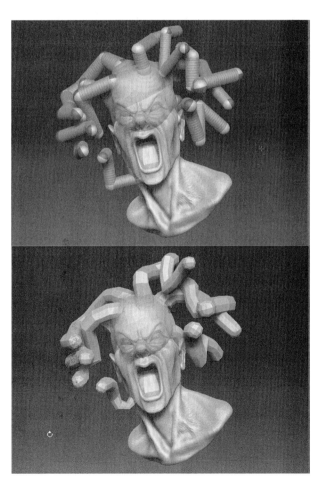

Figure 6.58

Eight snakes are created from the ZSphere tool.

16. When you are satisfied with the position of the snakes, add one more ZSphere to the end of each snake, and scale each one so that it is half the size of the ZSpheres in the chain. This will create a tapered end that will fit into the back of the snake heads (Figure 6.59).

17. When all eight snakes are in position, click the Make Adaptive button in the Adaptive Skin subpalette to create a mesh from the ZSpheres.

Figure 6.59

A small ZSphere is added to the end of each ZSphere chain.

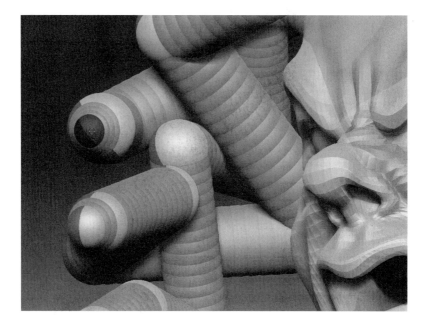

The spacing and number of shaded ZSpheres in a chain will determine the density of the mesh when it is converted to a Polymesh. This will also determine how much detail can be sculpted into the surface at higher subdivision levels. This doesn't mean you should make every ZSphere a shaded ZSphere, but keep in mind how much detail you intend to sculpt into your final Polymesh when you are spacing out the shaded ZSpheres in a chain.

18. Append the polymesh snakes to the head. You may delete the ZSphere subtool. However, you may want to clone it before deleting it and save the cloned version to your local disk drive in case you want to use it again.

19. Click the Divide button to add a subdivision to the snake subtool.

20. Use the Move, Inflate, and Smooth brushes to give the snakes a more serpentine look (Figure 6.60). ZSpheres create polygroups automatically; you can use the polygroups to isolate and mask individual snakes.

Figure 6.60

Use the sculpting brushes to give the snakes a more serpentine appearance.

The process of creating the snake head is fairly similar to making the Medusa head, with the exception that the snake head is not a human head. To see how the snake head is made, load the snakHead.mov movie and watch the entire process. A starter snake head tool is found in the Chapter 6 folder on the DVD. It is named snakHead_v1.ZTL. You can use it to create your own version of the snake head.

Creating Snake Fangs and Tongue

Creating fangs and a tongue for the snake is a simple exercise in ZSphere modeling. The same fangs and tongue will be saved out as separate objects so that they can be appended to the Medusa head as well.

1. Load the snakHead_v2.ZTL tool into a new ZBrush session. You can watch the snakeFangs.mov movie to see how the example file was created for this section.

2. In the Subtool subpalette, click the Append button and append a ZSphere to the snakeHead tool.

3. In the Transform palette, turn on the Active Symmetry button. Click the >X< and >M< buttons to make sure symmetry is mirrored across the x-axis. Even though a single fang is just a long pointy tube, you'll find that symmetry makes placing ZSpheres in a line much easier than if it would be if symmetry was off.

4. Click the Move button on the top shelf and position the ZSphere in front of the snake's head. Scale it down so that it is a little bigger than the snake's eye (Figure 6.61).

5. Turn off the visibility of the SnakeHead subtool.

6. Click the Draw button on the top shelf. Rotate the view so that you are looking at the ZSphere edge (hold the Shift key to snap to an orthographic view as you rotate). The dividing line between the two shaded halves should be horizontal. It doesn't matter if the darker or lighter side is on top (see Figure 6.62).

7. As you hold the brush over the ZSphere, you should see two red circular placement guides. If you see only one, you are most likely not facing the ZSphere on the proper axis; rotate the view of the ZSphere until you see two guides appear as you hold your brush over it, as shown in Figure 6.62.

8. Position the brush so that the two red circles are on top of each other at the center of the ZSphere. Drag across the ZSphere starting from this position. A new ZSphere will be added to the first; scale it up so that it is about the same size as the first (if you hold the Shift key as you add a new ZSphere, it will be drawn at the same size as the original).

9. Rotate the view to the opposite side of the original ZSphere, and repeat steps 6 and 7 to add another ZSphere on this side.

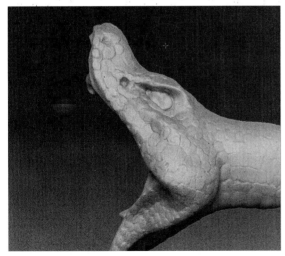

Figure 6.61

Position the ZSphere in front of the snake's head.

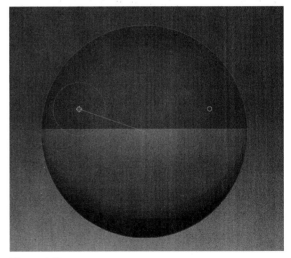

Figure 6.62

Using symmetry when adding ZSpheres makes positioning easier.

10. Press the a hotkey to see a preview of the three connected ZSpheres. It should look like Figure 6.63. If one of the ZSpheres is twisted, press the a hotkey to go back to the ZSphere view and rotate the ZSphere on the twisted end until the twisting is gone. This takes a little practice. Figure 6.63 shows the ideal ZSphere setup.

11. Once your ZSpheres are properly aligned, restore the visibility of the SnakHead sub-tool. Use the Move button on the top shelf to position the ZSpheres in front of the snake's mouth. There are two large bumps at the top of the snake's mouth; the final fangs will emerge from these bumps.

12. Add one more ZSphere to the chain and move it out a ways from the three original ZSpheres. Scale it down to a point.

13. From a side view, roughly position the ZSpheres so that they look like a fang. Use the A hotkey to test the position. Remember not to edit the adaptive skin mesh while in Preview mode; see Figure 6.64.

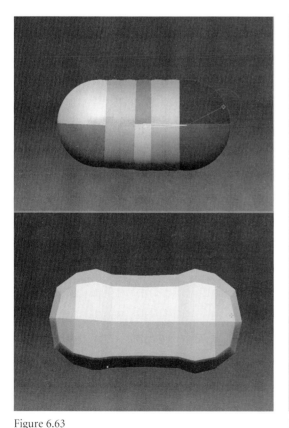

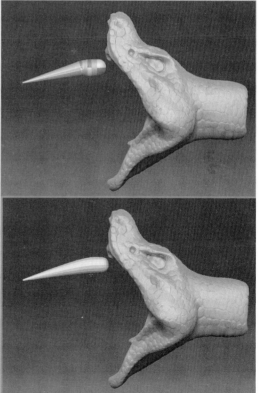

Figure 6.63

The ZSpheres are aligned. The adaptive preview shows no twisting between the ZSpheres.

Figure 6.64

The fang is positioned in front of the snake's head.

14. In the Adaptive Skin subpalette, set Density to 3 and turn the MC (Minimal Skin to Child) button on.

15. When you are happy that the fang is roughly in the right place, click the Make Adaptive Skin button in the Adaptive Skin subpalette.

16. Append the skin_fang tool to the SnakHead tool. Use the Rename button to name the subtool "Fang."

17. Make sure Active Symmetry in the Transform palette is off as you work with the Fang subtool. You can delete the ZSphere version of the fang and the SnakHead reference planes from the subtool palette.

18. Use the sculpting brushes to shape the fang into a tapered curving cone. The best way to do this is to use the Move brush to create the curving shape. Then to create the taper, use the Smooth and Inflate brushes with a very low Z intensity—somewhere around 5 should work.

19. Use the Transpose handle to scale, rotate, and move the fang into one of the holes in the snake's gum.

20. When you are happy with the fang's shape and position, follow the steps in the section on duplicating subtools to copy and mirror the fang to the other side of the snake's head (see Figure 6.65).

> To duplicate and mirror the fang, first set it to its highest SDiv level. Delete the lower subdivision levels and clone the Fang subtool using the Clone button in the Tool palette. Append the cloned fang as a new subtool, and then click on the Mirror button in the Deformation subpalette (make sure only the x-axis is activated on the Mirror button). Remember, subtools with multiple subdivision levels cannot be mirrored.

21. The snake's tongue is created using the same techniques as the fang; the only major difference is that the end of the tongue is branched. You create this split in the tongue by adding a symmetrical pair of ZSphere chains that branch out from the end. See Figure 6.66.

22. As a final touch, select the SnakHead subtool, then select the Snakehook brush from the Brush palette and set the Z intensity to 50. Use the brush to pull some very small teeth from the bottom of the snake's mouth. Make sure Symmetry is activated in the Draw palette. See Figure 6.67.

23. Save the tool as snakHead_v2.ZTL to your local drive.

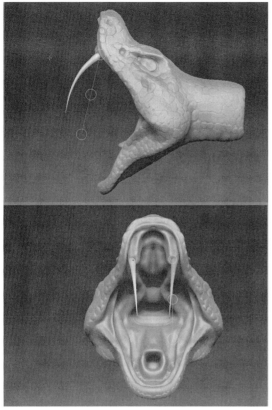

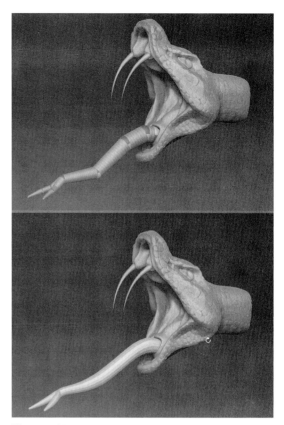

Figure 6.65
The fang is shaped and mirrored to the other side.

Figure 6.66
The snake's tongue is modeled the same way as the fang.

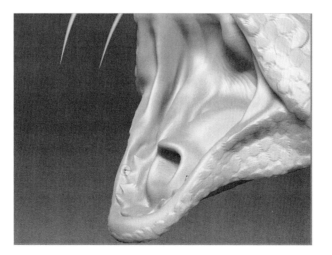

Figure 6.67
A small row of teeth is created on the lower jaw.

Combining Subtools into a Single Tool

The SnakeHead tool will be appended to the Medusa's head, but as it stands now, the snakeHead comprises several subtools. ZBrush will not allow a tool with subtools to be appended to another tool. To solve this problem, the snakeHead, fangs, and tongue will be combined into a single tool.

1. Load the snakedhead_v3.ZTL tool from the DVD or continue with the model from the previous section.

2. You'll want to use the fangs separately for the Medusa's head. Before combining the subtools, save the snakeHead tool as `fangs.ZTL`.

3. Click on each of the subtools in the model, make sure the highest SDiv level is active, and delete all of the lower subdivisions using the Del Lower button.

4. Select each subtool and click the Clone button to make a clone. These clones will appear in the Tool palette.

5. Once all of the clones have been made, open the tool inventory and select the cloned snakeHead. This tool should just be the snakeHead with no fangs or tongue subtools.

6. Click the Insert Mesh button in the Geometry subpalette of the Tool palette. From the inventory that pops up, select the first cloned fang tool. It will be added to the snake head as part of the mesh.

7. Repeat these steps for the other fang and tongue.

8. Save the tool as `snakHead_v4.ZTL`.

Adding the Snake Heads to the Medusa Tool

Adding the snakeHeads to the Medusa tool is a simple matter that takes a fair amount of work using the Transpose handle.

1. Load the snakHead_v4.ZTL tool into ZBrush.

2. Load the Medusa_v11.ZTL tool into ZBrush.

3. In the Subtool subpalette of the Medusa tool, click the Append button and select the snakHead_v4 tool to add it to Medusa. Use the Rename button in the SubTool palette to rename the subtool "snakeHead."

4. In the Subtool subpalette, select the snakeHead subtool. Use the Transpose handle to scale it down and position it at the end of one of the snakes coming from the Medusa's head (see Figure 6.68).

5. Use the Transpose handle to rotate it so that it faces the same direction as Medusa; the snakes on her head are all striking her victim at once.

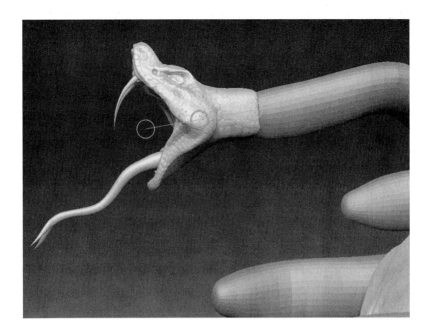

Figure 6.68

The snakeHead subtool is scaled and positioned in front of the end of a snake.

6. When you are happy with the placement of the snakeHead, switch to the Snake subtool. Click the Divide button in the Geometry subpalette to add another level of division.

7. To add another head, click the Clone button in the Tool palette, then add the cloned head using the Append button. The cloned head will appear at the same position as the original.

> Cloning the snake head saves time and labor as the clone will inherit the scaling and position of the original. This means you won't need to scale it down as you would if you had just appended another snakeHead tool.

8. Use the Transpose handle to position the cloned head at the end of another snake. Vary the size and rotation of the cloned heads.

9. Repeat steps 6 and 7 until you have a head at the end of each of the eight snakes (Figure 6.69). In Chapter 7 you'll remove the gap between the snakeHead and the snake body.

10. Remember, each snake body has an associated polygroup; you can easily isolate the snake bodies as you work to add each head.

11. Save the tool as `medusa_v12.ZTL`. Watch the `medusa_part12.mov` movie to see how the example scene was created.

Figure 6.69

The snakeHeads
have been cloned
and positioned so
that all eight snakes
have a head.

Adding Medusa's Fangs

One of the clear advantages digital tools have over their analog counterparts is that they can be effortlessly duplicated and reused. Rather than sculpt new fangs and a tongue for the Medusa, we can save time by reusing the ones created for her snakey friends.

1. Load the snakHead_part3.ZTL tool into ZBrush.

2. In the Subtool palette, select the snakeHead subtool and delete it.

3. Use the steps in the section "Combining Subtools into a Single Tool" to create a tool consisting of just the fangs and tongue (see Figure 6.70).

4. Save this tool as fangs.ZTL.

5. Load the medusa_9.ZTL tool into ZBrush. You'll use the version that was created before her head was posed to make modeling the interior of the mouth easier.

6. To create the interior of the Medusa's mouth, select the Medusa's head and click the Clone button to make a clone.

7. In the Tool palette's inventory, select the cloned head.

8. Make sure to Ctrl+Shift+click on the geometry inside the mouth to isolate the mouth polygroup. Use the marquee selection tool to hide any other parts of the geometry that are not part of the mouth (Figure 6.71).

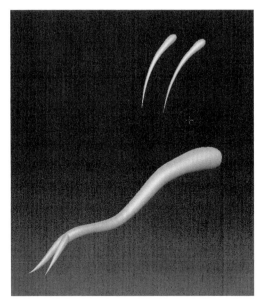

Figure 6.70

The fangs and tongue have been combined into a single tool.

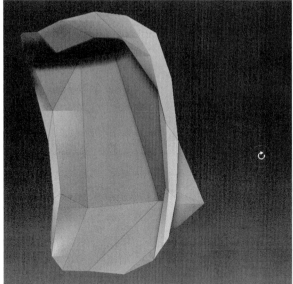

Figure 6.71

Isolate the geometry of the inside of the mouth.

9.   Move the SDiv slider down to level 2.

10. Make sure Pt Sel is activated in the Transform palette. Use the selection marquee (activating the Lasso button on the right shelf might make this easier) to hide the outer ring of polygons that form the lips.

11. Move the SDiv slider to level 5. Click the Del Lower button to remove the lower subdivision levels.

12. Click the Delete Hidden button to delete everything except the mouth.

13. Click the Divide button twice to add two levels of subdivision to the mouth interior.

14. Save the tool as `mouthInterior.ZTL`.

15. Turn on Symmetry in the Transform palette.

16. Append the fangs.ZTL tool. Use the Transpose handle to scale and position the fangs and tongue roughly so they match the mouth. You may need to mask parts of the tool to move the fangs separately from the tongue (Figure 6.72).

17. When the fangs and tongue are in position, switch to the MouthInterior subtool. Use the sculpting brushes to create the openings for the fangs and tongue. Use Figure 6.73 as a reference. An image search using an Internet search engine should turn up some good references as well. (The interior of a venomous snake differs from a nonvenomous one. Keep this in mind as you choose your references; consult your local herpetologist.)

Figure 6.72

The fangs are appended to the mouth interior as a subtool.

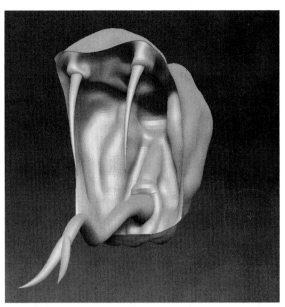

Figure 6.73

The inside of the mouth is sculpted to accommodate the fangs and tongue.

18. When you are happy with how the mouth interior looks, use the steps in the section "Combining Subtools into a Single Tool" to create a tool consisting of the mouth interior, the fangs, and tongue.

> If part of the tool turns black when you use the Insert Mesh button to combine subtools, don't panic. It's very easy to fix. Make sure the combined mesh is selected in the Subtool palette, set the color picker to white, and make sure the Colorize button in the Texture subpalette of the Tool palette is activated. On the top shelf, activate the RGB button (MRGB and M buttons should be off). Go to the Color palette and click Fill Object. The object is filled with a white color and should match the rest of the tool.

19. Save the tool as mouthInterior.ZTL.

20. Load the medusa_v12.ZTL tool into ZBrush. Append the mouthInterior.ZTL tool.

21. Use the Transpose handle to position the mouth interior inside the Medusa's mouth. You will want to use the Standard brush to push some of the geometry inside the Medusa's mouth back so that the mouth interior fits well (Figure 6.74). The easiest way to do this is to hide all of the geometry except for the mouth (remember, the

mouth interior is a polygroup, so you can isolate it by Ctrl+Shift+clicking on the geometry in the mouth), then use the Standard brush to paint the mouth from behind. Turn on the visibility of the appended mouthInterior subtool and use it as a guide. This is shown in the `medusa_part14.mov` movie.

22. Save the tool as `medusa_v13.ZTL`.

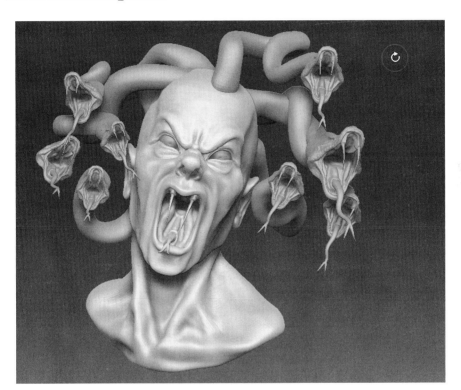

Figure 6.74

The mouth is added to the Medusa model.

Finishing Touches

You have finished the bulk of the sculpting work on the forms of the Medusa and her snakey friends. To add some extra drama, you'll add smaller worms to the head.

1. Load the Medusa_v13.ZTL file from the Chapter 6 folder of the DVD or continue with the tool from the last section.

2. Take some time to make some adjustments to the model as a whole. Create variations in the shapes of the tongues coming from the snakeHeads. Use Masking and Transpose tools to vary the amount each snake's mouth is open (Figure 6.75).

3. Select the head subtool and add another level of subdivision to the head.

4. Select the Snakehook tool. Set the Z intensity to 100.

5. Use the tool to draw out some snakey, wormy shapes from the skull; do this close to the base of each of the larger snakes. Vary the draw size as you work to add variety to the size of the worms. Be careful not to stretch the geometry too far using the Snakehook brush and avoid shearing of the polygons if you can (Figure 6.76).

Figure 6.75

Adjust the mouths of the snakes using the Transpose handle on unmasked portions of the snake's heads.

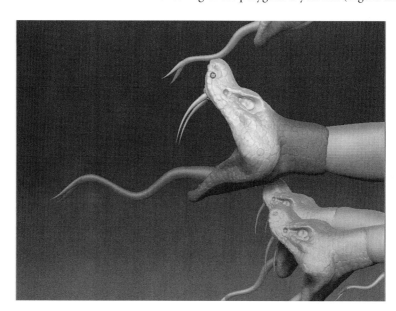

Figure 6.76

The Snakehook brush is used to pull wormlike shapes from the Medusa's skin.

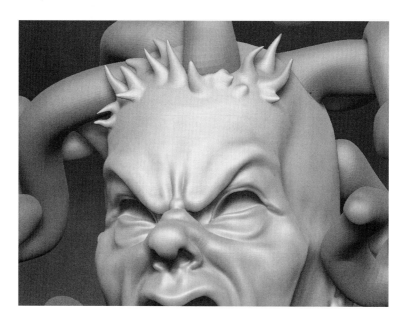

6. Pull a few snakes out from Medusa's face. Use the sculpting brushes to add heads, or parasitic orifices, to these snakes. Imagine that Medusa has worms crawling just beneath the surface of her skin—use the Inflate brush to create squiggly lines that connect to the worms created with the Snakehook brush. The Smooth brush will help you connect these shapes.

7. When you've added enough snakes to the head, save the tool as `medusa_part14.ZTL` (Figure 6.77).

8. Watch the `medusa_part14.mov` movie to see how the example file was created.

Figure 6.77

The Medusa is looking pretty mean.

Summary

Congratulations. You've completed a rather rigorous exercise in ZBrush sculpting. In this chapter you explored more advanced sculpting techniques, such as ZSpheres, subtools, masking, polygroups, and the Transpose handle. In the second half of Chapter 7 you'll finish the Medusa sculpture by adding scales to her face and the snakes on her head using alpha textures as a sculpting tool. You'll close the gap between the snake bodies and their heads and give the old girl a makeover using polypainting techniques.

This exercise should give you a taste of how to create an advanced sculpture in ZBrush. If it has been a challenge for you, that's good, there's no better way to learn. The main goal of these exercises is to get you familiar with a typical ZBrush workflow so that you can go on to make your own creations in your own style. If your Medusa does not look exactly like the one in the example, don't worry, you have plenty of time to perfect your techniques once you have the basic workflow down. If your Medusa looks better than the one in the example, post it on www.zbrushcentral.com.

CHAPTER 7

Color, Texture, and Alpha

The concepts of color, texture, and alpha as they are used in ZBrush can be a bit confusing to new users, mainly because all three are related and can be used in similar ways. In this chapter, you'll learn how each can be used to add detail to the Medusa maquette, but of course there are myriad more ways to use color, alpha, and texture that you can explore and invent once you have a handle on how they work.

This chapter includes the following topics:

- Color, texture, and alpha
- 3D layers
- Creating tiling textures
- Stencils
- Detailing the Medusa maquette
- Polypainting and cavity masking

Understanding Color, Alpha, and Texture

Color in ZBrush is quite simply a red, green, and blue (RGB) value that can be applied to the canvas or a 3D tool. As explained in Chapter 1, a computer displays color by mixing varying amounts of the colors red, green, and blue. The color you apply to the canvas or to a tool is determined by what RGB value is currently selected in the color picker. The color picker is located on the left shelf (see Figure 7.1). You can choose the hue of the color by picking a point within the outer square. The inner square allows you to choose the value and saturation of the color. You can drag from within the square to select any color on the canvas or the ZBrush interface. Another way to select a color is to press the c hotkey while holding the brush over replace with any color in the interface or on the canvas you want to select.

Figure 7.1

The color picker

Beneath the color picker are two rectangles. The large rectangle on the right shows the currently selected color; the smaller rectangle on the left stores a secondary color. You can switch between these colors at any time using the Switch button. To select a color to store as your secondary color, click on the smaller rectangle first, and then select the color from the color picker.

Color is easily confused with texture since both are ways to apply colors to the canvas or a 3D tool. A texture is a color 2D image, usually square in shape. When you expand the texture inventory, you see the standard textures that are loaded by default when you start up ZBrush (Figure 7.2). Textures can be created in other paint programs, such as Photoshop, and imported into ZBrush. You can also generate textures in ZBrush from the pixols on the canvas or from the colors applied to a tool. Textures can be exported from ZBrush for use on 3D models in other 3D applications such as Maya, 3ds Max, LightWave, and XSI. This is actually the most common use of textures in ZBrush and you'll learn about this technique in Chapter 9.

Figure 7.2

The texture inventory in ZBrush

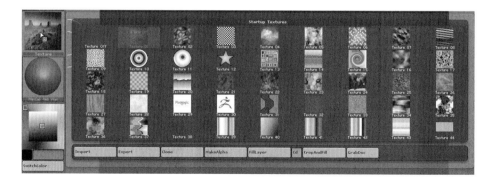

Alphas are similar to textures in that alphas are two-dimensional image files that can be created in paint programs and imported into ZBrush. Just like textures, alphas can be created from the pixols on the canvas. An alpha is essentially a grayscale texture. It has no color information. The alphas in the alpha inventory are loaded by default when you start up ZBrush (Figure 7.3). Alphas are most commonly used to modify the 3D sculpting brushes. They can also be used as stencils for detailing 3D tools. Both uses will be explored in this chapter.

> If you use Photoshop or another program to create an alpha, save the image as a Photoshop format file (.psd) for best results.

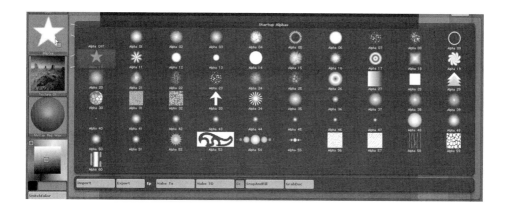

Figure 7.3
The alpha inventory

Working with Color, Alphas, and Textures

Follow this short exercise to get a quick understanding of how color, textures, and alphas are used in ZBrush.

1. Start up ZBrush, and click on the Load Tool button in the Tool palette. Browse your computer and choose the PolySphere.ZTL file from the Program Files\ZBrush3\ZTools folder. Draw the tool on the canvas and switch to Edit mode (Ctrl+t).

> The PolySphere tool on the startup screen is not the same thing as the Sphere 3D tool in the tool inventory. The Sphere 3D tool is a parametric 3D object; the PolySphere is a polymesh tool, and the geometry of the PolySphere is organized in a different manner than it is in the sphere3D tool. For more information on the difference between these tools, refer to Chapter 3.

2. From the Material palette, choose the Fast Shader material. Some materials have a built-in color, which can affect how colors and textures are seen on the object. The Fast Shader does not, so it's a good choice to use when working with color. Materials are discussed in-depth in Chapter 8.

3. Select a bright yellow color from the color picker. The sphere turns yellow. Change the color to orange and you'll see the sphere's color change to orange. If the color does not change, make sure there is no texture selected in the texture inventory. Also make sure that the large rectangle beneath the color picker is active, otherwise you're changing the RGB value of the secondary color and thus the polysphere's color will not update.

> No doubt you have noticed that the images in this book are in black and white, which can be vexing, particularly when the chapter is focused on color. A movie (color.mov) of this section is included in the Chapter 7 folder of the DVD so that you can see how the colors should actually look on the screen.

4. From the texture inventory, choose the image of the desert scene (Texture01). The color on the polysphere is replaced by the image (Figure 7.4).
5. Switch back to Texture Off. In the Tool palette's Texture subpalette, click the Colorize button (Figure 7.5). The Polysphere turns white.
6. Choose the Standard brush from the brush inventory. On the top shelf, turn off the ZAdd button and set Rgb Intensity to 100.

Figure 7.4

The Polysphere with a texture applied

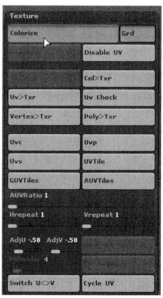

Figure 7.5

The Colorize button allows you to paint directly on 3D tools.

7. Paint on the surface of the PolySphere. The current color appears on the surface. This is known as *polypainting*. Each polygon vertex of the polymesh is being colored by the Standard brush. Change the color in the color picker and paint some more. The Grd button in the Texture subpalette smooths the painted strokes by blending the colors between adjacent polygons. If you deactivate this button, the paint strokes will appear blocky.

> Polypainting will not work on parametric 3D tools. You'll need to convert a parametric 3D tool into a polymesh by clicking on the Make PolyMesh 3D button in the Tool palette before you can paint on the surface of the tool. If you're using the Polysphere object (not the Sphere 3D object), you should be fine.

8. In the Geometry subpalette of the Tool palette, set the SDiv slider to 1. Notice that the smoothness of the painted strokes is affected by the number of polygons at the current subdivision level (Figure 7.6).

9. Paint some more strokes at SDiv level 1 and then move the slider back up to 3. The strokes painted at a lower subdivision level appear more blocky (Figure 7.7). When polypainting a 3D tool, it's always best to paint at the highest subdivision of the tool.

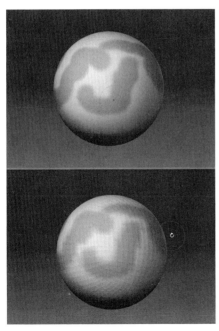

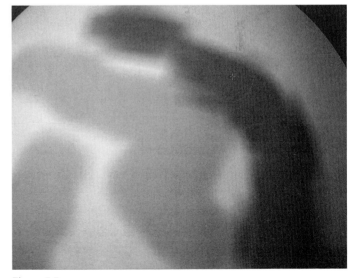

Figure 7.6

Colors are painted on the polysphere. The color will appear blocky at lower subdivisions.

Figure 7.7

Colors painted at lower subdivision levels will appear blocky when the 3D tool is at a higher subdivision.

10. Set the Rgb intensity on the top shelf to 4, select a new color from the Color picker, and paint some strokes. The opacity of the color is lower.

11. In the texture inventory, choose the star texture (Texture 12). Notice that parts of the polysphere appear transparent (Figure 7.8). If you try to paint a color on the polysphere, it will not show up; the color is being overridden by the texture.

12. Set the Rgb slider on the top shelf to 100. In the Texture subpalette of the Tool palette, click the Txr>Col button (Figure 7.9). The transparent parts of the texture turn black.

13. Paint some strokes on the polysphere. The texture has been converted to a color. Now any strokes you paint on the sphere will show up.

14. From the alpha inventory, select the star shape (Alpha 10). From the stroke inventory, select the DragRect stroke. Drag on the surface of the Polysphere. A star appears as you drag. It is colored using the currently selected color. The star shape is determined by the current alpha. As you drag, the star scales upward and rotates. Letting go will cause the star to be applied to the polysphere (Figure 7.10).

Figure 7.8

The Star texture makes parts of the polysphere appear transparent.

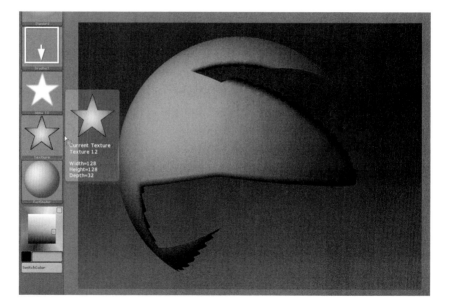

Figure 7.9

Use the Txr>Col button to convert a texture to a color.

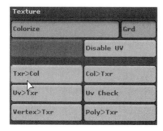

Figure 7.10

The star alpha allows you to paint stars on the poly- sphere.

15. Drag the brush from the color picker to different parts of the PolySphere. The current color is determined by the position of the brush on the polysphere when you let go.

16. In the Texture subpalette of the Tool palette, click the Col>Txr button. The current color is now converted to a texture that can be exported from ZBrush (Figure 7.11). Notice the cross shape of the texture. This is due to how the UV texture coordinates have been applied to the Polysphere. UV texture coordinates are discussed in Chapter 10.

Figure 7.11

The color can be converted to a tex- ture using the Col>Txr button.

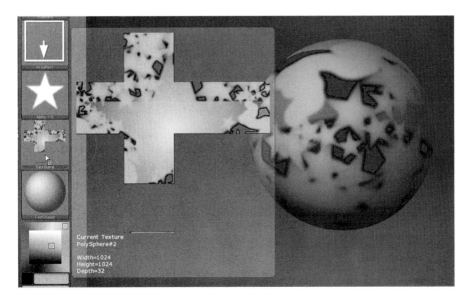

Experiment some more with these techniques. When you feel you have a basic understanding of how color, textures, and alphas work, you can move on to the next sections, which introduce more advanced uses of alphas.

3D Layers

3D layers should not be confused with document layers. They are completely different and unrelated. Document layers are discussed in Chapter 3 and are analogous to layers in a paint program such as Photoshop or Painter. 3D layers are only used with 3D polymesh tools.

The 3D layer subpalette (labeled Layers) is located in the Geometry palette (see Figure 7.12) and is similar in design to the SubTool subpalette. However, 3D layers serve a different purpose than subtools. You can think of a 3D layer as a container that holds whatever changes you make to a 3D polymesh tool. When you add a new 3D layer to a 3D polymesh tool, any changes you make to the tool while the layer is selected can be instantly removed by turning off the visibility of the 3D layer. The changes still exist but they are invisible as long as the 3D layer's visibility is turned off. They can be removed permanently if you decide you don't like them, or they can be made a part of a 3D polymesh tool. Furthermore, the intensity of the 3D layer can be adjusted and you can add as many 3D layers as you like to a 3D polymesh tool, each containing its own changes to the tool. This means you can use 3D layers to create a nonlinear sculpting workflow. In addition to having the Undo command to remove a change, you can store changes in 3D layers and remove them at any point while you create your sculpture, so you can add changes and decide later on whether you want to keep them or not. 3D layers work best for small changes and fine details. Large changes made with the Transpose handle can distort the tool and behave somewhat unpredictably. It's a good practice to use 3D layers once the basic shape of the model has been established.

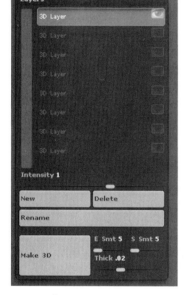

Figure 7.12

The 3D layer subpalette, in the Geometry palette, is simply labeled *Layers*.

The following exercise takes you through the process of using 3D layers. Later on in this chapter, you'll use 3D layers to add detail to the Medusa maquette.

1. Start up ZBrush, click on the Load Tool button in the Tool palette. Browse your computer and choose the Rhino.ZTL file from the Program Files\ZBrush3\ZTools folder. Draw the tool on the canvas and switch to Edit mode (Ctrl+t).

2. Expand the Geometry subpalette and click the Divide button three times to add three levels of subdivisions to the Rhino tool. Make sure the SDiv slider is on level 4.

3. Expand the 3D layers subpalette above the Geometry subpalette. Click the New button to add a 3D layer. You'll notice no change to the Rhino tool.

4. Click the Rename button in the 3D layer subpalette. Type **scars** in the layer title field (see Figure 7.13).

5. From the brush inventory, choose the Slash 2 brush. Set the draw size to 10 and the Z intensity to 50. In the top shelf, click the ZSub button. This will cause the brush to carve into the tool rather than raise a bump.

6. Zoom in so that the side of the Rhino fills the canvas, as shown in Figure 7.14. Draw six or seven scars on the side of the Rhino.

7. In the 3D layer palette, click on the eyeball icon to turn the visibility of the layer off. The scars disappear. Click on the eyeball icon again to turn the visibility back on. The scars return.

8. Notice that the Intensity slider at the bottom of the 3D layer palette is set to 1. Set it to 0. The scars disappear again. Set it to 0.1 and the scars reappear at 1/10 their original intensity (see the lower image in Figure 7.14).

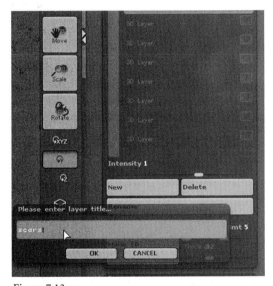

Figure 7.13

A new 3D layer is created and named scars.

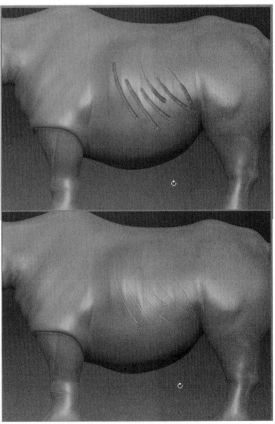

Figure 7.14

Draw scars on the side of the Rhino using the Slash 2 brush. Lowering the intensity of the 3D layer makes the scars less deep, as shown in the lower image.

Intensity settings above 1 will exaggerate the scars; negative values will reverse the direction of the scars, pushing the geometry out from the surface as opposed to digging in.

Clicking the Delete button at the bottom of the 3D layer subpalette will commit the changes to the tool. The layer will be gone, but all the changes made to the model will persist. If you'd like to remove the layer as well as the changes, set the intensity of the 3D layer to 0 and then click the Delete button in the 3D layer subpalette.

When you set the SDiv slider to a lower setting in the Geometry subpalette, the layer controls will become unavailable; however, the changes will remain. If you turn the layer's visibility off before moving the SDiv slider down, the changes will be invisible at lower SDiv levels.

Adding another level of subdivision while using layers can cause some strange behavior. If you move to a higher SDiv value with a layer visible, the changes will persist at the higher level and become subdivided with the model. If you then move back down to the SDiv level where the layer was created and turn the layer off, you may see a faint trace of the layer remain in the model even with the layer off. The only way to remove this is to use the Smooth brush. It's a good idea to either only use 3D layers at the highest level of subdivision or commit the changes made in the model using the Delete button in the Layer subpalette before adding another level of subdivision.

9. Set the intensity of the scar layer to 1 and make sure it is visible. Make sure the SDiv slider is at level 4. Click the New button in the 3D layer subpalette to add another layer. Click the Rename button and name this layer **bulges**.

10. Select the Blob brush, and set the intensity to 20 and the draw size to 30. Make sure the ZAdd button is activated on the top shelf.

11. With the bulges layer selected in the Layer subpalette, create some bulges on the surface of the Rhino using the Blob brush. Make sure some of the bulges are drawn on top of the scars (Figure 7.15).

12. Experiment alternating the visibility of the two layers to see how they work together. In some cases, the layers are not independent of each other. If you turn off the visibility of the scar layer, you may see traces of the scars in the bulge layer. To avoid this, you can try making changes in one layer while the visibility of the other layers is off and then restore the visibility of the other layers. It depends on what you are trying to achieve.

13. Create a third new layer, and name the new layer **large bulges**.

14. Turn off the visibility of the scars and bulges layers.

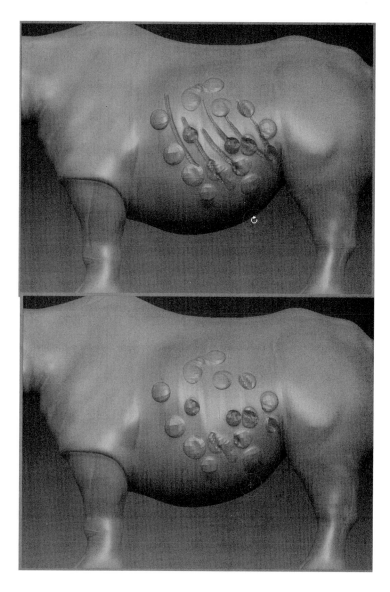

15. Select the Inflate brush from the brush inventory. Set the draw size to 25 and the Z intensity to 50.

16. Use the brush to create large bulges in the side of the Rhino.

17. With the large bulges layer selected, click the Make 3D button at the bottom of the Layers subpalette. This will create a subtool based on the difference between the original base mesh and the mesh in the 3D layer (Figure 7.16).

The thick slider at the bottom of the Layer subpalette adjusts the thickness of the subtool. The E Smt slider adjusts the edge smoothness of the subtool and the S Smt slider adjusts the smoothness of the subtool's surface. These sliders need to be set before creating a subtool from a layer using the Make 3D button (Figure 7.17).

The thickness and smooth settings will affect only the next subtool created. In most cases, you'll need to experiment with these settings to get the look that you want. If you click the Make 3D button and nothing happens, this means that the difference between the base mesh and the edits in the layer is not large enough for ZBrush to calculate properly.

18. To remove the new subtool, use the Delete button in the subtool subpalette. The Undo button will not remove the newly created subtool.

Creating subtools using layers is a great way to create armor and clothing for characters.

Figure 7.16

The difference between the layer and the base mesh is converted into a 3D subtool.

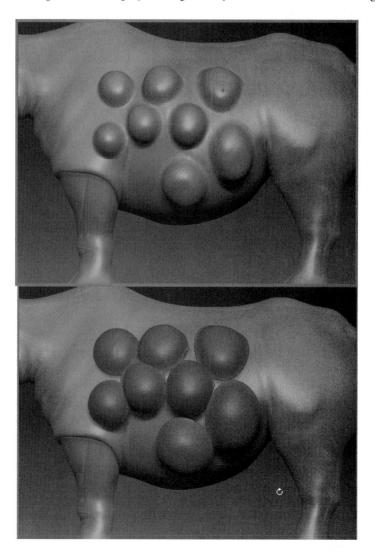

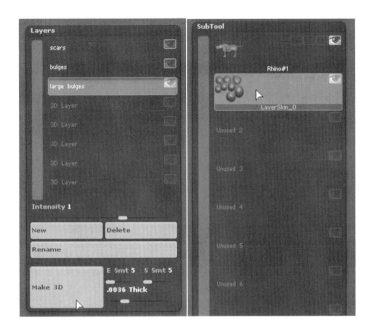

Figure 7.17
The Make 3D button converts the layer into a subtool.

You can use a similar technique to create a subtool from a mask painted on the surface of a polymesh. To do this, paint a mask on the surface of the polymesh (hold the Ctrl key while painting) and then click the Extract button at the bottom of the SubTool subpalette. You'll notice that E Smt, S Smt, and Thick sliders sit at the bottom of the SubTool subpalette. These work the same way as the buttons in the 3D layer palette (note that the 3D layer subpalette is simply labeled "Layer"), except that they adjust the smoothness and thickness of subtools created from masks using the Extract button in the SubTool subpalette.

Creating Tiling Alphas

There are a lot of ways alphas can be used for creating fine details. There are also many ways to create the alphas themselves. Along with the standard alphas located in the alpha inventory, you can import alphas created in paint programs such as Photoshop and Painter. ZBrush ships with a few example alphas from the Gnomon Alpha library. These are located in the `Program Files\Pixologic\ZBrush3\Gnomon Alpha Library` directory.

In this section you'll learn how to make a custom tiling alpha directly in ZBrush. The alpha will represent a common pattern of a snake's scales, which will be used later in the chapter on the Medusa maquette. A tiling alpha is one that repeats evenly on all four sides so that as the alpha is repeated; the seams where one repetition ends and the next repetition begins are not easily detectable.

1. Start a new, blank ZBrush document.

2. In the Document palette, turn off the Pro button to disable proportional scaling of the canvas size.

3. Set the canvas horizontal and vertical size to 1024 × 1024 and click the Resize button to resize the canvas (Figure 7.18).

4. In the Tool palette, click the Load Tool button. Locate the PolySphere tool in the `Program Files\Pixologic\ZBrush3\ZTools` directory. Load it into ZBrush.

5. Draw the polysphere on the canvas and switch to Edit mode (Ctrl + T).

   Typically, snake scales often appear as rounded, elongated diamonds. To create the alpha, you will fill the canvas with a repeating pattern of diamonds created from the polysphere. Follow the next steps to learn how to do this.

6. Set the SDiv slider in the Geometry palette to 1.

7. Rotate the polysphere while holding the Shift key so that it snaps to an orthographic view.

8. Activate the Move button on the top shelf to turn on the Transpose handle in Move mode.

9. Draw the Transpose handle down the center of the polysphere. Grab the control at the top of the action line and hold the Shift key as you drag it downward in a straight line. This will flatten the polysphere into a disc.

10. Activate the Draw button on the top shelf to turn off the Transpose handle. Rotate the polysphere while holding the Shift key to snap it into a position where the flat portion of the tool is facing the camera.

11. In the Transform palette, click the Activate Symmetry button. Click the >Y< and >Z< buttons as well as the >M< button. This will mirror symmetry across the x- and z-axes. Select the Move brush from the Brush palette. As you hover the cursor over the PolySphere, you should see four red dots indicating the position of the brush. If you don't, try a different combination of symmetry axes in the Transform palette, maybe >X< and >Z< or >Y< and >X< (see Figure 7.19).

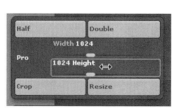

Figure 7.18

Resize the document using the settings in the Document palette.

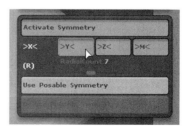

Figure 7.19

The symmetry settings in the Transform Palette.

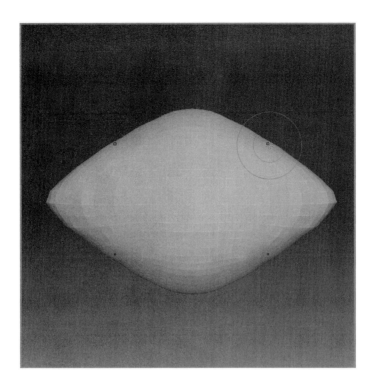

Figure 7.20

**The typical snake
scale looks like a
rounded diamond
shape.**

12. Use the Move brush to create a rounded diamond shape. See Figure 7.20 for an example.

13. Once you have a diamond shape, use the Save As button in the Tool palette and save the tool to your local disk as snakeScale.ZTL.

14. Turn the Activate Symmetry button in the Transform palette off. To create the tiling texture, scale the PolySphere down to about one-third the width of the screen and place it in the bottom-left corner of the screen.

15. Turn off the Edit button on the top shelf and turn on the Move button to activate the gyro. If you have not used the gyro, you should read "Using the Transformation Gyro in Draw Mode" in Chapter 2 for a quick review. The gyro is used extensively in Chapters 3 and 4 as well.

16. Make a snapshot of the PolySphere by clicking on the camera icon in the Transform palette (hotkey = Shift+s). Use the gyro to move the snapshot copy to the right of the first PolySphere (remember to drag the gyro by the outer ring; don't click on the center of the gyro or the rotation will change). Position the copy so that the two Poly-Spheres are almost touching at one end (Figure 7.21).

Figure 7.21

Move the snapshot of the PolySphere to the right of the original. Using the Gyro, fill the canvas with an overlapping pattern of diamond shaped scales.

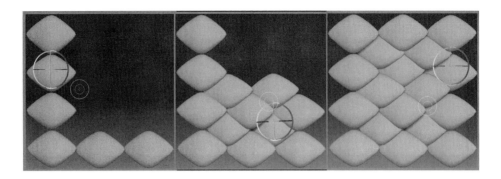

17. Use the snapshot and gyro to create a line of three polysphere diamonds that stretch across the screen. Then position a polysphere above the first polysphere (in the y-axis, not the z-axis). Make a column of polysphere diamonds that spans the y-axis of the screen; it should take four polyspheres to do this. Don't let any part of the polyspheres move off the screen. If you need to scale the last polysphere a little to fit it on the screen, that's okay. A little variation in the size of the polyspheres is fine—in fact, it will make the scales look more organic and natural.

Arranging the polyspheres in this pattern will take some trial and error to get the size just right. The undo action will not work while you're using the gyro control. To redo the action, you'll need to clear all the dropped polysphere diamonds from the canvas (Ctrl+n), scale the initial polysphere diamond, reposition, and try again. Be patient as you do this. Mastering the gyro is the most difficult challenge you will face while using ZBrush. Have faith that you will actually get the hang of it after some practice!

18. Continue placing snapshots of the polysphere in a pattern on the canvas. Fit the diamond shapes together but leave a slight gap between each copy. You may want to vary the size, rotation, and Z position of each snapshot a little. Use the gyro in Scale, Rotate, or Move mode to achieve this. Make sure none of the snapshots are off the screen.

19. When you reach a point where you can't fit any more polyspheres on the canvas without having part of a polysphere cut off by the edge of the canvas, activate the Draw button on the top shelf. Hold the tilde (~) key on the upper left of the keyboard (below the Esc key on most keyboards) and drag on the screen. You'll see the entire pattern of diamond polyspheres shift in the direction of the drag. The polysphere diamonds on either side will be repeated on the opposite side, likewise with the top and bottom (Figure 7.22).

20. Position the pattern so that any large gaps between the diamonds are centered on the screen. Draw a new polysphere diamond and scale it so that it fits within one of the spaces in the gap. Scale it so that it is about the size of the other polysphere diamonds.

21. Use the snapshot and gyro to place copies of the polysphere in the gaps.

22. You may need to move the pattern around to finish filling in all of the gaps; repeat steps 19 through 21 to do this. The finished pattern will repeat perfectly as any parts of the polyspheres that are off the sides of the canvas are completed on the opposite side.

23. Once the entire canvas is covered in a repeating pattern of diamond-shaped polyspheres, save the document using the Save As button in the Document palette (not the Tool palette). Save the document as snakeScalePattern.ZBR to a directory on your local disk.

24. In the Alpha palette, click the GrabDoc button at the bottom of the palette (Figure 7.23). This will create a new alpha by taking a snapshot of the depth information on the canvas.

25. The new alpha will be stored in the Alpha palette and inventory (Figure 7.24). Select the new alpha in the inventory and use the Export button at the bottom of the inventory to save the alpha to a directory on your local disk as snakeScale. You can save it as a PSD, TIFF, JPEG, or BMP—whichever format you prefer. PSD is usually a good choice since the image will not be compressed when saved.

26. To see a movie that goes through the process of creating the repeating pattern, load the tilingAlpha.mov file from the Chapter 7 folder of the DVD. The finished snakeScale.PSD alpha can also be found here.

Figure 7.22

The pattern on the canvas is moved so that each side, top, and bottom will repeat when the pattern is completed.

If you want to capture just a small section of the canvas as an alpha, you can use the MRGBZ-Grabber tool. It is located in the 2.5D brush section of the Tool palette. It will create an alpha as well as a texture based on the selected portion of the screen.

Figure 7.23

The GrabDoc button in the Alpha palette

Figure 7.24

A new alpha has been created and added to the alpha inventory based on the snake scale pattern on the canvas.

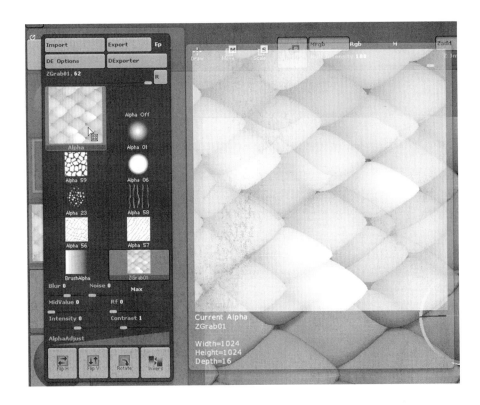

Using the Stencil

The alphas you create can be used with any of the sculpting brushes. In addition to this, you can create a stencil from an alpha. A stencil can be thought of as a moveable mask. In some cases, a stencil can allow for the most precise positioning of the pattern created by the alpha.

1. In the Preferences, click Init ZBrush to clear the canvas and start a new document.

2. Your custom alpha should still be available in the alpha inventory. If it's not, use the Load button at the bottom of the alpha inventory, or in the Alpha palette, and load the snakeScale.PSD alpha that you created in the previous section, or load the `snakeScale.psd` file from the Chapter 7 folder of the DVD.

3. In the Tool palette, select the Sphere 3D tool and draw it on the canvas.

4. Click the Edit button on the top shelf to switch to Edit mode (hotkey = Ctrl+t).

5. In the Tool palette, click the Make Polymesh 3D button to convert the sphere to a polymesh tool.

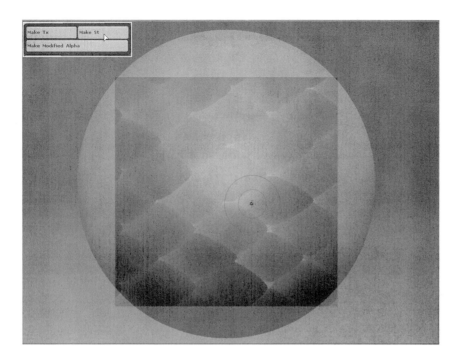

Figure 7.25

The Make St button in the Alpha palette (inset) makes a stencil from the current Alpha.

6. In the Geometry palette, click the Divide button three times to add three levels of subdivision; make sure the SDiv slider is at the highest level.

7. In the Alpha palette, select the snakeScale alpha.

8. Click the Make St button in the Alpha palette. You'll see a transparent version of the alpha appear above the sphere tool in the canvas (Figure 7.25).

9. In the Stencil palette, set Alpha Repeat to 3. This repeats the alpha pattern with the area of the stencil. Since the snake scale stencil tiles seamlessly, the repeating pattern is not as detectable.

10. Turn the Wrap Mode button on in the Stencil palette. This wraps the stencil around the surface of a 3D tool (Figure 7.26). The Res slider controls the resolution of the wrapping effect. The default value of 64 should be fine.

11. Zoom in on the sphere a little and notice that the size of the stencil does not change with the tool. If you want to keep the stencil pattern consistent, you should be careful not to zoom in while applying the stencil.

12. Choose the Standard brush from the Brush palette. Make sure Alpha Off is selected from the alpha inventory. Set the intensity to 5 and the draw size to 60.

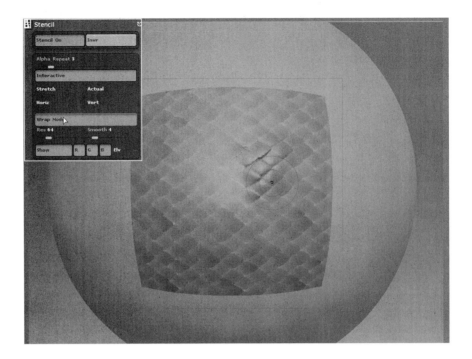

13. Paint a few strokes across the surface of the sphere; the brush is applied through the snakeScale pattern so the snake scales appear to rise from the surface of the sphere. The lighter parts of the pattern mask the brush stroke more than the darker parts.

> When the Grab Doc command is used, the pixols on the canvas are converted into an alpha using the Z-depth information embedded in the pixol. Pixols that are farther away from the front of the canvas appear darker in the captured alpha.

14. Hold the spacebar down. You'll see the stencil's Coin Controller appear (not another control!). The Coin Controller helps you position the stencil while you sculpt. Click on the bottom of the controller on the Mov label and drag. The stencil moves across the surface of the sphere.

15. To scale the stencil, drag on the right side of the coin on the Scl label. Dragging on the H or V on the right side will nonproportionally scale the stencil horizontally and vertically.

16. To freely rotate the stencil, drag on the Rot label on the left side of the Coin Controller. Dragging on the Z label will rotate the stencil around the stencil's normal, and dragging on the S label will rotate the stencil around the canvas normal. The pivot of the stencil is determined by the position of the brush on the canvas when the Coin Controller is first invoked by the spacebar.

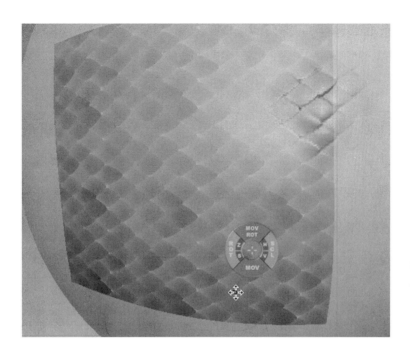

Figure 7.27

The Coin Controller allows you to reposition the stencil.

17. Dragging on the Mov Rot label at the top of the stencil moves and rotates the label at the same time using whatever is below the stencil as its center point (Figure 7.27). If you want to restore the rotation of the stencil so that it is parallel with the canvas, drag the stencil to a blank spot on the canvas by the top of the Coin Controller on the Mov Rot label.

> You can move, rotate, and scale the 3D tool while the stencil is active so you can move either the stencil around or the 3D tool or both, whichever works best for you. If you scale the 3D tool while the stencil is active, you can use the Coin Controller to reposition and scale the stencil based on the pattern you have sculpted into the surface.

18. Click Undo a few times to remove any changes you made to the sphere tool while experimenting with the Coin Controller. Position the snakeScale stencil over the sphere and paint a few strokes to add some scales to the sphere. Avoid painting along the edges of the stencil.

19. Use the Coin Controller to reposition the stencil so that it overlaps the edge of the sculpted surface. Use the shape of the scales to line the stencil up in such a way that the pattern will continue to repeat.

20. Paint a few more brush strokes across the surface to extend the snakeScale pattern. You can also use the Smooth brush (hold the Shift key while painting) to smooth the scales. You may want to lower the Z intensity of the Smooth brush to a value of 10 before doing any smoothing.

21. See if you can create a seamless scale pattern that wraps around the entire sphere. You'll have to both reposition the stencil and rotate the sphere to do this correctly.

22. When you are satisfied, turn off the Stencil On button to turn the stencil off. You should have a nice scaly sphere (Figure 7.28).

23. To see how the snakeScale alpha pattern is used as a stencil, open the snakeScaleStencil.mov file in the Chapter 7 folder of the DVD.

Figure 7.28

Snake scales have been sculpted directly onto the surface of the sphere using the stencil.

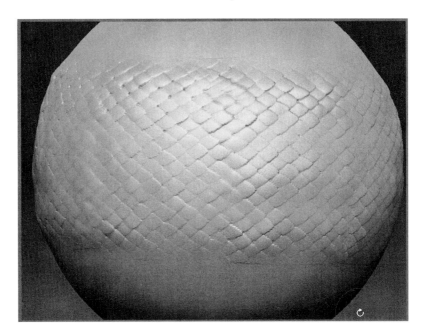

Detailing the Medusa Maquette

For the remainder of the exercises in this chapter, you'll return to the Medusa maquette created in Chapter 6. You'll add wrinkles, bumps, and scales and then color her skin using polypainting. Movies of each step in the process are available in the Chapter 7 folder on the DVD. It's a good idea to watch these either before or after you go through each section.

1. Start a new ZBrush session and use the Load button in the Tool palette to load the medusa_v15.ZTL tool. Select the medusa_v15 subtool and set the SDiv slider in the Geometry subpalette to 6.

2. In the SubTool subpalette, turn off all the subtools except for the Medusa's head. The easiest way to do this is to click on the eyeball icon next to the medusa_v15 subtool. This will turn off all of the subtool's visibility. The head remains visible since it is the currently selected subtool. Click on the medusa_v15 subtool in the Subtool palette (not the eyeball icon next to the subtool) to lock its visibility.

3. In the Geometry subpalette, click on Divide to add a seventh SDiv level. It may take a few seconds to calculate the subdivision. At SDiv 7, the head will have 2,293,760 polys, which should be enough for fine detail. You may be able to divide the head one more time depending on the available RAM in your computer but you shouldn't need to. Adding another level beyond 7 will give the head more than nine million polygons!

Creating Wrinkles

Before jumping into the task of creating wrinkles, it's a good idea to step back for a moment and think about the character of the maquette as well as her anatomy. This version of the Medusa will have scaly skin to match her snakey hair. If you think of her story, Athena cursed her, making her so ugly that the mere sight of her would turn men to stone. It seems unlikely that Athena, being the powerful and jealous god that she is, would let Medusa walk away with a nice complexion. On top of this, you can imagine that Medusa has been alone for years surrounded by the petrified bodies of her would-be slayers. The anger and loneliness she feels should be apparent in the wrinkles and folds of her skin. Her skin should be tough and fairly thick given its scaly nature. In this version of the Medusa, she also has worms and half-formed snakes emerging from her face and scalp, in addition to the vipers that live on her head. There are a lot of opportunities for accentuating the writhing subcutaneous parasites using the sculpting brushes and alphas.

When approaching the task of creating all of these wonderful details, it's best to think in terms of multiple passes using a variety of brushes and tools. A believable organic surface has layers of details—some subtle, some drastic—but they all should work together harmoniously to instill a sense of character and story to the maquette. To accomplish this, you'll begin by creating the larger, more obvious wrinkles that follow the contours of the Medusa's face and expression. The process involves a lot of back and forth between carving, raising, pinching, and smoothing the surface. It's not a straightforward, step-by-step process; it is more of a flow and a feel that you'll develop as you work. There is a lot of experimentation and personal preference involved as well. That being said, follow along with the exercises, but don't worry about precisely duplicating each step. To see how the wrinkles were created for the example, watch the medusa_wrinkles.mov movie located in the Chapter 7 folder of the DVD.

1. In the Brush palette, select the Smooth brush and set the Z intensity to 10.

2. In the Layers subpalette of the Tool palette, create a new layer and name it **wrinkles**.

3. In the Subtool palette, turn on both eyeball subtools.

The Head subtool has a different material applied to it than the rest of the subtools. This was done while sculpting the head so it would have a different material than the reference planes. To make the eyes and other subtools match the head, choose the MatCap White Cavity material from the material inventory. This will be applied to all of the subtools at once regardless of whether they are visible or not. Occasionally you may find that a subtool has spots where a number of polygons have a different material from the rest of the subtool. This usually happens after the subtool has a higher level of subdivision added to it. To fix this problem, you refill the subtool using the correct material from the Material palette. To do this, follow the instructions in the section "Applying Different Materials to Subtools" in Chapter 5.

4. Select the Standard brush from the brush inventory. In the Brush palette, set the BrushMod slider to 12. This will cause the Standard brush to pinch the surface a little as it pushes the vertices outward.

5. Set the Alt Brush Size slider to 1.3 in the Brush palette. When you use the Shift key to toggle on the Smooth brush, the Draw Size will automatically adjust to 1.3 times the size of the Draw Size settings on the top shelf.

6. In the Stroke palette, activate the LazyMouse button. Set the Lazy Radius to around 8. The LazyMouse feature is great for creating wrinkles as it helps you to draw smooth, straight lines on the surface.

7. Set the Z intensity of the brush to 15.

8. Before you begin to create details, you'll want to store a morph target. This captures the current state of the 3D tool and saves it in memory. One advantage of the morph target is that you can use the MorphBrush to undo changes you've made at very specific points. This is great for fading wrinkles at the edges. The Store Morph Target (StoreMT) button is at the bottom of the Tool palette in the MorphTarget subpalette.

9. The forehead is a good place to start as you begin to create wrinkles. The large surface allows you to test your brush settings and develop a feel for creating the wrinkles. Hold the Alt key down and start making vertical strokes on the surface of the forehead. You should keep the Z intensity of the brush fairly low as you work.

10. When you create wrinkles, you should work with quick, fluid stokes. Think about how flesh around the wrinkle behaves. Muscles are causing the skin to bunch up, therefore a wrinkle is more than just a line carved into the skin. It should have a matching raised line on one side (and sometimes both sides).

    Try carving a line into the surface by holding the Alt key while sculpting, and then draw a matching line next to it without the Alt key so that the surface next to the wrinkle is raised. Then hold the Shift key and smooth out both lines, especially at the ends of the wrinkle where it fades away (see Figure 7.29).

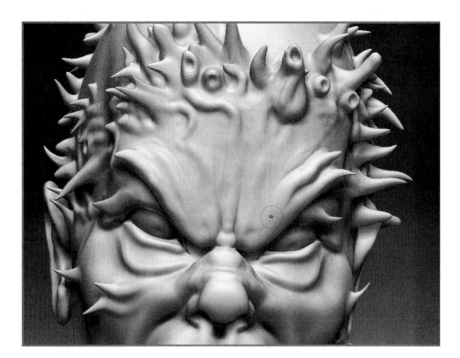

Figure 7.29

Use the Standard brush to draw wrinkles into the forehead.

The Ctrl+1 hotkey combination will repeat the most recent stroke.

11. Use the Inflate brush to raise the surface between wrinkles, and also try using the Pinch brush to refine the wrinkles. You can also use the Inflate brush to refine the shapes of the squiggly worms that appear at the Medusa's hairline as well as small bumps and dents on the forehead. Alternate brushes as you go: work over sections using a combination of the Standard, Inflate, Pinch, and Smooth brushes.

Holding the Alt key while painting with the Pinch brush will make the surface pinch inward rather than outward; this is great for wrinkles.

12. The Medusa's brows are squeezed together and forced downward at the center, creating a very exaggerated expression of rage. For this reason, it might be a good idea to create more vertical wrinkles than horizontal ones.

Vertical lines increase the energy of this particular expression, whereas a lot of horizontal wrinkles will actually undercut the look of rage. If Medusa's look were one of surprise, the opposite would be true; that is, horizontal creases would be more dominant than vertical creases. However, you can still add a few horizontal creases to suggest age; just make sure that they are not perfectly straight across and that they are not as deep as the vertical creases. The horizontal creases should dip downward at the center, following the contours of the expression. When in doubt, consult your photographic reference.

The *Artist's Complete Guide to Facial Expressions* by Gary Faigin (Watson-Guptill Publications, 1990) is a must read for anyone who wants to sculpt believable and dramatic facial expressions.

13. From the Brush Inventory, select the Morph brush. Set the Z intensity to 15. Paint over the ends of the wrinkles to fade them back into the surface. This brush is like an undo that you can paint over changes you've made. It is basically blending the surface where you paint between the current state of the tool and the state you stored as a morph target in step 8. As long as you have the morph target stored, you can use this technique to blend the details.

14. Watch the first 3 minutes of the `wrinkles.mov` movie in the Chapter 7 folder of the DVD. You'll see that dozens of lines are repeatedly drawn, smoothed, and redrawn to build of layers of wrinkly flesh.

15. You should vary the draw size of the brushes and the intensity fairly often to add variety to the wrinkles.

16. Once you have built up a fair number of wrinkles, set the SDiv slider in the Geometry subpalette to level 5. Increase the draw size of the brush and hold the Shift key to toggle the Smooth brush while painting over the forehead. Move the SDiv slider up to level 6. The wrinkles are still there; lightly dust the forehead again with the Smooth brush. Move the SDiv slider up to 7.

    The wrinkles still exist but their intensity is reduced. This technique of smoothing at lower subdivision levels is similar to lightly wiping a clay maquette with water or a solvent. It causes the fine details to melt together a little bit (see Figure 7.30).

17. When you feel satisfied that you have a good wrinkle technique working, move to the area around the eyes. Crow's-feet appear at the outside edges of the eyes. The wrinkles here should start from underneath the outside corner of the upper eyelid and arc upward following the contours of the skin (Figure 7.31).

You should not use Symmetry when you create fine details like crow's-feet. It's more work to detail each eye separately, but asymmetry in the end result is more organic and convincing.

18. The bags under the eyes are a good place for some extreme wrinkles. Overlap strokes to create slight crisscross patterns; this helps sell the look of skin.

19. The bridge of the nose and the bunched-up skin behind the nostrils should have some large wrinkles (Figure 7.32). Use the Morph brush to blend the ends of the wrinkles back into the surface.

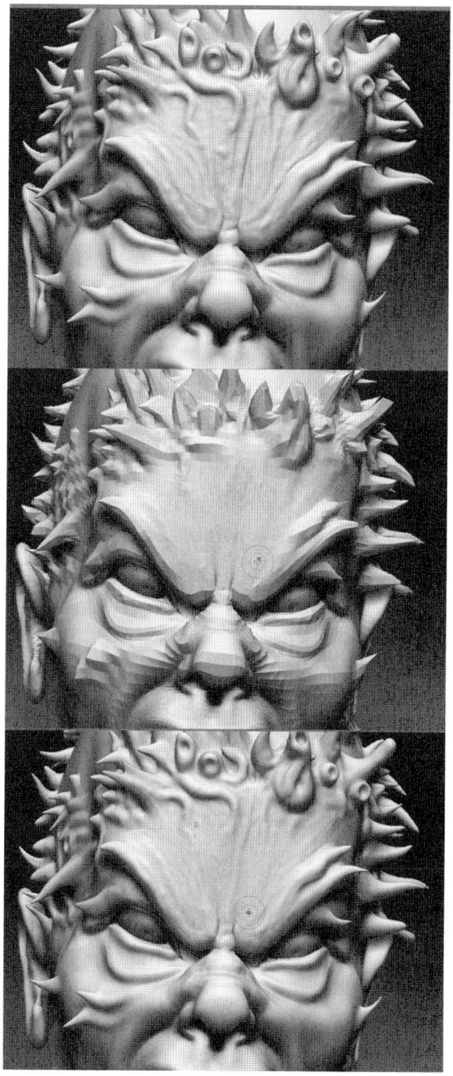

Figure 7.31
Crow's-feet are created at the outside corners of the eyes.

Figure 7.32
The bags under the eyes and the bridge of the nose are enhanced with wrinkles.

Figure 7.30
The Smooth brush refines the wrinkles on the forehead.

20. Draw long wrinkles down the side of the face above the nasolabial fold. These should start from the side of the nose and wrap around downward beneath the chin. The crisscross pattern of overlapping wrinkles is obvious as the skin wraps around the jaw in Figure 7.33. The skin bunches up below the chin when the mouth is opened wide, so be sure to add some deep creases here as well.

21. Use wrinkles to add details to the squirming worms that live in the side of the Medusa's face.

22. The striated muscles that lie beneath the skin of the neck can be detailed with overlapping passes of long lines and wrinkles. This adds energy to the pose as well as an aged and worn look to the skin (Figure 7.34).

This skin is not quite like human skin. Eventually it will be covered in scales, so it's okay to overdo the wrinkles a bit. In addition, since all of these wrinkles have been sculpted using a 3D layer, their intensity can be reduced later on if you decide that they are too much.

Figure 7.33

Wrinkles are added to the cheeks and the side of the face and below the chin.

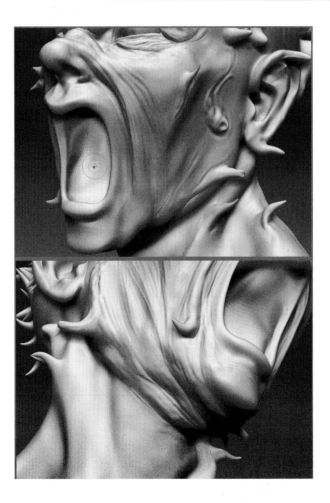

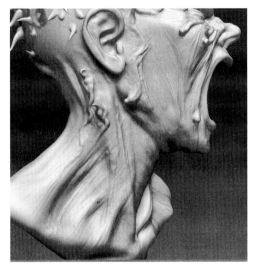

Figure 7.34

The skin on the neck is enhanced with long overlapping lines.

Figure 7.35

The MalletFast brush is used to create the lip details.

23. Create some horizontal wrinkles just below the nose and above the upper lip. These form as the upper lip pushes the skin up toward the nose.

24. The MalletFast brush is a good choice for creating the look of the lip tissue. Set the draw size to 10 and the intensity to 40. Make sure the ZAdd button is active on the top shelf. Make small strokes that move vertically across the lips, as in Figure 7.35.

> The MalletFast brush works very well on high-resolution surfaces. Like the Clay, ClayTubes, and Mallet brushes, it behaves as if you were adding (or removing, depending on the mode) small blobs of soft clay to the surface.

25. To finish the lip details, you can use the Standard, Pinch, and Smooth brushes to enhance the marks made with the MalletFast brush. Then make some thin horizontal creases across the lips with the Standard brush. Remember that the lips in this pose are stretched, especially along the sides (Figure 7.36).

26. Once you are happy with the wrinkles you've made on the Medusa's skin, save your changes as medusa_v16.ZTL using the Save As button on the Tool palette.

Figure 7.36

The wrinkles on the skin of the Medusa

Adding Scales to the Medusa Head

To create Medusa's scaly skin, you'll use the snakeScale alpha created earlier in the chapter and apply it to a sculpting brush. The scales will be applied on top of the wrinkles, which will help give the skin a thick and leathery appearance.

1. Load the medusa_v16.ZTL tool into ZBrush; you can use the one you've been work-ing on or load the medusa_v16.ZTL file from the Chapter 7 folder of the DVD.

2. Select the medusa_v16 subtool and set the SDiv slider to 7. Hide the other subtools.

3. In the Layers subpalette, create a new 3D layer and name it **scales**.

4. In the alpha inventory, click the Import button. Find the snakeScale alpha you created earlier or load the snakeScale.psd file from the Chapter 7 folder on the DVD.

5. Select the Standard brush from the brush inventory. Set the Draw Size to 34 and the Z Intensity to 15.

6. In the Alpha palette, make sure snakeScales is selected, and set the RF slider to 10. This slider controls the radial fade. It adds a blurred circular shape to the edge of the alpha. Increasing the value of the slider increases the amount of blur applied to the edge. Set the Blur slider to 15 to soften the alpha.

7. In the Brush palette, set Align to Path to 25. Activate LazyMouse in the Stroke palette, set LazyRadius to 5. Set LazyStep to .75.

8. In the Alpha palette, click the Rotate 90 Degree button; this will rotate the scale pattern so that the scales move vertically as opposed to horizontally as you paint on the surface with the brush.

9. Rotate the Medusa tool so that you can see a blank spot on her scalp, and paint some test strokes on the surface. Adjust the settings in the Alpha palette and the LazyMouse subpalette until you get a nice scaly pattern that flows with the direction of the brush stroke (Figure 7.37).

10. Use the Standard brush to paint the snakeScale pattern all over the Medusa's head. Try to stroke along the contours of the face so that the direction of the scales flows with the shapes created by the skin and muscle (Figure 7.38).

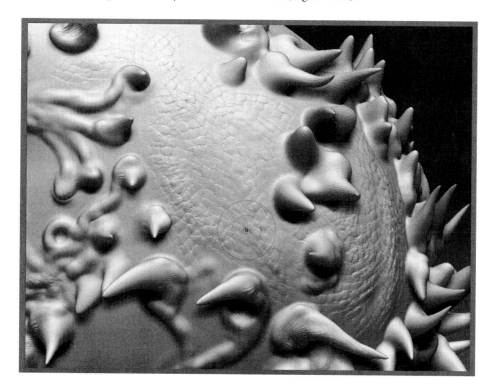

Figure 7.37

Use the snakeScale alpha applied to the Standard brush to sculpt scales onto the scalp.

Figure 7.38

The Medusa's face is covered in snake scales.

The draw size is relative to the scale of the object. To maintain a consistent size to the snakeScale pattern, remember to adjust the draw size accordingly whenever you change the scale of the tool. However, there's really no need to make an absolutely perfect snake scale pattern on the face. Variations in size and intensity will create a more organic look to the flesh on the skin. If you look at your own skin, you'll notice that the texture of your face differs from region to region. Likewise, although the size of the scales on a snake's body is generally consistent, you'll notice that the size of the scales on the face change to accommodate the shape of the head.

11. After you cover the face in scales, you can refine some of the scales individually if you feel they need to be touched up. The best way to do this is to use the MalletFast brush with a Z intensity of 40 and a draw size of 4. Try selecting Alpha number 12 from the

alpha inventory to use with this brush. Make sure ZAdd is activated on the top shelf. You can then paint on top of scales in spots where the Standard brush may not have been sufficient (Figure 7.39). Resist the temptation to paint over every scale on the entire head unless you have a lot of free time on your hands.

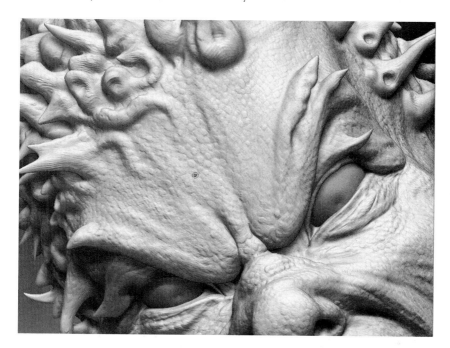

Figure 7.39
Use the MalletFast brush to refine individual scales.

The Medusa's face will no doubt still look somewhat faceted, meaning that the square shape of individual polygons is visible, especially close up. Before you try dividing the mesh again (remember, adding another division will result in over 9 million polygons for the head alone, not including the snake bodies and snake heads!), consider that Quick mode is enabled in the Transform palette. Quick mode helps optimize 3D tools so that the performance of ZBrush on your machine does not suffer even when you work on dense meshes. You can turn Quick mode off, which will help smooth the appearance of the head a little. You can also set the DSmooth slider in the Display Properties subpalette of the Tool palette to 1. This will remove the faceted look of the face, but it will cause the model to update more slowly when you're modeling, moving, or rotating it. It's good to check out how the model looks with the DSmooth slider set to 1 every once in a while, but keep working with the DSmooth slider at 0 and Quick mode activated.

12. When you are happy with the appearance of the scaly skin, you can experiment by varying the intensity of the Wrinkles and Scales 3D layers in the Layers subpalette. If you feel you lost the detail of the wrinkles after you added the scales, you can either lower the intensity of the Scales layer or increase the intensity of the Wrinkles layer, or both or the reverse. Figure 7.40 shows Medusa with a number of different intensity settings for the two layers.

13. The final example image of the head, shown in Figure 7.41, uses an Intensity value of 1 for the Scale layer and an Intensity value of 1.2 for the Wrinkles layer.

14. Save your changes as medusa_v17.ZTL using the Save As button on the Tool palette. To see how the scales in the example file were created, watch the medusa_scales.mov QuickTime movie in the Chapter 7 folder of the DVD.

Figure 7.40

Changing the Intensity of the 3D layers creates a number of possible looks for the finished head. Clockwise from the upper left, the Intensity value for the Wrinkles layer has been set to 0, 0.5, 1, and 1.5.

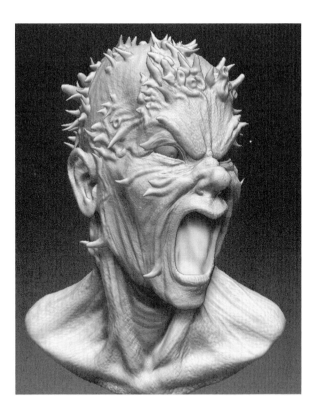

Figure 7.41

The final version of the Medusa head

Combining the Snake Heads and Bodies

Before you can detail the snakes that make up the Medusa's hair, you'll need to combine the heads and the bodies so that the noticeable gap between them can be hidden.

1. Open the medusa_v17.ZTL tool from the Chapter 7 folder on the DVD or continue using the model from the previous section.

2. Draw the tool on the canvas and switch to Edit mode.

3. If you're using the medusa_v17.ZTL file from the DVD, the subtools should be named; if you're using another version or your own version of the tool, take a few minutes to rename the subtools using the Rename button in the Subtool subpalette. Name the snake hair **snakes**. Name the heads **snakeHead1** through **snakeHead8**. It does not matter which head is 1 or 2, just as long as they are organized. This will help when you start to clone the subtools in the next steps.

4. Select the snakes subtool. Click the Clone button on the top of the Tool subpalette.

5. From the Tool subpalette, select the new Snakes tool. It should look exactly the same as the snakes in the original version, but it won't have any other subtools in the Subtool subpalette (see Figure 7.42).

Figure 7.42

The snake hair is cloned and turned into a separate tool.

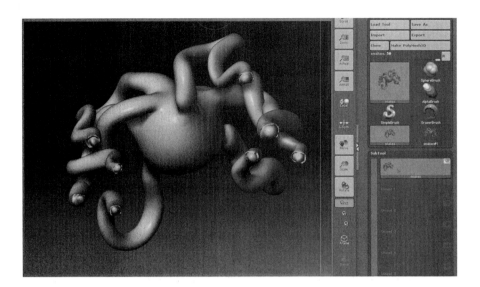

6. Set the SDiv slider in the Geometry subpalette to the highest level.

7. Click the Divide button to add another level of subdivision.

> You may want to subdivide twice in step 7, but it depends on how much your system can handle. In the Preferences palette, you can adjust the max number of polygons each mesh (or subtool) can have using the MaxPolyPerMesh slider in the Mem subpalette. This limit is specified in millions of polygons per mesh (a limit of 12 means 12 million polygons). Each subtool is a mesh—so in a tool composed of subtools, each subtool can have up to the maximum number of polygons set in the Preferences palette. However, if you use the Insert Mesh button to combine two subtools into a single mesh, the resulting mesh must be under the limit. The example files on the DVD and in these exercises are kept under a certain limit so that people with slower machines can use them. If you have a fast machine, you can try subdividing the snake bodies even more so that the scale details sculpted on in a later section look good.

8. Make sure the SDiv slider is set to 7 (or the highest level you have). Click the Del Lower button to remove all of the lower levels of subdivision.

9. Ctrl+Shift+click on the big sphere at the center of the snakes. All of the snakes should disappear, leaving only the center visible. Remember that because the snakes were originally created using ZSpheres, the mesh was automatically divided into polygroups when the ZSpheres were converted to an Adaptive Skin polymesh. So you can still selectively hide and show parts of the mesh.

10. Ctrl+Shift+click again on the center sphere. The visibility of the tool will be inverted so now you see just the snakes but not the center sphere.

11. Click the Del Hidden button at the bottom of the Geometry subpalette to permanently remove the sphere at the center of the snakes (Figure 7.43).

12. From the Tool palette, select the original medusa_v17 tool.

13. In the subtool palette, select each snakeHead subtool one at a time and click the Clone button at the top of the palette. This will make a clone of each snakeHead subtool at its current position. As you make clones of each snakeHead, you'll see the Tool palette fill up with copies of the snakeHead subtools (see Figure 7.44). Because you took the time to rename the subtools, you can easily see which ones have been cloned and which ones haven't. The snakehead subtools in the original medusa_V17 will have a # symbol added to their name in the Subtool subpalette.

Figure 7.43

Delete the sphere at the center of the snake bodies.

Figure 7.44

Clones of each snakeHead are added to the tool inventory.

You can assign a hotkey to the Clone button to make your life a little easier. Hold the Ctrl key, click the Clone button, and then enter the hotkey you'd like to assign. Alt plus a numeric key is usually a safe bet since they are not assigned to any commands in ZBrush by default.

14. Select the Snakes tool from the Tool palette to switch back to the isolated snake bodies.

15. Click the Insert Mesh button at the bottom of the Geometry subpalette. Select snake-Head1 from the tool inventory to combine the snakeHead with the snake bodies. Notice that it is not added as a subtool; it is now combined with the snake body as a single tool.

The Insert Mesh button works only with tools that have the same number of subdivisions or have only a single level of subdivision.

16. Repeat step 15 to add snakeHead2 through snakeHead8 to the snake bodies. They should appear at the end of each snake body.

17. Save the tool as snakeHair.ZTL (see Figure 7.45).

Figure 7.45

The snake heads have been combined with the snake bodies.

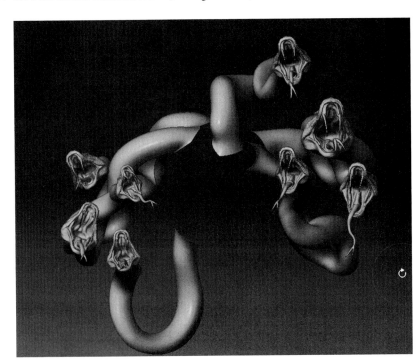

Refining the Snakes

To close the gap between the head and the snake, you'll use a combination of the Clay and Smooth brushes.

1. Select the Smooth brush from the brush inventory and set the Z intensity to 20.

2. Select the Clay brush from the brush inventory. Set the alpha to Off and the Z intensity to 30.

3. Scale the snakes so that you are zoomed in to the point where one of the bodies meets one of the heads.

4. Paint over the end of the snake head while holding the Shift key to smooth away some of the scales.

5. Paint over the seam between the head and the body with the Clay brush; this will fill in the gap. Use the Smooth brush to refine the strokes made with the Clay brush. It may take a few passes to get it seamless. Your main concern should be continuity between the head and the body, but don't get too hung up on erasing the seam perfectly because it won't be visible from a distance (see Figure 7.46).

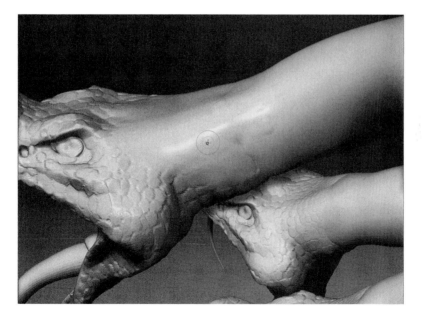

Figure 7.46

Use the Clay brush to conceal the gap between the body and the head of each snake.

Adding Scales to the Snake Bodies

The process of adding scales to the bodies of the snakes is similar to adding scales to the head of the Medusa. The scales on the snake bodies should be more uniform in size and direction than those on the face of the Medusa. The easiest way to apply the snakeScale pattern is to use the DragRect stroke type with the Standard brush.

1. In the alpha inventory, click the Import button. Import the snakeScale.psd file if it is not already in the Alpha palette.

2. Select the Standard brush, and set the Z intensity to 30.

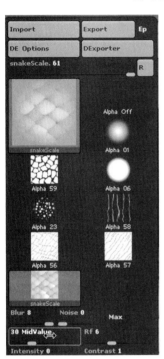

3. In the Alpha palette, select the snakeScale alpha and set the RF (radial fade) slider to 6. Increase the MidValue slider to 30. This will lighten the darker areas of the alpha, which will keep the brush from creating too much of a lumpy look as you drag copies of the alpha on the snake's body (Figure 7.47).

4. In the Stroke palette, select the DragRect stroke. If the DragRect is already selected, select another stroke type and then reselect the DragRect. Occasionally the DragRect stroke type will not work properly with the Standard brush unless this is done.

5. Drag on the surface of the snake; you should see the impression created by the alpha appear as you hold the brush down and drag. As long as you hold the brush to the surface, you can rotate and scale the stroke until you let go.

6. It takes a few minutes of practice, but you can start carefully positioning the brush strokes on the surface of the snake. Scale each stroke upward and rotate so that it matches the other strokes. You may find yourself undoing a few brush strokes until you get the position correct—it will most likely take a little bit of practice, but you should get the hang of it after a few tries (see Figure 7.48).

Figure 7.47

Adjust the properties of the snakeScale alpha pattern in the Alpha palette.

7. Use the brush to cover the snake from the back of the head to the end of the body with the scale pattern. Leave the bottom of the snake body alone.

As you're using the Standard brush to create the scale pattern, you may notice that occasionally the DragRect stroke type jumps in size or becomes hard to control. This usually happens when there is another part of the tool behind the tool you're painting on (such as another snake). If you can rotate the tool so there is only blank canvas behind the snake you are editing, you'll have more control over the brush. You can still isolate the snake body and hide the other snakes by Ctrl+Shift+clicking on the snake you want to edit.

8. Do some touch-up with the MalletFast brush once you've finished applying the snakeScale pattern.

9. Use the ClayTubes brush to create the long thin scales on the underside of the each snake (Figure 7.49). The ClayTubes brush works well with dense polymesh tools. It works a lot like pressing tubes of clay onto a real clay sculpture.

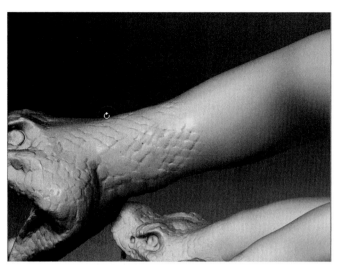

Figure 7.48

The snakeScale alpha pattern is stamped onto the snake geometry.

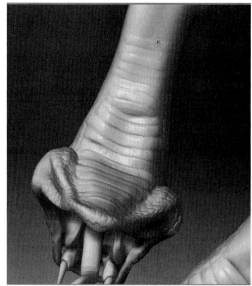

Figure 7.49

Use the ClayTubes brush to create the long scales on the underside of the snake.

By the time you finish all eight snakes, you should be a master of the DragRect stroke type. Wax-on Wax-off Daniel-san!

10. Save the Snake tool as snakeHair.ZTL. Save often while working on this tool; it's a lot of work and you won't want to have to redo it.

To watch a movie that goes through the process of combining and detailing the snakes, watch the snakeHair.mov QuickTime in the Chapter 7 folder of the DVD.

Polypainting

Painting believable skin is similar to creating wrinkles; it's best to work in passes, building upon layers of color. Working with skin is a very creative process, ripe for experimentation. You can have a lot of fun seeing how using different alphas and brush types can lend subtle detail to the color. The following exercise describes the process used in the skinPaint.mov file located on the Chapter 7 folder of the DVD. Try this technique out and then see how you can add your own personal style to the Medusa's skin.

Polypainting is actually vertex painting, meaning that the RGB values you paint onto the surface of the tool are stored with each vertex of the polymesh tool. The color values between two adjacent vertices are blended across the surface of the polygon between them. The more vertices a tool has, the more detail you can paint onto the surface.

Snakes come in every possible color, with a variety of markings. For simplicity's sake, a classic greenish blue was chosen for the example in this chapter. The images in this chapter are black and white, so for a better look at how the colors are applied, watch the skinPaint.mov file on the Chapter 7 folder of the DVD.

1. Load the medusa_v18.ZTL tool into ZBrush.

2. Select the medusa_v18 subtool.

3. In the Texture subpalette of the Tool palette, make sure the Colorize button is on.

4. On the left shelf, make sure there is no texture selected for the tool.

5. In the color picker, choose a grayish green. An RGB of 100, 114, 93 should work well.

6. Select the Standard brush from the Brush palette. Make sure ZAdd is off. Set the Rgb intensity to 30.

7. Set Stroke Type to Color Spray. The Color Spray brush varies the hue of the colors in the spray as you paint.

8. Set Draw Size to 46.

9. Paint over the entire Medusa head. This pass is a simple base coat of green with some variation created by the color spray. You'll layer additional colors over this (see Figure 7.50).

Figure 7.50

Paint a green color on the Medusa's face.

10. Once you have the Medusa's head fairly well covered, set the color picker to a more saturated bluish green (RGB = 56, 140, 92).

11. Choose Alpha 7 from the Alpha inventory. Set the draw size to 29.

12. Paint the bluish color on top of the base coat of green. Don't completely cover the head in this new color; instead, use it to bring out the larger facial features.

13. Now for some contrast: Pick a grayish purple (RGB = 101, 86, 91). Layering contrasting shades is a great way to add depth and visual interest, especially to skin. It also helps to tone down the saturated greens a little.

14. Choose Alpha 22 and set the stroke type to DragRect. Set the Rgb intensity to 10.

15. Use quick, short strokes to drag copies of the stroke all over the face. Rotate and scale as you drag, layering the vein pattern created by the alpha. It seems unlikely that you would see veins through the Medusa's scaly skin, but as you layer the vein pattern, you'll see that it breaks up the green color in a very organic way. Use this technique on the neck and the back of her head as well. Don't go so far as to color her completely in purple.

16. Once you're satisfied, you can do another pass with green to knock the purple back a little. Set the stroke type to Color Spray. Choose Alpha 23. Set the color picker to a light bluish green (RGB = 123, 140, 143), Rgb Intensity to 19, and Draw Size to 44. Go over the head with this brush, just enough to knock the purple color down a little.

17. To bring out some of the detail you'll do another quick pass with a grayish blue (RGB = 71, 110, 101). You can use the same settings as in step 13. Paint around the eyes, the eye bags, the end of the nose, and areas of the cheeks. Don't be overly neat or careful about this; you want a nice organic look, so random blotchy patches are what you want to achieve. Apply this color to the center of the neck and the eyebrows as well.

18. For the lips, choose a dark grayish blue (RGB = 46, 71, 65). Set the alpha to Alpha_08 and the stroke type to Dots. Set the RGB intensity to 26 and the draw size to 23. You don't need to make the lips a solid color, unless you think she needs lipstick (Figure 7.51).

19. You can use this same color on the inside of the nostrils and the eyelids.

> If you accidentally paint outside the lip area, you can easily fix your mistake. Hold the brush over part of the skin outside the lip. Click on the c hotkey to sample the color, and then paint over the areas you need to fix.

20. Use a dark gray to accentuate some of the larger wrinkles and folds in the skin. Paint very lightly in the crevices of the wrinkles.

Figure 7.51

The lips are painted dark blue.

Cavity Masking

Once you have a good overall skin color going, you can use cavity masking to add contrast to the scales on the surface of the skin. Cavity masking restricts the color to the raised parts on the geometry, such as the folds of skin between wrinkles or the tops of the scales. You can reverse the masking as well so that only the spaces between bumps on the surface receive color.

1. Select the Standard brush from the brush inventory.

2. Select Alpha 8 and set the stroke type to Dots. Set the Rgb intensity to 25.

3. In the Brush palette, activate the Cavity Mask button. By default, the cavity mask is set to paint only on the raised areas of the surface. You want to paint in the crevices. To reverse the action of cavity masking, either you can adjust the slope of the Edit curve so that it is the reverse of the default—that is, sloping down from left to right (Figure 7.52)—or you can set the cavityMaskInt (Cavity Mask Intensity) slider to -100.

   The cavity masking is controlled using an Edit curve. The curve controls the intensity of the masking. When you make a sharp peak on the left side, color is restricted only to the crevices and indentations in the mesh surface. It's a good idea to experiment by painting a few strokes across a less-visible portion of the mesh. When you have the settings you like, you can try it out on the face. Use Figure 7.52 as a guide for adjusting the cavity masking Edit curve.

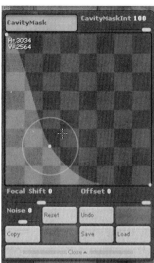

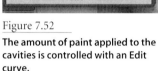

Figure 7.52

The amount of paint applied to the cavities is controlled with an Edit curve.

Figure 7.53

Painting with Cavity Mask applied causes the scales to stand out on the surface.

4. Paint a dark green color (RGB = 30, 112, 63) on the Medusa's face using the Standard brush with Cavity Mask. Make sure you vary the Rgb intensity occasionally as you paint to keep the surface looking organic (Figure 7.53).

> Cavity masking will be disabled when a tool is at its lowest level of subdivision or if the tool does not have more than one level of subdivision.

5. When you've covered a good portion of the head with this pass, choose a dull yellow color (RGB = 166, 155, 105) in the color picker.

6. In the Brush palette, alter the Edit curve for cavity masking so that it is the opposite of the curve shown in Figure 7.52 (i.e., it slopes upward sharply from left to right).

7. Set the Rgb intensity to 17 and paint on the Medusa's head. This will add a subtle yellowish color to the raised areas of the surface, giving her complexion a dusty, dirty appearance. It also adds a slight yellow tinge to the worms protruding from her head.

8. In the Alpha palette, click the Import button and browse your computer to the `Program Files\Pixologic\ZBrush3\Gnomon Alpha Library` directory. ZBrush ships with several examples from the extensive Gnomon library of alpha textures. Choose the Scaly `skin_22.psd` file from the Scaly Skin directory.

9. In the Alpha palette, increase the intensity of the alpha to .34 and the contrast to 3.14.

10. Set the stroke type to DragRect.

11. In the color picker, choose a grayish green (RGB = 124, 173, 140). Set the RGB intensity to 15.

12. Use the brush to drag copies of the pattern created by the alpha across the skin. This pass will bring back some of the green color and knock down the cavity masking passes a little, just to even things out.

13. Switch to a darker green (RGB = 55, 81, 73). Set the Rgb intensity to 10 and the stroke type to Freehand. Add a little more shading to some of the long wrinkles and details. At this point you should be able to see how all these layers of color work together to create the look of believable scaly skin.

14. For one final touch, set the color in the color picker to a pinkish orange (RGB = 186, 158, 130). Set the Rgb intensity to 12.

15. Set the stroke type to Freehand and set Alpha to Alpha_08. Paint lightly over the worms that are coming from the Medusa's face and scalp. This will separate them a little from the skin and help them to read more as organisms that are embedded in her skin (Figure 7.54).

Figure 7.54

The skin of the Medusa has been created using numerous passes of color.

The hardest part about the process of painting skin is knowing when to stop. You can really just keep going, adding more passes of color using various alphas and stroke types forever. It can be a lot of fun, especially when the subject is an imaginary creature such as the Medusa. Realistic human skin is also a great challenge. The translucent nature of skin can reveal subtle changes in hue as well as the color of veins and blood vessels just beneath the surface.

You use similar techniques to paint the skin of the snakes emerging from the Medusa's body. Figure 7.55 shows the completed maquette with color applied. Refer to the color insert at the center of the book to see the final image properly. The process used to create the final color is the same as the one outlined in this chapter but with many more passes. For a complete discussion of the polypainting technique, read Scott Spencer's *ZBrush Character Creation: Advanced Digital Sculpting* (Wiley, 2008).

Figure 7.55

The completed maquette.

Summary

In this chapter you've taken the Medusa maquette from a basic sculpture to a highly detailed piece of artwork. The alpha, texture, and color tools not only allow you to sculpt very organic surfaces, they also allow you to add color to your sculptures. In the next chapter you'll explore how materials work as well as lighting and rendering.

The final Medusa maquette was completed using many of the same techniques described in this chapter. The snakeHair subtool was combined with the head subtool using the technique described in the section titled "Combining the Snake Heads and Bodies." The Clay brush was then used to fill in the gaps and smooth the transition between the scalp and the snakes. To see a movie that shows how the Medusa was finished, watch the `finishingMedusa.mov` QuickTime movie file in the Chapter 7 folder of the DVD.

CHAPTER 8

Rendering, Lighting, and Materials

Pixols on a ZBrush canvas contain material information along with their x-, y-, and z-coordinates. The materials give a pixol its surface quality, and reflectivity, transparency, translucency, and other qualities define a material. Pixols also react to lighting changes on the canvas and can cast shadows. Materials are also applied to polymesh objects in Edit mode.

Lights in ZBrush are easy to use and can be a helpful sculpting aid. Likewise, the myriad properties of ZBrush materials offer an unlimited creative resource when creating illustrations. This chapter provides a number of short, hands-on tutorials designed to get you comfortable with rendering, lighting, and materials in ZBrush.

Topics in this chapter include:

- Rendering
- Lights
- Standard materials
- Material capture tool

Rendering Basics

Rendering in ZBrush defines how the pixols and 3D polymesh objects look on the canvas based on the colors and materials applied, the lights in the document, and the rendering style selected in the Render palette. By default all pixols and 3D polymeshes are constantly rendered in Preview mode while you work in a typical ZBrush session. Preview mode features preview shadows, reflection, transparency, basic lighting, and simplified materials and textures (Figure 8.1).

The three other render modes are activated using the Flat, Fast, and Best buttons, which are on the Render palette. You can see examples of the render modes in Figure 8.2. Flat render mode renders only the color of the pixols and 3D polymesh objects. It is quick and it allows you to view the colors applied to a polymesh, through polypainting or through textures, without the distraction of lights, materials, and shadows. Fast is similar to preview rendering; however, no shadows are visible. Best mode renders accurate shadows, reflection, global illumination, and other effects. It takes more time than the other modes and is used most often for finalizing a completed composition in ZBrush. Rendering a 3D polymesh is useful for when you want to present your digital sculpture as part of a portfolio. You can also export variations on a lighted ZBrush document and use them to create a composite in Photoshop.

Figure 8.1

ZBrush renders the canvas in Preview mode by default.

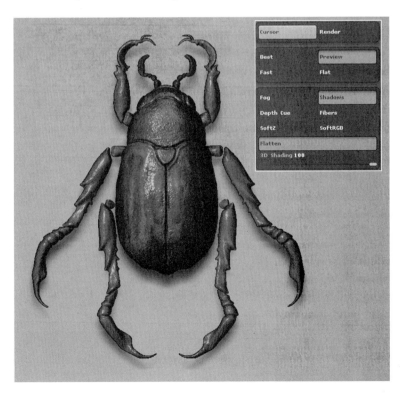

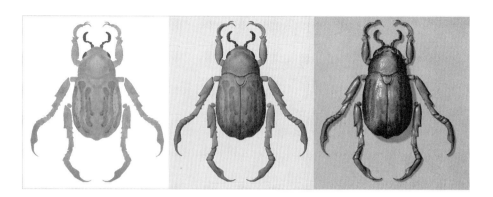

Figure 8.2

Flat, Fast, and Best render modes

This section is a brief overview of how to use the Render palette. Rendering is very closely tied to lights and materials. After you have a basic understanding of how to use the Render palette, you will learn more advanced rendering techniques in the sections on lights and materials. This first exercise goes through the process of creating a render using Best mode.

1. From the Chapter 8\ZDocs folder on the DVD, open desertScene.ZBR. This is a simple scene showing a couple of cacti and a rather drab desert floor (Figure 8.3).

2. The document will open larger than the document window. To see the whole image, you will need to zoom out. On the right shelf, click the AAHalf button.

Figure 8.3

A simple desert scene in ZBrush rendered in Preview mode

Figure 8.4

The AAHalf button reduces the magnification of the canvas by 50 percent, which aids anti-aliasing.

The AAHalf button shrinks the document to half its original size. When the document is reduced to half size, it is anti-aliased so the edges of the shapes on the canvas are smoother when the document is rendered. What this means is that when you start a composition in ZBrush (as opposed to sculpting a 3D polymesh tool), you should set the document window to double the size you want. You can do this using the Double button in the Document palette. When you activate the AA Half button, the document will be exported at half the dimensions specified in the Document palette and the anti-aliasing will be applied (Figure 8.4).

3. Place the Render palette in the tray so that the controls are available (Figure 8.5).

4. Click the button labeled Flat. Only the colors applied to the pixols will be displayed.

5. Click the Fast button. The image will render with no shadows.

6. Click Preview. The image will render with shadows. Notice that the shadows are not correct. The shadow cast by the cactus in the foreground falls on the plane without any perspective, as shown in the top half of Figure 8.6.

Figure 8.5

The Render palette contains controls for the four render modes.

Figure 8.6

The top image is rendered at Preview quality; the bottom image is rendered at Best quality.

The purpose of the preview shadows is to help you visualize the shape of 3D poly-mesh tools, to inform you of the position of tools and pixols in relation to each other on the z-axis, and to give an indication of where the light in the document is coming from.

7. Click the Best button. The image will render with more accurate shading and shadows, as shown in the bottom half of Figure 8.6. The look of the shadows is determined by the settings in the Light palette. Those will be discussed later on.

When you render using Best quality, a progress report on the status of the render will appear above the top shelf. The display shows the amount of time that has passed since the render was initiated, an estimate of the time left, and a gray progress bar that moves from left to right across the screen.

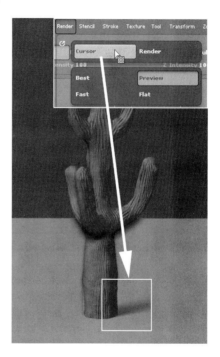

Figure 8.7

The Cursor button allows you to render a small square of the canvas to test the settings.

As long as one of these modes is selected, any change you make on the canvas or with the lighting will cause the canvas to be rendered again. Most of the time this isn't noticeable, but if Best is selected, the canvas will keep rendering at high quality, which can take a fair amount of time. To stop a Best quality render, press the Esc key. The canvas will switch to Preview mode. Changing a setting will cause the render to start again at Best quality, unless you switch to Preview render mode. If a Best quality render does not start for some reason, you can click the Render button (hot key = Ctrl+Shift+r).

8. Start a render at Best quality, then press the Esc key to stop the render. Click the Cursor button at the upper left of the Render palette and drag down to a spot on the canvas, near the base of the cactus in the foreground. This will render a 128×128 square area where you let go of the cursor (Figure 8.7). To return to canvas rendering mode, click the Render button.

When rendering documents, save often. It is easy to accidentally create a setting that can crash ZBrush, causing you to lose your hard work.

You can render a 3D polymesh tool using Best quality while still in Edit mode. Rendering the 3D tool will not cause it to be dropped to canvas.

Fog and Depth Cue

There are a couple of settings that can increase the sense of dimension in a ZBrush composition. Fog creates a haze that can obscure pixols further back along the z-axis, giving them a sense of distance. Depth cue blurs parts of the canvas based on their position on the z-axis.

1. Switch the render mode to Preview. Click the Fog button in the Render palette. The canvas will be covered in a white haze.

2. Expand the Fog subpalette in the Render palette. Set the fog intensity to 60.

3. Click on the Depth1 slider and drag the cursor to the base of the cactus in the foreground. This sets the start point for the fog on the z-axis.

4. Click on the Depth2 slider and drag to the base of the cactus in the distance. This sets the end point, or the point of greatest intensity for the fog. You can also use the sliders to set these points numerically.

5. Set the color picker to a dark blue in the Fog subpalette. Click on the white color swatch on the left and drag to a medium blue color on the color picker. This sets the color of the fog at the start point.

6. Click on the color swatch on the right and drag all the way across the canvas to a light blue color on the center square of the color picker. This sets the color of the fog at the end point.

    The two slots at the center allow you to choose a texture to apply to the fog either as a color or an alpha. You may need to render using Best quality to see the how the texture is applied to the fog.

7. Use the Edit curve to control the density of the fog. The left side of the curve represents the foreground; the right side represents the background (Figure 8.8).

8. Render the scene using Best render mode (Figure 8.9).

9. Switch to Preview render mode. Turn off the Fog button in the Render palette and turn on Depth Cue.

10. In the Depth Cue subpalette, click on the Depth1 slider and drag the cursor to the base of the cactus in the foreground (-.3328). This sets the start point for the depth cue on the z-axis where the blur intensity will be at its minimum.

11. Click on the Depth2 slider and drag the cursor to an area of the ground just behind the foreground cactus (-.1258). This sets the end point for the depth cue blur on the z-axis where the blur intensity will be at its maximum.

12. Set the intensity of the depth cue to 100 and the softness to 7. Higher blurs take longer and can crash ZBrush. Adjust the Edit curve so that it resembles Figure 8.10.

13. Render the canvas using the Best render quality (Figure 8.11).

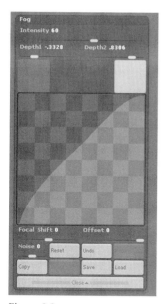

Figure 8.8

The Fog settings are tuned using the Edit curve.

Figure 8.9

The cactus scene rendered with fog

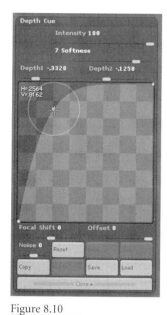

Figure 8.10

The settings for the depth cue Edit curve

Figure 8.11

The cactus scene rendered with Depth Cue. The blurring effect on the distant canvas is subtle.

There is a texture slot that can allow you to use a texture to determine the depth cue. The color value is used to filter areas of the image.

Depth cue, in many cases, is extremely subtle. If you need to create a more intense depth of field, you'll need to render with Best quality, bake the render in the layer, and then use the Blur brush (in the 2.5D Brush section of the Tool palette) to blur the areas. Baking layers is discussed later in this chapter.

A number of settings in the Antialiasing subpalette can help smooth the edges of the pixols on the canvas when they are rendered at Best quality. Higher settings in the Super Sample setting can create better image quality, but it will take longer to render (Figure 8.12).

Figure 8.12

The Antialiasing settings in the Render palette

Using Lights

Lights in ZBrush are very simple to use and provide a way for you to change the lighting in a composition at any point during its creation. Lights are also an important aid to the sculpting process. Clay sculptors in the real world will continually move and adjust their lights so that they can literally see their work in a new light. This helps when you are defining forms and also while you are sculpting details. The following exercise shows you how to adjust the lighting on the canvas while working with a 3D polymesh tool.

1. Start ZBrush. From the startup window, choose the Other option to create a blank document.

2. From the `Chapter 8\Ztools` folder on the DVD, select the clayHead.ZTL tool.

3. Draw the tool on the canvas, switch to Edit mode (Ctrl+t), and choose the Basic material from the material inventory.

4. Rotate the tool to a front view.

5. Put the Light palette into a tray so that you can access the settings easily.

6. Set the render quality in the Render palette to Preview.

7. In the Light palette, drag across the sphere icon. This repositions the light. You'll see the lighting on the surface change accordingly. If it doesn't change, make sure you have the Basic Material selected in the Material palette.

   It's a good idea to change the position of the light frequently while sculpting a 3D polymesh tool. You'll notice problems that you might not see otherwise (see Figure 8.13).

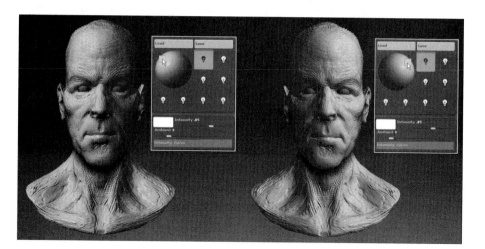

Figure 8.13

Dragging across the preview sphere in the Light palette will change the position of the light in the scene (sun and spot light types only).

Only the Start Up Standard materials in the lower section of the material inventory will react to the settings in the Light palette. The Start Up MatCap (material captured) materials at the top of the material inventory are created with the lighting information built into the material. All materials made with the MatCap tool contain their own lighting information. Repositioning the light has no effect on tools using MatCap materials. Materials are discussed later on in this chapter.

8. Expand the Zplugin palette. In the Misc Utilities subpalette, click the InteractiveLight button (Figure 8.14). As you move your brush (don't drag on the canvas, just move the brush over it) across the canvas, the lighting will follow the position of the brush until you click on a blank part of the canvas.

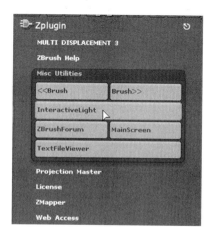

Figure 8.14

The Interactive Light plug-in allows you to position the light in the scene using your brush.

9. Hold the Ctrl key down and click the Interactive Light button in the Misc Utilities subpalette. Then click Alt+1. This will make Alt+1 the hotkey for the Interactive Light plug-in so you can call it up anytime you need it.

> If the preview sphere in the Light palette goes dark, it means that the light has gone behind the sphere and the 3D polymesh on the canvas. Just click on the front of the preview sphere to bring it back to the front.

10. In the Light palette, click on the lightbulb icon that is colored orange. This will turn the light off. Click it again to turn it back on. The border around the icon indicates that the light is selected. Changing the settings in the palette, such as Intensity and Light Type, will affect the selected light only, even if the light is off.

11. Click on the next lightbulb icon in the Light palette once to select it and again to turn it on (Figure 8.15). A second light is added to the canvas. You can add up to eight lights in a single document.

12. With the second light selected, set the Intensity slider to .25. Click on the color swatch next to the Intensity slider and drag it down to the color picker, to the blue region to change the light color. The second light on the preview icon in the Light palette is blue. However, the light color in the document has not changed—it's just dimmer. To see changes in light color, render with Best quality mode.

13. Expand the Intensity edit curve. This curve adjusts the intensity of the selected light. The left side of the curve refers to the intensity falloff. Reversing the curve can create some interesting negative exposure effects (Figure 8.16).

14. In the Light palette, click on the lightbulb icons that are highlighted in orange, and turn both of the lights off.

15. Increase the Gdi slider below the Intensity edit curve to a value of 80. Even though the lights are off, the clayHead tool appears brightly lit. This slider controls the global diffuse intensity. The Light palette limits you to eight lights in a scene; however, you can use the Global Diffuse Intensity slider to create an overall diffuse light for all strokes and tools on the canvas (Figure 8.17). Other lights in the scene can be used to create other effects.

16. Click on the sphere labeled DefaultDiffuse. The texture inventory will open. From the texture inventory, select texture 41. This will map the texture to the global diffuse intensity.

Figure 8.15

To turn a light on, click on a light-bulb icon in the Light palette.

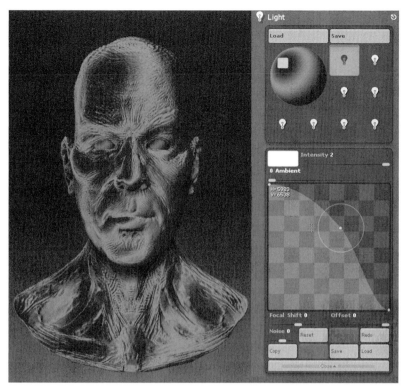

Figure 8.16

Reversing the Edit curve for the Intensity slider can create some interesting effects.

Figure 8.17

The Global Diffuse Intensity slider increases the overall diffuse lighting in the document.

17. In the Render palette, select Best quality. The canvas will render and you'll see how the color information in the texture is mapped to the lighting on the canvas (Figure 8.18). You can create your own textures for use with the Global Diffuse Intensity settings. This can replace complex lighting arrangements using the lights in the Light palette. For instance, if you create a 2D texture file with cool colors in the upper left and warm colors in the lower right, these colors will be applied to the diffuse lighting of the pixols on the canvas with cool colors coming from the upper left and warm colors coming from the lower right. Then you can add additional lighting to the scene, thus circumventing ZBrush's 8-light limit.

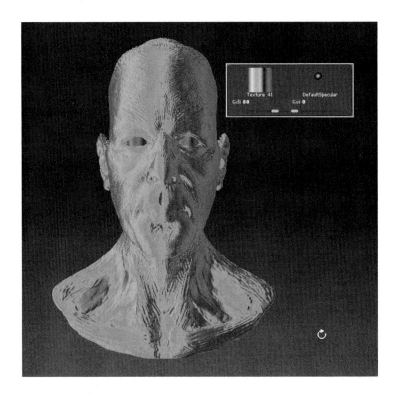

The Global Specular Intensity slider works the same way as the Global Diffuse Intensity slider. However, the slider and any textures you use apply only to specular highlights on a 3D tool. A specular highlight is a reflection of the light source on the surface of a tool. The lighting on the canvas is also affected by settings in the materials applied to strokes and 3D tools.

Light Types

ZBrush uses four types of lights to illuminate the strokes and 3D tools on the canvas. The default light type in a new ZBrush document is a sun light. Sun lights have no point source—all of their rays are cast in parallel. You place sun lights using the sphere icon in the light window.

The other three types of lights are point, spot, and glow. To change the type of light you are using, click on one of the buttons in the Type subpalette. This will change the type of the currently selected light. Remember that the lighting you see on the canvas may not be coming from the currently selected light. Make sure that the currently selected light is turned on when you change the settings if you want to see the lighting update accordingly.

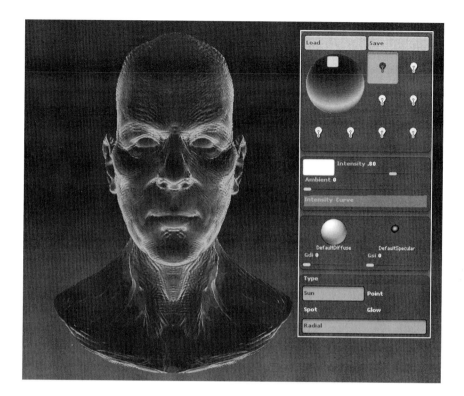

Figure 8.19

The Radial button can change any light into a fill light.

The Radial button changes the behavior of the currently selected light so that the areas of the strokes or 3D tools that face away receive the light. This creates a good fill lighting effect (Figure 8.19). Radial lights can't cast shadows. Any of the light types can be modified using the Radial button.

The following exercise will illustrate some of the differences between the types of lights.

1. Start up ZBrush, or click on the Init ZBrush button in the Preferences palette if ZBrush is already open. This will reset the changes made to the lighting in the last exercise.

2. Load the clayHead.ZTL tool from the `Chapter 8\Ztools` directory on the DVD.

3. Draw the clayHead tool on the canvas and switch to Edit mode (Ctrl+t). Choose the Basic material from the Material palette. Rotate the head so that it is facing the front of the canvas.

4. Place the Light palette in a tray so the settings are easily accessible. Make sure only one light is on by clicking on the orange highlighted lightbulb icon in the Light palette (if it turns off, click the icon again to turn it on).

5. Drag across the sphere icon in the Light palette to change the position of the light. Set the position so that clayHead is lit from the upper right.

6. Set the Ambient slider below the Intensity slider to 0. This removes ambient light from the lighting on the canvas.

7. Click the Radial button in the Type subpalette. Reposition the light by dragging across the sphere icon in the Light palette. Move the light to the upper left.

8. Set the intensity to .15.

9. Add another light by clicking on another lightbulb icon. Click once to select it and again to turn it on.

10. Set the position of the second light to the upper right. Set its intensity to .75 and its color to white (click on the swatch next to the Light Intensity slider; it will change to the current color in the color picker, which is white by default).

11. The first light is now acting as a fill light. Turn the first light on and off, and compare how the clay head looks with and without the first light. The preview sphere in the Light palette shows how the combination of lights affects the scene (Figure 8.20).

12. Turn the second light off. Make sure the first light is on. Set its intensity to .75 and turn off the Radial button so the light is a standard sun light again.

Figure 8.20

The clayHead with a fill light

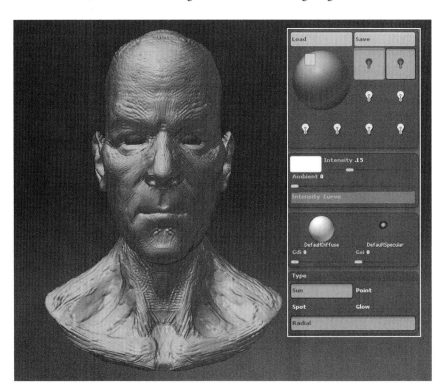

13. Set the type to point. Change the render mode in the Render palette to Best. Point lights do not show up well in Preview mode.

14. Expand the Placement subpalette. To change the position of a point light, drag from the P button in the Placement subpalette on to a spot on the front of the clayHead tool, on the tip of the chin. Use the settings in the Placement palette to change the position of point, spot, and glow lights.

15. In the Placement palette, set the radius to 1.25. A point light emits light in all directions from a single point in space, like a candle (Figure 8.21). The radius determines how far the light from the point light travels in the scene.

16. In the Shadow subpalette, activate the Shadow button. The point light will cast shadows on the face, making the lighting look a bit more natural.

17. Click the Radial button to see how the point light reacts to the 3D tool when this setting is on.

18. Turn off the Radial button and change the light type to spot.

19. Drag from the P button in the Placement subpalette to the forehead of the clayHead tool to set the position where the spotlight hits and illuminates the tool.

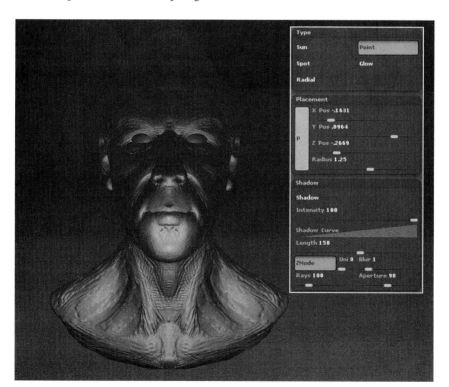

Figure 8.21

A point light behaves much like the light emitted from a candle.

20. Drag across the sphere icon in the Light palette to set the source of the spotlight—the position where the light comes from (Figure 8.22).

21. Change the Radius slider to change the cone size of the spotlight.

Figure 8.22

Use both the Position subpalette and the light preview sphere to position the spot light.

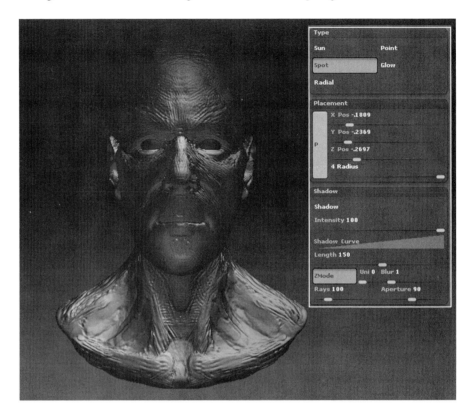

22. Change the light type to glow. The glow light creates even lighting on strokes and tools on the canvas. The light emits from a point, just like the point light.

23. Set the radius to .7 and drag the P button in the Placement subpalette to the tip of the figure's nose.

    When positioned strategically, glows can be used in combination with other types of lights to create the look of translucent materials. You can export a version of the document that uses only a point light (such as the one in Figure 8.23) and use it as the basis of a depth pass for blurring and shading effects in Photoshop.

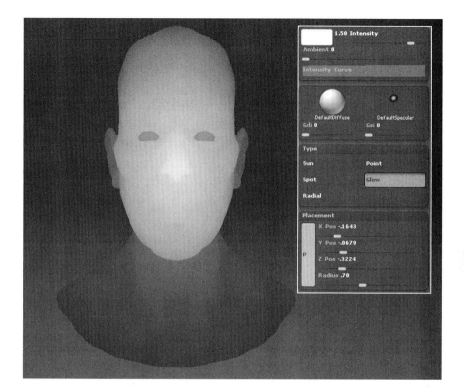

Figure 8.23

The glow light type creates even lighting on the surface of a tool.

Using Shadows

Sun, spot, and point lights can all cause strokes and 3D tools on the ZBrush canvas to cast shadows. Since a ZBrush document is not the same as a 3D scene in a 3D animation program such as Maya, the way ZBrush tools cast shadows may seem a little different. However, with some work, you can create convincing shadows on a ZBrush canvas that will add to the depth of your compositions. Shadows in ZBrush will not compare with realistic shadows created in 3D applications with more advanced rendering options, such as mental ray.

1. Start ZBrush. Load the desertScene.ZBR document from the Chapter 8\ZDocs folder on the DVD.

2. Click the AAHalf button on the right shelf so that the canvas fits on the screen. The original document was created at double the final resolution so that when you reduce it by half with the AAHalf button, the anti-aliasing is improved and the pixols on the canvas appear smoother.

3. In the Render palette, click the Best button. ZBrush will take a couple minutes to render the image. Notice the shadows cast on the ground by the cactus.

4. In the Light palette, select the orange highlighted lightbulb icon. Change the position of the light to the upper right by dragging the marker across the surface of the sphere icon. The image will re-render. Notice that the position of the shadows has changed based on the new light position, as shown in Figure 8.24. (If the image does not render automatically when you change the position of the light, then click the Render button in the Render palette [Hotkey = Ctrl+Shift+r].)

5. Set the Aperture value in the Shadow subpalette to 60 and render the canvas again. The shadows are much blurrier and more spread out.

6. Set the Aperture value in the Shadow subpalette to 5 and render the canvas again. The shadows are crisper and more defined (Figure 8.25).

Figure 8.24
Changing the light position changes where the shadows will be cast.

Figure 8.25
A higher Aperture setting creates blurry, spread-out shadows. Lower aperture settings create well-defined shadows.

Increasing the value of the Rays slider improves the accuracy of the shadows, but the image will take longer to calculate. You'll most likely want to keep the ZMode button on. ZMode produces more accurate shadows by considering the ZDepth of shadow-casting pixols when calculating the shadow. Sometimes a shadow created with ZMode on will have holes in it if shadow-casting strokes on the canvas intersect shadow-receiving strokes.

The Uni slider adjusts the unified shadow setting. This slider is available when ZMode is on and can help to reduce artifacts and decrease render time.

Creating convincing shadows often requires a fair amount of experimentation with these settings. The Shadow Edit curve and the Blur slider can also help tune the look of the shadows. The Edit curve controls the fade of the shadows. The x-axis of the graph represents the distance from the shadow-casting object, and the y-axis of the graph represents the amount of fade.

Remember that the shadow settings are for the selected light. Another light can have a completely different arrangement of shadows at the same time.

7. Set Shadow Length to 300, Rays to 500, Aperture to 5, and Uni to 100. Edit the shadow curve so that the orange portion nearly fills the graph, as in Figure 8.26.

Figure 8.26

Realistic shadows can be created by experimenting with combinations of the shadow settings in the Light palette.

Understanding Materials

Materials in ZBrush determine the quality of the surface of pixols on the canvas. If you create a red shiny ball in ZBrush, the red color is determined by the color or texture applied to the ball and the material determines the shiny quality. In some cases, a material will influence the color as well, but for the most part color and material are separated but work together to create the look of pixols on the canvas.

Materials cannot be exported from ZBrush for use in other 3D programs. All of the settings you create for materials exist only within the ZBrush document. You can save your materials and special material files (ZMT files); however, these files can only be used within ZBrush.

There are two major categories of material: standard materials and MatCap materials. Standard materials are determined by the shader settings in the Modifiers section of the ZBrush palette. A shader is a category of settings, and more than one shader can be used in a single standard material. The settings in each shader are combined to create the final look of the material.

ZBrush includes 78 standard material presets (Figure 8.27). These presets are based on four types of materials, which in some cases are combined into a single material. The section on standard materials discusses how to use and customize them.

MatCap (Material Captured) materials are created by sampling parts of an image. You can import a photo into ZBrush and use it as the basis for a MatCap material. MatCap materials do not react to changes in lighting in a ZBrush document. They have their own set of modifiers. ZBrush includes 24 MatCap presets. Later in this chapter I'll show you how you can create your own MatCap materials.

Figure 8.27

The material inventory shows all of the available presets.

Materials can add realism or special effects to the images you render in ZBrush. They can also be used as a sculpting aid. Different materials can reveal different aspects of your 3D tools. Changing materials every once in a while during the sculpting process can help you to see aspects of your sculpture you might not otherwise notice.

The Flat Color Material

Flat Color is the simplest material available. In fact, it's not really a material at all. Just like the Flat Color render mode, it only shows the color on the surface. It has no modifiers at all. What makes it a useful material is that when it is applied to a 3D tool such as the clay-Head tool, it can serve as a sculpting aid.

The silhouette of a sculpture is an important compositional element, and when you apply Flat Color you can create a silhouette. Working with just the silhouette of a 3D tool can open up avenues of creative exploration. The Flat Color material may not seem as exciting as the metallic or reflective materials, but it's actually much more useful.

1. Start ZBrush, or if ZBrush is open, click the Init ZBrush button in the Preferences palette to restore ZBrush to the initial settings.

2. In the Tool palette, click the Load button, and load the clayHead.ZTL tool from the `Chapter 8\ZTools` directory on the DVD.

3. The tool will load with the MatCap Red Wax material applied by default. Expand the material inventory and choose the Flat Color material.

4. Rotate the head to a profile view, holding the Shift key while rotating so that the head snaps into place (Figure 8.28).

Figure 8.28
The silhouette of the clay head is clearly seen using the Flat Color shader.

5. From the brush inventory, select the Move brush.

6. In the Transform palette, click the Activate Symmetry button. Make sure the >X< and >M< buttons are on so that the symmetry is mirrored across the x-axis.

7. Set the Z intensity to 70, the draw size to 100, and the focal shift to 25.

8. Use the Move brush to pull and push large areas of the front of the face. Pull the forehead up, the chin down, and the nose back into the face.

   You can completely change the character of a sculpture very quickly (Figure 8.29). Some changes will spark ideas you may not have thought of before. You can use a base head sculpture to create an endless amount of variations. That's not to say that you couldn't do this with any other material, but seeing the sculpture as a pure silhouette will keep you focused on form and structure and prevent you from being distracted by details.

9. Rotate to the front view and see what other changes you can make to the model just based on the silhouette. The profile view works a little better usually.

10. From the material inventory, select the Basic material. No doubt the model will need some cleanup in some areas (Figure 8.30).

While you are working on a sculpture, make it a practice to use the Flat Color material as you go just to check that the silhouette stays true to the form you want to create or as a way to experiment with new ideas.

Figure 8.29

Changing the silhouette of a sculpture quickly changes its character.

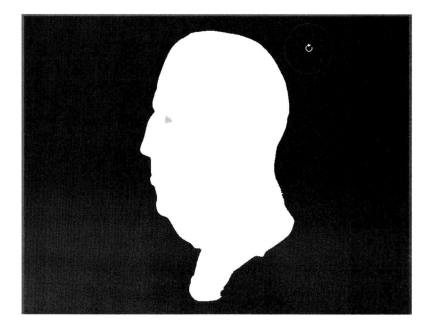

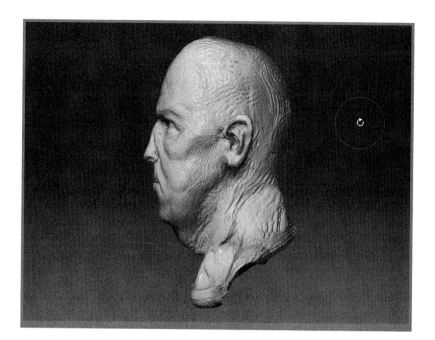

Figure 8.30

A new character has been created in about 45 seconds.

Standard Materials and Shaders

In this section, I'll introduce you to the standard materials. These materials are found in the lower half of the material inventory. You can create your own standard materials by adjusting the settings on the presets and then saving the material as a ZMT file. Changes you make to materials are saved with ZBrush documents. They are not saved with ZBrush tools.

1. Start ZBrush, or if ZBrush is open, click the Init ZBrush button in the Preferences palette to restore ZBrush to the initial settings.

2. In the Tool palette, click the Load button and load the Beetle.ZTL tool from the Chapter 8\Ztools folder on the DVD. Draw the tool on the canvas and switch to Edit mode.

3. Rotate the Beetle tool so that you're facing its top.

4. From the material inventory, select the Basic material (Figure 8.31).

5. Place the material inventory into a tray.

   The top of the material inventory shows the current material in the large icon. The smaller icons represent more recently used materials. Hold the brush icon over any of the material icons and you'll see a preview of what the current tool will look like with the material applied (Figure 8.32).

Figure 8.31

Figure 8.31

The Beetle tool with the Basic material

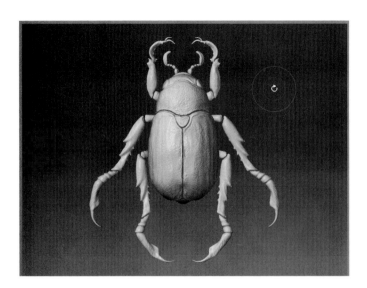

Figure 8.32

A preview of the 3D tool in any of the material presets appears when you hold the brush over the presets in the material inventory.

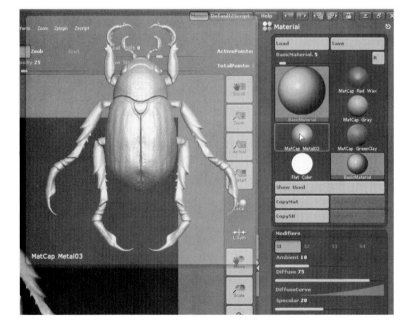

6. Click the Show Used button below the icons. This will reduce the upper palette to show only the materials currently in use. The Flat Color material is always in use as part of the canvas.

7. Expand the Modifiers subpalette for the Basic material. Modifiers alter the settings of a material. Notice at the top that there are four slots labeled S1, S2, S3, and S4. Only the S1 slot in the Basic material is available. The others are grayed out.

   A material is made up of one or more shaders. The shaders are sets of modifier settings. The long list of settings and sliders you see in the Modifiers subpalette of the Basic material is essentially its shader (Figure 8.33). The Basic material has only one shader available; other materials may have more.

8. Select the TriShaders material at the bottom of the material inventory and expand its Modifiers subpalette. The shader is immediately applied to the entire Beetle tool (see Figure 8.34).

9. The TriShader has three of the four shader slots available. Click the S2 button and set the Diffuse slider to 1. You'll see the beetle become slightly darker.

10. Click the S1 button and the Diffuse slider changes. However, the material on the beetle does not.

    What's going on here is that you are switching between two of the three shader settings applied to the beetle. The TriShaders material uses three sets of the basic shader settings loaded into slot S1, S2, and S3. These settings are initially identical. When the beetle is rendered at Preview or Best quality, the settings from the three slots are combined. You cannot add or remove shader slots from a material, but you can change the settings in each slot and save the material as a ZMT file. You can also copy shaders from one material to another.

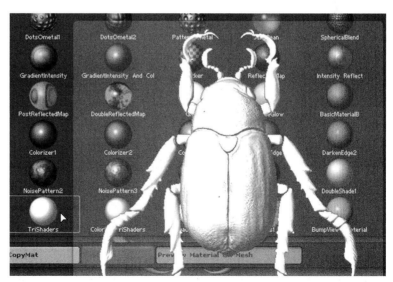

Figure 8.33

A shader is a group of settings within a material.

Figure 8.34

The TriShaders material in the material inventory

11. Click on the Reflected Map material and it will be applied to the beetle (there are two materials named Reflected Map; pick the gray one).

12. Click the S1 button to view the first shader settings. Notice that the modifiers are different in S1 and S2.

13. Click the Copy SH button. This will copy the shader settings to memory (Figure 8.35).

14. Expand the material inventory. You'll see that the TriShaders material has been moved to the top section (Figure 8.36). Click on the TriShaders material again. The beetle will have the TriShaders applied to it again.

15. Click the S1 button in the TriShaders' Modifiers subpalette.

16. Click on Paste SH button to replace the TriShaders' S1 settings with the Reflected Map's shaders currently in memory. This replaces all of the settings as well as the sliders available in the TriShaders' S1 slot (Figure 8.37).

    Materials are not saved with the tool but they are saved with the document. You can also save a customized material to the `Program Files\Pixologic\ZBrush 3\Start Up\ Materials` folder and it will appear in the inventory the next time you start ZBrush.

17. Click the Copy Mat button in the Material palette.

Figure 8.35

A shader setting can be copied using the CopySH button.

Figure 8.36

Edited materials are moved to the User Material's section of the material inventory.

18. In the Material palette, select the JellyBean material. This material normally has only one shader slot.

19. Click the Paste Mat button. All of the shaders and settings for the Jelly Bean shader will now be replaced with the shaders and settings from the TriShaders material. Notice that the JellyBean material now has three shader slots, just like the TriShaders material (Figure 8.38).

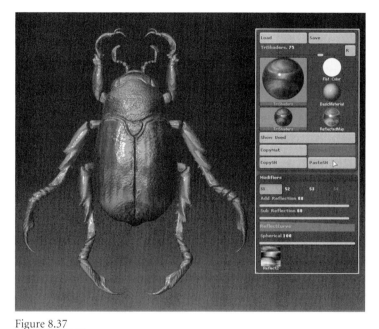

Figure 8.37

The first of the TriShaders material's three shaders has been replaced with the first shader from the Reflected Map material.

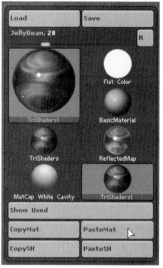

Figure 8.38

A material preset can be copied over another preset, replacing all of its settings and shaders.

Ambient, Diffuse, and Specular Channels

There are several types of shaders that can be used within materials. Many materials combine the basic shader settings with other modifiers, and some use multiple versions of the same shader with different settings.

1. Select the Fast material from the material inventory. It will be applied to the beetle automatically.

2. Expand the Modifiers tab. The Fast Shader has only two channel sliders: Ambient and Diffuse (Figure 8.39).

    The Ambient slider determines how strongly the ambient light in the document will be reflected by the material. It does not change the ambient lighting in the light panel, just how the material reacts to ambient light. Ambient light does not have a source: it's basically the light that is reflected by an environment.

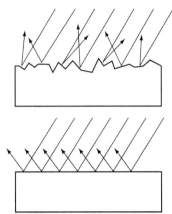

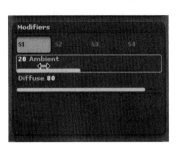

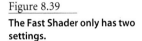

Figure 8.39

The Fast Shader only has two settings.

Figure 8.40

A rough surface (top) diffuses light as it is reflected back into the environment. A smooth surface (bottom) reflects the light back into the environment more evenly.

The diffuse slider controls how the material diffuses the light that comes directly from a light source. Imagine zooming in microscopically close to a surface that is rough, such as a brick. Photons of light hit the rough surface and bounce in all directions, diffusing the reflected light so more surface color is reflected back into the environment. Smooth surfaces such as glass do not diffuse the light as much. Instead, a reflection of the light source bounces directly back into the environment and appears as a specular highlight on the surface (Figure 8.40). The color of the environment is reflected rather than the color of the surface. A mirror is a smooth surface that has a low diffuse value. It reflects nearly 100 percent of the light that hits it back into the environment. Some surfaces, such as glossy paint, are actually made of layers. A smooth, reflective coating is combined with the color material that diffuses light so that you see a specular highlight as well as the color of the paint.

3. Select the Basic material. It will replace the Fast Shader on the beetle.

   The modifiers in the Basic material are used for many of the presets in the material inventory (Figure 8.41). You can create many different variations using only the settings in the Basic material's single shader. To get an idea of what each setting does, hold the brush over the setting and press the Ctrl key. Some of the more common settings are described in the next few steps.

4. At the top of the Modifiers list, set the Diffuse slider to 90. The beetle will appear brighter even though the lighting has not been changed.

5. Expand the Diffuse curve. Change the slope of the curve so that it rises sharply on the right side (Top image in Figure 8.42).

   Many settings in the material modifiers include both a slider and a curve. The slider sets the overall value of the channel; the curve allows you to fine-tune how the setting is applied. The value of the slider determines the 100 percent value used by the curve.

6. Click the reset button beneath the curve so that it becomes a straight line from the lower left to the upper right.

7. Adjust the points on the curve so that it is reversed; make the curve slope from the upper left to the lower right.

   The left side of the curve controls the intensity of the light on the parts of the surface that face away from the light source; the right side controls the intensity of the light on the parts of the surface that face the light source. Reversing the curve creates a negative effect that is reminiscent of the appearance of objects seen through an electron microscope (bottom image in 8.42).

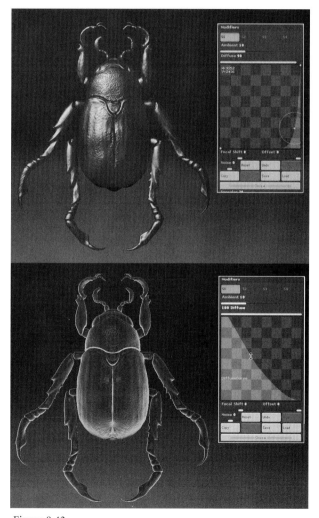

Figure 8.41

The Basic material shader has a long list of settings.

Figure 8.42

The Diffuse curve alters the diffuse lighting on the 3D tool (top image). Reversing the Diffuse curve creates an electron microscope look (bottom image).

8. Increasing the Noise slider will add noise to the curve, which adds a grainy look to the diffuse channel.

9. Select the basicMaterial 2 material from the Users Materials section at the top of the material inventory. Expand the Diffuse curve and click the Copy button below the curve.

10. Select the basicMaterial from the material inventory. Expand the Diffuse curve and click the Paste button. This will replace the changes made to the curve with the settings copied from the basicMaterial2 diffuse curve.

The specular intensity and curve work in the same way as the Diffuse controls. The Specular channel controls the reflection of a light source on a material's surface. Matte surfaces have a low specular value and a high diffuse value, while shiny surfaces are the opposite.

Transparency Channel

The transparency channel works only when there is more than one document layer. The Flatten button in the Render palette needs to be disabled as well. The following steps show how to work with transparent materials.

1. Start ZBrush, or if ZBrush is open, click the Init ZBrush button in the Preferences palette to restore ZBrush to the initial settings.

2. Click the Texture button on the left shelf to open the texture inventory; click the Import button at the bottom, and load the flowerTexture.PSD file from the Chapter 8\Textures directory on the DVD.

3. In the material inventory, select the Flat Color material.

4. With the texture selected in the texture inventory, open the inventory and click the Crop and Fill button at the bottom. This will resize the document to match the texture file and fill the canvas with the texture.

5. Use the Zoom button on the right shelf to zoom out so that the image fits inside the ZBrush interface.

6. In the Layer palette, click the Create button to create a new layer (Figure 8.43).

7. In the Tool palette, click the Load Tool button and load the Beetle.ZTL tool from the Chapter 8\Ztools folder on the DVD. Draw the tool on the canvas and switch to Edit mode.

8. In the material inventory, select the Basic material.

9. In the Render palette, turn off the Flatten button (Figure 8.44).

10. In the Modifiers subpalette of the Material palette, increase the Transparency slider to 75. You'll see the beetle become transparent (Figure 8.45).

Figure 8.43

A new layer is created in the Layer palette.

Figure 8.44

Turn off the Flatten button in the Render palette.

Figure 8.45

The Beetle becomes transparent.

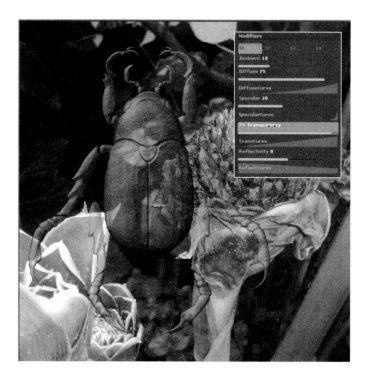

If you set the Transparency slider to a negative number, the transparency will be determined by the texture or color applied to the surface of the tool.

The way the Transparency curve works is similar to the way the Diffuse curve works. When you set the Transparency slider to a positive number, the right side of the curve controls transparency for surface areas that face the viewer and the left side controls areas that face away.

Reflectivity Channel

There are a number of ways to create a reflective material. This exercise demonstrates some of these methods.

1. Start ZBrush, or if ZBrush is open, click the Init ZBrush button in the Preferences palette to restore ZBrush to the initial settings.

2. In the texture inventory, click the Import button and load the `flowersTexture.PSD` file from the `Chapter 8\Textures` directory on the DVD.

3. In the Tool palette, click the Load button and load the Beetle.ZTL tool. Draw the tool on the canvas and switch to Edit mode.

4. Select the Basic material in the material inventory. This will be applied to the Beetle tool automatically.

5. Expand the Modifiers subpalette. Scroll to the bottom of the list of modifiers. Click on the square labeled Text00. This will bring up the texture inventory. From the inventory choose the `flowerTexture.PSD` file.

6. Scroll up the list of modifiers. Increase the Reflectivity slider to 100. The texture can be seen reflected in the surface of the Beetle tool.

7. Expand the Reflectivity curve to match the left image in Figure 8.46. The curve adjusts the intensity of the reflectivity just like the Transparency curve.

   The left side of the curve controls the reflective intensity of surface areas that face away from the viewer. The right side controls the intensity for surface areas that face the viewer. In the real world, many materials are more reflective on the parts that face away from the line of sight. The line of sight is known as the incidence angle.

   If the Reflectivity slider is set to a negative value, this changes the behavior of the Reflection curve. In this case, the left side determines the intensity of the reflectivity of dark colors applied to the surface (as a color or a texture) and the right side determines the reflective intensity of light colors applied to the surface (as a color or a texture).

8. Set Reflectivity to zero.

9. Scroll down the list of modifiers and set Env. Reflection to 80.

10. In the Render palette, expand the Environment subpalette. Click the Texture button, click the right-hand button below it, and choose the `flowerTexture.PSD` file from the texture inventory.

11. Set the render quality to Best. The beetle will render with no reflection, and when it is complete, the reflection will appear on the surface. You can see the Env. Reflection setting when you use Best render quality. See the right image in Figure 8.46.

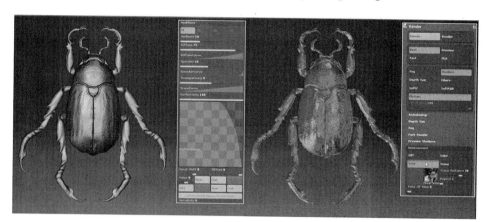

Figure 8.46

The Reflection slider (left image) and the Env. Reflection slider (right image) offer two ways to create reflections on the surface of a 3D tool.

12. In the Environment subpalette of the Render palette, click the Scene button. Now the beetle will reflect the other strokes and tools on the canvas, including itself.

   The Trace Distance slider determines how far from the surface the reflections will be calculated. The larger the distance, the longer the render time will be. The Repeat slider tells the reflection map how many times to repeat the reflection. The maximum is 5. And the Field of View slider calculates the angle of the field that can be seen on the reflections on the surface.

   Clicking the Color button will cause the surface to reflect a flat color instead of the scene or a texture.

13. In the Environment subpalette of the Render palette, click the Scene button. Set Trace Distance to 60 and Field of View to 90.

14. In the modifiers for the Basic material, set Reflectivity to 90 and Env. Reflection to 30.

15. Do a render using Best quality. The two reflection settings will be combined so that the beetle reflects a texture as well as the scene, including itself. The dark gray reflected on the surface is the actual canvas being reflected on the surface.

16. Switch the render quality to Preview.

17. From the Material palette, select the Fast Shader material.

18. In the Tool palette, expand the Texture subpalette and click the Colorize button.

If the beetle turns black, don't panic. This happens occasionally when a tool has been created using several combinations of subtools. To fix it, set the color picker to white, make sure only the Rgb button is enabled on the top shelf, expand the Color palette, and click the Fill Object button. This fills the object with the current color. If the Fill Object button is grayed out, make sure there is no texture active in the texture inventory.

19. Select the Standard brush. Make sure ZAdd is off; only RGB should be activated on the top shelf.

20. Set the stroke type to Drag Rect and choose Alpha 23.

21. Set the color picker to black.

22. Drag across the surface of the beetle to create dark spots on its back.

23. From the material inventory, select the Reflected Map material. Click the S1 button to switch to the first shader.

24. Set the Add Reflection slider to 100 and the Sub Reflection (subtract reflection) slider to 0. The dark spot reflects the image in the texture slot (left image in Figure 8.47).

25. Reverse the sliders so that the Add Reflection slider is at 0 and the Sub Reflection slider is at 100. Now only the light parts reflect the texture in the texture slot (right image in Figure 8.47).

26. The Spherical slider controls whether the texture in the texture slot is mapped as a sphere or as a flat plane.

Notice that the reflected Map material has two shaders. The S2 slot contains the Basic material settings, including a Reflection and Env. Reflect slider. These are both set to zero, but they can be set to combine a second reflection setting with the settings created in the S1 slot.

Figure 8.47

In the left image, the reflection is seen on only the dark parts of the surface. In the right image, the reflection is seen on only the light parts of the surface.

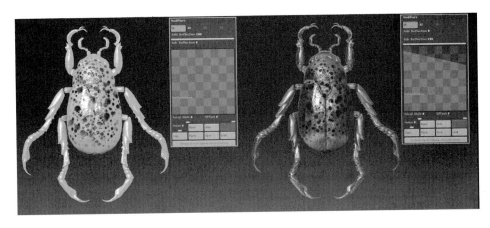

Other reflective materials include the Gradient Sky material and the Intensity Reflect material. Gradient Sky is a two-shader material. The first shader slot contains the gradient controls. The materials reflect the colors chosen for the gradient. The gradient is horizontal, so you can quickly create the look of a simple reflected ground and sky. The Intensity Reflect material contains two shaders. The first shader is a simple reflection intensity slider based on the colors of a texture. The second shader is the basic shader settings.

Baking Materials

Materials can be painted on a surface just like colors. In this section, you'll create a unique look for the Beetle tool and gain a deeper understanding of more of the settings available in materials. You'll begin by creating a simple patch of dirt. The materials and colors will be set and then baked into the layer to decrease render times.

1. Start ZBrush, or if ZBrush is open, click the Init ZBrush button in the Preferences palette to restore ZBrush to the initial settings.

2. From the Tool palette, select the Plane3D tool, and draw it on the canvas.

3. Switch to Edit mode and rotate the plane so that it is parallel to the canvas.

4. Scale the plane so that it fills the canvas

5. Select the Basic material from the material inventory.

6. Turn Edit mode off and click the Move button on the top shelf.

7. Expand the Transform palette. In the Info subpalette, set Z Component to 1500. This will move the plane back along the z-axis. If the plane disappears behind the canvas, lower this value (Figure 8.48).

8. Select the Simple brush from the Tool palette; a pop-up box may ask you if you want to switch tools and drop the plane to the canvas. Click the Switch button.

9. On the top shelf, click the Rgb button. Make sure ZAdd, ZSub, and ZCut are off.

10. Set the color picker to brown (RGB = 100, 70, 40). Set the stroke type to Spray, the RGB intensity to 25, and the alpha to 44. Set the draw size to 40.

11. Use the brush to cover the plane with brown dots.

12. Select the Blur brush from the tool inventory. Set the Rgb intensity to 75. Use the brush to blur the colors on the plane.

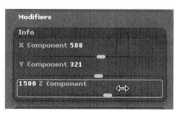

Figure 8.48

Setting Z Component in the Transform palette to 1500 will move the plane back in space.

13. Add the Material palette to the tray.

14. In the Materials modifiers, set Diffuse to 75 and Specularity to 5.

15. Set the Noise slider to .125. This adds a noise pattern to the material.

16. Set Noise Radius to 8. This changes the scale of the noise pattern.

17. Set Color Bump to -4. Color Bump adds a bumpiness to the material based on the colors applied to the surface (Figure 8.49). A negative number will cause lighter areas to appear raised and darker areas to appear recessed. Color Bump can be seen only when the render quality is set to Best.

Figure 8.49

Color Bump raises the lighter parts of the surface.

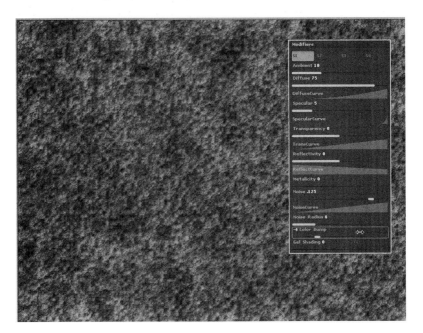

18. Save the document as beetleScene_v1.ZBR.

19. Switch to Preview render mode. Select the Directional brush and turn off the Rgb button on the top shelf. Turn ZAdd on.

20. Set the texture to Texture Off.

21. Set Z Intensity to 55 and choose Alpha 25. Set Stroke Type to Drag Rect.

22. Use the brush to create cracks on the surface of the plane. Rotate the alpha as you drag copies of the brush on the plane. Layer the brush strokes using different sizes so that the repeating pattern of the brush becomes less noticeable (Figure 8.50).

23. Choose the Bump brush from the Tool palette. Set Z Intensity to 50. Turn off Mrgb on the top shelf; only ZAdd should be activated.

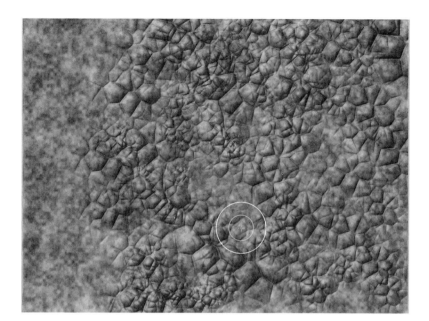

24. Paint on the surface in a sketchy manner, inflating the crack pattern on parts of the plane surface. Try not to be too uniform in the application of this brush.

25. Set the render mode to Best. The combination of the Color Bump setting and the details painted on the surface should make for a nice earthy texture.

26. In the Materials modifiers, set Cavity Intensity to 1000. This will darken the recessed areas on the plane.

27. Set the color picker to a dark brown. Click the cavity color swatch at the bottom of the Material modifiers.

28. Increase Cavity Colorize to .6. This adds the color chosen in the cavity color swatch to the dark color in the cavities.

29. Set Cavity Diffuse to .10. This adjusts the diffuse quality of the color in the cavities. Increasing this value lightens the color of the cavity a little.

30. Render the dirt using Best quality (Figure 8.51).

31. In the Layer palette, click the Bake button. This bakes all of the material and lighting information into the layer (Figure 8.52). Now when you switch to Preview render mode, the plane will look the same as it does in Best render mode. The only drawback is that the ground no longer responds to changes in lighting.

32. Save the material as Dirt.ZMT and the document as beetleScene.ZBR.

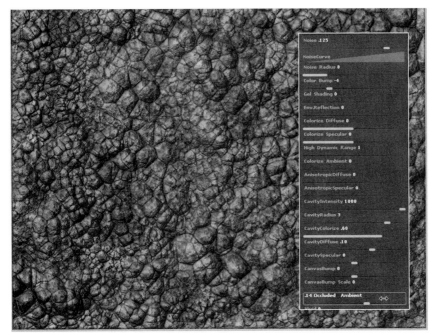

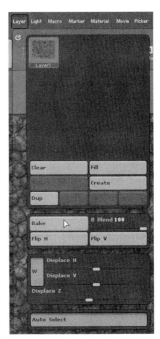

Figure 8.51

The combination of the material and the details on the surface create a nice dirt texture.

Figure 8.52

Baking the layer makes the material and lighting information a permanent part of the surface.

Painting Materials

Materials can be painted onto a 3D tool, just like colors. In this section you'll add the beetle model on a new layer and paint materials onto it.

1. Continue with the same document from the previous section or load the beetleScene_v1.ZBR document from the Chapter 8\Docs folder on the DVD.

2. Create a new layer in the Layer palette.

3. In the Tool palette, click the Load button and load the paintedBeetle.ZTL tool from the Chapter 8\ZTools folder on the DVD.

4. Draw the tool on the canvas and switch to Edit mode (Ctrl+t).

5. Rotate the tool so that the back of the beetle is facing you. Use the Shift key while rotating to snap it into place.

6. From the Material palette, choose the Basic 2 material; this will be applied to the beetle automatically.

7. On the top shelf, turn off ZAdd. Turn on the M button so that only material is applied.

15. Save the tool as paintedBeetle_v2.ZTL. A pop-up window will ask if you want to save the current alpha with the tool; since the alpha you are using is included in the Startup alpha inventory, you can click No.

16. Expand the Texture palette and click the Import button. Choose the plantTexture from the Chapter 8\textures folder on the DVD.

17. From the Material palette, select the JellyBean material. This material has the same controls as the Basic material. The settings stored with the material cause it to behave differently than the Basic material. Adjust the following settings:

    - Set Ambient to 27.

    - Set Diffuse to 70.

    - Set Specular to 75.

    - Set Reflectivity to 55.

    - Set Metalicity to 78. Metalicity mixes the color of the surface into the specular highlights, giving more of a metallic look.

    - Set Gel Shading to 1. Gel Shading adds a translucent quality to the surface.

    - Set Env. Reflection to 10.

    - Set High Dynamic Range to 2. This intensifies the lighting on the surface, seen mostly in the specular highlights. The slider value acts as a multiplier for all the shader values. The overall effect is to emulate the intense lighting range seen in the real world.

    - Set Anisotropic Specularity to .3. This alters the spread of specular highlights across the material. A rough metallic surface, such as brushed metal, tends to spread out the reflection of the light source. Anisotropic specularity emulates this effect.

    - Set Occluded Ambient to -.17. This creates ambient shadows in recessed parts of the surface.

    - In the Texture00 slot, add the plantTexture.PSD file.

18. Save the material using the Save button in the Material palette. Name it beetleWing.ZMT.

If ZBrush crashes while working on the materials, you can load the saved document, create a new layer, load the paintedBeetle2.ZTL tool that you saved, select the JellyBean material, and then load the beetleWing.ZMT material using the Load button in the Material palette. This will replace the JellyBean material painted on the wings with your saved material. All of these files are also available in the Chapter 8 folder of the DVD. Load the plantTexture.PSD file into the Texture palette. The beetleScene2.ZBR has the scene set up with painted materials; however, the Beetle layer has been dropped to canvas so the Beetle tool can no longer be rotated.

8. In the Color palette, click the FillObject button. This fills the object with the current material.

> In the Tool palette's Texture subpalette, the Colorize button needs to be activated to assign the material directly to the polygons.

You won't see any change in the Beetle tool, but if you switch to a different material in the material inventory, the material on the beetle will not change. However, you will be able to use a brush to paint a material directly on the beetle.

9. Select the JellyBean material from the material inventory.

10. From the Brush palette, select the Standard brush. Turn off the ZAdd button on the top shelf and turn on the M button so that the brush only paints the current material.

> You can use the Mrgb button to paint both material and color (Rgb) at the same time. Some artists prefer to paint the colors and the materials in separate passes.

11. Set Draw Size to 30 and Alpha to 01. There is no Intensity slider for materials. They are always applied at 100 percent intensity.

12. In the Transform palette, turn on the Activate Symmetry button. Click the >X< and M buttons so the symmetry is mirrored across the x-axis.

13. Paint the beetle's wings using the Standard brush (Figure 8.53).

14. Switch to the Darken Edge material, and use the same brush to paint this material on the beetle's legs and antenna.

Figure 8.53

The JellyBean material is painted on the beetle's wings.

19. Select the Darken Edge material, expand the Modifiers subpalette, and adjust the following settings:

    • Set Ambient to 20.

    • Set Diffuse to 40.

    • Set Specularity to 70.

    • Set Diffuse Power to 7. Higher settings reduce the spread of diffuse light across the surface of the material.

    • Set Specular Power to 135. This will reduce the size of the specular highlight.

    • Set Outer Intensity to 100. This will cause the edges of the tool where this material is applied to appear darker.

20. Save this material as beetleLeg.ZMT.

21. In the Environment subpalette of the Render palette, set Reflections to Scene.

22. Save the document.

23. Render the canvas using Best quality. Shadows will not be cast on the dirt layer because the lighting has been baked in; however, the dirt will show up in the environment reflections.

Painting Shadows

Since the lighting is baked into the dirt layer, the beetle can no longer cast shadows on the ground. This makes the composition look flat and awkward. Painting a quick drop shadow is a very easy fix for this problem.

1. In the Layer palette, turn off the visibility of the dirt layer. To do this, click it once so that the border of the layer icon is not highlighted, then click on the Beetle layer twice to select it. The dirt layer should become hidden.

2. With the Beetle layer visible and selected, open the Alpha palette and click the Grab-Doc button at the bottom. This will create an alpha based on the Beetle layer.

3. In the Alpha palette, the beetle alpha should be selected. Set the Blur slider to 8.

4. In the Alpha palette, click the MakeSt button to create a stencil from the alpha (stencils are covered in Chapter 7).

5. In the Layer palette, click on the ground layer twice, once to make it visible and again to select it.

6. In the Stencil palette, click the Actual button. This will set the size of the stencil to match the beetle.

7. Hold the spacebar to call up the stencil's Coin controller. While holding the spacebar, drag on the MOV at the bottom of the Coin controller to position the stencil beneath

the beetle. Make sure the stencil is slightly offset from the beetle, just as a drop shadow would be.

8. Select a dark brown or black in the color picker.

9. From the Tool palette, select the PaintBrush. In the top shelf, turn off ZAdd. Turn on Rgb. Set Rgb Intensity to 40.

10. Use the PaintBrush to paint over the stencil. This will darken the dirt layer based on the shape of the beetle, creating a nice drop shadow (Figure 8.54).

Figure 8.54

The beetle rendered at Best quality with a painted drop shadow

Creating MatCap Materials

MatCap (Material Capture) materials are designed to help artists integrate ZBrush strokes and tools seamlessly into photographs. Using the MatCap tool, the material quality of an object can be sampled directly from a photograph and applied to a 3D tool. ZBrush ships with 24 MatCap presets located at the top of the Material palette. This exercise will take you through the process of creating your own MatCap material.

MatCap materials include color information as sampled from the original images. Color applied to a stroke or tool using a texture or polypainting will be combined with the color of the MatCap material. MatCap materials also have lighting information baked into them, so they will not react to changes in the lighting of a scene.

To create a MatCap material, you'll start with one of the presets in the material inventory, make changes using the MatCap tool, adjust the settings, and save the material to your disk using a different name than the original preset.

1. Start ZBrush, or if ZBrush is open, click the Init ZBrush button in the Preferences palette to restore ZBrush to the initial settings.

2. In the texture inventory, click the Import button, and load the egg.PSD file from the Chapter 8\textures directory.

3. Select the Flat Color material.

4. In the texture inventory, click the Crop and Fill button. This will resize the current document to match the eggs1.PSD file's dimensions. It will fill the canvas with the texture.

5. In the Tool palette, select the Sphere3D tool, draw it on the canvas, and switch to Edit mode. Position the Sphere3D tool in the upper right, away from the eggs in the image.

6. From the Material palette, choose MatCap White material. This will be applied to the Sphere3D tool, you can use it as a guide as you work on creating the MatCap material (Figure 8.55).

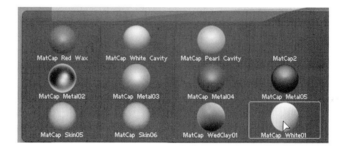

Figure 8.55

The MatCap White material makes a good starting place for creating your own MatCap material.

7. In the Transform palette, turn off the Quick Mode button.

8. From the Tool palette, select the MatCap tool. You may get a warning asking if you want to switch tools: click Switch to accept the warning.

9. Click on part of one of the eggs, near the center but not on the white highlight. An arrow with a circle will appear. As you move the brush, the angle of the arrow will change. The tool will sample the color from the point where you hold the brush.

   When you sample a color from the image and then set the normal angle by adjusting the MatCap tool's arrow icon, the polygons or pixols with a normal angle that matches the sample will receive the sampled color (Figure 8.56).

   You want to make the arrow point as if it's coming out of the surface of the egg, along the egg's normal. Imagine a toothpick sticking out of the egg, through the shell, pointing toward the center. Align the arrow as close as you can to the angle of the imaginary toothpick; that's basically the angle of the normal. The color you sample will be applied to any part of the 3D tool that has a matching normal. Since this is the first color sampled, it will be applied to the entire material. You'll see a preview of the material next to the arrow. The sphere you drew on the screen will also provide you with a preview of how the material will look. This explanation sounds much more complex than the actual practice of sampling the color. As you create more samples, it should become clearer.

10. Click on another part of one of the eggs, and position the arrow to match the direction of a surface normal coming from the egg. You don't need to have absolute precision here, just enough to get an idea.

11. Create seven or eight more sample points; you can use any of the eggs in the image. Notice how the preview circle updates with each sample. Sample the very outer edges of the egg as well as various points in the middle.

12. To sample the specular highlight on the egg, click on the highlight on one of the eggs. Hold the brush down (or hold the left mouse button) and press the Ctrl key. While holding the Ctrl key, drag the brush toward the right side of the screen (Figure 8.57). You'll see a highlight appear on the preview circle. As you drag to the right, the highlight becomes smaller and sharper; as you drag to the left, it becomes larger and blurrier.

Figure 8.56
The MatCap tool samples colors from the image and assigns them based on the normal angle you specify.

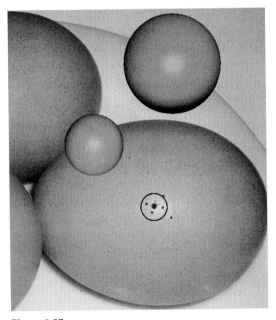

Figure 8.57
The radius of the highlight is set by sampling the color and dragging while holding the Ctrl key.

13. Use the brush and Ctrl key combination to create a highlight that matches what you see on the egg. The bumpy quality of the egg's surface will not be seen in the highlight you create; that's not part of the Mat Cap material. If you want to reproduce the egg exactly, you can sculpt that bumpiness into the surface. What you want to duplicate is the size of the highlight. On the egg, it's a fairly wide highlight.

14. Move the brush over the egg image without pressing on the mouse button or pressing on the tablet and you'll see dots appear at the positions where you sampled the image. If you position the brush over these spots, the arrow will reappear, allowing you to change the normal angle of the sample. You can remove the sample markers by holding the Alt key while clicking on the markers.

15. When you've set the highlight to match the egg in the photo, save the material using the Save button in the Material palette. Save it to your local disk as `MatCap_brownEgg.ZMT`.

16. Don't close ZBrush or change tools; continue with the next section to learn how to modify the material.

Modifying MatCap Materials

There are two sets of modifiers for the MatCap materials. Both sets are found in the Material palette when you have the material selected. The smaller set of modifiers will work only when the MatCap tool is the currently selected tool in the Tool palette. These modifiers affect how the tool samples the image, so they work while the tool is active. The second set of modifiers is found in the Modifiers subpalette of the Material palette when the material is selected in the inventory. These modifiers affect the look of the material, and you can change them at any time just like standard materials. This section discusses both sets of modifiers.

1. Continue with the document from the previous section. Make sure the MatCap tool is still the current tool. Set the render mode to Best to get a better idea of what the material will look like when rendered at full quality.

   Look at the settings at the bottom of the Material palette (not the settings in the Modifiers subpalette). These settings can be left alone if you're happy with the egg. If you do decide to change them, make your changes using very small increments; the sliders are sensitive (Figure 8.58).

Figure 8.58

The MatCap tool has a number of settings that adjust the look of the samples.

2. Set Gloss to 2.78. It adjusts the shiny gloss on the Egg material.

3. The Refine slider is slightly mysterious in what it does; you can adjust it very slightly and see if it makes the shader look more or less like the edges in the image. Try setting Refine to 12.

4. The Intensity slider adjusts the overall intensity of the material. Set it to 1.02.

5. Set Saturation to .88 to make the colors look a little less saturated and more natural.

6. The Contrast slider adjusts the dynamic range of the material. A low contrast will flatten the look of the material; higher contrast makes it look more dimensional. Set the contrast to 1.10.

7. The BackLight slider adjusts the colors at the edge of the material, helping to separate pixols and tools with the material applied from the rest of the image.

8. The Specular slider can help if the sampled specular highlight is not working as well as you'd like. For the egg, you can leave it at 0.

9. The Sample slider adjusts the sample radius of the tool. Changing the setting may have some effect on the material you create; for the egg you can leave it at 4.

> The MatCap button refreshes the markers and the material map. Click this button if the material is not updating.

10. Expand the Modifiers subpalette. These settings are available whenever you have this material selected regardless of the current tool. Notice that the material has only one shader channel. Also, at the very bottom you'll see an image of a sphere. This is the shading map.

11. Hold the mouse cursor over this image and an enlarged view appears in a pop-up window (Figure 8.59).

Figure 8.59

The shading map preview is seen at the bottom of the Modifiers subpalette for the MatCap material.

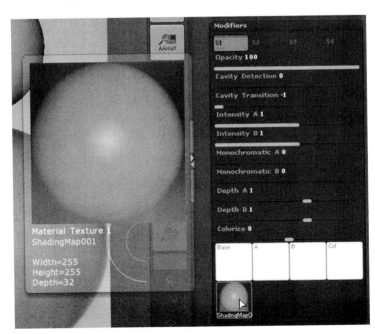

12. Click the B button in the Mat Cap tool Modifiers palette (next to the MatCap button) and take another sample from the image of the eggs. The B button creates a second shading map. You'll see that the shading map preview now has two spheres in it.

    The sphere on the left is a shading map for the raised areas on the pixols or 3D tools that have the material applied. The sphere on the right is the shading map for the recessed areas, or cavities. While the B button is activated, any samples you take from the image using the MatCap tool will be applied to the sphere on the right of the preview and thus all the recessed areas in the material. You can create an entirely different map for the recessed areas. The MatCap Red Wax material is an example of a material that uses two shading maps.

13. Take a few more samples from the image using the MatCap tool so that the B map looks different from the A map (Figure 8.60).

14. Delete some of the markers over the specular highlight on the image by clicking on them while holding the Alt key. Try to make the B map more of a matte (unshiny) surface.

15. In the Tool palette, select the Simple brush. Activate the ZSub button on the top shelf. Make sure the Mrgb, Rgb, and M buttons are off.

16. Set Draw Size to 16. Make a few small dents in the sphere that you drew on the canvas. This will help to see how the material reacts in the cavities created on a surface.

17. The Opacity slider blends between a flat color and the color of the material; leave it at 100 for now.

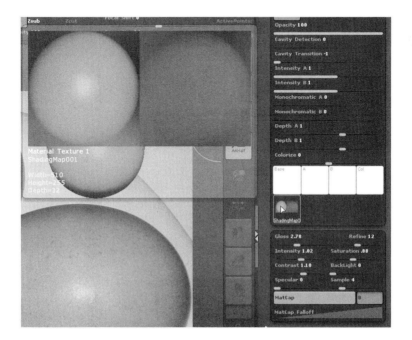

Figure 8.60

A second shading map, seen as an additional sphere in the preview, determines the coloring for the recessed areas of a surface with the material applied.

18. Set the Cavity Detection slider to 1. This controls the sensitivity of the material to the raised and lowered parts of the pixols or the 3D tool.

19. Set the Cavity Transition slider to -.5. This setting smoothes the transition between the recessed and raised areas. If you set this slider to .5, you will reverse the A and B channels so that shading map A (the preview sphere on the left) is applied to recessed areas and shading map B (the preview sphere on the right) is applied to raised areas.

20. Take a few moments to experiment with the other A and B sliders. These basically fine-tune the look of the A and B shading map channels. Increase the intensity of the B slider to 1.28 to give a translucent look to the material.

21. The four white swatches at the bottom of the modifiers add color to the A and B channels. You can drag from the swatch to a point on the image to sample the colors. Most often anything below the color white will darken the appearance of the material.

    The swatch on the far right affects the color that is added using the Colorize slider. The final MatCap texture is shown in Figure 8.61.

22. To see a movie (in vibrant color) demonstrating this process, open the matCap.mov file from the Chapter 8\movies folder on the DVD.

Figure 8.61

The final brown egg MatCap material

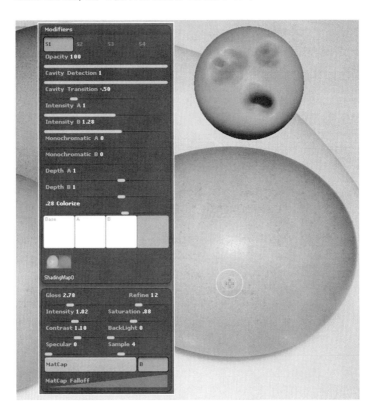

MatCap materials can be a lot of fun to make. The `Chapter 8\Textures` folder contains several other images that you can use to create your own MatCap materials. There are several example MatCap materials in the `Chapter 8\materials` folder that were created using the images. Load them into the Material palette and see how they react on 3D tools.

Summary

This chapter introduced you to the concept of rendering, lighting, and materials. Take advantage of the lights and materials as you create your digital sculptures, and remember that the properties of materials we covered in this chapter are just the beginning.

As you practice, you'll become more proficient at using lighting, materials, and rendering together to form cohesive compositions. You will quickly learn that ZBrush offers lots of possibilities for creating both realistic and stylistic images. You can also render passes using variations on lighting. These passes can be composited together in paint programs such as Photoshop.

CHAPTER 9

ZBrush with Other 3D Applications

ZBrush has become an important part of the production pipeline at many effects studios because of its unique modeling capabilities. It is often used to add detail to models created in other 3D applications. The workflow typically involves importing a preexisting model, sculpting details in ZBrush, and then exporting the modified version along with bump, normal, and displacement maps generated in ZBrush. ZBrush is also excellent for painting color, specular, and other maps that can be integrated into the models' shader networks in the rendering application.

This chapter includes the following topics:

- UV mapping
- ZBrush and Poser
- Bump, normal, and displacement maps
- ZBrush and Maya

UV Mapping

UVs are texture coordinates. Just as x-, y-, and z-coordinates tell you where an object is located in space, u and v coordinates tell you where a point exists on a surface. Imagine a dot drawn on a cardboard box. The u and v coordinates specify the location of that dot on the surface of the box. If you unfold the box and then place a grid over the flattened box you can plot the position of the dot using the grid. One axis of the grid is the u-coordinates; the other axis is the v-coordinates. 3D software uses u- and v-coordinates to determine how textures should be applied to 3D objects. UV mapping refers to the process of determining these coordinates for polygon objects. *UV layout* is a term that refers to the 2D configuration of the UVs on a surface, like a picture of the unfolded box on a grid taken from above (Figure 9.1).

Editing a texture "by hand" refers to the practice of exporting a 2D texture that has been to a 3D tool or object and then painting the texture in a 2D paint program such as Photoshop. The UV layout can act as a guide to help a texture artist understand which parts of the model are being painted. You can edit textures by hand in ZBrush by filling the canvas with the current texture and then using the 2.5D paint brushes to paint changes into the texture.

Figure 9.1

The basic UV layout for a cube resembles an unfolded box.

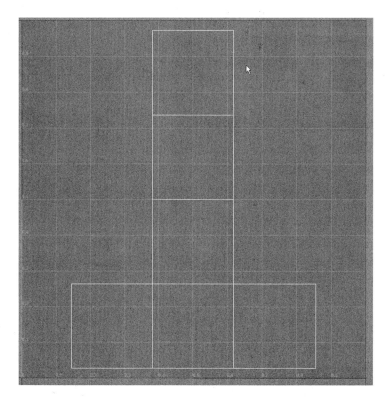

ZBrush has several basic controls for creating and applying UV maps on a 3D tool. These are located in the Texture subpalette of the Tool palette (Figure 9.2). Load the DemoHead.ZTL tool and draw it on the canvas to enable the controls in the Texture subpalette.

The following list provides a brief description of what each button does.

Enable UV and Disable UV The Enable UV button activates UV mapping for the polymesh tool. All of the UV mapping buttons are unavailable unless this button is active.

> Disable UV actually deletes any UV mapping applied to a tool. Use this button with caution!

Uv>Txr The Uv>Txr button creates a color-coded texture based on the UV layout (Figure 9.3). You can use it as a guide for painting 2D textures in ZBrush or in another paint program.

Uv Check The Uv Check button also creates a texture based on the UV layout applied to the 3D tool. The texture it creates is shaded red wherever UVs overlap in the model (Figure 9.4). Overlapping UVs can cause texture maps to render incorrectly and can often cause the software to crash when rendering.

Vertex>Txr and Poly>Txr The Vertex>Txr and Poly>Txr buttons create color-coded texture maps based on the position of individual vertices and polygons, respectively.

Figure 9.2

The Texture subpalette in the Tool palette has basic controls for editing UVs on a 3D polymesh tool.

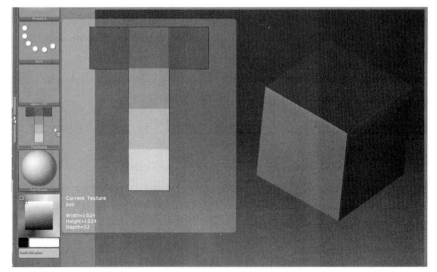

Figure 9.3

The Uv>Txr button creates a color-coded texture displaying how the UVs are mapped on the 3D polymesh tool.

Figure 9.4

**The Uv Check button
creates a texture
that is colored red
(shaded dark gray in
this image) where
the UVs overlap.**

Uvc, Uvp, and Uvs The Uvc, Uvp, and Uvs buttons create a simple UV layout based on the shape of a cylinder, plane, and sphere, respectively. It's unlikely that these buttons will be useful unless you are working with very simple objects.

UVTile The UVTile button applies UV mapping to each individual polygon and applies the entire texture to each polygon. This button is best used with seamless textures such as the snake scale texture created in Chapter 7.

GUVTiles The GUVTiles button creates groups of UVs and assigns the texture based on these groups (Figure 9.5). This is similar to automatic UV mapping methods used in other 3D programs. The UV mapping is generally even, but the resulting 2D layout does not bear an obvious resemblance to the shape of the model, which makes it difficult to edit the texture by itself.

AUVTiles The AUVTiles button creates a grid of square tiles and maps a square portion of the texture to each tile. Larger polygons receive more tiles than smaller polygons. This button makes for a very even UV mapping, but the resulting texture can't easily be modified by hand (Figure 9.6).

The sliders and controls below these buttons allow you to tune the manner in which the UV mapping is applied.

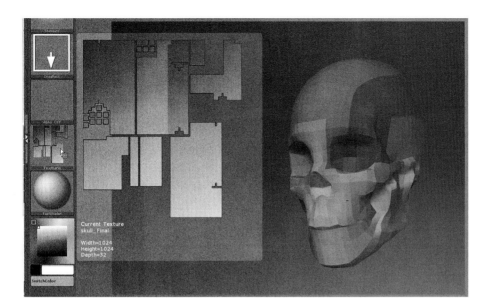

Figure 9.5
**Group UVTiles
creates a simple
UV layout for the
3D polymesh tool.**

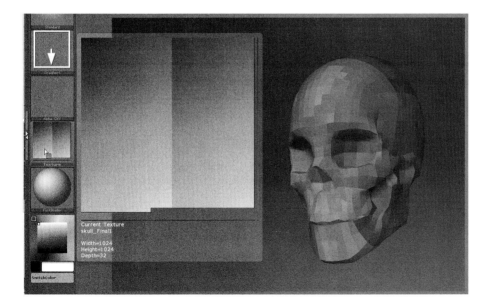

Figure 9.6
**AUVTiles creates
a grid of UVs.**

In practice, while these controls are useful for very simple objects or in situations where no further editing to textures needs to be done, you will generally want to take the time to lay out the UVs thoughtfully and carefully, just as you model creatures. UV mapping is like doing your taxes; it's no fun, and sooner or later you have to do it (although no one has yet been arrested for failing to map UVs properly). In production situations, UV mapping is usually done in another 3D application such as Maya, 3ds Max, LightWave, or XSI. There are also applications that are devoted solely to UV mapping, and these are generally worth investigating. UV Layout by Headus (www.uvlayout.com) is particularly good.

There are several important things to keep in mind when creating a UV layout for models that are imported into ZBrush. You should avoid overlapping UVs at all costs, the UVs should lie within the borders of the UV mapping grid, and ZBrush can work only with models that have a single UV set. Figure 9.7 shows a proper UV layout created in Maya and imported with the skull model.

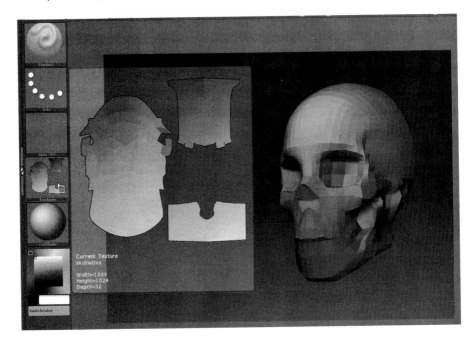

The most useful button in the Texture subpalette is the Check UV button. Make it a practice to check your UVs every time you import a model from another program. If there is a problem, fix the UV outside of ZBrush, re-import, and check it again.

It is possible to create an original 3D tool in ZBrush and then use another program to create UVs for the 3D too. You need to export the 3D Tool as a Wavefront OBJ format model at a low subdivision level, import it into another program, such as Maya, and create the UVs. You then export the model with its UVs as an OBJ and import it back into ZBrush. The updated UVs will be imported with the model.

ZBrush and Poser

Curious Labs Poser is a 3D character generation application often used for illustration and animation. It comes with a wide variety of 3D characters that can be customized, posed, and animated. You can easily export models from Poser into many other 3D applications, including ZBrush. Likewise, objects made in ZBrush can be imported into Poser.

In this section you'll learn a basic workflow for importing a skeleton model created in Poser into ZBrush. You will then use ZBrush to sculpt a muscle that you can export from ZBrush, bring back into Poser, and add to the original skeleton. If you're not familiar with or do not have Curious Labs Poser, that's okay. Reading through the section will give you a basic idea for how you can use a similar technique to import and export ZBrush tools into other 3D applications. You may want to watch the `sternomastoid.mov` movie in the Chapter 9 folder of the DVD to see how the example project was created.

Exporting from Poser

This demonstration uses Poser 6; however, this same workflow should work for other versions of the programs.

1. In Poser, start with a skeleton model and a simple standing pose.

2. From the File menu, choose Export → Wavefront object (Figure 9.8).

3. A dialog box opens asking for the frame range of the exported object. Choose Single Frame (Figure 9.9).

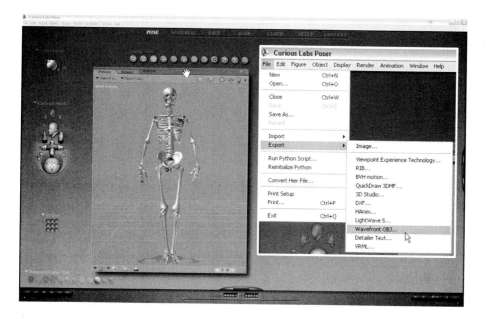

Figure 9.8

A skeleton model is exported from Poser as a Wavefront object.

Figure 9.9

**Export a single
frame from ZBrush.**

4. A second dialog box opens that shows the hierarchy of objects in the scene. You want to export only the skeleton, not the rest of the scene. From the hierarchy, deselect the Universe and Ground boxes. The box below this will be the name of the current pose (in the example, JamesCasual is the name of the pose applied to the skeleton). Choose this current pose, and all objects below it should remain selected (Figure 9.10).

5. Save the file to your local disk as skeleton.obj.

6. After you name your file (skeleton.obj) and save it to a location (your local disk), a third dialog box opens. Select only Weld Body Part Seams; leave all others unselected.

Figure 9.10

**Select the parts of
the hierarchy you
want to export.**

Importing into ZBrush

The skeleton model will be imported into ZBrush as a 3D polymesh tool.

1. Open a new session of ZBrush. From the startup window, choose Other.

2. Click the Import button in the Tool palette (not the Document palette), and then browse your computer and find the `skeleton.obj` file you exported from Poser. You can also use the `skeleton.obj` file included in the Poser directory in the Chapter 9 folder of the DVD.

3. Draw the Skeleton tool on the canvas and switch to Edit mode (Ctrl+t).

4. The tool is a single polymesh; however, the polymesh itself is composed of a number of parts. You can separate these parts into polygroups, which can make working with the tool much easier if you need to mask or hide parts. The polygroups are visible on the tool when the Frame button on the right shelf is activated.

   In the Tool palette, expand the Polygroups button and click the Auto Groups button (Figure 9.11).

5. Ctrl+Shift+click on the skull and the rest of the skeleton will be hidden. Ctrl+Shift+click on a blank spot on the canvas and the visibility is restored.

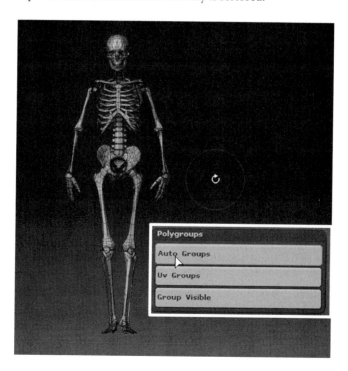

Figure 9.11

Separate the skeleton into polygroups by clicking the Auto Groups button.

Creating the Sternomastoid Muscle

For this example you'll use ZBrush to create a simple sternomastoid muscle. This muscle connects the skull from behind the ear to the collarbone and the sternum. The sculpting techniques are similar to those used on the skull in Chapter 5 and the Medusa in Chapter 6. Once again, a good anatomy reference is helpful in understanding the shape of the muscle. A quick search on the Internet for "sternomastoid" should also yield some useful reference diagrams.

1. In the Tool palette, click the Load button. Browse your computer to the `Program Files\ Pixologic\ZBrush3\Ztools` directory and load the PolySphere object. It will load onto the canvas; most likely it will appear quite large.

2. In the Tool palette, select the Skeleton tool to switch back to the skeleton.

3. Ctrl+Shift+drag the selection marquee around the skeleton's head, neck, and collarbones. When you let go of the marquee, the parts of the skeleton that lie outside of the green selection marquee should disappear. If it doesn't work, then Ctrl+Shift+ click on a blank part of the canvas to unhide the rest of the skeleton and try again (Figure 9.12).

4. Expand the Subtool palette. Click the Append button and choose the PolySphere tool from the menu. The PolySphere will be much larger than the skeleton (Figure 9.13).

5. In the Subtool palette, select the PolySphere subtool. Click the Rename button and name it sternomastoid.

6. Expand the Deformation subpalette in the Tool palette. Click the Unify button. The sternomastoid will scale to the same size as the skeleton (Figure 9.14).

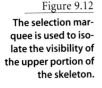

Figure 9.12

The selection marquee is used to isolate the visibility of the upper portion of the skeleton.

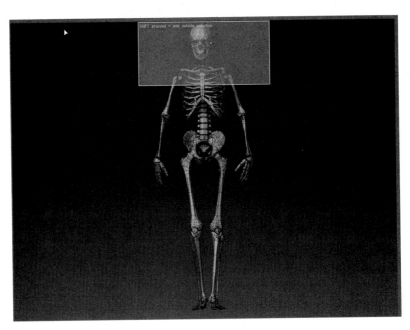

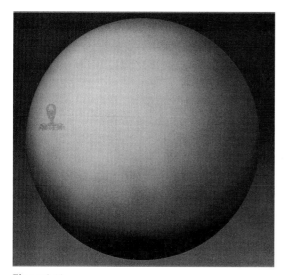

Figure 9.13

The appended PolySphere is much larger than the skeleton.

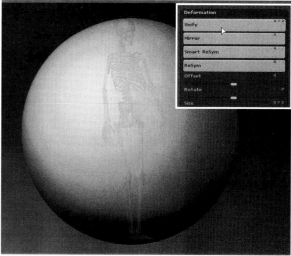

Figure 9.14

The sternomastoid is scaled to match the size of the skeleton using the Unify button in the Deformation subpalette.

7. In the Geometry subpalette, set the SDiv slider to 1. Click the Reconstruct Subdivision button twice to add two lower subdivision levels to the tool (working with subdivision levels is covered in Chapter 5).

8. With the sternomastoid subtool still selected in the SubTool palette, turn on the Scale button (hotkey = e) on the top shelf to activate the Transpose handle.

9. Click on the upper-left corner of the PolySphere and drag diagonally to the lower right. This will draw the Transpose handle across the front of the polysphere.

10. Click on the inside circle of the Transpose handle at the lower right and drag upward to scale the polysphere so that it fits roughly between the bottom of the skull and the collarbone (Figure 9.15).

11. Click the Move button on the top shelf (hotkey = w) to set the Transpose handle to Move mode. Draw the Transpose handle across the surface of the sternomastoid again and drag on the center circle to position the sternomastoid subtool at the left side of the skull.

12. You can use the Transpose handle to nonproportionally scale the sternomastoid while the Move button is still activated. In fact, this approach works better in some cases than using the Transpose handle in Scale mode. When you use Transpose with Move, you move the vertices near the outer handles, which is in effect the same as nonproportional scaling.

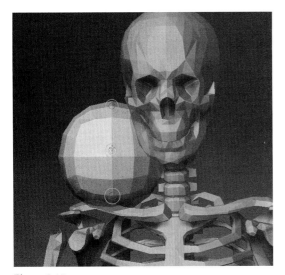

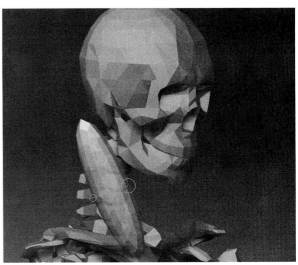

Figure 9.15

The Transpose handle is used to scale and position the Sternomastoid subtool.

Figure 9.16

The sternomastoid is shaped into an elongated sphere.

Drag on the circles at the end of the Transpose handle to scale the sternomastoid. You want to shape it into an elongated ellipse. Then use the Transpose handle in Rotate and Move mode to position the muscle so that it stretches diagonally from the bottom of the skull to the sternum. Use Figure 9.16 as a guide.

13. Click the Draw button on the top shelf. From the brush inventory, choose the Move brush. Set the draw size to 30 and the Z Intensity slider to 100.

14. Stretch the sternomastoid so that it reaches the base of the skull and the top of the sternum.

15. Select the Smooth brush from the brush inventory. Set the Z Intensity slider to 20. Use the brush to smooth the shape of the muscle (Figure 9.17).

Figure 9.17

The Move and Smooth brushes are used to shape the sternomastoid.

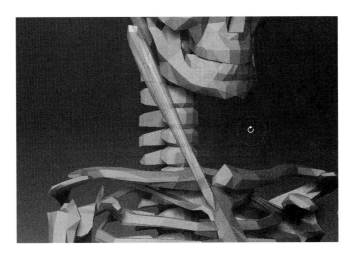

Sculpting the Muscle

The sternomastoid muscle splits into branches at the bottom: one branch attaches to the collarbone and the other to the sternum. It's a good idea to add some extra geometry on the original polysphere for the branch that attaches to the collarbone. The best way to do this is to add some edge loops to the sternomastoid. Creating edge loops is covered in Chapter 6. The following steps are a quick review.

1. In the Transform palette, click the Pt Sel button; this will enable you to select polygons by any one of their points.

2. Turn off the visibility of the Skeleton subtool.

3. Zoom in so that you can see the back of the sternomastoid geometry. Click the Frame button on the right shelf so that a wireframe is drawn on the geometry. This will help you see when you are trying to select individual polygons.

4. You want to hide all of the polygons that make up the sternomastoid muscle except for those on the back. To do this, Ctrl+Shift+drag a selection marquee around the polygons you want to hide. Release the Shift button so that the marquee turns from green to red. Then let go of the Ctrl button. Repeat this process until all the polygons you want to hide are hidden. The sternomastoid.mov QuickTime movie in the Chapter 9 folder of the DVD shows how this is done.

> Remember that you can activate the Lasso button on the right shelf to set the selection marquee to Lasso mode. You may find it easier to draw your selections using the lasso instead of the default square selection marquee.

5. The edge loop will be created around the remaining visible polygons. In the Geometry subpalette of the Tool palette, click the Edge Loop button. This will create a ring of polygons that surround the visible part of the sternomastoid.

6. Polygroups are automatically created when you perform an edge loop action. These polygroups are indicated by the different colors applied to the polygons. Ctrl+Shift+click on one of the polygons on the outer edge on the edge loop to hide them. This process does take a little practice to master. Don't get too frustrated if it doesn't work immediately for you. Once you have it down, it will become second nature.

7. Click the Edge Loop button again to create another group of polygons (Figure 9.18). The added geometry created by the edge loops will help you to build the second branch of the muscle and reduce a lot of the stretching you might otherwise encounter.

8. Ctrl+Shift+click on a blank part of the canvas to restore the visibility of the rest of the sternomastoid subtool.

9. Turn the visibility of the Skeleton subtool back on.

10. Use the Standard, Move, Smooth, Inflate, and Pinch brushes to create the shape of the muscle (Figure 9.19). The `sternomastoid.mov` movie in the Chapter 9 folder of the DVD shows how the muscle was sculpted for the example file.

Figure 9.18

Edge loops are created to add geometry to the subtool.

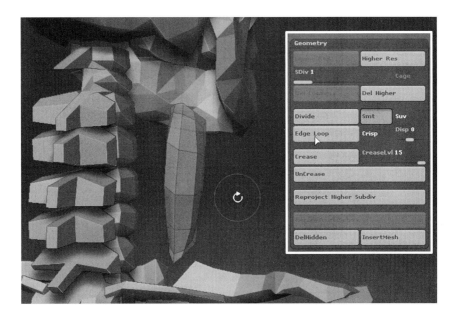

Figure 9.19

The muscle is shaped using the Move, Smooth, Inflate, Standard, and Pinch brushes.

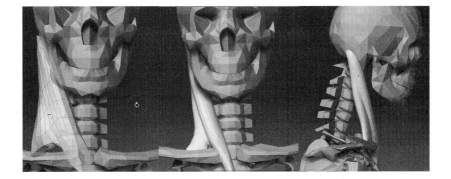

The sculpting process is no different than those used in Chapter 5 to create the skull. Remember to rough out the shape as best as you can at subdivision level 1, then increase the SDiv slider in the geometry palette to the next level and make more changes. Avoid jumping to a high subdivision level immediately when shaping the model. Each time you move up a subdivision level, you'll probably need to do some smoothing. For this exercise, the final muscle does not need to be any higher than SDiv 3. In fact, it should work just fine at SDiv 2.

Painting the Muscle

You can paint colors onto the muscle in ZBrush, export the color as a texture map, and apply it to the muscle when it's imported into Poser.

1. Continue with the file you created in the previous section, or load the skeleton2.ZTL tool into ZBrush. Draw the tool on the canvas and switch to Edit mode (hotkey = Ctrl+t).

2. From the material inventory, select the Fast Shader material.

3. In the Tool palette, select the Sternomastoid subtool.

4. Turn off the visibility of the Skeleton2 subtool.

5. In the Tool palette, expand the Texture subpalette. Click the Colorize button (Figure 9.20).

Figure 9.20

Activate the Colorize button in the Texture subpalette to enable polypainting.

6. From the brush inventory, choose the Standard brush.

7. On the top shelf, turn off the ZAdd button; make sure the Rgb button is on and set Rgb Intensity to 100.

8. Select a red color from the color picker. Paint the muscle red.

9. Select a white color, lower the Rgb Intensity slider to 30, and paint on the ends of the muscle where the muscle is attached to the bone.

10. Set the SDiv slider in the Geometry subpalette to level 1 to move to the lowest subdivision level. This is required when creating UVs for a 3D tool.

11. The PolySphere tool has UV coordinates already mapped out. However, when you added edge loops to the polysphere, these coordinates became invalid. Generate new coordinates by clicking the GUVTiles (Group UV Tiles) button in the Texture subpalette. This creates a very basic UV map that should be fine for your simple muscle shape.

12. To create the texture from the painted colors, click the Col>Txr button in the Texture subpalette of the Tool palette. This will generate a texture map and place it in the texture inventory (Figure 9.21).

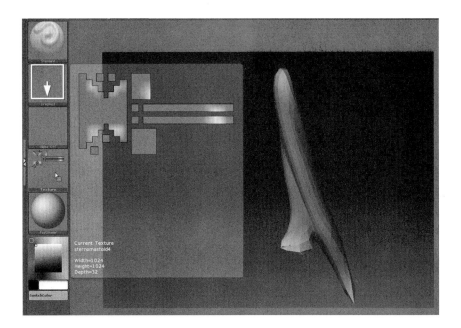

13. Open the texture inventory and you'll that see a new texture is created in the upper part of the inventory. The shape of the texture map reflects how the UVs were created for the muscle.

14. Click the Export button at the bottom of the inventory and save the texture to your local disk. Save the file as a bitmap (.bmp) file; Poser prefers this file type for textures.

Exporting the Muscle from ZBrush

You're ready to export the sternomastoid tool from ZBrush as a Wavefront OBJ format object.

1. Select the Sternomastoid subtool in the Subtool palette.

2. Expand the Export subpalette at the bottom of the Tool palette.

3. Activate the Obj button so that the format of the exported file will be a Wavefront OBJ file.

4. Click Qud so that the exported geometry is all quadrilaterals. This may not be absolutely necessary for Poser files, but it's a good habit to keep when exporting for use in other programs.

5. You don't need subgroups to be exported, so deactivate the Grp button. You also don't need to merge the UVs or flip the normals, so you can keep the Flp and Mrge buttons deactivated.

6. Click Export and save the file to your local disk (Figure 9.22).

Figure 9.22

The settings in the Export subpalette

Importing the Muscle into Poser

Importing into Poser is extremely easy. You can use this technique for any props that you would like to make for your Poser characters.

1. Start Poser and load the skeleton.ps3 file from the Chapter 9 folder of the DVD.

2. Choose File → Import → Wavefront Object and select the sternomastoid.obj file (Figure 9.23).

3. In the pop-up window, deactivate all of the check boxes except the one labeled "Make polygon normals consistent." Deactivating these options will ensure that the muscle appears in the proper position relative to the skeleton.

4. The texture should be automatically applied to the muscle object. Do a test render to see.

5. If the muscle renders with a black color applied, it may be because ZBrush and Poser interpret UV coordinates slightly differently. To fix the problem, you'll need to go into the Materials → Advanced tab and set the V coordinates to -1 for the texture. This will flip the texture upside down (Figure 9.24).

6. Open the skeleton2.ps3 file from the Chapter 9 folder of the DVD to see a version with the muscle imported (Figure 9.25). You may get a pop-up box asking for the location of the texture file exported from ZBrush.

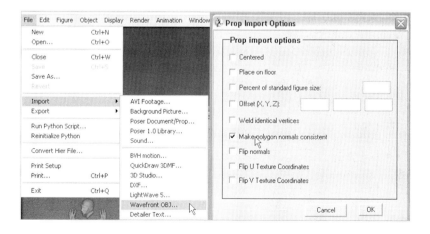

Figure 9.23

The import settings in Poser

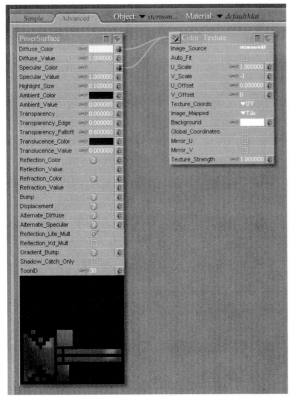

Figure 9.24

The texture coordinates in Poser are flipped in the Advanced tab of the Materials editor.

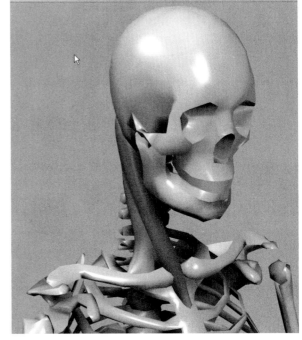

Figure 9.25

The skeleton and muscle are rendered in Poser.

Bump, Displacement, and Normal Maps

Bump, displacement, and normal maps are all types of 2D textures that you can use to add detail to a 3D object at render time. The technology used to calculate these types of textures differs, but they all share the same purpose: to add a fine level of detail to a 3D object that would be otherwise difficult or impractical to create directly in the geometry of the 3D object.

As you are well aware by now, ZBrush can easily handle extremely dense, detailed meshes. You're more likely to use bump, displacement, and normal maps in another 3D application such as Maya, 3D Studio Max, LightWave, or XSI. ZBrush is designed to convert the sculpted details you make for your model into any of these types of texture maps. So a typical workflow would be either to create an original model as a 3D polymesh tool in ZBrush or to import a low-resolution model created in another 3D application, sculpt the details at a higher subdivision level in ZBrush, and then export the 3D polymesh tool from

ZBrush as a 3D object at a low subdivision level. Then you would generate bump, normal, or displacement maps (usually some combination of these) for the details that exist on the tool at higher subdivision levels and export them as 2D textures from ZBrush. You then apply the textures to the object in the other 3D application, and with a little work, when the object is rendered it will look just like the highly detailed object you created in ZBrush.

The following sections briefly describe how bump, displacement, and normal maps generally work in most 3D applications. Different applications will have some variation in how they apply and calculate these textures, but for the most part, they all work the same way.

Bump Maps

A bump map is a grayscale image that causes a surface in a 3D program to appear bumpy at render time. The lighter parts of the texture tell the 3D application's renderer to make the surface appear as though it is raised; the darker parts tell it to make the surface appear lower or indented. Bump maps calculate fairly quickly, but they do not actually alter the geometry of the object. If you look at the silhouette edge of a surface that has been rendered with only a bump map, you'll notice that the surface is not actually bumpy; it just appears as though it is on the parts of the surface that face the camera. Bump maps do not actually produce shadows either (Figure 9.26). Bump maps are best used for fine details such as pores on skin. When used properly, bump maps can add realism to an object without adding too much to render time. They are usually best used in combination with displacement maps.

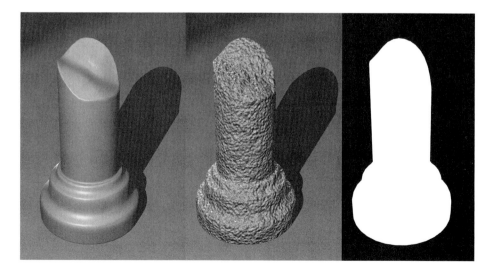

Figure 9.26

A texture is applied to the bump channel of an object rendered in Maya. Notice that the silhouette, shown in the alpha channel on the right, does not show the effect of the bump map.

Displacement Maps

A displacement map is similar to a bump map in that it is a grayscale image designed to produce a bumpy look on a surface at render time. Just as with bump maps, the lighter areas of the image raise the surface, the darker areas lower the surface. However, unlike bump maps, displacement maps do actually change the surface of the geometry. This means that the silhouette edges of geometry rendered with a displacement map reflect the changes in the geometry created by the displacement map. Displacement maps cast shadows as well (Figure 9.27). They are ideal for larger details such as wrinkles and scales. They can add a significant amount of time to renders, so it's best to optimize the use and application of displacement maps as much as possible.

Because a displacement map interprets the light and dark of a 2D texture as changes in surface elevation, you should be aware of how you use certain brushes when creating details intended for use in a displacement map. The Pinch and Inflate brushes (and several others, such as Blob and Magnify) move the surface of the geometry based on the normals of the surface. The details that appear squeezed or pushed apart in ZBrush will not necessarily look the same when converted to a displacement map and rendered in another 3D package. That's not to say that you should avoid these brushes altogether; just be aware that when converted to a displacement map, the details you create with these particular brushes may not look exactly the same when rendered in another application.

Figure 9.27

A texture is applied as a displacement map of an object rendered in Maya. Notice that the silhouette, shown in the alpha channel on the right, does show the effect of the displacement map.

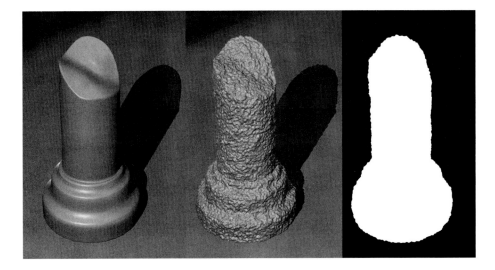

Normal Maps

A normal map is similar to bump and displacement maps in that it is a 2D texture that makes a surface appear bumpy at render time. However, a normal map differs significantly in how it is generated. A surface normal defines the direction in which a polygon is facing relative to the camera as well as to the lights in the scene. Think of a normal as a line that points out 90 degrees from the surface of a polygon. A normal map uses the red, green, and blue channels of a texture to change the direction in which the normal faces without actually changing the orientation of the polygon. The lights in the scene react to the altered position of the normal, giving the appearance of more detail. The renderer very quickly calculates normal maps. This makes them well suited for use in games and real-time rendering engines.

The diagram in Figure 9.28 shows a normal at a 90-degree angle from the surface of a single polygon. The circle at the left is a light that shades the polygon at render time. In the second diagram, the polygon is tilted away from the light. It is shaded gray to show that less light is hitting the polygon, thus making it appear darker than the top diagram. The third diagram shows what happens when a texture is applied as a normal map. Even though the orientation of the polygon is the same as in the top diagram, the normal map bends the normal and causes the polygon to appear shaded, as if it were tilted the same way as in the second diagram. The red, green, and blue colors in the normal map determine the x-, y-, and z- directions in which the normal is bent.

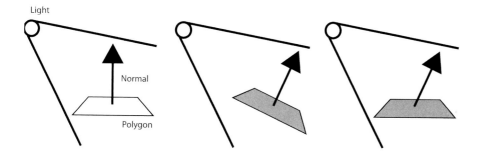

Figure 9.28

The diagram shows how normals are affected when a normal map is applied.

A normal map stores information in the red, green, and blue channels of a texture map. Each color channel stores a value that tells the lights in the scene which way each normal on the surface is facing when the object is rendered. Since displacement and bump maps use a simple grayscale image, they can easily be created and edited in a 2D painting program such as Photoshop because a texture artist can easily interpret how the light and dark areas of the texture relate to the surface of the object. The same is not true for normal maps. The normal map's red, green, and blue colors do not give an artist an intuitive sense of how a surface will look when it is rendered using a normal map. For this reason, normal maps can only be generated automatically by the software; it is impossible for an artist to paint a correct normal map. ZBrush can translate the details sculpted into a surface into a normal map that can then be exported from ZBrush for use in other 3D packages.

There are two types of normal maps: object space normal maps and tangent space normal maps. Object space normal maps are generated with the assumption that the normal direction is relative to object space coordinates. In other words, a normal pointing upward is assumed to be pointing toward the top of the object. Tangent space maps are generated with the assumption that the normal's direction is relative to the direction in which each polygon faces. So "up" to a tangent space map refers to up, away from the surface of the polygon, regardless of whether that polygon is on the top or the bottom of the model. Object space maps are generated very quickly and are best used for nondeforming models such as buildings. Tangent maps take longer to generate and are best used for objects that deform, such as animated characters. Some 3D packages, such as Maya 8.5, will use tangent maps for all types of 3D objects. Maya 2008 allows both tangent and object space normal maps (Figure 9.29).

Normal maps are gaining popularity as an alternative to bump maps. The choice to use one over the other depends on your software and the specific requirements of your scene. A complete discussion of the merits of one over the other is beyond the scope of this book.

Figure 9.29

A texture is applied to the bump channel of an object as a tangent space normal map and then rendered in Maya. Notice that the silhouette, shown in the alpha channel on the right, does not show the effect of the normal map.

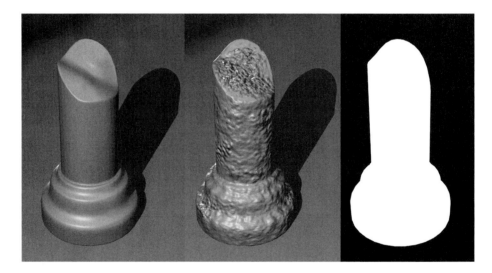

ZBrush and Maya

ZBrush can be easily used with any 3D package, and in this exercise we will use Maya as an example external 3D application. The specific techniques used will differ for other packages, but the general ideas will be similar. The ZBrush documentation contains comprehensive guides on using ZBrush with most of the more popular 3D animation applications. Really, the techniques used within ZBrush are the same; the only difference is the settings and techniques used in each individual application.

For this section, you will export a simple model of a broken marble column from Maya, import it into ZBrush, and edit it. Then you will export the model and various texture maps from ZBrush and import them back into Maya for rendering.

Exporting from Maya

Polygon objects created in Maya should be exported as Wavefront OBJ format files. Before exporting from Maya, there are a few things you should do to prepare your model. In the case of the broken column model in this exercise, you will make some changes in ZBrush and create bump, normal, and displacement maps as well as color texture maps. The edited model and the maps will be brought back into Maya and the column will be rendered using mental ray.

If you have Maya, open the column.mb file from the Chapter 9\introducingZBrush\scenes directory. If you are using another 3D application, import the column.obj file from the Chapter 9\IntroducingZbrush\data directory; you should be able to follow along fairly easily.

1. Select the column in Maya and take a look at its topology. Generally, when you export for editing in ZBrush, you will want the polygons in the model to have a relatively even size. This is so that when you sculpt detail into the model in ZBrush, the details do not appear stretched or blocky in areas where there are fewer polygons.

All models must be exported as polygons, if you are using a NURBS or subdivision surface model, you'll need to convert it to polygons before exporting as a Wavefront OBJ.

The main cylinder of the column has been divided in Maya so that it can support sculpted details. The edges at the base of the column have several closely spaced divisions so that the profile of the edge shape is maintained when the model is subdivided in ZBrush (Figure 9.30).

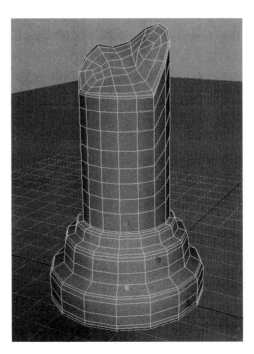

Figure 9.30

The column model as modeled in Maya

2. With the column selected, open the UV texture editor (Window → UV Texture Editor).

The UVs have already been prepared for the model (Figure 9.31). Notice that they have been mapped in such a way that if the textures need to be edited in a 2D paint program, the texture artist can easily see which parts of the 2D texture relate to the parts of the 3D model. Also notice that much more space has been given to accommodate the UVs on the top of the column than at the bottom. In this shot the column is standing upright; the bottom will not be seen, so it does not need to have much texture space devoted to it. There will be a fair amount of detail on the top so the UVs that relate to the top occupy a large portion of the UV layout. Notice also that the UVs lie within the borders of the grid and not on the very edge.

Figure 9.31
The UV layout in Maya

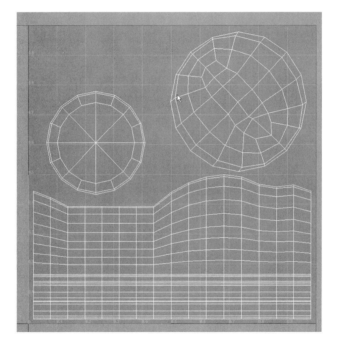

3. To export the model, select it in Maya and choose File → Export Selection→ Options. Select the OBJ format for export. Use the default settings (Figure 9.32). Name the file `column.obj` and save it to a local directory on your disk. The UVs will be exported with the model.

If the OBJ format does not appear in the export options, you may need to load the OBJ Exporter plug-in. To do this in Maya, choose Preferences→ Plug in Manager, find the `objEx-port.mll` plug-in in the list, and check the box next to Loaded. Apply the settings in the plug-in manager and try exporting again.

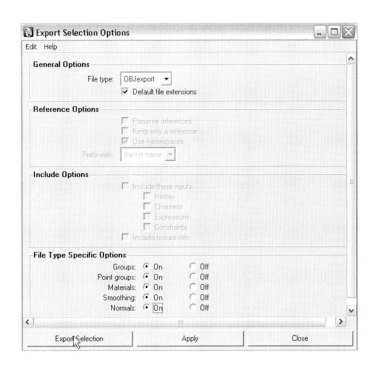

Figure 9.32

**The export options
in Maya**

4. Close Maya and open ZBrush. From the startup screen, choose Other.

5. In the Tool palette, click the Import button. Browse your computer and load the `column.obj` file that you exported from Maya, or load the `column.obj` file from the `Chapter 9\IntroducingZbrush\Data` folder on the DVD.

6. Draw the column tool on the canvas and click the Edit button on the top shelf to switch to Edit mode (Ctrl+t).

Sculpting in ZBrush

You will make some simple changes to the column. The shot calls for a broken, worn marble column. The column will appear large in the shot, so you will need to sculpt a fair amount of detail into the model.

1. In the Texture subpalette of the Tool palette, click the UV Check button. A texture will be applied to the model. The texture should be completely gray (Figure 9.33); if there are any problems with the texture, the problem areas will be colored red. Switch the texture back to Texture Off in the texture inventory once you have confirmed that there are no problems with the UV mapping on the 3D tool.

2. In the Material palette, select the Fast Shader.

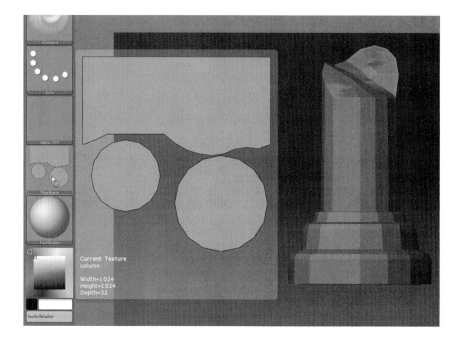

3. In the Geometry palette, click the Divide button four times to give the model a total of five subdivision levels (128,000 polygons).

4. In the Brush palette, select the Smooth brush and lower the Z Intensity slider to 20. This way, when you toggle smoothing using the Shift key, your work won't be completely obliterated by the Smooth brush.

5. Select the Standard brush. Set the Draw Size to 30 and the Focal Shift to -45. Set the Z Intensity to 40. The Stroke Type should be Freehand.

6. In the Transform palette, click on the Activate Symmetry button. Set the axis to Y (turn off X). Turn on the radial symmetry (R) and set the radial count to 8. Make sure the mirroring button >M< is also activated.

7. In the Stroke palette, activate the LazyMouse button. Set LazyRadius to 200.

8. Rotate the column so that the tallest side is facing the front of the canvas.

9. Position the brush above the base of the column on the side. Hold the Alt key and slowly drag upward. Because of the large lazy stroke radius, there is a significant delay before the brush starts to do anything to the column. Use this delay to make sure the red line that indicates the lazy mouse is vertical and straight. This will ensure that the flutes are sculpted perfectly straight into the side of the column.

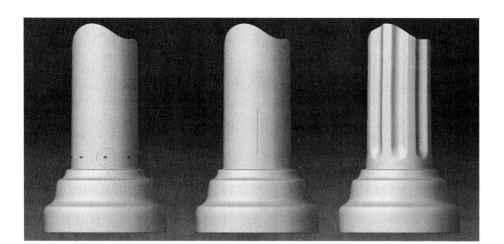

Figure 9.34

The LazyMouse setting makes it easy to draw straight fluting on the column.

10. Pull upward on the brush, keeping it straight, until you are well past the top of the column. You want the flutes to appear as though they extend past the broken top of the column (Figure 9.34).

11. Select the Clay brush. Choose Alpha 25 and set the Stroke Type to Spray. Set the Draw Size to 25 and the Z Intensity to 15.

12. In the Transform palette, deactivate the Activate Symmetry button. Click the ZSub button on the top shelf, or hold the Alt key as you sculpt. Use the Clay brush to sculpt nooks and crannies into the top of the column to give it the appearance of broken marble.

13. Worn marble has an almost melted quality to it. Use the Smooth brush to smooth patches into the detail.

14. Use the Clay brush to sculpt broken and warn patches on the sides and base of the column. Vary the Draw Size and Z Intensity as you go to avoid producing a uniform look to the details.

15. Use the Standard brush with a Draw Size of 5 and a Z Intensity of 20 to make cracks and pits in the column. Choose the Freehand brush stroke type and hold the Alt key as you paint so that the cracks are carved into the surface (Figure 9.35).

16. When you are satisfied with the sculpting, save the tool to your disk as `column.ZTL`. You do not need to save the current alpha with the tool if ZBrush asks.

Figure 9.35

**The column is
sculpted to appear
worn and broken.**

Using the Bump Viewer Material

Creating bump maps in ZBrush is very easy and a lot of fun. Bump maps are best suited for creating a fine level of detail on the surface of a rendered 3D object. To create a map in ZBrush, you simply paint a grayscale map on the surface of the tool, export the map as a texture, and apply the texture as a bump map in your object's shader in your external 3D application. To make bump map painting easier, ZBrush ships with a special material that shows how the grayscale texture you paint will look on the object as a bump map. The next exercise shows you how to use the bump viewer material to create a bump map for the column.

1. Load the column tool you created in the last section into ZBrush or load the column.ZTL tool from the Chapter 9\Ztools directory on the DVD.

2. Open the material inventory on the left shelf. Choose the BumpViewerMaterial located at the bottom right of the material inventory (Figure 9.36).

3. In the Transform palette, turn off the Quick Mode button. In the Display Properties subpalette, set the DSmooth to 1.

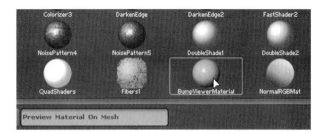

Figure 9.36

The BumpViewer-
Material in the mate-
rial inventory

4. Select the Standard brush. Turn off the ZAdd button and set the draw size to 56.

5. Set the color in the color picker to a dark gray (Rgb = 55, 55, 55). Set the Rgb Intensity to 5.

6. Choose Color Spray from the stroke inventory and choose Alpha 23.

7. Paint across the surface of the column. You'll see that the surface becomes bumpy as if you are sculpting the column, but that's not actually what's happening (Figure 9.37).

8. Set the material to Fast Shader. You'll see that the bumps you created are actually a dark grainy texture.

9. Set the material back to the BumpViewerMaterial.

10. Continue to cover the column with a nice stony bump. Select the Smooth brush and turn off the ZAdd button on the top shelf. Set its Rgb Intensity to 20. The Smooth brush will blur textures painted on the surface of the column. Use the Smooth brush to make some areas of the column smooth so the texture seems organic. Edges of the column around the base and the top that are more exposed to wear and tear should be smoother than the rest of the column.

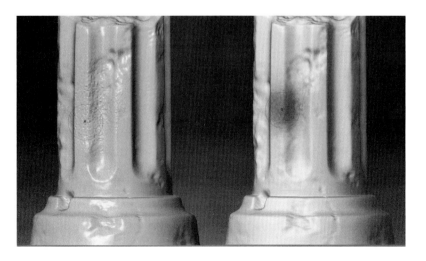

Figure 9.37

The BumpViewer-
Material (left) shows
light and dark values
painted on the col-
umn (right) as
bumps sculpted in
the surface.

Exporting the Bump Texture

When you are satisfied with the bumps you have painted on the surface, you'll need to convert them to a texture to export as a bump map in Maya. If you click the Col>Txr button, it will convert the colors applied to the column into a texture and add it to the texture inventory. By default, this texture will be 1024 × 1024. However, you may want to choose a different size for the bump texture.

1. Open the Texture palette (the Texture palette on the top menu, not the Texture sub-palette in the Tool menu) and set the Texture Size Width and Height sliders to 2048 (Figure 9.38).

Figure 9.38

The sliders deter-mine the size of the next texture you create.

2. Click the New button. The column will turn completely smooth, causing you to panic. Don't worry; the colors/bumps you painted on the column still exist; they are just hidden by a flat gray color applied as a texture.

3. Set the Rgb Intensity slider to 100.

4. Click the Col>Txr button in the Texture subpalette of the Tool palette. The colors will be converted to a texture that is added on top of the new texture you created in step 2 (Figure 9.39).

> The Rgb Intensity slider controls the intensity of textures created with the Col>Txr button. If you set it to a value lower than 100, it is added on top of any current textures at that intensity. This is kind of like setting the color's opacity before merging it on top of the texture.

5. When you are satisfied with the bump map, open the texture inventory. Click the Export button at the bottom of the texture inventory and save the texture as columnBump.TIF to your local directory.

You can take a look at an example bump file by loading the columnBump.TIF texture from the Chapter 9\Introducing ZBrush\sourceImages directory on the DVD and applying it to the column. Look at the texture using both the BumpViewerMaterial and the Fast Shader material. Compare the two.

> To save the colors you painted on the column with the tool, save the column using the Save As button in the Tool palette. However, save the tool with a different name, such as column-BumpColors.ZTL. You'll want to keep an unpainted version of the tool as well, so don't over-write the column.ZTL tool you saved earlier!

Figure 9.39

The completed
bump texture
appears in the tex-
ture inventory.

Painting a Color Map

To create a convincing color for the column, you'll paint a color map using cavity masking.

1. Continue with the same column tool from the previous section or load the
   column.ZTL tool from the Chapter 9\Ztools directory on the DVD.

> If you continue with the same column tool from the last section, you'll need to set the texture
> to Texture Off. You'll notice that the colors you painted for the bump map are still there. To
> remove the colors, set the color picker to white, make sure the Rgb button is on in the top
> shelf, set the Rgb Intensity to 100, and click the Fill Object button in the Color palette. Or you
> can simply reload your saved version of the tool using the Load Tool button in the Tool
> palette.

2. Set the material in the material inventory to Fast Shader.
3. Click the Colorize button in the Texture subpalette of the Tool palette.
4. In the color picker, set the color to a dull yellow (RGB = 163, 155, 121).
5. In the brush inventory, select the Standard brush. Turn off the ZAdd button on the
   top shelf and set the Rgb Intensity to 100.
6. In the Color palette, click the Fill Object button.
7. Set the Rgb Intensity to 15; the color picker to 94, 89, 67; the stroke type to Color
   Spray; and the alpha to 12.

8. In the Brush palette, turn on the Cavity Mask button and set the cavity mask to -80. Paint across the surface of the column; fill the dents and cracks with this color.

9. Select the Smooth brush from the brush inventory. Turn off the ZAdd button on the top shelf and set the Rgb Intensity to 15. Use the Smooth brush to blur the edges of the strokes you painted in step 8. Occasionally, cavity masking will paint blocky artifacts on the tool, which are caused by the geometry in the tool. The Smooth brush can blur out these artifacts.

10. Choose the Standard brush again with the Color Spray stroke type. Set the color to 204, 204, 177 and set the CavityMask strength to 100. Paint lightly over the column to add white spots around the raised areas of the surface, especially on the edges of the flutes. This will sell the worn look of the column. Use the Smooth brush to lightly smooth the edges of these details.

11. In the Brush palette, turn off the CavityMask button. Set the color to 228, 228, 204. Set the stroke to Freehand and the Rgb Intensity to 35. Choose Alpha 46 and set the Draw Size to 3. Paint light vertical stripes on the surface of the column.

12. Smooth out any artifacts in the paint job with the Smooth brush. Don't overdo it—you don't want to lose too much detail.

13. Follow steps 1 through 4 in the previous section to create a color texture map at 2048×2048.

14. Export the color texture from the texture inventory. Save it as `columnColor.TIF` to your local drive (Figure 9.40).

15. To see the texture created in the example, load the `columnColor.TIF` file from the `Chapter 9\Introducing ZBrush\sourceImages` directory on the DVD.

Figure 9.40

The completed color texture appears in the texture inventory.

Painting a Specular Map

Painting a specular map is very similar to painting a color map. The specular map will be applied to the specular color of the shader in Maya. This will make some parts of the column reflect highlights. The smoother parts of the column, such as the edges that are more exposed to wear and tear, should be slightly more reflective than the rough parts.

1. Set the texture to Texture Off.

2. Reload the column.ZTL tool. Use the one you saved or load the tool from the Chapter 9\Ztools directory.

3. In the color picker, set the color to a dark gray (RGB = 40, 40, 40).

4. In the brush inventory, select the Standard brush. Turn off the ZAdd button on the top shelf and set the Rgb Intensity to 100.

5. In the Color palette, click the Fill Object button.

6. Set the color picker to a slightly lighter gray (RGB = 90, 90, 90).

7. Set the stroke type to Color Spray. Select Alpha 23 from the alpha inventory. In the Brush palette, set Alpha Tile to 6. In the Stroke palette, set the flow to .02.

8. Spray over the column to create a spattered texture.

9. Set the color to black and the Rgb Intensity to 25. Do another pass using the same stroke type to lightly knock down the gray created in step 8.

10. Set the RGB color to 168, 168, 168. Select Alpha 07. Choose the Freehand stroke and set Alpha Tile back to 1.

11. Turn on CavityMask in the Brush palette, and set the Rgb Intensity to 100. Color along the edges of the column where you feel the marble might be more worn and smooth.

12. Follow steps 1 through 4 from the section "Exporting the Bump Texture." Create a texture that is 1024 × 1024 for the colors you've painted on the column. Generally a specular map does not need to be as high resolution as a color map, and a smaller-resolution map will make rendering faster and more stable in your external 3D application. You may even want to make it as small as 512 × 512. Save the texture from the texture inventory as columnSpec.TIF (Figure 9.41).

13. To see the texture created in the example, load the columnSpec.TIF file from the Chapter 9\Introducing ZBrush\sourceImages directory on the DVD.

14. You can save a version of the column with these colors applied, but don't overwrite the column.ZTL tool you saved earlier.

Figure 9.41

The specular color texture appears in the texture inventory.

Creating a Displacement Map

ZBrush has a number of ways to create a displacement map from the details sculpted at the higher subdivision levels of the model. ZBrush 3.1 ships with the Displacement Exporter plug-in, which can take some of the work out of creating a displacement map. This plug-in will be discussed in Chapter 10. In this section, you'll learn the more classic method of creating a displacement map using the tools in the ZBrush interface.

1. Load the column.ZTL tool into ZBrush and make sure you are in Edit mode. You can also load the column.ZTL tool from the Chapter 9\Ztools directory on the DVD.

2. Set the SDiv slider in the Geometry subpalette to 3.

ZBrush creates displacement maps by comparing the difference between the current subdivision level and the highest subdivision level. Depending on the model, it may take some experimentation to decide the best subdivision level to use when creating the map. You definitely do not want the tool to be at the highest subdivision level when you're creating the map.

3. Expand the Displacement subpalette in the Tool palette.

4. Set the DPRes to 2048. This will create a displacement map at 2048 × 2048.

5. Click the Adaptive button. This will optimize the creation of the displacement map so that areas with more detail are more detailed.

6. Leave Intensity at 0 and Mid at 50. The intensity of the displacement map can be easily adjusted in Maya.

7. Click the Mode button. Without this button activated, the displacement map will not be generated (Figure 9.42).

8. Click on Create DispMap. It will take a few seconds to create the map (much longer for highly detailed maps). The displacement map will be stored in the Alpha palette (Figure 9.43).

9. In the alpha inventory, select the displacement map and click the Export button at the bottom. Save the file as columnDisplace.TIF.

Figure 9.42

Displacement settings modify the next displacement map created.

These steps describe how to create a 16-bit displacement map using the standard ZBrush workflow. In production, many studios are switching to 32-bit displacement maps. The method for creating these in ZBrush involves using the Multi Displacement Exporter plug-in. This is described in Chapter 10.

Figure 9.43

The new displacement map appears in the alpha inventory.

Creating a Normal Map

You can use the ZMapper plug-in to create a normal map. This section gives a brief description of how to use ZMapper. A more detailed explanation of the controls can be found in Chapter 10.

1. Load the column.ZTL tool into ZBrush and make sure you are in Edit mode. You can also load the column.ZTL tool from the `Chapter 9\Ztools` directory on the DVD.

2. Set the SDiv slider in the Geometry subpalette to 3.

> The normal map is created by comparing the difference between the current subdivision level and the highest subdivision level. You should have the SDiv set to a lower SDiv level to create a more accurate map. However, the original SDiv level might not have enough detail to calculate accurately. You may need to experiment with these settings on your own models.

3. Click the ZMapper button on the upper left in the top shelf.

   A small control panel appears at the bottom of the canvas with a dizzying array of controls. For the most part, you need to worry about only a few buttons.

4. Under the Display controls on the far right of the control panel, click the Tangent space N. Map button. Since Maya 8.5 uses Tangent maps, you'll create this type. To create an Object space map, you can click on the Object space N. Map button above this control.

5. Click on the Normal & Cavity Map tab in the lower left to expand these controls.

6. Increase the Sharpen Hires Mesh Details slider in the lower left. Set it to about one-third of the way to the right (see Figure 9.44).

7. Click the Create NormalMap button to create the map; it will take a few minutes.

8. When the map is completed, click the Exit button in the upper-left portion of the ZMapper control panel. This will take you back to the standard ZBrush canvas. The normal map is stored in the texture inventory (Figure 9.45).

9. Select the normal map in the texture inventory. Click the Export button at the bottom of the inventory and save the file as `columnNormal.TIF`.

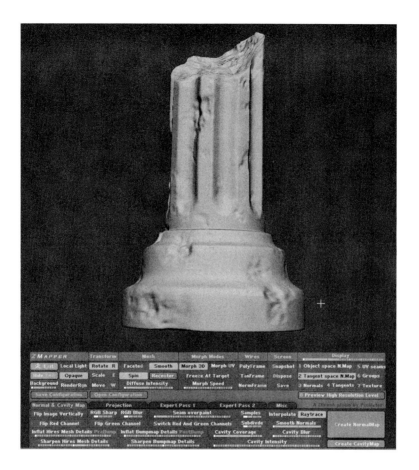

Figure 9.44

The ZMapper interface

Figure 9.45

The normal map appears in the texture inventory when ZMapper is finished.

Exporting from ZBrush

The final task in ZBrush is to export the column tool as an OBJ. The lowest subdivision level may not have enough detail to support the changes made by the displacement map. You'll export the tool at SDiv level 3.

1. Load the column.ZTL tool into ZBrush and make sure you are in Edit mode. You can also load the column.ZTL tool from the `Chapter 9\Ztools` directory on the DVD.

2. In the Geometry palette, set the SDiv slider to level 3. ZBrush will export a tool at the current SDiv settings.

3. Expand the Export subpalette at the bottom of the Tool palette.

4. Activate the Obj button so that the exported file will be a Wavefront OBJ file.

5. Click Qud so the exported geometry is all quadrilaterals.

6. You don't need subgroups to be exported, so deactivate the Grp button. You also don't need to merge the UVs or flip the normals, so you can keep the Flp and Mrge buttons deactivated.

7. Click Export and save the file to your local disk. Save the file as `columnExport.obj`.

8. Close ZBrush.

Creating Map Format Files

You may have noticed that all the textures exported from ZBrush are in TIF format. Although it doesn't like them, the Mental Ray renderer in Maya will work with TIF files. In fact, large TIF files often cause Mental Ray to crash. There is a special format that mental ray does prefer. Converting your TIF files (or files in any format) to the MAP format (`.map`) ensures that Mental Ray will be much more stable when rendering. The conversion process is done through a command-line program that ships with Maya called Imf_Copy.

1. In Windows, open the command prompt from the Programs menu.

2. Change the current directory in the command prompt to the directory that contains your textures.

3. To run the program, type `Imf_copy filename.ext filename.map`. In the case of the color map, type `Imf_copy columnColor.tif columnColor.map`. After a second, if there are no errors in your typing, the C prompt will return. It looks as though nothing happened (Figure 9.46), but if you look in the directory where you made the conversion, you'll see that a new `columnDisplace.map` file has appeared.

4. Repeat this process for the columnBump, columnSpec, columnNormal, and columnDisplace files.

5. Make sure all of these map files are placed in your sourceImages directory in Maya. You can also use the map files that are in the `Chapter 9\introducingZbrush\sourceImages` folder on the DVD.

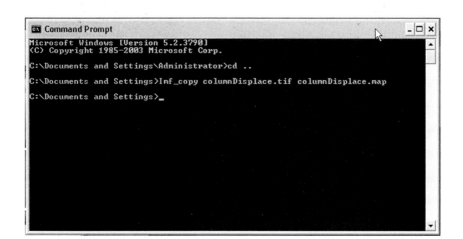

Figure 9.46

Imf_copy converts image files to the MAP format.

Importing into Maya

Now you are ready to import the column object and all its maps into Maya. for this section, it is assumed you have working knowledge of basic shader assignment and editing in Maya.

1. Open the column.mb file from the Chapter 9\IntroducingZbrush\scenes directory.

2. Choose File → Import → Wavefront Object. Select the columnExport.obj file.

3. In the Import Options dialog box (Figure 9.47), make sure Create Multiple Objects is set to False. This ensures that the point numbering on the model is not changed during the import process. This step is very important if you decide you need to bring the model back into ZBrush for further editing.

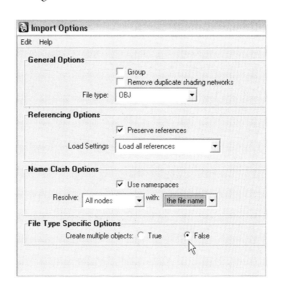

Figure 9.47

The import settings in Maya

4. When the file loads, the column you created in ZBrush will appear on top of the original (Figure 9.48). Open the Outliner, select the column object, and delete or hide the object (Display → Hide Selected).

5. Select the column and open its Attribute Editor; in the Section labeled Displacement Map, turn off the Feature Displacement check box (Figure 9.48).

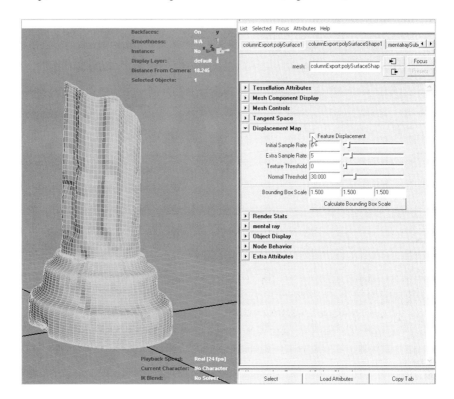

6. To ensure that the geometry can subdivide properly to create a displacement map, you need to add a subdivision approximation node. Select the object and choose Windows → Rendering Editors → mental ray → Approximation Editor. When the window opens, make sure the column is still selected and click the Create button in the section labeled "Subdivisions (Polygon and Subd. Surface)" (Figure 9.49).

7. Open the Attribute Editor for the column object and select the mentalRaySubdiv-Appox1 tab. Set the preset menu to Spatial Quality. Set the Min Subdivisions to 3, the Max Subdivisions to 5, and the length to .1.

8. Create a Blinn shader for the column and open the Hypershade Editor (Windows → Rendering Editors → Hypershade). Middle mouse button (MMB) drag the Blinn shader to the work area or select the shader and graph the input and output connections.

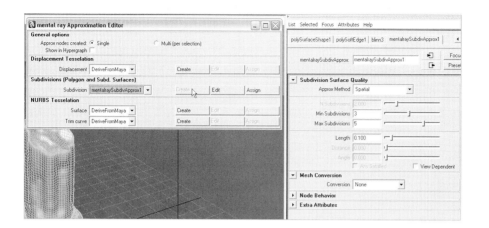

Figure 9.49

A subdivision approximation node is created from the column model

9. In the left column of the Hypershade, click on the Displacement node to create a displacement shader.

10. MMB drag the displacement shader on top of the Blinn shader. From the pop-up menu, choose Displacement Map.

11. Select the Blinn shader and click the Graph input/output connections button. Select the Displacement shader node. In the Attribute Editor, click the Texture button (the tiny checkerboard) next to the Displacement value. In the dialog box that opens, choose Apply a File Texture.

12. In the file texture's Attribute Editor, click the File button and choose the columnDisplace.map file from the sourceImages directory in your project.

13. Graph the connections for the Blinn shader; it should look like Figure 9.50.

Figure 9.50

The Blinn shading network in Maya

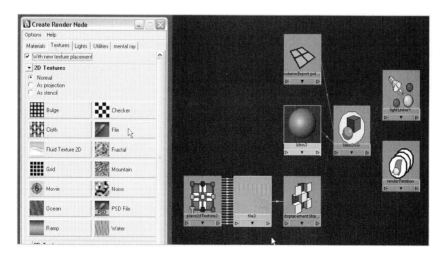

14. ZBrush interprets UVs so that the textures it creates are flipped vertically when imported into Maya. To correct this problem, you'll need to flip the texture in the place2DTexture node attached to the file used for the displacement shader (as well as any other textures imported from ZBrush). To do this, open the place2DTexture node in the Attribute Editor and set the repeat V value to -1, as in Figure 9.51 (the V value is the second field of the boxes labeled Repeat UV).

Figure 9.51

The texture needs to be flipped in the place-2DTexture node.

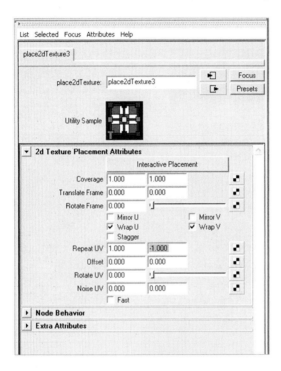

ZBrush and Maya interpret the color gray in displacement maps differently. Gray to ZBrush means a displacement value of 0, while in Maya a displacement value of 0 is indicated by the color black. A quick expression in Maya will make it easier to adjust the intensity of the displacement map.

15. Open the file node that is connected to the displacement shader in the Attribute Editor. In the Color Balance section, right-click over the Alpha Offset field and choose Create New Expression.

16. In the Expression Editor's Expression field, type the expressive expression `alphaOffset= -.5*alphaGain;` (see Figure 9.52).

17. Click the Create button to apply the expression.

18. Check the box labeled "Alpha is Luminance" just below the Alpha Offset slider. This is necessary for .MAP files.

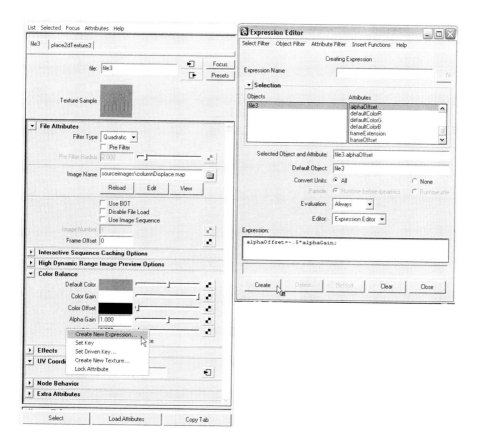

Figure 9.52

An expression is entered into the Alpha Offset field.

19. Set the Alpha Gain slider to .35 and switch to the renderCam in the perspective window. Do a test render to see how the displacement map looks. Make sure you have mental ray selected as your renderer. You can adjust the intensity of the displacement map using the Alpha Gain slider. To see these settings applied to the column model, open the columnDisplacementSettings.mb file in the Chapter 9/introducingZBrush/scenes folder.

20. Add the columnColor.map file to the color channel and the columnSpec.map file to the specular color channel. Remember to set the V value in Repeat UV attribute of the place2DTexture nodes to -1 for each of these files.

21. Add the columnBump.map file to the bump channel and set Bump Depth to .2. Remember to set the V value in Repeat UV attribute of the place2D Texture nodes to -1 for each of these files.

22. In the Render Setting, set the Render to mental ray. In the mental ray tab, set the Quality preset to Production. Do a test render from the renderCam to see how the column looks (Figure 9.53).

23. To test the normal map, select the File node attached to the bump channel and change the file to the `columnNormal.map` file. In the Bump node, change the Use As menu to Tangent Space Normal. Render the file and compare it with the previous render.

You can actually view the effect of the normal map in the perspective window. In the menu at the top of the perspective panel choose Renderer > High Quality Rendering.

24. To see a finished version of the file, open the `column1.mb` scene from the `Chapter 9/introducingZBrush/scenes` directory (Figure 9.54).

Figure 9.53

Test renders are created for the column model. The far left has only displacement applied. The center image uses displacement, color, specular, and bump. The image on the far right substitutes the normal map for the bump map.

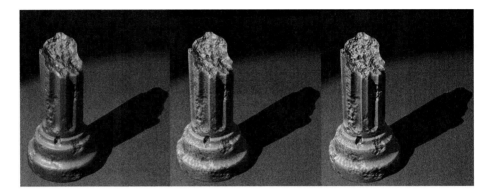

Figure 9.54

The column is rendered using an advanced lighting set up.

The example in this chapter uses Maya 8.5. The subdivision approximation editor in Maya 2008 has been changed and results may differ. For information on how to use displacements with Maya 2008, please refer to this thread on ZBrushCentral: `http://www.zbrushcentral.com/zbc/showthread.php?t=56061`.

Summary

This chapter shows how models created or edited in ZBrush can easily be incorporated into any rendering and animation pipeline. ZBrush can not only sculpt and refine models created in other programs, it is also useful for creating and editing textures. For details on how to use ZBrush with other popular 3D packages, consult the ZBrush help files. Changes and updates to these guides are added frequently and can be downloaded from ZBrushcentral.com.

The final chapter in this book will cover useful plug-ins and scripting tools that allow you to expand ZBrush's capabilities.

CHAPTER 10

Plug-ins and ZScripts

ZBrush's capabilities can be expanded using plug-ins and ZScripts. A plug-in is a module written by programmers that adds additional functionality to an application. All the plug-ins discussed in this chapter either come with ZBrush or are available as a free download from Pixologic. A ZScript is a module written in ZBrush's own ZScript language.

This chapter includes the following topics:

- Projection Master
- Displacement Exporter
- Transpose Master
- ZAppLink
- ZMapper
- ZScripts and macros

Projection Master

Projection Master allows you to use the 2.5D brushes on a 3D polymesh tool without having to drop the tool to canvas. Actually, it does drop the tool to canvas, but only temporarily. When you activate Projection Master, it freezes your tool and temporarily converts the polygons in the mesh to pixols, and you can edit the tool using any of the tools in the tool inventory—including the 2.5D paintbrushes. When you finish, your tool will be converted back into a polymesh 3D object so you can then pick it up, reposition it, and freeze it again for more detail work in Projection Master.

The following exercise offers a brief tour of Projection Master.

1. Start a new ZBrush session. In the Tool palette, load the column1.ZTL tool found in the Chapter 10\Ztools directory.

2. Draw the tool on the canvas and switch to Edit mode (Ctrl+t) (Figure 10.1).

3. In the Transform palette, turn off the Quick Mode button. In the Tool palette's Display Properties subpalette, set DSmooth to 1. This will remove the faceted look from the 3D polymesh.

4. Rotate the column holding the Shift key so that it snaps into an orthographic view.

5. Choose the Fast Shader material from the Material palette.

6. Use the Scale button on the right shelf to zoom in closely to the top of the column.

Figure 10.1

The column1 tool is loaded into ZBrush and drawn on the canvas.

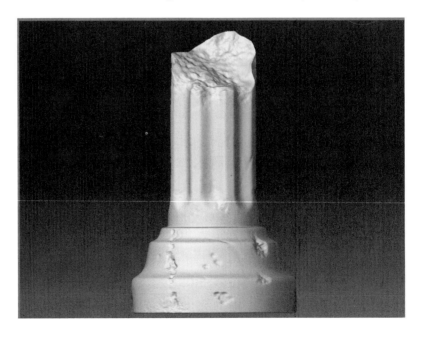

7. In the upper-left corner of the top shelf, click the Projection Master button (Figure 10.2). A dialog box opens, displaying the options for the Projection Master session. You'll want to first try sculpting with Projection Master, so turn off Colors and Material and turn on Deformation (Figure 10.3).

Figure 10.2

A button on the top shelf activates Projection Master.

8. Click the Normalized button. This will cause any sculpted details to be made relative to the surface normal. The sphere icon on the lower half of the dialog box previews the differences between sculpting with normalize on or off.

9. Turn the Fade option on. Fade creates a falloff to details made on the edge of a model; again, it's more noticeable when large changes are made to the model.

10. Click Drop Now to start the Projection Master session. ZBrush will look the same, but you'll notice that you can no longer rotate the 3D tool, just as though you had dropped it to canvas. Don't panic. You'll be able to pick it up again when you end the session.

11. You'll notice that all of the tools in the Tool palette are available for use. Select the Directional brush from the 2.5D Brush section of the tool inventory (not the brush inventory!). Set the stroke type to Drag Rect, and select Alpha 07 from the alpha inventory.

Figure 10.3

Select the Deformation option on the Projection Master startup screen.

12. Turn off the Rgb, M, and Mrgb buttons on the top shelf. Turn on the ZSub button. You can paint materials and colors in this session; however, since you selected Deformation as the only option when you started Projection Master, colors and materials painted on the surface will disappear when you exit Projection Master. Only the sculpted changes will remain.

14. Select the Sphere 3D tool from the 3D Brush section of the Tool palette.

15. Click the ZSub button on the top shelf and set the intensity to 100. Use the Sphere3D tool to make some pits in the surface of the column (Figure 10.4).

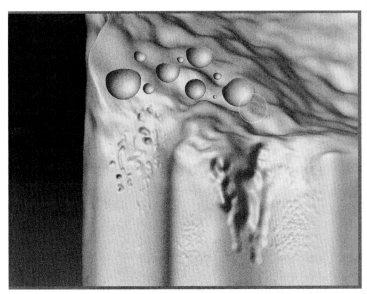

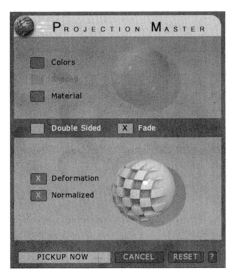

Figure 10.4

Details are painted on the column surface with 2.5D brushes and the Sphere3D tool is used to cut pits.

Figure 10.5

The Pick Up Now button converts the tool from pixols back into a polymesh 3D object.

16. Try some of the other 2.5D tools on the surface of the column. Turn on the ZAdd button on the top shelf, select the Blur brush, and use it to smooth some of the details on the surface of the column.

17. After you have made a few changes, click the Projection Master button on the top shelf again. In the dialog box, click the Pick Up Now button (see Figure 10.5).

After a few seconds the column will return to regular Edit mode. Notice that the details that looked very fine while in Projection Master are not nearly as refined when you leave Projection Master (Figure 10.6). This is because you are zoomed in very close on the model, and this illustrates an important point when working with Projection Master.

It is important to understand the pixol-to-polygon ratio when you work in ZBrush. When you work with a tool in Projection Master, the parts of the tool that are visible on the screen are temporarily converted to pixols. When you leave Projection Master, the changes you made using pixols are translated into changes to the polygons of the 3D tool. If the size of the polygons is larger than the size of the pixols, the polygons will not be able to represent changes made in Projection Master accurately. You'll want to use Projection Master only at the highest subdivision level of the tool. Keep the pixol-to-polygon ratio in mind when you scale the model up before starting a Projection Master session. If you scale too much, you may be disappointed that the translation of the details you create don't hold up when you exit Projection Master.

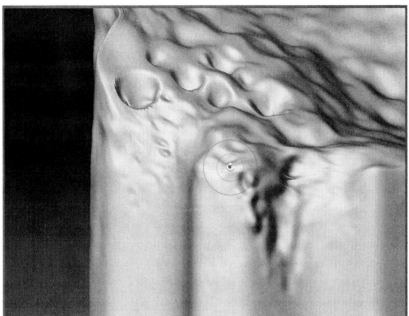

It's also important to understand that if you scale the model down so that the polygons are smaller than the pixols painted in Projection Master, you may lose much of the pre-existing detail on the model because the details created by painting pixols will be translated uniformly to all of the polygons. In practice, you may need to do a little experimentation to find a safe range for creating detail with Projection Master based on the number of polygons in the model and how closely you've zoomed in on the tool before starting Projection Master.

Using undo (Ctrl+z) immediately after exiting Projection Master will undo all of the changes you created while in Projection Master.

Painting Color and Material with Projection Master

Projection Master can be used to paint both color and material on the surface of a 3D tool. While painting straight color is probably better done using the polypainting techniques described in Chapter 7, there are some interesting effects you can achieve painting materials onto objects.

1. Start a new ZBrush session. In the Tool palette, load the column1.ZTL tool found in the Chapter 10\Ztools directory.

2. Draw the tool on the canvas and switch to Edit mode (Ctrl+t).

3. In the Transform Palette, turn off the Quick Mode button. In the Tool palette's Display Properties subpalette, set DSmooth to 1. This will remove the faceted look from the 3D polymesh.

4. Rotate the column holding the Shift key so that it snaps into an orthographic view.

5. Make sure the Perspective button is off in the Draw palette.

6. Select the Fast Shader material from the Material palette.

7. Click the Projection Master button in the upper-left portion of the top shelf.

8. In the Projection Master dialog box, select Material. Turn off Color and Shaded and Deformation. Click the Drop Now button to start Projection Master (Figure 10.7).

9. After clicking the Drop Now button, you'll see a warning pop-up that tells you to create a texture before using Projection Master to paint color or material (Figure 10.8). If you click Yes, a texture will be created for you. By default the texture is 1024 × 1024.

Figure 10.7

Choose the Material option when starting Projection Master.

Figure 10.8

A warning lets you know that you need to create a texture before you can paint materials or color in Projection Master.

10. Choose the Simple Brush from the 2.5D brush section of the tool inventory, and from the Material Inventory, choose the ReflectedMap material (Figure 10.9).

11. On the top shelf, click the M button so that only material will be painted on the tool.

12. Paint some strokes on the surface of the column. The reflective material appears where you paint.

13. Click the Projection Master button on the top shelf and choose Pick Up Now. When you exit Projection Master, you can rotate the tool and see how the materials have been applied to the column (Figure 10.10).

14. In the Texture palette, set the Height and Width sliders to 2048, make sure the color picker is set to white, and click the New button to create a new texture. It's a good idea to make a texture before you start Projection Master so that you can determine the size ahead of time (Figure 10.11).

Figure 10.9

Choose the ReflectedMap material from the material inventory.

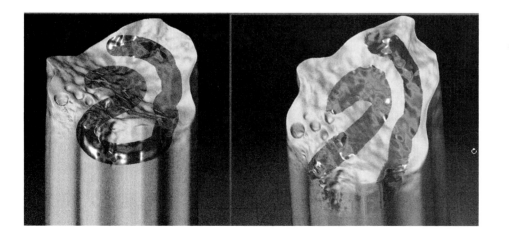

Figure 10.10

The ReflectedMap material is painted on the column. The view on the left shows the material painted in Projection Master. The view on the right shows the tool after it has been converted back to a 3D polymesh with the material painted on.

Figure 10.11

Create a new texture before starting Projection Master.

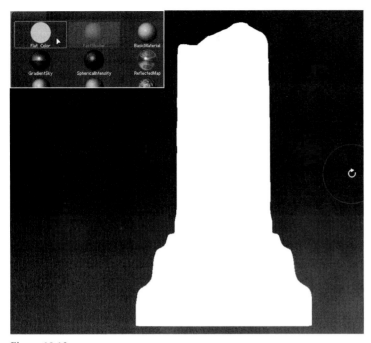

Figure 10.12

Flat color is chosen as the column's material.

Figure 10.13

Select Colors and Shaded at the start of the Projection Master session.

15. In the Material palette, choose the Flat Color material. Scale the column so that the entire tool fits on the canvas (Figure 10.12).

16. Click the Projection Master button. In the options, choose Colors and Shaded (Figure 10.13). Turn off Material and Deformation and make sure Fade is on. Click Drop Now.

    The Shade option allows you to bake lighting and material information into a texture. Materials themselves can't be exported from ZBrush for use in other programs, but you can use Projection Master with the Shade option to create an exportable texture from the materials.

17. Choose the Simple brush from the 2.5D brush section of the tool inventory (Figure 10.14). Click the M button so that only material information is painted on the surface.

Figure 10.14

The Simple brush is chosen from the tool inventory.

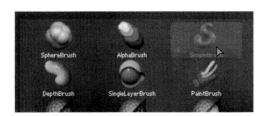

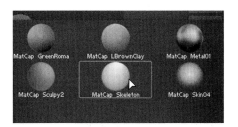

Figure 10.15
Choose the MatCap Skeleton material from the Material inventory.

18. Set the stroke type to Drag Rect and the alpha to "Alpha to Off".

19. Make sure the ZAdd button on the top shelf is off.

20. From the Material inventory, select the MatCap Skeleton material (Figure 10.15).

21. Drag across the surface of the column so that it is covered in the Skeleton material (Figure 10.16).

22. Click the Projection Master button and choose Pick Up Now to end the Projection Master session.

23. Once Projection Master has closed, take a look in the Texture palette. The lighting and shading that are part of the Skeleton material have been *baked* into the texture applied to the column. You can export this texture as an image file, which can then be used as the basis of a texture map for use in another 3D program (Figure 10.17).

Figure 10.16
Paint the Skeleton material on the surface of the column.

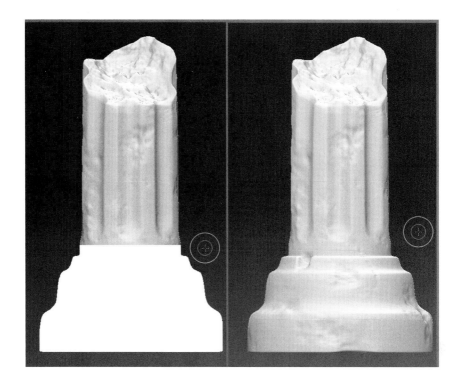

ZAppLink

ZAppLink is a plug-in that is very similar to Projection Master in execution. ZAppLinkIt temporarily freezes your model and then links to an external digital painting program such as Adobe Photoshop or Corel Painter. ZAppLink is free, but you'll need to download and install it to run. You'll also need to have a digital paint program installed on your machine. This example uses Photoshop CS3.

Installing ZAppLink:

1. Download ZAppLink 3 from `www.pixologic.com/zbrush/ZAppLink/`.

2. Close all programs and run the installer.

3. Start ZBrush.

4. The ZAppLink button is found in the Document palette. Click the button, and in the ZAppLink window, click the ZAppLink the Set Target App button. In the File dialog, browse your file directory and select a paint program such as Photoshop or Painter. The file you select must be an executable (`.exe` extension).

Running ZAppLink:

1. In the Tool palette, click the Load button and load the seaCreature.ZTL tool.

2. Draw the tool on the canvas and switch to Edit mode (Ctrl+t).

3. In the SubTools subpalette, select the seaCreature subtool. Set the SDiv slider in the Geometry subpalette to 7 (Figure 10.18).

4. Rotate the seaCreature so that it is visible from the top. Position the tool so that the body fills most of the canvas.

5. Select the Fast Shader material from the Material palette.

6. Click the ZAppLink button in the Document palette (Figure 10.19). A warning appears telling you that you need to either create a texture first or enable Colorize mode so that the tool will use ZAppLink for polypainting. Select Enable Polygon Colorize.

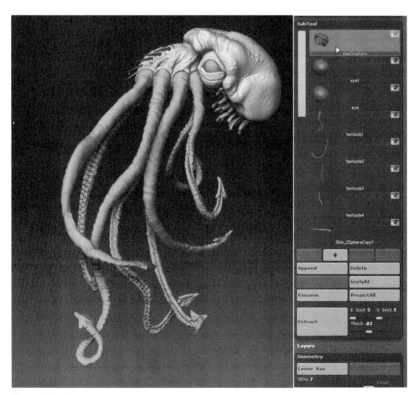

Figure 10.18
Load the seaCreature tool and draw it on the canvas.

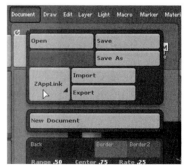

Figure 10.19
The ZAppLink button is found in the Document palette.

Figure 10.20

**Set the options
before starting
ZAppLink.**

7. The next dialog box will present a number of options. Select Fade from the options and leave the others unchecked (Figure 10.20).

8. Click Drop Now. Photoshop (or whichever target app you have chosen) launches automatically if it is not already open. An image of the canvas and tool will appear in a new document in your paint program. Do not close ZBrush while working in your paint program.

9. In the Layer palette in Photoshop, you'll see several layers: ZShading, Layer 1, and Full ZShading (Figure 10.21). Do not edit the ZShading and Full ZShading layers. Only paint on Layer 1. You can add additional layers for editing, but they must be merged before returning to ZBrush.

Figure 10.21

**An image of the
ZBrush session
opens in Photoshop
with a predefined
layer arrangement.**

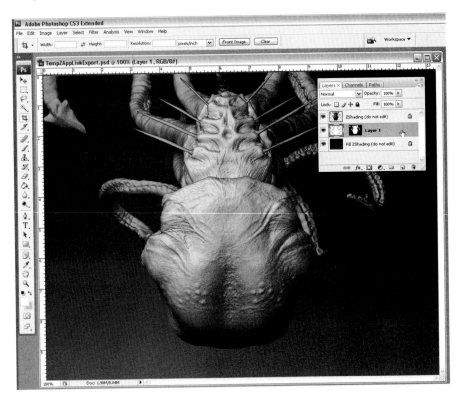

10. Use the paintbrushes in your paint program to create some detail on the image of the model.

11. When you are finished, choose Save from the file menu in Photoshop (or your paint program).

12. Click on ZBrush, and in the pop-up window, click Re-Enter ZBrush.

13. Your model updates with the new texture, but it is still frozen on the canvas. Click Pick Up Now if you'd like to return to Edit mode (Figure 10.22).

14. Rotate the tool to another view and reactivate ZAppLink. The file in your paint program will be overwritten with a new image of the ZBrush canvas. You can make changes in your paint program, save, and return to ZBrush to accept the changes.

> ZAppLink will allow you to paint on all visible subtools while in Photoshop; however, when you pick up the tool in ZBrush after exiting ZAppLink, the changes you made while using ZAppLink will be applied only to the currently selected subtool.

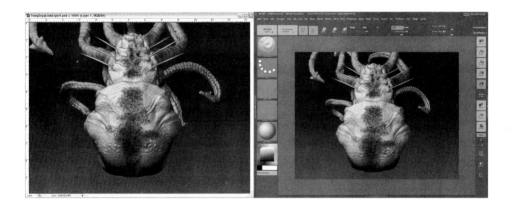

Figure 10.22

The changes created in Photoshop are transferred automatically to the 3D tool in ZBrush.

Multi Displacement Exporter

In Chapter 9 you learned a simple workflow for creating a displacement map in ZBrush. ZBrush ships with the Multi Displacement Exporter plug-in that adds some powerful features for creating displacement maps. Multi Displacement Exporter can store settings that can be reused each time you need to make a displacement map. If you are using ZBrush with a specific 3D animation package, such as Maya, you only need to create the settings for Multi Displacement Exporter once; then you can reuse those same settings for all your 3D tools whenever you need to create a displacement map. Multi Displacement Exporter can export several displacement maps with different settings at the same time, and it can export normal maps as well.

Multi Displacement Exporter ships with presets for use with more popular 3D applications, and you can also enter a quick code that will automate the settings. Quick codes can easily be shared between users, and many of these codes are posted on website forums such as ZBrushcentral.com.

Try the following exercise to see how Displacement Exporter works:

1. Start ZBrush from the startup screen and choose Other.

2. In the Tool palette, click the Load button and load the column1.ZTL tool from the `Chapter 10\Ztools` directory of the DVD.

3. Draw the tool on the canvas and switch to Edit mode (Ctrl+t).

4. In the Geometry palette, set the SDiv to level 2 (Figure 10.23). Select the Fast Shader from the material inventory.

5. In the ZPlugin palette, expand the Multi Displacement 3 subpalette. Hold the brush over the various settings to get a brief description of each.

6. Set MaxMapSize to 2048; this determines the size of the exported maps (Figure 10.24).

7. Click Export Options to open the Multi Displacement Exporter options panel (Figure 10.25).

Figure 10.23

Set the column tool to subdivision level 2.

Figure 10.24

The main settings for Multi Displacement Exporter

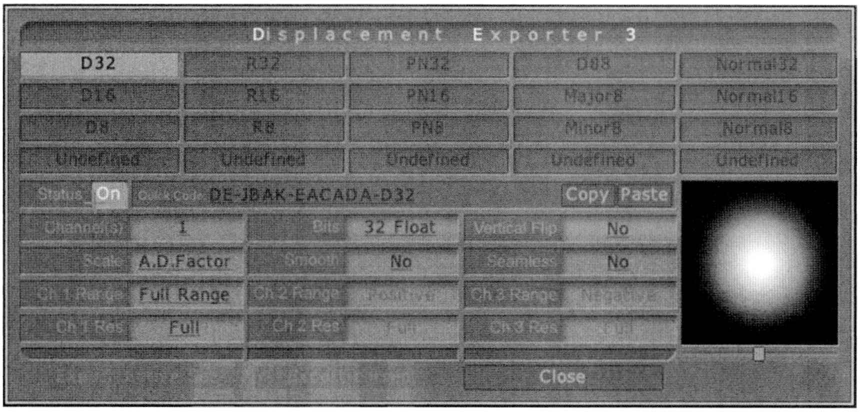

Figure 10.25

The options panel
sets the type of
displacement
maps that will be
exported.

8. The numbered boxes at the top contain all of the displacement map presets that are available plus some empty slots (labeled Undefined) where you can store your own custom presets.

9. Click on D32 in the upper corner. Set the Status button to On. When this is on, Multi Displacement Exporter will create a displacement map based on the settings in the D32 slot.

10. Click on D16 below D32 and set its status to On as well. Now two maps will be created using the D32 and D16 settings when you run the exporter.

11. Under D16, click on the Bits field. Clicking on the number in this field will cycle between 8, 16, and 32 bits for the settings. Notice that the quick code also changes. You can change the settings in preset by clicking on the fields under each preset.

12. Set the Bits field to 16 again. Click the Copy button in the middle row.

13. Select one of the undefined buttons and then click Paste. This will paste the settings for D16 into this field, creating a new preset.

14. Move the slider under the icon in the lower right. Click on the slider to create the setting. This slider adjusts the intensity of the displacement map.

15. Click on the Quick Code field. When the dialog opens, you can enter a quick code into this field and all the settings for the preset will be changed.

16. Highlight the field and then press the right arrow key on your keyboard to move the cursor to the end of the field. Press the Backspace key three times and replace *D-32* with *Test*. Click OK, and the new preset will be renamed Test (Figure 10.26).

17. Click on the Normal32 field in the upper right, and set its status to On (Figure 10.27).

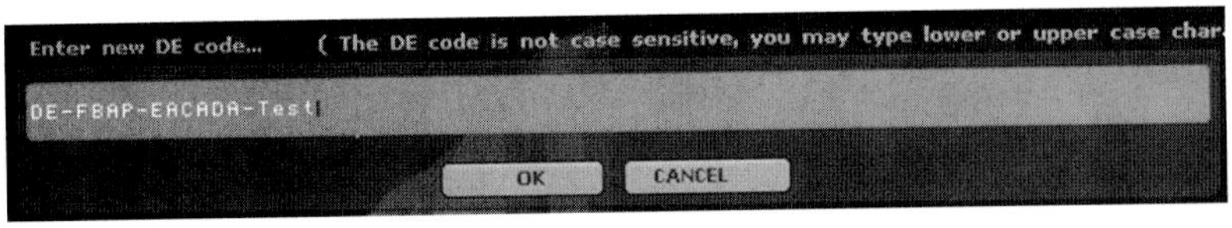

Figure 10.26

The last three letters of the quick code determine the name of the preset.

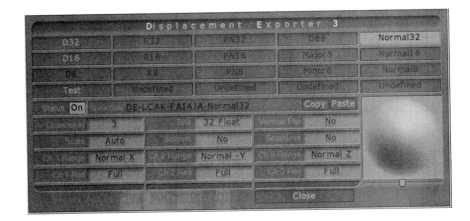

Figure 10.27

Normal maps can also be generated using the Multi Displacement Exporter.

18. Click the Close button to close the Multi Displacement Exporter options.

19. In the Multi Displacement subpalette of the ZPlugin palette, click the Create All button. In the File dialog box, set the filename to MDETest.

20. ZBrush will perform the calculations to create a displacement map for each of the activated settings (D32, D16, and Test) as well as a normal map for the activated Normal32 preset. These files will be saved to your hard drive: they will not appear in the ZBrush interface when they are done.

Files of the same name will be overwritten without warning, so be careful not to have multiple presets with the same name (e.g., two D32 presets), and mind how you name the files when you run Multi Displacement Exporter.

You can use the icon in the lower left to preview the displacement map settings. To do this, first create a displacement map using the classic method as described in Chapter 9, section "Creating a Displacement Map." Select the displacement map in the Alpha palette and then open the Multi Displacement Map export options. The preview window displays a preview based on the currently selected alpha; if a displacement map is selected in the Alpha palette, you can use it to preview the settings.

The name of each preset describes the type of file it will create. You can look at the bottom two rows (labeled CH Range and CH Res) in the interface to see what information will be contained in each channel.

- D8, D16, and D32 all create a single channel displacement map using 8, 16, and 32 bits, respectively.

- R8, R16, and R32 all create a three-channel file with the displacement in the red channel. The other two channels are unused. The bit depth per channel is also 8, 16, and 32, respectively.

- PN8, PN16, and PN32 all create files with three channels. Positive displacements are in one channel, negative displacements are in another, and the third channel is unused. The bit depth per channel is also 8, 16, and 32, respectively.

- D88 exports displacements where major displacements are in the first channel, minor displacements are in the second, and the full range is in the third.

- Major and Minor each create a file with either the major or minor displacements contained in a single channel.

- The final column creates 8-, 16-, and 32-bit normal maps.

> One of the biggest advantages of using the Multi Displacement Exporter is that you can use the same settings for all the maps when you import them into your favorite 3D application. For instance, when you apply a 32-bit displacement map exported from the Multi Displacement Exporter to a model in Maya, you can set the Alpha Gain of the map to 2.2 and the Alpha Offset to -1.1. These numbers will be the same for every model that uses a 32-bit displacement map created with the Multi Displacement Exporter. This saves you the trouble of having to constantly adjust the Alpha Gain and Alpha Offset of the displacement map texture in Maya to match the look of the model created in ZBrush.

Transpose Master

Transpose Master allows you to pose a character composed of multiple subtools. This can save a great deal of time and effort. Without Transpose Master, you need to either pose each subtool individually or use a complex import and export workflow that includes another 3D application, such as Maya, to pose all of the subtools.

Transpose Master creates a low-res version of your current tool, where all subtools have been merged into a single object. You can pose the low-resolution version of the mesh and then Transpose Master will copy the pose back on to each of the subtools in the original mesh. Transpose Master is a free plug-in, but you'll need to download and install it before using it.

Installing Transpose Master:

1. Download the plug-in from `http://download.pixologic.comPlugins/TransposeMaster _ver1.2E.zip`. (Please check the Pixologic site and see if updates are available.)

2. Unzip the folder and move or copy the contents to your `Program Files\Pixologic\ ZBrush3\ZStartup\ZPlugs` directory. Do not change or omit any of the contents or the plug-in will not work.

Using Transpose Master:

1. Start ZBrush, and in the Tool palette, click the Load Tool button. Select the Demo-Soldier.ZTL tool from the `Program Files\Pixologic\ZBrush3\ZTools` folder.

2. Draw the DemoSoldier on the canvas and switch to Edit Mode (Ctrl+t).

3. In the ZPlugin palette, click the TPoseMesh button (Figure 10.28). This will create a low-resolution version of the DemoSoldier.

4. Click the Lasso button on the right shelf. Hold the Ctrl key and drag a selection over the soldier's legs and lower torso. Be careful not to select any of the hands or arms (Figure 10.29).

5. Click the BlurMask button in the Masking subpalette of the Tool palette.

6. Click the Rotate button on the top shelf to activate the Transpose handle.

7. Hold the Shift key and drag the handle up from below the belt to the top of his head.

8. Select the center circle of the Transpose control and drag upward so that the soldier turns to the right. Use the Transpose handle in Move mode to reposition his upper torso if necessary.

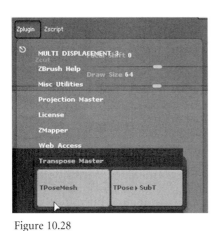

Figure 10.28

The TPoseMesh button creates a low-resolution copy of the 3D tool.

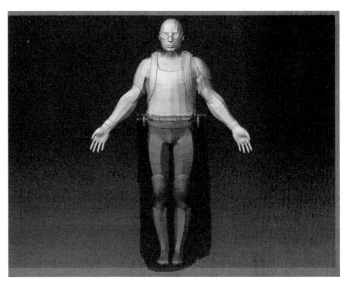

Figure 10.29

Use the Lasso to mask the soldier's legs.

9. Clear the mask by clicking the Clear button in the Masking subpalette of the Tool palette.

10. Mask other parts of the tool and make additional changes using the Transpose handle (Figure 10.30).

> You may notice that the multiple meshes that make up the low-resolution version of the soldier are easier to mask using the selection marquee (i.e., dragging a selection box while holding the Ctrl key) than dragging a mask directly on the surface with the Transpose handle.

11. When you are done posing the soldier, click the TPose>SubT button in the ZPlugin palette. ZBrush will go through each subtool and apply the changes (Figure 10.31).

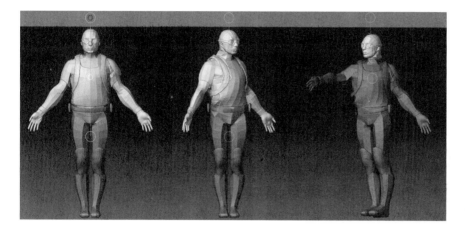

Figure 10.30

Several changes are made to the low-res soldier using the Transpose handle.

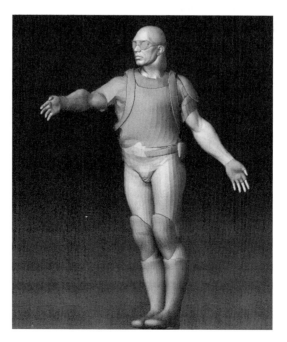

Figure 10.31

The pose is transferred to the hi-res mesh and all of its subtools.

ZMapper

The ZMapper plug-in is an advanced normal map generation tool that ships with ZBrush. You used it briefly in Chapter 9 to create a normal map for the column. ZMapper boasts a lot of features that go beyond the scope of this book. Many of them are detailed in the ZBrush documentation. In this exercise, you'll take another look at ZMapper so that you have a better idea of how it works. If you just need to create a simple normal map for a 3D polymesh tool, you only need to worry about a few of the settings in the ZMapper interface. Most of the other buttons are for advanced use.

1. In the Tool menu, click the Load button and load the column1.ZTL tool from the `Chapter 10\Ztools` folder on the DVD.

2. Draw the tool on the canvas and switch to Edit mode (Ctrl+t). Select the Fast Shader material from the Material palette.

3. Open the alpha inventory, and click the Import button. Load the `columnBump.psd` file from the `Chapter 10\Texture` folder on the DVD (Figure 10.32).

4. Make sure the bump map is selected in the Alpha palette. Having a bump map in the Alpha palette will cause ZMapper to include the bump texture in the normal map that it creates for the tool.

5. In the Geometry palette, set the SDiv slider to level 2. ZMapper calculates the difference between the current SDiv level and the highest SDiv level when it creates a normal map. Therefore, if you start ZMapper at the highest SDiv level, you'll get an error. In fact, ZMapper won't open if the tool is at the highest SDiv level.

Figure 10.32

The column is loaded and drawn on the canvas. The bump map is imported into the Alpha palette.

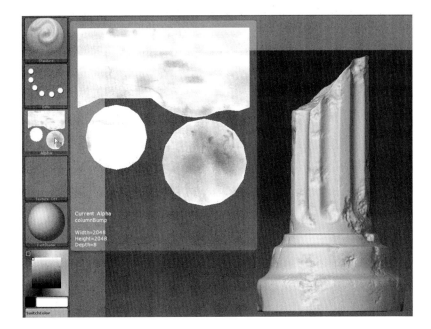

Figure 10.33

The ZMapper button is on the top shelf.

Figure 10.34

The ZMapper controls are organized into columns.

6. Click the ZMapper rev-E Button on the top shelf (Figure 10.33). The ZMapper interface loads on the canvas.

7. Click on the ZBrush interface outside of the canvas and ZMapper will close. You can open it up again by clicking on the ZMapper button (Figure 10.34).

8. The column tool will spin automatically while ZMapper is active. Drag on the tool to rotate it to another view. Let go while dragging and the column tool will continue to spin in the direction you drag.

9. Click the Spin button in the Mesh column to stop the spinning.

10. The Rotate, Scale, and Move buttons in the Transform column allow you to switch between different transform modes. The letter highlighted in yellow indicates the hotkey for each command.

11. Click the Morph UV button in the Morph Modes column to see the tool animate between its current shape and a layout of the UVs. The Morph 3D button in the Morph Modes column animates the tool moving between its current shape and any morph targets that may have been applied to it (the column has no morph target, so this button will do nothing). This helps you diagnose any potential stretching problems your normal map may have in specific positions.

12. Click the PolyFrame, TanFrame, and NormalFrame buttons in the Wires column to display the wireframe, tangent, and normals on the tool.

13. Click the Snapshot button in the Screen column to drop a copy of the tool in its current position to the canvas. The Save and Dispose buttons save or delete the snapshot copy.

14. Click the Local Light button in the far left column and a yellow cube appears, representing a point light. You can drag on the cube to change the position of the light in ZMapper (Figure 10.35).

Figure 10.35

The light's position is represented by a yellow cube.

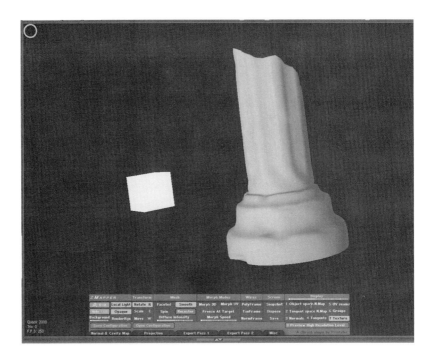

15. Click the Object space N.Map button in the Display column. This displays what the tool will look like with an object space normal map. If the tool appears dark, turn on the Local Light button on the far left and position so that you can see the tool. More importantly, the Object space N.Map button sets the maps creation mode to object space.

16. Click the Tangent space N.Map button in the Display column. This displays what the tool will look like with a tangent space normal map. If the tool appears dark, turn off the Local Light button on the far left. More importantly, the Tangent space N.Map button sets the map creation mode to tangent space. (Object and tangent normal maps are explained in the section "Normal Maps" in Chapter 9.)

17. Clicking the UV seams, Groups, Normals, and Tangents buttons in the Display column will display these features on the tool.

18. The Preview High Resolution Level button on the far right shows what the model will look like with the normal map applied, including any bump maps that are currently active in the Alpha palette.

19. Click on the Normal & Cavity Map tab in the lower-left portion of the ZMapper control panel. This will open the controls for the actual creation of the normal map. The Projection and Expert 1 and 2 Passes tabs are meant for fine-tuning of normal maps

for very specific applications, a topic that is beyond the scope of this book. You will most likely not need to use the controls in these tabs (Figure 10.36).

Figure 10.36

The Normal & Cavity Map tab contains controls to adjust the bump and cavity map strength.

The sliders in the Normal & Cavity Map tab are used to fine-tune the creation of the normal map. Each slider is described in the ZMapper reference that is available in the ZBrush documentation. This section will describe some of the more notable controls.

- The Flip Image Vertically button automatically flips the normal map when it is created, which accommodates other 3D programs that map textures with the vertical V value the reverse of ZBrush (such as Maya). This button can save you the trouble of having to remember to flip the normal map once you import it into your other 3D application.

- The Inflate Hires Mesh Details and Inflate Bumpmap Details sliders adjust the intensity of these details when the map is created. If there is no bump texture in the alpha channel, the Inflate Bumpmap Details slider will have no effect on the normal map.

- The Samples and Subdivide sliders increase the quality of the normal map but add to calculation time.

- The Cavity Intensity slider creates a normal map that darkens the cavities and indentations in the final render of the model. You can also use this slider to generate a separate cavity map that gives a preview of how the darkness of the cavities in the model will look. The cavity map can also be used in the model's shader to create the look of ambient occlusion.

Ambient occlusion is a shadowing effect created when ambient light is blocked from entering corners and cavities in an object. It can greatly increase the realism of a render. It is often created in the rendering either by using a raytracing technique or as part of a global illumination pass. You can use ZMapper to create a cavity texture map for a model that can then be plugged into the channel of the model's shader. Doing this can eliminate the need for ambient occlusion calculation during render and thus speed up the rendering process.

Once the settings are adjusted the normal map can be generated.

1. Adjust all the settings listed earlier to your liking and then click the Create Normal-Map button to make the map (Figure 10.37). The type of map created will be determined by whether tangent space normal map or object space normal map is selected in the Display column. The normal map will also include a bump map if one is selected in the Alpha palette.

   After the map has been created it can be seen on the tool in the ZMapper interface by clicking on the Preview High Resolution Level button.

Figure 10.37

The normal map can take a few minutes to calculate.

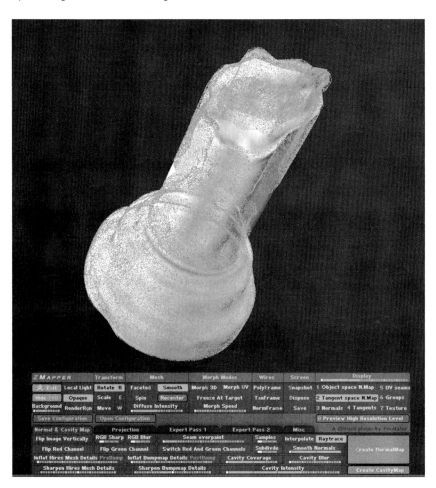

2. Click the Create CavityMap button to create a separate cavity map for the tool (Figure 10.38).

   The normal map may take a few moments to calculate depending on the settings and type of map (tangent space maps take longer to calculate than object space maps). The

ZMAPPER **419**

finished normal map will appear in the texture inventory (Figure 10.39). Every time you create a normal map during a ZBrush session, this texture will be overwritten. You may want to export the map each time ZMapper finishes creating it. Clicking the Create Cavity-Map button will also overwrite the current normal map texture in the texture palette!

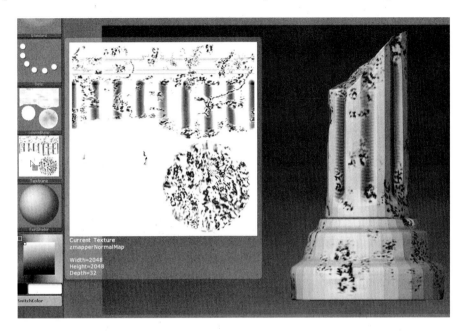

Figure 10.38

A separate cavity map can be created and stored in the texture inventory.

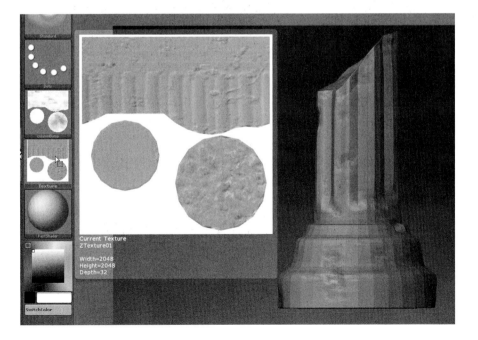

Figure 10.39

The finished map appears in the texture inventory.

ZScripts

A ZScript is a short piece of computer code written in ZBrush's ZScript language. When you run a macro, you are actually executing a ZScript. This section discusses how to load a ZScript as well as how to record a macro.

Loading a ZScript:

1. Expand the ZScript palette.

2. Click the Load button (Figure 10.40).

Figure 10.40

ZScripts are loaded using the ZScript palette.

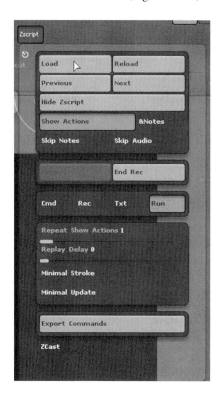

3. From the Chapter 10\Macros folder on the DVD, select the ringTwist.ZSC file.

4. You'll notice that nothing much happens. Expand the bottom tray by clicking on the arrows below the canvas.

5. Click the ringTwist button in the bottom tray (Figure 10.41). You'll see a ring 3D tool drawn on the canvas. The ring is deformed using the Twist deformer.

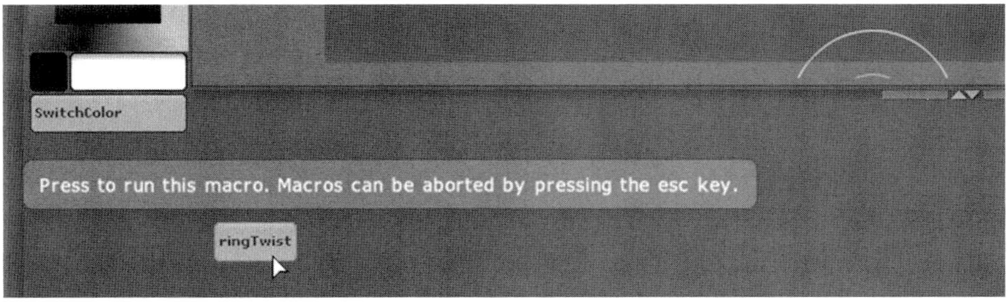

Figure 10.41

A button appears in the bottom tray. Clicking it will start the ZScript.

This action is essentially a macro—a recording of a ZBrush session. ZScripts can be as simple as this or they can be more complex, including their own custom functions and graphical interfaces. The ZBrush documentation includes a guide to ZScripting and more in-depth discussion is available in Scott Spencer's book *ZBrush Character Creation: Advanced Digital Sculpting* (Wiley, 2008). The next section describes how to record a ZScript as a macro.

To record a Macro:

1. Expand the Macro palette.

2. Click the New Macro button. The macro will start recording all the actions you perform in ZBrush once this button is clicked.

3. From the Tool palette, select the Sphere 3D tool. Draw the tool on the palette and switch to Edit mode (Ctrl+t).

4. In the Macro palette, click the End Macro button.

5. Save the macro to your local disk as drawSphere.txt.

6. Use a text editor such as Notepad to open the drawSphere.txt file. In the file you'll see text describing the actions you performed in ZBrush.

7. In the second line of the text, change IButton,???, to IButton,drawSphere and save the file. Now when you load the ZScript, the button in the bottom shelf will be labeled drawSphere instead of ???(Figure 10.42).

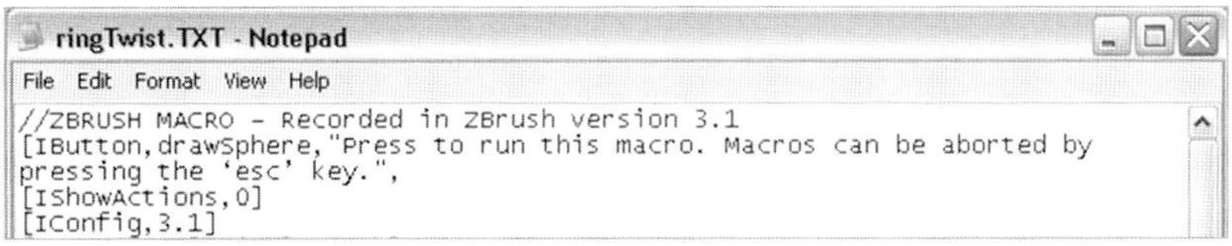

Figure 10.42

You can change the ZScript label by editing the text of the ZScript.

8. Follow the steps described in the section "Loading a ZScript" to run the drawSphere script.

9. After running the script, you'll notice that two files, drawSphere.ZSC and drawSphere.PSD, have been saved to the same directory as the original text file. The ZSC format file is a copy of the text file in ZScript format; you can run either the ZSC or the TXT version of the file. The PSD format file is an icon created from a screen grab of the script.

ZScripts can be aborted at any time by pressing on the Esc button.

Summary

Using plug-ins is a useful way to expand the powerful sculpting and painting tools in ZBrush. The plug-ins described in this chapter represent only a small portion of those available. Check the Pixologic and ZBrushCentral websites frequently for updates to these plug-ins as well as for news and information about new plug-ins.

About the Companion DVD

In this appendix:

- What you'll find on the DVD

- System requirements

- Using the DVD

- Troubleshooting

What You'll Find on the DVD

The following sections are arranged by category and provide a summary of the content you'll find on the DVD. If you need help with installing the items provided on the DVD, refer to the installation instructions in "Using the DVD" later in this appendix.

Trial, demo, and *evaluation* versions of software are usually limited by either time or functionality (such as not letting you save a project after you create it).

Chapter Files

In the Chapter Files directory, you will find all the files for completing the tutorials and understanding concepts in this book. This includes sample scene files, sample texture files (PSD format images), and ZScripts as well as video files that provide screen recordings of the tutorials in progress. Sculpting is an artistic process that cannot always be described with words alone. You're strongly encouraged to view the movies that accompany some of the exercises in the chapters to see how the example files were created. The text for each chapter will specify the corresponding movie files.

Each directory on the DVD is divided into subdirectories so that the files can be found easily. ZBrush tools are located in each chapter's ZTools directory, ZBrush documents are located in each chapter's ZDocs folder, movies are located in each chapter's Movies folder, and so on. Note that the content for each chapter varies, so not every chapter will necessarily have a ZTools directory. Chapter 9 includes a Maya project directory structure (`Chapter 9\introducingZBrush`). Again, the text in each chapter will point you to the folder where you can find the content.

ZBrush Trial Software

Trial version. For Windows.

The ZBrush 3 30-day trial provides free access to the software for noncommercial use. This product is subject to the terms and conditions of the end-user license agreement that accompanies the software.

For more information, software updates, and an impending Mac version, visit `www.pixologic.com`.

System Requirements

Make sure your computer meets the minimum system requirements shown in the following list. If your computer doesn't match up to most of these requirements, you may have problems using the software and files on the companion DVD.

- Preferably a PC running Microsoft Windows XP or Windows Vista. ZBrush requires at least Windows 2000. You can use ZBrush on an Intel-based Mac running Windows emulation software such as Boot Camp or Parallels, but there may be some stability issues with ZBrush plug-ins such as ZMapper.

- Preferably your computer's processor should be a fast Pentium 4 or newer (or equivalent such as AMD) with optional multithreading or hyperthreading capabilities. ZBrush requires at least a Pentium 3 processor.

- You should have at least 1024MB of RAM, preferably 2048MB for working with multi-million-poly meshes. ZBrush requires at least 512MB of RAM.

- An Internet connection.

- A DVD-ROM drive.

- Apple QuickTime 7.0 or later (download from www.quicktime.com).

For the most up-to-date information, check www.pixologic.com/zbrush/system.

Using the DVD

To install the items from the DVD to your hard drive, follow these steps.

1. Insert the DVD into your computer's DVD-ROM drive. The license agreement appears.

Windows users: The interface won't launch if you have Autorun disabled. In that case, click Start → Run (for Windows Vista, Start → All Programs → Accessories → Run). In the dialog box that appears, type **D:\Start.exe**. (Replace D with the proper letter if your DVD drive uses a different letter. If you don't know the letter, see how your DVD drive is listed under My Computer.) Click OK.

2. Read through the license agreement, and then click the Accept button if you want to use the DVD.

The DVD interface appears. The interface allows you to access the content with just one or two clicks.

Troubleshooting

Wiley has attempted to provide programs that work on most computers with the minimum system requirements. Alas, your computer may differ, and some programs may not work properly for some reason.

The two likeliest problems are that you don't have enough memory (RAM) for the programs you want to use or you have other programs running that are affecting the installation of a program or how it runs. If you get an error message such as "Not enough memory" or "Setup cannot continue," try one or more of the following suggestions and then try using the software again:

Turn off any antivirus software running on your computer. Installation programs sometimes mimic virus activity and may make your computer incorrectly believe that it's being infected by a virus.

Close all running programs. The more programs you have running, the less memory is available to other programs. Installation programs typically update files and programs, so if you keep other programs running, installation may not work properly.

Have your local computer store add more RAM to your computer. This is, admittedly, a drastic and somewhat expensive step. However, adding more memory can really help the speed of your computer and allow more programs to run at the same time.

Customer Care

If you have trouble with the book's companion DVD-ROM, please call the Wiley Product Technical Support phone number at (800) 762-2974. Outside the United States, call +1(317) 572-3994. You can also contact Wiley Product Technical Support at `http://sybex.custhelp.com`. John Wiley & Sons will provide technical support only for installation and other general quality control items. For technical support on the applications themselves, consult each program's vendor or author.

To place additional orders or to request information about other Wiley products, please call (877) 762-2974.

Index

Note to the Reader: Throughout this index **boldfaced** page numbers indicate primary discussions of a topic. *Italicized* page numbers indicate illustrations.